Systemic Therapy as Transformative Practice

Systemic Therapy as Transformative Practice

Edited by
Imelda McCarthy and Gail Simon

First published 2016 by
Everything is Connected Press
9-11 Main Street, Farnhill, UK, BD20 9BJ

Copyright © 2016 to Gail Simon and Imelda McCarthy for the edited collection, and to the individual authors for their contributions.

The rights of the contributors to be identified as the authors of this work have been asserted in accordance with sections 77 and 78 of the Copyright, Designs and Patents Act 1988.

All rights reserved. No part of this book may be reprinted or reproduced or transmitted in any form or by any electronic, mechanical, or other means, now known or hereafter invented, including photocopying and recording, or in any information storage or retrieval system, without permission in writing from the publisher.

Trademark Notice: Product or corporate names may be trademarks or registered trademarks, and are used only for identification and explanation without intent to infringe.

British Library Cataloguing in Publication Data
A.C.I.P. for this book is available from the British Library

ISBN 978-0-9930723-2-1 (pbk)
ISBN 978-0-9930723-3-8 (ebk)

Systemic Therapy as Transformative Practice
Edited by Imelda McCarthy and Gail Simon
Layout by Shelagh Aitken

www.eicpress.com

Systemic Therapy as Transformative Practice

This compilation of chapters from leading systemic therapists and researchers offers inspiration to the reader in opening fresh horizons of creative possibilities in the field of systemic practice and therapy. The range of illustrated practice applications combines a deep appreciation of seminal theoretical foundations with contemporary philosophical understandings. In so doing the reader is offered a breadth of resources and inspiration relevant to current developments in the fields of social care, mental health and education. The transformative qualities of systemic therapy to matters of human distress are abundantly displayed in this fresh exposition of the evolution and creative development of systemic therapy and its refined application in practice. The humanity of each author shines through in their ability to combine rigorous thinking with imaginative co-creative practice. The versatility of each author to explore the generative qualities of systemically informed therapy is evident in each chapter. Therapists and practitioners will find in this book a confirmation of the continued benefit of systemic ideas and their creative potential to inform and enthuse.

Jim Wilson, Systemic Psychotherapist & past Chair,
The Family Institute, Cardiff

This timely book illuminates the crucial contribution of systemic ideas to creative therapy, organisational work, training and research and it is particularly welcome at a time when we face increasing inequalities and constraints on our freedoms. Grounding their work in the ideas of such key systemic thinkers as Gregory Bateson and Gianfranco Cecchin, the authors demonstrate their innovative, generative and reflexive systemic approaches in an impressively wide range of contexts. Systemic approaches continually move between levels of context, and the contributors highlight processes of connecting these different levels explicitly for themselves and for those with whom they are engaged. Systemic thinking has always had the capacity to be revolutionary and I am confident that this book will inspire with its range of creative and emancipatory ideas and practices.

Charlotte Burck, PhD. Honorary Systemic Psychotherapy Consultant,
Tavistock Clinic

This book is a landmark in the field of systemic theory and practice. It brings together contributions from leading European and North American practitioners and academics on a wide range of topics relevant to systemic practice and couple and family therapy. The book shows how practices based on systems theory and social constructionism can transform lives in a world recovering from an economic and social crisis. It is scholarly and thought provoking, but also immensely practical and a 'must-read' for all family therapists.

Alan Carr, Professor of Clinical Psychology, University College Dublin &
Couple and Family Therapist, Clanwilliam Institute, Dublin

In an increasing neo-liberal word where the emphasis is on individualistic models of practice and on economic discourses of human support and help, I am so pleased to welcome this volume. Imelda McCarthy and Gail Simon offer an impressive collection of European and North American systemic practitioners that critically, creatively and competently show how systemic ideas are transformative. McCarthy and Simon have succeeded in providing an important contribution to the field that focus on human and community flourishing. This impressive work will be an invaluable resource for students, scholars and practitioners!

Ottar Ness, Professor of Mental Health Care, University College of Southeast Norway & Taos Associate

This book is an excellent resource in the systemic literature and is a distillation of work from established systemic practitioners, researchers and scholars. The ecological view, the Batesonian legacy to the field, aligned with the politics and philosophy of subjective experience is the common thread connecting the chapters. The contributors describe work that is contextually engaged, reflexively guided and participative. Grassroots activism as a sister movement gives energy and conviction to the many practices described here, where communities are honoured in their need, resilience and entitlement. In places, the whimsical, the personal and the poetic are literary artifices that mark aesthetic and ethical aspects of the field. Reading it is a lovely journey, revisiting some trusted landmarks and arriving at new places.

Dr Nollaig Byrne, Co-Founder of Family Therapy Training Programme, Mater Misericordiae University Hospital, Dublin

Contents

Foreword   x
Monica McGoldrick

Preface   xiii
Gail Simon & Imelda McCarthy

Part I - Times of Change and Solidarity

1. Systemic Psychotherapy on the Move: Following Ariadne's thread in changing clinical contexts
Jane Dutton   3

2. The Inner and the Outer Sides of the Wind: Collaborative practice in the Solidarity Social Medical Centre of Thessaloniki, Greece
Fany (Fotini) Triantafillou, Dimitra Pouliopoulou, Elektra Bethymouti & Efrossini Moureli   17

3. A 'Fifth Wave' Systemic Practice Punctuating Liberation: Reflective practice and collective social action
Taiwo Afuape   43

4. Fourfold Vision and Cybernetic Unity: Therapist as scientist, theorist, humanist and artist
Hugh Palmer   62

5. The Event. On experimenting with complex systems
Christopher J. Kinman   79

6. Looking for a Home: An exploration of Jacques Derrida's notion of hospitality in family therapy practice with refugees
Lucia De Haene & Peter Rober   94

7 A Systemic-Dialogical Perspective for Dealing with Cultural Differences in Psychotherapy
Andrea Davolo & Laura Fruggeri ... 111

8 Living Supervision in Practice: Structuring accountability with men therapists working alongside women and gender-variant persons with precarious lives
Vikki Reynolds & Andrew Larcombe ... 125

9 Family Therapy in an Emerging Professional Life: One story among stories
Therese Hegarty ... 139

10 Reflexive Processes in Higher Education: Systemic dilemmas in teaching research methodology by means of 'polyphonic dialogue'
Eleftheria Tseliou, Georgios Abakoumkin, Vicky Kokkini, Katerina Nanouri & Fani Valai ... 154

11 Systemic Practice as Systemic Inquiry as Transformative Research
Gail Simon ... 169

12 Framing the Symmetry
Nora Bateson ... 192

Part II - Transformative Conversations

13 Community Work and Psychotherapy as Two Sides of the Same Cooperative Practice
Umberta Telfener ... 209

14 The Aesthetics of Interruption: Points of entry in systemic therapy
Ged Smith ... 222

15 Restoring Communities for Children and Separated Parents Caught in Demonising Fights
Justine Van Lawick ... 233

Contents

16 Creating Islands of Safety for Victims of Violence: Critical systems approach
Catherine Richardson/Kinewesquao — 250

17 Systemic Practice in a Complex System: Child sexual abuse and the Catholic Church
Marie Keenan — 269

18 Hope and Risk: Systemic practices for supervision and assessment in child protection
Ernst Salamon & Imelda McCarthy — 284

19 'Double Jeopardy' and 'Professional Jeopardy': Stories of shared identity
Gill Goodwillie — 298

20 Paths to Transformative Conversations
Francesca Balestra & Laura Fruggeri — 316

21 Systemic Conversations with Military Families: Research as intervention
Ann-Margreth E. Olsson — 331

22 Heresies from Practice: A Case of Obsessive–Compulsive Disorder
Padraic Gibson & Don Boardman — 345

23 Family Semantic Polarities as a Guide for the Therapeutic Process
Valeria Ugazio — 362

24 Beyond Biology and the Linguistic Turn: Event, singularity, sense and the work of imagination
Marcelo Pakman — 386

25 Systemic Psychosexual Therapy: A guided tour
Desa Markovic — 401

26 When You Say, "It's not Sickness, it's Love", there will be a Powerful Change of Context
Mia Andersson — 419

Notes on Contributors — 432

Foreword

Monica McGoldrick

Systemic Therapy as Transformative Practice offers a crucial revitalisation of systemic thinking at this moment when our global circumstances so require it. The editors have brought together a broad group of outstanding and creative authors into this rich collection of writings. Our field and our world are in great need of these perspectives. This book is a gratifying reminder of the importance of the systemic ideas we have struggled so hard for the past fifty years to develop into practice for healing and transformation.

We live in a period of such a degree of rapid change and pressure to constrict our thinking that very often the centre does not hold. It becomes hard to see the patterns in which our lives are embedded and to remain grounded to help clients clinically. Many forces in our society have been constraining our theory and practice to narrowly defined "evidence based" service delivery – where "evidence" is measured only in terms of numbers, finances of the drug and insurance industry, and the politics of healthcare. *Systemic Therapy as Transformative Practice* is a refreshing challenge to that thinking, offering us a rich array of writings on systemic theory, policy and practice for our rapidly changing "liquid times," as Jane Dutton refers to them in her chapter.

The dominant societal forces that are currently in control of mental health delivery do not support our assisting clients who are most in need and least able to access our services. These forces are undermining our ability to work collaboratively. Without time to share and collaborate on developing coordinated and integrated interventions, our clients experience fragmentation and disruptions at every level of our service delivery.

The increasing mobility and diversity of our society make the need for collaborative thought more important than ever for effective intervention. We are being pressed ever harder to provide quick, present oriented solutions that take no account of the cultural or life cycle contexts of our clients' lives, or their need for continuity in a rapidly changing world. We are given no time for learning about the structure, contextual stresses, and historical events that are essential for systemic engagement with our clients. To learn about our clients' experiences and to co-evolve healing strategies, therapists must hold on tight to their beliefs

Foreword

about the importance of systemic, historical, contextual and collaborative thinking.

Systemic Therapy as Transformative Practice offers a wide variety of perspectives from theoretical challenges to clinical practice, to exciting suggestions for service delivery in difficult contexts, to specific applications with particular populations such as refugees and veterans, and questions for expanding therapist's personal challenges to their therapeutic interventions.

For example, Marie Keenan offers and important theoretical challenge to linear thinking in our definitions of victim and perpetrator in relation to the sexual abuse within the Catholic church, even as, of course, we need to hold priests accountable for their behaviour. Her challenging dissection of our language and the complexities of our clients' lives reminds us that we all have experiences of victimisation and of being perpetrators, but also many life experiences beyond either of these definitions. A systemic understanding requires that we keep the awareness of the complexities of our lives and our connections in our consciousness.

At the level of programme design, Van Lawick contributes a brilliantly constructed 10-session multifamily intervention programme to help chronically warring divorced couples who have been engaging in terrible battles for years. This subtle systemic intervention is aimed at expanding parents' awareness of the impact of their 'demonising" behaviour on their children with encouragement and support from their own social networks. Their children are facilitated to convey their experiences in creative and protected ways to promote their parents' strengths as are parents in their realisation of the need to stretch themselves on their children's behalf. Van Lawick's examples demonstrate very creatively the power of systemic thinking in designing interventions for our most difficult cases.

Systemic Therapy as Transformative Practice offers also rich exploration of work with particular populations including veterans, victims of violence, the seriously mentally ill and, very pertinent in our era, work with refugees. De Haene and Rober's contribution, for example, offers a fascinating discussion of working with refugees using Derrida's challenging ideas about hospitality toward the person who comes to your door requiring an unconditional welcome. The authors challenge clinicians to examine their own stance in careful listening to be sure they take responsibility where appropriate for their part in the dominant group's judgmental attitudes about outsiders.

At the level of service delivery, Triantafillou, Pouliopoulou, Bethymouti and Moureli offer a creative antidote to our traditional programmes and policies, suggesting they are like a Greek Chorus of Modern Greece in its most critical hour. They have developed a collaborative service where they treat anyone who walks through their doors free of charge in all areas of health and mental health care. In the face of the most dire circumstances, they function collaboratively and with a sprit of solidarity. They work to overcome the fragmentation and objectification of patients in traditional health care services. Just in the circumstance where most would restrict their perspective, this group's effort is expansive, redefining those seeing their services as "incomers" rather than "clients" or "patients" in an effort to promote inclusive language for their health community and to join in collaborative engagement with those who seek their services.

These are just a few examples to illustrate why *Systemic Therapy as Transformative Practice* is such an important contribution to our field. We must use and develop systemic practice at a time when it is so crucial for survival. We have worked so hard to develop these ideas over the past many decades, drawing, on systemic insights that have been many generations in their evolution. The editors deserve tremendous credit for creating this rich text which goes a long way toward regenerating our hope for the power of systemic theory, application and policy design to guide our practice.

Monica McGoldrick

Preface

"What is happening with this word 'systemic'?" someone asks at a workshop, in supervision, over coffee. "Isn't it enough to just say, 'relational' or 'dialogical' or 'collaborative' or 'eco-systemic'?" These are questions of our time. So how come the word 'systemic' survives – or even thrives? These other terms are all important and, while often used by the same people, are not interchangeable. The interest in relational ethics and relational aesthetics has become deeply important to many practitioners. And sometimes, the critical understanding of language as a social construction can be taken as meaning, we made up all these words so does it matter which of them we use? There are, as we see it, wider contexts which warrant continued and conscious use of the term "systemic" For example, the influence of liberal humanism, while an understandable response to dehumanising practices on a global scale, distracts our attention away from systemic contextualising to individualising discourses. In these times of systemic global crises, we need to situate our understanding of small systems and local exchanges within wider, national or global, and transdisciplinary systems so we can see how everything is connected, so we can make visible and critique power relations and watch how they play out in the world – and with what consequences for different peoples.

As we see it, systemic practice is not simply an approach but a movement. The systemic movement is a community of critical thinkers about change and stasis in systems and the power relations influencing both. It is imbued with the ethic of wellbeing for all. Systemic practitioners are trained to pay attention to where and how power relations play out at different levels of context in society and impact of the wellbeing of all people – not simply within our teams and the clients with whom we are working. When we come across signs of what could be regarded as "illness", we reframe the struggles of an individual as an understandable response to problems in wider social and political systems, not simply within their intimate relationships. When we watch the news or struggle to participate in the world, we do not put our systemic thinking to one side.

The scientific search for a fixed, reproducible one-size-fits-all method uses individualising discourses to justify the backgrounding of context. This renders invisible people's membership of community, their knowledge and contributions, the links between personal, social and political.

This approach not only isolates individuals coming for therapy it defines change as movement towards a notion of better health occurring within a limited biological or social system. In systemic practice, the emphasis is on collaborative re-search, where the "re-" denotes looking again at familiar and old ways of being, doing, talking and performing. One of the things which struck us in each of these chapters is how the writers describe how they are moved (on) in response to what they see, hear, feel, realise. They describe movement in and between people. They describe improvisational practices arising out of a reflexive openness and collaboration with all those involved in the conversation.

This is often difficult in a world in which public services are increasingly dominated by market-led forces, method-led practices and a determination to situate expertise within decontextualised therapeutic practices. Such practices are dependent on the generation of a certain kind of data to defend the methods used to justify particular economic models. However, this means i) only certain mono-cultural practices count as therapy or counselling; ii) practitioners have less power to provide ways of working which respond to local need; and iii) there is proportionately little research being conducted into innovative systemic practice. The systemic movement has rejected fixed methods and theories seeing them as products of time, place, culture and economic investment. Rather, it has developed a philosophical curiosity in dialogical artistry, in improvisational ways of working through difficulties and exploring how change in one part of a system has transformational influence in unexpected ways and places immediately and/or elsewhere.

We are using the word "systemic" to portray fluidly responsive practices with an ethical preoccupation about what makes a difference, for whom and how. Working descriptions of "systemic" emphasise which values, theories and practices it might include and promote rather than what shape it must take. We see "systemic" as inclusive of a contextually, relationally and personally reflexive collective of working practices, ethical positionings, and a metaphor about how our world works. "Systemic" involves practitioners being committed to exploring the critically reflexive movements in the relationships between context, ideology, theoretical propositions, methods and relational activities. This allows the systemic movement to be open to new theoretical and ethical punctuations of practice, to change ourselves and ways of being and doing in the world to fit with or influence the multiple and overlapping local and global systems within which we live and work as systemic activists. Reflexivity is our ethical guiding light. Self and relational reflexivity, local

Preface

and global reflexivity encourage situated and joined up ethical thinking about the contexts we are each acting out of and acting into.

This book arises in response to the creeping shift towards reproducibility and the shadowing by formulaic ways of working of practice knowledge and know-how. It is an attempt to redress the side-lining by market led forces of professional knowledge. Each of the twenty-six chapters showcases creative systemic practice with different groups of people in very different places of work. Writers make new connections with theories and philosophies, tell old stories new ways, tell us new stories old ways! Throughout these chapters this community of practitioners address socio-political, familial and discursive contexts which reflexively inform, deform, reform our thinking, our comfort, our beliefs and our practices. Writers elegantly show robust systemic practice which is transformative, co-creative, collaborative and deeply sensitive to contexts which can promote social justice and critical of contexts which effectively stifle it.

We invited the writers in this book to write what they consider to be contemporary systemic practice in changing times. What we have is a collection of chapters with different and connected aspects of contemporary systemic practice. The title arose out of the content. On reading early drafts, the themes of movement and transformation, and critical thinking about the influence of wider contexts were jumping out at us from the texts. It became clear to us that writers were emphasising the transformative aspects of our work and our worlds.

These chapters are written from within the moral, existential, and creative challenges and opportunities presented by our turbulent times: a historical and evolutionary moment in which a "perfect storm" of an unprecedented number of global crises is brewing. Our political, social, economic, financial, cultural, agricultural, and religious dynamics – as well as healthcare, education, media, and other institutions and infrastructure – are all in serious crisis *simultaneously*. For many years in Europe, North America and many other parts of the world there has been a reduction and contraction of public services justified under the rhetoric that our societies could no longer support the most needy. Before our eyes, the unbelievable is happening. Social progress is deliberately confused with economic growth and stability and economics used to justify the systematic undoing of social values of care and care provision. Refugees, people with additional needs, those on the margins are left to fend for themselves in dangerous circumstances. Alongside the demise of social infra-structure, there is evidence that while the poor are getting poorer, the rich are getting richer. Instead of downward redistribution we are witnessing upward redistribution.

If we see ourselves as participant-observers, as opposed to simply observers or victims in this global crisis, then systemic practice can create opportunities to navigate with consciousness of our power in the global crisis. In subscribing to a systemic worldview, it becomes incoherent to defer responsibility for the world crisis to political, corporate, and celebrity "masters of the universe". Systemic thinking unlocks opportunities to generate transformation of human culture and human services.

Our systemic movement is always working towards a more collective, inter-related, interactive and cooperative coherence and game change. This way of being and thinking in the world is inevitably not only transformative but transgressive in that we take a stand against the systematic, intentional maintenance of poverty, persecution, displacement and inequality. Having a systemic critique enables us to resist the "consensus trance" of neoliberal discourses intended to numb and dumb people down into disconnection, separation and self-interest at the expense of communal and environmental wellbeing and interconnection. Systemic irreverence towards any theories, our own or those of others, is helpful in creating out of the box thinking and action for responding creatively and sensitively to need. The ethical stance of theoretical and structural irreverence supports the conviction to continuing identifying and responding to need, to continue to think, to articulate, while still retaining an aesthetics of care in relationships and in our writings. It generates the vigour, humour, verve, and penetrating clarity that the systemic movement brings to finding ways forward together. These chapters provide some shade and light to further nurture the green shoots of systemic sensibility and action. They echo the surge of renewed interest systemic practice.

The book is divided into two main sections, the first called *Times of Change and Solidarity*, while the second section is entitled *Transformative Conversations*. When we received the rich diversity of material for the book, it seemed to us that these two headlines seemed to best way of speaking of the content.

The enthusiasm of the contributors to this book working alongside us on this venture has strengthened a sense of a contextually innovative systemic community in which we feel honoured to participate.

Gail & Imelda

Times of Change and Solidarity

Systemic Psychotherapy on the Move
Following Ariadne's thread in changing clinical contexts

Jane Dutton

On the first day they sat in awe on the stone steps outside the shop, watching the street and seeing a universe of frightening chaos. Gradually, they perceived the river of traffic in the street, and, within it, the currents of handcarts, bicycles, bullock carts, buses and the occasional lorry. Now they learned the wild river's character. They were reassured that it was not all madness and noise, there was a pattern in things.

Mistry 1996, p.116

In this chapter I consider the responses clinicians make to bewildering movements in organisational contexts, whist working day to day with children and families in high-risk situations. Through reporting on guided conversations with systemic therapists, I look at different experiences of bewilderment, including uncertainty, exhaustion, losing a safe haven, loss of identity, as well as the capabilities people show when they rise up and meet challenges that face them when they locate in new contexts after dislocation from old ones. I begin with two stories, ancient and modern, that directly address these issues. The first is the legend of Ariadne and Theseus. When Theseus is facing his dreaded journey into and through the labyrinth to kill the Minotaur, Ariadne offers him a red thread that he unspools as he goes, so he can remember where he has come from, and how he needs to return. It is, from her perspective, a practical expression of her attachment to him. From his perspective, perhaps it is no more than a logical marker for a way in and a way out from the prospect of endless, lost wandering. Between them, it is a compact and a promise of continuity – a way out of feeling endlessly bewildered. The second story is offered from within Rohinton Mistry's novel *A Fine Balance*. Two young men, migrating from rural contexts to a highly charged urban environment, face the volume and velocity of a city for the first time. In the quote above, Mistry captures their slow reorientations, from bewilderment to sense making, allowing them to be seen as observers, being still, and gradually understanding the patterns of movement swirling around them. These two stories of following threads, or generating sense out of what appear to be unpredictable, alien, and perhaps hostile contexts, are used here as frames for considering the kaleidoscopic challenges that clinicians face in seeking to help others, as well as themselves, in being able to live, and live on in complex times and in fast moving contexts. I consider how we find ways to hold on to our red threads that allow us to stay connected to the journeys we undertake, without becoming lost.

Thinking about yourself in context

Think of yourself in a space that creates composure for you – a space in which your mind expands, to think, to travel. As it does so, consider what this mind tells you about who you are, personally, professionally, and relationally. How have you come to know these things? What are the types and levels of influence in that telling from cultural and social contexts, from family, historically and in the present, from your working life? And how has that sense you have of your identity, of who you are within yourself, and in relation to others, been affected, altered, reinforced, by events and movement. As you think about this story about yourself, take this with you into these pages, think about what resonates for you.

Zygmunt Bauman (2007) observes that we live and work in "liquid times", that is to say, we are part of contexts where:

> "Social forms and institutions no longer have time to solidify and cannot serve as frames of reference for human actions and long-term life plans – so individuals have to find other ways to organise their lives. They have to splice together an unending series of short-term projects and episodes that don't add up to the kind of sequence to which concepts like 'career' and 'progress' could meaningfully be applied. Such fragmented lives require individuals to be flexible and adaptable...In liquid times the individual must act, plan actions and calculate the likely gains and losses of acting (or failing to act) under conditions of endemic uncertainty." (Bauman, 2007)

In such contexts, I would suggest that in relation to professional identities, the tasks of systemic therapists are increasingly labile and not as solid as they were. While once we worked in contexts where our professional identities and roles were relatively stable, an increasing emphasis on functions and tasks has moved us from solid to liquid, from the "who" of our identities, further towards the "what" and the "how". In adapting to such pressures as systemic therapists we have begun to show a malleable side, and learnt to live professionally with dispersed and permeable identities. For example, we might have a role with a different title from Family and /or Systemic Therapist, in a school, in Social Care or in a community based setting. This can be seen as a threat to the hard won identity of the profession, and also as an opportunity to expand the horizons of systemic practices. We may see these changes as a political erosion of public sector mental health services, and work hard within these constraints to provide therapeutic services within these public contexts. In this chapter I will consider the relationship between tradition and innovation embedded in these stories of movement and migration, and how we as clinicians draw on these experiences to generate connections with those with whom we work. These encounters frequently occur at points of Mistry's (1996) characters' observation of "frightening chaos", and our collaborative endeavours to see pattern over time creates at best a capacity to think and reflect for all involved, to develop a rhythm and tempo of attuned listening. How to feel alive, how to be human in these points of connection, are questions which can at times feel fundamentally shaken by the contexts around them. Fear in our lives can shut down places of composure. Creating capacities to think and reflect can re-open them.

Finding red threads in a fearful maze

An organisation that responds fearfully to economic and political forces may unwittingly create a context of fearfulness in its work force. Fearfulness influences how we talk, how we think about to whom we talk, what we talk about. In the high risk scenarios in which many in children's services are working today, communication within and across agencies has been identified as an essential component in keeping children safe. (Working Together to Safeguard Children 2015; The Munro Review 2011). Whilst the need to communicate effectively is established within policy documents, the practice of doing so seems to be inhibited again and again in situations which can seem paralysingly chaotic to the practitioner. Creating organisational contexts that support the possibility of maintaining the red thread of effective communication within trustworthy networks of protection and care provides a safe base from which to think and to work. Additionally, promoting training and the use of theoretical ideas and techniques to add confidence to observation, can help clinicians in their varied contexts to observe pattern and their place within it.

My interest in writing this chapter came partially from a professional rupture. After two years of talking and hoping through doing so for continuity in maintaining and developing our service, and working hard towards this goal, the context to which my colleagues and myself were passionately committed was organisationally reshaped and altered, becoming a different service. In response to this reorganisation many of us moved to other settings, taking with us the collaborative approaches to our work we had established together. The systemic practices of our team, and of the wider systemic community, are being reshaped, or we are reshaping them, to address changing and complex legal, policy and practice contexts, to hold on to the tradition of inherited knowledge and continuity of relationship as roots whilst developing innovative practices in the shifting landscapes of public service.

These "enforced migrations" are very different from the experiences of many people to whom we provide services. They have had to manage severe and traumatic ruptures of family and community life, faith, country and identity. This professional experience has however made us pause, reappraise our professional identities, and consider what living on means in these circumstances. In so doing, the questions we have asked of ourselves have had some resonance with our perceptions of the experiences of those with whom we are involved clinically.

As I thought about "the universe of frightening chaos" that the young men in Mistry's (1996) description were observing, I remembered a different chaotic view I experienced as a young social worker. I had been called out following a phone call to Social Services by the wife of a man in a nearby estate. He had a history of mental health difficulties and was reportedly showing great distress and expressing some suicidal thoughts. I would be the social work component of a mental health assessment, to include his doctor and ambulance back up in case of need.

I reached the flat before my colleagues and his wife answered the door. She said that her husband was quieter but still distressed, and that he was now standing on their small balcony. I asked if this was making her frightened for his safety. She said that it was, but he had not expressed a desire to jump. I asked if I could talk a little to him from the living room and she agreed. I sat in the chair nearest the balcony, and introduced myself, explaining that his doctor and I had been called because his wife was worried about him. I asked him how I could understand his distress. If there were ways to do this? Could it be spoken of? He did not think it could but as our conversation about the unspeakable continued I asked if I could join him on the balcony. He agreed, and we continued our talking.

As we spoke we looked down at the street several floors below, and saw his doctor park and open his car door. As he did so a car came round the bend in the road and knocked into the car door. At that moment the ambulance appeared. Ambulance staff got out to attend to the doctor and the other driver, both of whom were clearly shocked. They also called the police, who then arrived to take statements. We became engrossed in the scene unfolding below us, and we talked of what we were seeing together. I asked him if he would like to talk about it with his wife, and we moved back into the living room where he retold the story he had witnessed. I then talked with them both about how his distress was now, and whether they would like to go with me to see his doctor as the planned visit was not now going to happen. I said that I thought we needed to know whether his distress would continue to be manageable for him, or whether he and his wife needed any other help with the managing. We set off together to his GP's surgery.

I think as clinicians we are often faced with people who have become lost inside themselves in different ways. In this instance, using the circumstances of the moment, I worked to establish a "red thread" to which the man could connect, and return from the internal maze to his home and help.

In entering the family's bewildered moment, I was myself at risk of being bewildered. Using my training, and myself, gave me a thread by which to inch myself forward and find my way back. Now, in considering Cronen and Lang's "grammar of living" (Cronen and Lang 1994), I can think about my legal responsibility in that situation (the domain of production), and how circumstances created an unexpected opportunity to co-create a reflexive space (domain of explanation), in which the person could become the "primary interpreter of their own experience" (Fredman 2004), even if the outcome was not that which they would have chosen.

In telling the story of the car accident together, and in his re-telling to his wife, her husband was able to take a meta-position to a scene of chaos, to which he was the audience. In becoming the storyteller, he came back into connection from the separation that brought him to the brink. In facilitating the narrative of the story unfolding below, he was able to step into an observing role and become part of an observing system, thus moving from the isolation of a first order observation, wherein he himself, and what he saw around him, were all objects in chaos. The meta-observation of the story we were witnessing together connected us to the red thread, guiding him back through the labyrinth towards reconnection to himself and his relational context. This in turn could lead him to connect with the wider health system. In accompanying him, his wife and I were maintaining some continuity and companionship in the isolating context of his distress.

Continuity, companionship, and finding ways to author and find choices in our professional circumstances have been part of my own and my colleagues' experiences in entering new territories and finding new identities within them.

How do I remain the same as I change?

In fast moving times, everything appears fluid. Holding threads of belonging to our trainings, and where possible to some of our work colleagues, has been an important part of understanding the "grammar" (Cronen and Lang 1994) of new languages, and "establishing and re-establishing a sense of belonging" in order to move forward with confidence.

In thinking about taking systemic ideas into new contexts, and wanting to understand different perspectives on managing some of the rapid changes, I had guided conversations with several colleagues around the following four topics.

How has migrating from one context to another influenced you, and how have you influenced the context?
These are some of the views that were voiced:

> *Being a newcomer makes one feel more tentative, and aware of the importance of relearning trust and trusting in a new context.*
> *It is easy to feel diminished if your service is threatened; someone having belief in you helps to maintain pride.*
> *If migrating exposes a dissonance between the past and the present it provides an opportunity to re-examine your own assumptions about work and the values which underpin that work.*

Comment
This makes me think about a family I met soon after my own change of work context. This was a piece of intercultural work which I approached as I would have done in my previous setting. Detailed tracking of the contexts in which the "problem" held by the adolescent in the family

occurred, produced what seemed to be some useful talk, with an acknowledgement of new information and some new ways of seeing the solutions employed by the young person whom I thought was articulate and thoughtful. However, towards the end of the session I sensed that my engagement with the parent was tenuous. I did not feel clear about how this was happening and I felt tentative about voicing this with her. Although we did agree to meet again, the process of agreeing reinforced my sense of this being a tenuous agreement.

After the session I sat and thought about the family. I thought about how, in my previous context, I would have thought carefully about what I and the organisation of which I was a part, might embody for a family. Here the newness of my position and context had I felt inhibited my thinking about the experience of unfamiliarity for the parent. I was too caught up in "performing" a new role. I thought about issues of pride and shame which may have been stirred for her by the referral. I wondered about the fluency of the young person, whether this might have made the parent feel less so, and whether I had paid enough attention to this identity. I considered how my own hesitancy as a newcomer to the organisation made me underestimate the mother's sense of newness in this professional context. I had not thought about the experience of stepping over the threshold with the same rigour as I might have done previously. I then considered what feeling tentative meant in this context for all of us in the room.

I decided to write to the parent. I said that I had not thought sufficiently about their experience of the referral, and what it might have been like for them coming to the first session, to a new place, with someone they had not met. I acknowledged how difficult this was for anyone, and how they might have thought that I would not really be able to understand their situation or help them as I thought I had not talked to them enough about this. I commented on how fluently the young person had spoken about their difficulties, and how they must have learnt how to do this from their parent, as in my experience many young people were not able to speak up for themselves in this way. I said that I hoped they would feel able come again, so that we could talk together about some of these things.

I had a rich and impassioned letter back, full of thinking about the young person's fluency and sensitivity and how this could be supported further. Extending a thread of possible connection brought a much stronger thread in return, a promise of continuity.

This was not of course the end of my clumsiness, or of difficult moments, but the family had helped me to interrogate the meaning of the context, and myself in that context, with fresh eyes. I had seen a new "pattern in things".

How might continuity of relationships maintain or inhibit your identity through your migration to new work contexts?
I think migration can be a bit like being part of a reconstituted family; old relationships are shaped differently, as well as providing some continuity.

It is important to find a foundation for this change – for me it is my faith.

I hold a story about my own father, who had to leave his high status position due to political risk in his country of origin. His story of having a friend who believed in him and helped him to success again has helped me maintain my own narrative of possibility in different contexts.

Being accompanied rather than unaccompanied is comforting, and has made me feel I have a stronger voice and can be a stakeholder. Continuity of relationship has helped me to maintain optimism and retain a pride in our work when it might have been eroded by reductions in public services.

It has been important to form new relationships with old colleagues in order to remain open to possibility and re-examine my work, rather than assume old ways due to the comfort of familiarity.

Comment
Negotiating new relationships within and between family members, professional networks and ourselves is a central component of our working lives. In the fast running currents of organisational life, and the experience of those who collide with them as providers and users of services, creating a listening space in which the effect of tradition on professional or personal identity can be freshly examined can allow new ideas to grow.

In thinking about the importance of continuity of relationship, and of using this as a stepping-stone to new developments we established clear spaces in working lives to talk across disciplines and across relationships about complex clinical dilemmas. In other words, we committed ourselves to cross-pollination. We spoke about how this could feel quite exposing but the potential for new learning provided opportunity. An example of this for myself was outlined above when, I realised that my approach to managing one such meeting had been congruent with the conduct of business in one organisation but did not quite fit with the other. Being still, and observing myself in action, allowed me to re-examine my approach, think afresh about how different colleagues might be experiencing it, and consider how to move forward.

Where does change and innovation create fault lines, and where might new horizons be possible?
It has taken some time to create trusting relationships with colleagues. I think the importance of these connections in helping us manage complexity with confidence and thoughtfulness often goes unrecognised in organisational contexts.

Migrating into a new context has created the opportunity to make new connections, to bring the value of collaboration.

Both contexts have given me a sense of pride and belonging, being part of something worthwhile to me.

A constant state of change is exhausting-there needs to be some settlement.

Comment
We are usually meeting families at a point of significant rupture, but often in quite compacted time frames, due to organisational and legal rules and requirements. My colleagues' reflections made me think again about the importance of time in our work, holding apparently contradictory positions, observing pattern together, creating space for talking, reflecting, trying out new ways of relating, whilst working swiftly to tight deadlines or a limited session allowance. Families will usually have had extensive experience already of working with services in their lives, and exhaustion may at times be interpreted as disengagement. Their thoughts also clarified for me the importance of standing up for working with families over time, challenging the idea that "one size fits all".

How does your thinking about these experiences resonate with your clinical work?
In my work with refugees, many have come to this country with degrees and publications, and have to start again. They have to

keep hold of an idea: this is who I was and who I am, in spite of and through any story of suffering.

This is part of my work as a therapist – uncovering and holding on to stories of pride.

I am in a minority position in some of my new work, which has encouraged me to use my theoretical knowledge as a systemic therapist to look at recursive loops of influence, and develop further confidence in contributing to others' professional growth through training and consultation.

This makes me think of our work in the court context, where we are constantly thinking with parents about what they think they need to do to shift perceptions of themselves as parents.

It makes me think of thickening stories of self-esteem in being a parent, through spotting moments of potential and amplifying these with clients and other professionals.

Established trust, and developing trust, has been containing for me as a clinician, and helped me to be containing when working in complex circumstances.

Comment

In our work with families whose children have been removed, or are at risk of removal, making the process explicit and transparent is key to the first stage of our work together. Whilst the "facts" of the court proceedings, and the reasons for these maybe ostensibly be explicit, the adversarial context can encourage polarisation between all parties – professionals and family members. Whilst working within a legal framework in which we have identities as "assessors", and "expert witnesses", we attempt to "co-create a therapeutic space in mind, conversation and relationship that invites ambivalence and resists the impulse towards categorical impositions" (Byrne and McCarthy 2007). In talking to create "shared meanings" (Burnham 2005), we aim to understand the parents' experience of entering this powerful system, to hear their story of how they have arrived at this point and who has helped or hindered along the way. In sharing our thinking and our written notes about these conversations, we invite responses and make visible alterations to our reports according to the parents' views (or young person's, depending on age and capacity). At times, alteration may not be possible, but any disagreement can be made visible as such, thus "thickening" the parental or young person's voice in the assessment process.

In one such situation, as the disagreement was made visible within the courtroom and I was asked to defend my own position, I was also asked by the parent's barrister what I thought about the expressed difference between their views and mine, as indicated in my report as well as their own statements. I was then able to talk about how we had arrived at these differences, and what sort of therapeutic work might, in my view, make a difference for future family relationships. The parent's barrister then commented to the court that whilst his client did not agree with my recommendations, he wanted to say that he thought I had arrived at them justly. In my view, this conversation "thickened" the court's experience of the parent, as someone who could think about different perspectives and acknowledge difference. It also showed a potential capacity to engage with therapeutic work. Inviting some ambivalence into a linear system created an indication in the moment of the potential for a different story to emerge with further therapeutic and practical help thus visibly supporting this aspect of the recommendations. One year later, the children and parent were living together again.

Having the confidence to question our identity

Entering new territories offers the opportunity to question ourselves, to see our work anew through new lenses, as my colleagues commented. However, this is hard to do without companionship. In order to bring the best of ourselves to a new context we need to consider how we bring a sense of belonging with us, and how we maintain that continuity whilst changing and developing new ways of working. I am always particularly attracted to methods of "thickening" (White 2007) collaborative endeavours, trying to bring disciplines together to think about practice and working together across culturally varied professional boundaries. As with any intercultural practice, this also entails creating a safe haven from which to venture forth. This may be a small haven of one or two companions or a larger group, who importantly share a common goal and possibly discipline, and are supported in the creation of this haven by those with more organisational power. The "exhausting" nature of change referred to above, can undermine the practising of balance and stability so essential in establishing and re-establishing a sense of belonging. Practising collaboratively creates new energies, raises new questions, encourages self-scrutiny and helps "maintain optimism", as a colleague identified, although the shapes and form of these collaborations may be difficult to forecast.

The nature of the collaborative practising space will vary across and within organisations. Other practitioners might wish, as we did, to develop a model incorporating some of Harlene Anderson's thinking (Anderson 2007). The opportunity for inner and outer dialogue is created through the process of uninterrupted telling (a story of practice) and on-hold listening (to inner dialogue about the listening) in order to generate multiple perspectives in both the telling and the listening. At times, asking colleagues to perform the on-hold listening from the perspective of a character in the story has enriched understandings of the possible inner conversations of that character, and the impact of these on the practitioner.

In the language of current dominant organisational discourses around evidence gathering and productivity, this may sound like the antithesis of valuable "performance indicators". However, there is an increasing recognition (Keegan 2015) that an engaged and resilient workforce provides an optimum return on investment. My colleagues and I would argue that engagement and resilience are fostered through trusted alliances, creating contexts for new alliances to be formed, being open to questions about practice, and a sense of belonging, both old and new.

These in themselves are questions for our practice. They bring to my mind working with a colleague in a high profile safeguarding situation where the referring agency (Social Care) was feeling highly scrutinised and worried. I asked this colleague to join me as I would be working across culture and language, and I knew my colleague, born in the same country as the older family members and able to speak family language fluently, would bring a different level of knowledge and understanding from my own. Having lived and worked in intercultural contexts throughout my career I thought carefully about what I might embody for the family when we met in their home. Through our bodies "social divisions become embodied, and through them we exercise our human agency and act on the world." (Malik and Krause 2005). How I was dressed, how I greeted family members of different genders and age, how I accepted food, were all important and available to me to think about and discuss with my colleague. Likewise the significance of the extended family, as a protective factor, as an ally in complex territory, as providing a sense of belonging and continuity at a time of rupture, were crucial considerations. I even thought I had a sense of the importance of faith for the family members, in similar and different ways across the generations. Without my own ally and companion, and the use of a collaborative practising space created by her and her colleagues, I would have really not understood how the most important "red thread" for the family, the meaning of forgiveness could be held through faith. Even though that faith was talked about and practised differently by different members, forgiveness became a collaborative endeavour, again practised in different ways by family members, but all with a similar aim. In our final meeting with the family, all members came, some having travelled far, and each gave their account of their contribution and support, in the present and the future.

A year later I received a phone call from one of the family members. He needed me to corroborate a relative's presence in the country at a particular time which I was able to do as we had held a family meeting on the day in question. He said the family still spoke of our final meeting and reminded each other of their commitment to each other on that day. I said that I and my colleague also held that day in mind when we had learned about the family's commitment to standing together through such difficult times.

When my colleagues spoke of thinking about families we have known and how they wondered what was happening for them, I thought about the stories lodged with us and with them, and the collective memories held somewhere. I thought about the impact of these memories on our working lives, and how these moments live on, inform and develop the tapestries of our practices.

Looking back — looking forward

Our responsibilities in the contexts in which we work are profound. Interrogating our own positions, how we perform these, and with what effect is an essential component of thinking respectfully, about ourselves, our work, about others and about how identities are supported and eroded. In these "liquid times", when dislocation and uncertainty are often prevailing stories in our work, we seek and find stories of resilience and fortitude.

The ripples from any rupture continue over time, and the end point of these journeys is not known and will go through many transformations. Old relationships take their shape and form into new contexts, which add to and at times reshape them. New connections are made. In our work with families we usually meet at a point where the ripples are strongly resonating from the rupture and where questions of living and living on are powerfully present. In our slow listening we seek to retrieve, remember and witness the moments of connection, which provided something good amidst the gravitational pull of catastrophe. We work on the creation of possibility through collaborative talk as a counterweight to that force.

References

Anderson, Harlene (2007). Creating a space for a generative community. In Harlene Anderson and Per Jensen (Eds.), *Innovations in the Reflecting Process*. London: Karnac Books.

Baumann, Zygmunt (2007). *Liquid Times: Living in an Age of Uncertainty*. Cambridge: Polity Press.

Burnham, John (2005). Relational Reflexivity: a tool for socially constructed therapeutic relationships. In Carmel Flaskas, Barry Mason, Amaryll Perlesz (Eds.). *The Space Between: Experience, Context and Process in the Therapeutic Relationship*. London: Karnac Books.

Byrne, Nollaig & McCarthy, Imelda (2007). The Dialectical Structure of Hope and Despair: A Fifth Province approach. In Carmel Flaskas, Imelda McCarthy, Jim Sheehan (Eds.). *Hope and Despair in Narrative and Family Therapy: Reflections on Adversity, Forgiveness and Reconciliation*. Sussex: Routledge.

Cronen, Vernon & Lang, Peter (1994). Language and Action: Wittgenstein and Dewey in the practice of therapy and consultation. *Human Systems. The Journal of Systemic Consultation and Management*. 5(1–2), 5–43.

Fredman, Glenda (2004). *Transforming Emotion: Conversations in Counselling and Psychotherapy*. London: Whurr Publishers Ltd.

Keegan, Sheila (2015). *The Psychology of Fear in Organizations*. London: Kogan Page Ltd.

Malik, Rabia & Krause, Inge-Britt (2005). Before and Beyond Words: Embodiment and intercultural therapeutic relationships in family therapy. In Carmel Flaskas, Barry Mason, Amaryll Perelsz (Eds.), *The Space Between: Experience, Context, and Process in the Therapeutic Relationship*. London: Karnac Books.

Mistry, Rohinton (1996). *A Fine Balance*. London: Faber and Faber.

Munro, Eileen (2011) *The Munro Review of Child Protection: Final Report. A Child Centred System*. London: Department of Education.

White, Michael (2007). *Maps of Narrative Practice*. New York: W.W. Norton and Co.

Working Together to Safeguard Children (2015). London: Department of Education.

The Inner and the Outer Sides of the Wind
Collaborative practice in the Solidarity Social Medical Centre of Thessaloniki, Greece

2

Fany (Fotini) Triantafillou, Dimitra Pouliopoulou, Elektra Bethymouti & Efrossini Moureli

Fotini: So, how should we map a place such as The Solidarity Social Medical Centre? Would a metaphor, a poem, or an image do?

Dimitra: What if we attempted some kind of combination of a metaphorical description with a formal or even an academic one?!

Electra: I would love to connect anything with anything else! After all, this is an *Everything is Connected Press* book, isn't it?

Fotini: Fine! And, if we mixed up metaphorical and formal descriptions would that be a kind of double description?! Dear old Gregory, will you forgive the audacity?

> *I bring to the readers' attention a number of cases in which two or more information sources come together to give information of a sort different from what was in either source separately.* (Gregory Bateson, 1980)

Fotini: So, any metaphors flowing around?

Electra: An image has just popped up in my mind, an image that moves me a lot, actually... Remember Mirorad Pavic's, *The Inner Side of the Wind* (1993)?

> *"The inner side of the wind is the one that remains dry when the wind blows in the rain..."*

That is, the wind has an outer and an inner side. When it blows towards one direction, its interior, although not apparent, blows towards the opposite direction...

Fotini: I like it! Let's make something of it! Where would you put the Solidarity Social Medical Centre (SSMC) on this image/ map/metaphor?

Electra: Everywhere! The SSMC could be every single part of this image and at the same time, all of it!

Fotini: Meaning?

Electra: Meaning that this small but yet so complex system, called "The Solidarity Social Medical Centre", is the wind with its inner and outer sides; it is the rain, too, and the human being half dry, half wet insisting to walk on the inner side against the wind...

Dimitra: We could also say that the inner side of the wind stands for the "new" (ideas, attitudes and procedures) as they have been created, step-by-step, by all its people – both its members and its visitors – by the relationships between all of them, as well as by their actions and interactions, by their dialogues, their voices and the polyphony thus co-created.

Fotini: It must be a safe place, then! With the storm blustering outside...

Dimitra: It feels as such! Mind you though, there are unavoidable inner storms too! How else could it be in such a polyphonic place?

Electra: Well, I myself would like to think of the inner side of SSMC's wind as being created mainly by its members' collaboration, self-organisation and horizontal operations. By sharing common goals and working together, the members aspire to co-create a wide field of activity, enthusiasm, determination and strength.

Dimitra: On the other hand, the SSMC's visitors (we call them "incomers"), citizens of a winter-beaten economy, find a friendly welcoming place, respectful to their personalities and needs which provides primary medical and pharmaceutical treatment.

Fotini: Well, let's have a closer look! What is the story here?

Efrossini: The SSMC was created within the storm of this century's crisis: all of a sudden, Greek society entered into a vortex of multiple losses – a lot of people (most of them of the middle and lower class) lost their jobs, their salaries and pensions, their houses... They had basic utilities ("common goods", actually) like electricity and water cut off. Their work and insurance rights disappeared – indeed, a total social disaster has taken place during a period of supposed peace!

The Inner and the Outer Sides of the Wind

Dimitra: Health care, the educational system, standards of living, social relations, all in vertical decay...

Electra: Society in despair and enfeeblement. People full of questions and disappointments, feeling accused, being paralysed and confused, seeing no way out...

Efrossini: A society humiliated, in the lap of wicked and devouring profiteers... People unprotected, people oppressed!

Fotini: My God! You sound like a moaning Ancient Greek Tragedy chorus!

Efrossini: You know, we might as well be a chorus – not of the ancient but of the Present Greek Tragedy...

Electra: And yet, within all this falling apart of values, still the values of "family", "self-organisation" and "solidarity", the meanings of which is incarnated through many forms and ways, have been emerging as the best resources – like how parents and the grandparents are using their small pensions to support unemployed children, grandchildren and their families.

The self-organisation of people's groups and collectives, like this SSMC, have been contributing mostly in the support of uninsured patients, providing food and taking care of people with low or no income at all, pressing for the re-connection of electricity in darkened houses ... The SSMC's prefix is: *No one should be left alone in this crisis.*

Dimitra: The sense and the actions of self-organisation and solidarity raise the moral, elicit dignity, and generate resistances while re-enforcing a strong spirit of people wanting to question and overturn existing structures. After all, one of the slogans of SSMC is "Solidarity is an action of resistance".

Αντιδρώντας έμπρακτα σε πολιτικές που εξαθλιώνουν τον άνθρωπο, κατασκευάζουν στρατιές ανέργων, δημιουργούν χιλιάδες ανασφάλιστων, καταργούν τη δημόσια υγεία. **Απαντάμε** υλοποιώντας στην πράξη, την αλληλεγγύη, τη συλλογικότητα, την αυτοδιαχείρηση στο κοινωνικό πεδίο. Από **7 Νοεμβρίου 2011** λειτουργεί το **Κοινωνικό Ιατρείο Αλληλεγγύης** προσφέροντας δωρεάν ιατροφαρμακευτική & οδοντιατρική περίθαλψη σε Έλληνες & αλλοδαπούς ανασφάλιστους.

Fotini: Very interesting! Let's have an even closer look at this place of Solidarity, the image it presents to the public, starting from its logo:

A quite welcoming-looking house, I see!

Efrossini: In fact, the SSMC is housed in a city-centre, relatively small basement flat, which was offered by the Labour Centre of Thessaloniki. It is a quite narrow place, really, facilitating at same time, though, closeness and direct communication...

Fotini: How would SSMC members present this place of solidarity they have co-created?

Efrossini: We had better refer to our formal communal description:

> *The Solidarity Social Medical Centre of Thessaloniki, Greece is a social health care collective which provides primary medical and pharmaceutical treatment to all the uninsured citizens who can walk freely in, without any distinctions and discriminations, in terms of ethnicity, race, religious affiliation, gender, sexual orientation and age. As a primary health structure it exerts pressure on political society to secure universal, free of charge, secondary and tertiary medical care, hospitalisation and rehabilitation. The SSMC takes part in the movement for a universal, free and public health system in Greece and it is part of the anti-racist and anti-fascist movement. It also takes part in the social solidarity networks that are active in the fields and sectors of life, which currently have proven indispensable for the preservation of a humane way of life and social cohesion. A primary aim has been the re-establishment of those relations and modes of being that restore the sense of the collective and practically oppose individualism, competition and the exploitation of human by human.*
>
> *The SSMC operates on a daily basis and holds regular clinics (pathology, dentistry, neurology, paediatrics, otolaryngology, dermatology). It is also supported by a large group of psychotherapists-psychologists-psychiatrists, a group of midwives, a physiotherapy group and a pharmacy that serves the needs of the clinics and twice a week provides medication to patients with chronic diseases. It is also affiliated with a network of external associates/private physicians (microbiologists, gynaecologists, surgeons) that serve the health care needs not provided by its clinics (i.e. diagnostic tests), a network of pharmacists who, in their private pharmacies, collect medicines for the SSMC and with a*

network of hospital MD's who facilitate the access of the patients to the National Health Service.

Fotini: Well, it seems that it provides quite a lot of services, through a whole network of people and relationships! Well done! But how is it done?

Efrossini: First of all, its main characteristic and inspiring asset is solidarity!

Fotini: In what sense?

Efrossini: The SSCM members acknowledge solidarity as resistance and subversion. Solidarity means giving something that is substantial to you, not something you have in excess. Of course, in this context, giving is considered as a circular and not as a linear process. Still, we have not yet found a satisfying solution so that the incomers could equally give back to us something else than their gratitude... It is true that the SSMC's members have been trying very hard, indeed, to promote solidarity, internally and externally, by building bridges with the social groups and movements of the area. Being independent of the State and the E.U., the Church, the Government, Political Parties and the Market has been one of their great values.

Fotini: Well, this is news! Not taking into consideration THE Market???? And especially within the context of a third memorandum, the latest financial "arrangement" between the European Commission, the International Monetary Fund and Greece???!

Dimitra: I believe that SSMC does make a difference by making a difference in almost any level of operation...

Fotini: Is this difference so big that it overthrows the need for money?!

Efrossini: Not at all! SSMC accepts donations, but only from individuals (e.g. artists giving concerts) or other social collectives and associations. It neither advertises nor receives sponsorship. You see, I believe the most important thing in relation to the Market is that SSCM offers us the opportunity to subvert our own alienation, which is the result of the expropriation of our capabilities by the market through money. The commercialisation of people's potentials leads towards a social life, which is estranged and infiltrated strongly by the significance given by the institutions to their professions. For example, a doctor is considered as having: power, knowledge and importance. I think, in SSCM, the non-commercialisation of our potential might make us emerge as non-commercial subjects, as people capable of collaborating on the basis of ideas and common visions.

Fotini: Quite an interesting political comment, you attempt here, I think! And as far as the organisational aspects and the management are concerned?

Electra: This is it! The SSCM declares and celebrates its autonomy! There is a system of self-management, that is, the collective itself takes and realises all decisions. Most importantly, the SSCM tries to operate on a direct democracy basis.

This means that all SSCM members, as social subjects, in their attempt to create a unique social space with the others, have been trying to achieve a balance between the needs of the individual and collective aspects of their personality and the needs of the group. This process sometimes becomes problematic for all concerned but it seems that the common goal obliges all to continuously test, revise and create anew this delicate balance, within a context in which:

- The general assembly is the decisive body of the SSCM.
- Each "department" (subgroup) operates through its autonomous assembly that plans and organises the workload. Its members debate over and propose the issues to the general assembly.
- The permanent committees that organise events deal with finances and the Press and they implement the decisions of the general assembly.
- There are also action groups dealing with the publication of a calendar, posters and sanitation and working groups elaborating on issues that are disseminated to its members and presented to the assemblies.
- In contradistinction to the ruling representative democracy, the SSCM operates on the basis of delegation (with specific space-, time- and issue- limits) and rotation, attempting to apply direct democracy principles.
- Preferably, decisions are reached with maximum participation and on the basis of substantive convergence or consensus – namely unanimously. Whenever this is not possible, decisions are taken

with majority vote while the minority is granted due recognition (dissensus is recorded and the decision is subject to re-evaluation).

Fotini: It sounds quite challenging to me! There must be a lot of wind (both a fair and an "un-fair" one) in this home of direct democracy!

Efrossini: Well, yes, as happens with any human group. Sure, at times, there are conflicts that are painful, tiresome and consuming of mental energy, with members resigning and leaving, but on the whole, I hope we learn a lot about how our own behaviour contributes to the conflict and/or its resolution.

Fotini: Well, now, I get more curious about the persons and the processes involved... How long has this solidarity "experiment" been going on?

Dimitra: The SSCM has been going on for four years. Its members respect the principles of Collectivity, (irrespectively of the partisan affiliation of some of them), Collaboration, Equality and Parity among themselves. No one is more important than the other persons. We collectively decide on our principles, rules and modes of operation and equally we abide by them. In general, we oppose philanthropy, individualism, hierarchical relations and practices.

Fotini: Mmm... I feel that this way of working must be very fulfilling and at the same time quite wearisome for the members... Perhaps it serves their personal, collective, medical, social and subversive needs? Could this be some kind of reward and satisfaction?

Efrossini: It could. There are some moments and some situations that bring us real joy. For example, when we manage to find the rare medication some refugees need, or intervene and put pressure on a hospital to accept a patient for surgery, when we succeed in reaching a decision in an easy and friendly way and so on so forth.

It is invaluable, I think, this sense of freedom and strength we experience while trying to make a health service be different or when we organise a medical group to go to the country's borders to support the refugees who continuously cross them...

At the same time, we come across much pain and suffering that affects us greatly. Tragic stories and total losses carried by human beings walking endlessly towards their destiny. On which side ("inner" or "outer"?), of which "wind" (history's perhaps?) is the road of all these people walking against all odds?

Electra: Anyway, we basically believe that health is a fundamental good that should be provided to all without any preconditions such as insurance. It should be a corner stone of a society. Health is not a right, because the right needs someone to secure it, or not, as it is the case today.

So we struggle for:

- A universal, free and public health system.
- The establishment of solidarity among people.
- The subversion of power relations and subordination.
- And ultimately, for Health as a social good.

Fotini: Revolution in action, then!

Electra: Well, yes, the SSMC could be a subversive action unto itself!

Fotini: In that case, it is almost natural that this kind of organisation invites a lot of new ideas and practices to emerge! I am sure there are systemic practitioners who find a nice place there for developing their ideas!

Dimitra: True! I think systemic thinking and acting fits with SSMC practices. There is certainly space for systemic contributions, which understandably perturb the status quo of traditional Medicine, Psychiatry and Psychology...

Fotini: An example?

Electra: The wish, the attempt and the experimentation of some SSMC members, (two of which are authors of this text, E. Moureli and D. Pouliopoulou) to make room for an "alternative" medicine and medical care in collaboration with SSMC medical doctors and others specialists.

Fotini: And...?

Efrossini: Hang on! First, I think we should make a distinction between the dominant paradigm of Medicine and the "alternative" ones. I suppose you agree that the paradigm followed by status quo Medicine is based on various separations and dissociations: the separation of psyche/soma, human beings – environment/contexts, patient/doctor...

Fotini: Well, yes! The glorious paradigm of Science fragmenting and objectifying everything!

Efrossini: Furthermore, conventional Medicine divides constantly its field of operation into sub-disciplines talking past each other. But most importantly, it divides the human organism, rendering it fragmented, which is not re-united. Thus, status quo Medicine misses the opportunity to identify and acknowledge the overall patterns that integrate the parts into a whole, to appreciate the complexity and the capabilities of the human organism as a whole. From this point of view, the effectiveness of the alternative forms of Medicine might depend on their perception of the human organism as a unity, as a whole.

Dimitra: Consequently, in our Western Societies, instead of having a health-orientated Medicine taking care of the bio-psycho-social human well-being, we have ended up with a damage-focused and technologically governed Medicine. Instead of a humane relationship between patient and doctor, we usually have a symptom-medication, symptom-medical-act relation!

Efrossini: We should also take into consideration that the medical science is enchained to the complex of pharmaceutical/medical technologies and is directly affected by the interests they represent. So, it constantly expands its field of application by incorporating areas previously treated as social. Prominent amongst those is the medicalisation of childhood, wherein children's resistance to excessive channelisation of their lives is pathologised and medicalised.

Fotini: So, do you mean that in SSMC the systemic approach... has been trying to talk with conventional Medicine on an equal basis?

Dimitra: You might say this. Starting from our wish to approach as far as possible the wholeness of human beings and participate in a qualitative transformation of the therapeutic relationship, we have been making attempts towards this direction in clinical practice. Mind you, this is not an easy thing at all!

Fotini: And what is the vision of the SSMC "alternative Medicine" group?

Efrossini: A medical science that does not simply perceive, explain and deal with the symptom but treats it as a part of the whole human being's life. Namely, the human being should be seen as a physical/psychic unity

– like two pages of the same sheet – that cannot be possibly separated without abolishing its unity as a whole.

Dimitra: In this sense and reflecting on equality and parity, in the SSMC, we agreed to welcome the incomers as indispensable, active and energetic participants in their own treatment/therapy, as we consider them to be in their own life. That's why we use the word "incomer" instead of visitor or the usual "client" or "patient", relying on the constructing power of language and knowing that in this health community we are all incomers...

Fotini: Okay, but how about the doctor-patient and the therapeutic relationship, which you envisage to qualitatively transform? After all, it is quite an intense relationship based very much on Medicine's institutional power coming mainly from societal reasons....

Efrossini: Sure! The conventional doctor-patient relationship reflects the authoritarian regulation of the social field that treats the doctor as the bearer of the power of knowledge as far as the physical, mental, psychic and, by extension, social aspect of the human existence are concerned. And, on the other hand, it treats the patient as a passive and child-like "object" of study.

Fotini: Isn't it true, though, that in the modern world, plagued as it is by the so-called "authority crisis", doctors' authority appears to be the sole survivor?!

Efrossini: Yes. I suppose so, and this can be credited, also, to patients' consent, which in turn is predicated upon the universal acceptance of Science.

Fotini: Ah, yes, Science the "new" God of the "New Age"! But how have you proceeded with this "alternative medicine" project?

Dimitra: Acknowledging our common desire to criticise the dominant paradigm of medical science, at first, we started reflecting and dialoguing! A lot of our discussions were focused on the relations developing among all of us (the incomers, the members and the "experts") and on issues concerning the therapeutic relationship. Almost naturally, within the context of this social health care collective, our wish to start experimenting with new forms of collaboration in clinical practice become true. So, as a systemic therapist, I "joined forces" with two other members of the "alternative Medicine" group, a male intern in the beginning with whom we created the "joint sessions" as we called them, and then – till today – with a female family doctor with whom we continue developing these sessions in which a "psychologist" and a "medical doctor" together converse with incomers complaining of physical problems. This was one of the initiatives of the alternative Medicine group.

Mind you, this new form of collaboration is an "experimental" co-creation in process. It has been developing through a continuous dialogue between the collaborators and the participant incomers in the joint sessions. It has also been discussed and reflected upon in the "alternative Medicine" group and at times presented at the assemblies of SSMC.

Fotini: How was this new idea and practice received by SSMC, at first?

Dimitra: Well, some of the members expressed their enthusiasm, were really interested and curious to know more about it and were supportive to this initiative! Others were ambivalent and others expressed some perplexity and objections (e.g. "We have too many incomers and we are struggling to manage to see them all, why should we have two members spending so much time with one case?")

Fotini: Did any power issues come up?!

Efrossini: Of course! Power has been an issue for our systemic field. I think the concept and the praxis of "power" is an issue for SSMC, too. Some members seem to deny the power that the institution of Medicine gives to doctors or they think that SSMC doctors manage not to get involved in power relations!

Dimitra: I agree, but I would also add that this kind of collaboration and therapeutic context brings out the issues of the "unknown" and of "uncertainty" which at first could provoke a sense of fear, and could in turn be expressed as a rejection of any new idea. So, the issue of power and the need to control could emerge as a "response" or a kind of "solution", which is illusive in my opinion, especially within these inevitable human conditions. In any case, I think, it is what doctors are facing in their everyday working life... So, after dealing with these kind of issues and going through quite a few ups and downs (the inner side of the wind...), today, almost two years later, although still on an experimental basis, this collaborative practice, I think, is more accepted by SSMC members.

Also, it is always open to psychotherapists of different approaches and to more family doctors or interns to participate if they wish to do so.

Fotini: In this course, which theoretical winds have been blowing you away?

Dimitra: Well, let's say that at first, each one of the collaborators came to the joint sessions, with their clinical experience, training, theories, epistemology, expectations about therapy, and so on, but as well as with their personalities, their whole life, really. In this sense, our practice in the joint sessions is a composition of different practices. It is a meeting of lived experiences of different approaches. Until now, our joint sessions have been informed mainly by collaborative approaches to therapy (Anderson & Gehart 2007); reflecting (Andersen 1991) and dialogic processes – the approach of Open Dialogue has been and still is a great inspiration, (Seikkula 2006); systemic ideas and practices – a lot of them coming from the Milan School tradition (Boscolo, Cecchin, Hoffman, & Penn 1987); general medicine, (Stephenson 2004); holistic medicine, (Bauer 2014), classical medicine and systemic medicine (Asen, Tomson, Young & Tomson 2004), all of them "in dialogue".

Fotini: Who is referred for these joint sessions?

Dimitra: Look, first, all incomers contact the SSMC Reception and from there they are referred to the doctors according to their problems and quests. As far as joint sessions are concerned, we have noticed that the incomers who usually are considered as "difficult" by SSMC medical doctors (i.e. people wanting to see the interns or family doctors too often, people who have a large medical file or create difficulty or distress to doctors and SSMC members), and the incomers with non–specific symptoms associated with psychological issues might be referred for joint sessions by the family doctors or the interns, after at least one conventional medical visit. Additionally, incomers with chronic physical complaints, with a serious and sudden disease, those having to face an imminent or a recent death or post-surgery conditions could also be referred for joint sessions. The incomers enter the context of joint sessions if they accept this proposal otherwise they follow the usual SSMC's procedure.

Fotini: Would you say a bit more about the joint sessions' particulars?

Dimitra: Each collaborative joint session lasts about one hour (when there is only one incomer participating) or one hour and a half (if they come with their significant relationships). Before and after each session, the family doctor and the psychotherapist usually spend some 15-30 minutes to discuss the topics related to the therapy of the incomer, as well as issues concerning the development of joint sessions' process and context, and the collaboration of the two "experts". Additionally, a session form has been co-created by the psychotherapist and the family doctor, including questions of joint interest, which is filled jointly by them before and after each session.

As far as the actual space (the doctor's office) is concerned, each time is rearranged. As you know, traditionally, the doctor usually sits behind her/his desk; during the joint sessions everybody is sitting in front of the desk, in a circle.

Fotini: And how about the conversational process?

Dimitra: The family doctor and the psychotherapist meet with the referred incomers. First, we introduce ourselves and then we give information about the general context of SSMC and the particular context of the proposed joint sessions. We proceed as soon as the incomers give their consent. So far, there has been no objection or rejection by any incomer. Following the systemic and dialogical tradition, from the start or at a later stage, those comprising the incomers' significant relationships are invited to participate. These could be: family members, close friends, caregivers and relationships that have been developed by sharing similar conditions due to the effects of crisis on their lives. When this is not possible or wanted by the incomer, the dialogue "includes" the absent persons through circular questions (Boscolo, Cecchin, Hoffman, & Penn 1987).

Fotini: Go on! Describe more of this dialogue!

Dimitra: I would say that it is a process that invites all participants to get involved in a circular "narrative dance", if you like. During this dialogue, correlations gradually start emerging and connecting the physical complaint, its investigation and examination, the incomers' important life events (loss of employment is very common these days) and of their important relationships, their life history and the history of their treatments and therapies. So, you see, within this kind of process, the medical examination shifts form the partial to the whole, from the physical complaint to the vicissitudes of the incomer's whole life...

Fotini: These vicissitudes, I gather, depend a lot on the recent social and economic Greek situation!

Dimitra: Certainly! The present oppressive social and economic situation in Greece affects the manifestation and aggravation of physical symptoms as well as the outcome of medical treatment. Naturally then, it has been steadily "present" in these joint sessions, connecting, thus, the person, her/his family and other significant persons, and the joint conversation and therapeutic context with the wider social context.

Fotini: I am curious, though, in this dialogical process is there any "proper" medical, physical, examination? And how is it done?

Dimitra: Well, this is a difference! The medical examination of the incomer is a part of the whole conversational process. It all happens within the circular sitting and dialoguing arrangement.

At some point, depending on how the dialogue goes and when medical examination is deemed necessary, the doctor moves from the description to the medical examination which often takes place in parts, according to the various parts of the body, like a dialogue traversing the entire body. While dialogue is continuing, more physical symptoms, values and feelings could be highlighted, connected and correlated. So, you understand that an "alternative" medical examination takes place within the circle of this multilevel dialogue but when needed, the doctor might invite the incomer to sit on a medical couch for a while. If the incomer's significant relationships participate in the dialogue, the procedure of the medical examination doesn't change, unless all the participant discussants wish otherwise.

It is interesting that in this context, a "proper", conventional medical examination takes place very rarely since logos (the principle) seems to contain everyone and everything.

Fotini: Maturana's (1988) "bodyhood" enmeshed in and even shaped by discussion!

Dimitra: Possibly! We are still experimenting on it!

Fotini: And the position of the psychotherapist?

Dimitra: The psychotherapist, being a participant acting observer (Cecchin 1992) either connects the information coming up from anyone present or she could preserve an attitude of careful listening and observing or at other moments she could ask the family doctor to elaborate on a medical term (e.g. a diagnosis) that sounds incomprehensible, inviting all to talk about it afterwards so that dialogue goes on...

But you know, while the incomers usually feel quite at ease with this process, trusting us, I suppose, the collaborating "experts" seem more concerned with this kind of situation. After all, we are all simultaneously present in a doctor's office (with its awe-inspiring atmosphere) and in a psychologist's office (which is quite different from the medical one), embedded all in a dialogical space!

Fotini: I see... I imagine, though, that for the family doctor this kind of dialogue might have been a bit awkward, at least in the beginning... And you, how did you feel?

Dimitra: Sure, being present at these "medical" moments is a particular condition for the psychotherapist since she finds herself in front of an "unknown" way of thinking and naming. Still, I feel that this condition is very special, too; since it allows me to be in front of the sanctum of a psycho-somatic-social relationship. In fact, I feel that it connects me with the whole human spectrum and that it enriches invaluably our dialogue.

Both of us, the family doctor and I, feel that this kind of process facilitates a strong confidential relationship among all the participants.

Fotini: What would the family doctor have to say?

Dimitra: I can share with you some of our thoughts from our conversations. From the point of view of the family doctor, the main difference is the active participation / collaboration, on "equal" dialogical terms, of the "patient" in her/his own therapy. The process of joint sessions shifts away from the standards of conventional medical care, often unable to resolve complex "symptoms" within the usual vertical and univocal medical therapeutic context. Even in the Family General Medicine, the professionals are used and trained to talk to the patient (and decide for her/him). So, in our case, it seems that it is a big change for them to talk with the patient.

There also another big difference: the joint sessions help to plan together with the incomers their medical care and rehabilitation. The plan of medical intervention is co-constructed by all -incomers, family doctor and psychotherapist.

The interaction and the dialogue enlighten all the spectrum of the physical symptom and help us to go deeper and understand complex situations better.

You could say that we have been attempting to transcend the conventional physical-psychic-social split and go towards a holistic approach forging cross-disciplinary collaborative relations...

But we are still at the beginning. So, we are investigating whether this procedure could be saving time for all of incomers and "therapists". We are thinking that it could be saving physical and mental energy for the incomers, in particular, as we see that it spares them from numerous and time consuming medical examinations, referrals or visits to various doctors and or from getting lost in an inhuman-disconnecting health care system.

And eventually, we start wondering whether this kind of joint sessions could be a suggestive idea for the saving of human and financial resources in the development of an alternative Health care system... Ambitious? Dreamy? Perhaps...

Fotini: Well, I am sure that within this kind of process there are various benefits to be gained by all participants...

Dimitra: It is very important, I think, that being mainly dialogical (before, during and after the actual sessions), the joint sessions could become for all participants a context of active learning. If each voice could be heard, acknowledged and accepted – then, through interaction, it influences the other voices, points of view, epistemologies, specialties!

Isn't this one of the "charms" of a polyphonic dialogue?

Fotini: Ah! Yes, the charms coupled with the sense of the unknown, the complexity and the power of the polyphonic dialogue or the "dialogic collaboration"!

The Inner and the Outer Sides of the Wind

Electra: Perhaps we are dealing here with an inner side of the wind – collaborating humans walking hand in hand against the outer sides of the wind...

Dimitra: Quite! We have seen, by now, how the joint sessions could broaden the domain of interaction; how they could begin to inspire and promote a more reflecting stance in the conversations and research; how they could open up horizons of creativity, and knowledge; and all these within a context of wishing to improve the incomers' well-being.

Fotini: So, how do you feel, as one of the initiators of this endeavour of the alternative Medicine group?

Dimitra: You know that this kind of dialogical process facilitates connections and correlations. So, not only the physical complaint is variously connected and reframed but also the relationship between the incomer, the doctor and the psychotherapist is greatly facilitated. The whole process appears as an invitation to all participants and a challenge for equality and parity between all of them, particularly between the doctor and the incomer.

Still, as a therapist, I feel that the most significant thing for me is the vicissitudes of therapy and their connection to relationships and life events.

Fotini: So, in this very "inner side of the wind", could we say that the psychotherapist's position of reverence and irreverence, curiosity, and a "relational" point of view gradually, within a dialogical context, has been structurally coupled with the doctor's sensitivity and careful medical examination, ending up in the formation of a collaborating "therapeutic couple" with a common relational point of view?

Dimitra: Yes, we might say that! Practically, I think this kind of process widens the scope both of systemic therapy hypotheses and the medical "diagnoses" – if there still exist any traditional ones!

More importantly, though, I have seen this "wind" blowing away and moving all participants emotionally, relationally, mentally, physically...

Fotini: Any feedback from the participating incomers?

Dimitra: They seem interested in and generally content. The other day, one incomer commented on the process: "*I think my physical and* mental health is a kind of give and take process, anyway. Yes, I think, all this is helping me. But it is helping you, too, to understand better... You know, with this kind of discussion, I feel that I have a base to stand on. I have two persons who think about me and try to help me. This is very important to me. It gives me hope that something good exists and will come out, shedding light on my case".

Fotini: So, in this inner side of the wind light is shed on new descriptions, new narratives...

Dimitra: Yes! The incomer, the doctor and the therapist become conversational "partners" and develop a collaborative relationship. Within a dialogical process, new meanings and new narratives as well as new questions are co-constructed by all of them. The certainties of each "expert" are challenged. Not to mention that the co-existence of the representatives of the two specialties in the same room and during the same examination hour signifies the sectionalism of knowledge and the necessity for the scientific fields to be and act as complementary with each other.

Fotini: ... Fitting very well with the SSMC's ideology!

Dimitra: Yes! I think that the collaborative joint sessions could contribute to the modification and subversion of authority relations between specialties and between "patient" and "doctor" They could also contribute to the criticism of the dominant scientific knowledge, the critical discussion and the renewal of science's meaning. Possibly, they could transform clinical practice so that it aims to the emancipation of the person by constituting a community for the promotion of health and, eventually, by establishing health as a common, social good and right.

Fotini: Mmm... The inner and the outer sides of the wind interacting! By the way (!), have they been any intense conflicts inside the SSMC?

Electra: Of course! As they could have been in any living system! I believe that conflicts cost a lot emotionally but at the same time they emancipate collective life.

Fotini: So, I presume that there is an inner side of the wind inside the SSMC that keeps the person dry and well while the wind blows in the rain and an inner side that could become quite difficult... Or, perhaps an

The Inner and the Outer Sides of the Wind

inner side that it could get the person a bit wet considering all the upsets and the losses any change brings.

Electra: True. On the other hand, the outer blowing wind, on a level, could represent all the old things its members carry with them: individualism, dominance, control, personal authority, the attribution of responsibility, monologues and silence...

The "new" (the dry or half-dry inner side) has been emerging with difficulty. It appears fragile but moving. It gives inspiration and strength to the difficult work and to the enormous human effort to understand. Nothing is taken for granted – neither equality, nor non-authority, or, mainly, direct democracy. Everything demands its definition right from the start and continuously. But it is here, in this inner side of the wind that the endless effort opens up new ways of collective life...

Efrossini: Together with a lot of questions!

- What is an authoritative relationship, and what is its opposite? What is "dominant" and what "dominated"? How could or should we avoid conflict? When is a conflict useful and in what ways?
- How can a "useful" coupling be facilitated? Is our hypothesis true that if each SSMC member carried inside them the "whole" of SSMC and had it in mind in every action, it could result in a better coupling? How could we go about it?
- What does "solidarity" among the SSMC's members mean? How could the SSMC inspire solidarity to its incomers?
- What kind of "things" cultivates thinking and dialogical processes? How could SSMC show its difference from other services?
- And finally, what kind of humans do we become within SSMC's context?

Electra: We envisage that in this route, helped by the wind of creativity, a new "human being" will emerge; the collective subject. A human being, part of a wider collaborative whole, which takes decisions jointly, appreciates group inclusiveness that multiplies individual potentials. The "new" human being puts forward activity, not passivity; dignity, not humiliation; group spirit, not loneliness.

Dimitra: I suppose, though, for the time being, these coming "new" human beings are struggling in between the old and the new approach;

they are striving, first, inside them, then in their small community, then, out in the wider society.

Electra: True! The "new"takes different names... You could feel it at some blessed moments, while it is born in action, while it strengthens the group spirit and makes our journey worthy. Still, the "old" as the outer side of the wind, does keep on blowing! Privatisation and Nationalisation enclose the common goods; the National Health System breaks down in misery, in an atmosphere of terror and colonisation. We attribute to the "old" the delegation, a deep-seated idea that somebody else will manage for us and decide about the things that concern us, like the common goods.

The "old" could also be shown in some of our own ways of still serving the status quo Medicine, Psychiatry and Psychology.

Efrossini: And of course, in the ever-present struggle for power!

Dimitra: And yet, in this small system created by all the SSMC's members, the "new" takes particular forms: self-organisation, autonomy, decisions taken collectively, various working groups, relations with communities and engagement of communities...

Efrossini: Let me tell you about our experience with such a community! It has been such a gift for us! Once upon a time (very recently, that is), in a very beautiful area of Northern Greece, Chalkidiki, a Canadian ore mining company, started digging to find gold, exploiting the earth, the people and the environment. It is well known that gold mining brings out toxic components, such as arsenic and other heavy metals, contaminating and poisoning the earth, water, air and the food chain, causing absolute and irreversible damage to the environment. From the start, the local communities reacted, resisted and fought against the Gold Company but the State's oppression and suppression on them, until recently, has been very strong.

One day, the representatives of one of the local communities came to SSMC asking for psychological help for their children. A lot of parents had been worried that the conflicts, the arrests and the imprisonments of their friends and relatives would damage their children's mental health. A group of psychiatrists and psychologists (some of them systemically orientated) decided to respond to this request.

The Inner and the Outer Sides of the Wind

Dimitra: Of course, a lot of conversations took place in SSMC concerning this experience.

Efrossini: And a lot of questions emerged pressing for some answers:

- How do we con-verse with a community, which is faced with a (pseudo) double bind: protection of the environment or a job in the mine in times of great unemployment?
- What is our position on this issue? Being against the gold mining ourselves, how are we disposed towards them?
- How could we protect their personal data while at the same time we would respond to their questions? How could we avoid psychologising the social and vice versa?
- In this meeting, how much could we be in solidarity and how much would we be "professional experts" with them? What kind of meeting would we like to organise?
- What kind of consequences would this meeting have on their morale?
- How do we feel in front of people who fight for the survival of themselves and of their homeland?

Fotini: What was your main concern, would you say, while preparing for this meeting?

Efrossini: The central question appeared to focus on what kind of processes should be developed in this coming meeting. First of all, we were thinking that as a SSMC activity, the process should be very different from the hierarchical medical/psychiatric model, which favours giving advice and prescriptions to passive receivers. It should secure both personal differentiation and participation. There should be a safe place for the parents to reveal any personal issues and for the SSMC members to express their own opinion. The process should have the elements of collaboration and collectivity while promoting personal reflection and choice in a context of equality.

These kinds of thoughts almost dictated the way we finally organised this public meeting. We decided to use our ideas about large group discussions, systemic investigating discussions, reflecting and dialogic processes.

In the end, the whole process developed as follows: the meeting took place on a Saturday afternoon, in a schoolyard of this long-suffering area, in May 2014. It lasted some six hours, until midnight. In this meeting there participated twelve SSMC members, three men and nine women, (five of which were systemic therapists), and sixty five parents, most of them women.

Fotini: A big community, then, inside the inner side of the wind of solidarity! How did you proceed?

Efrossini: First, we introduced ourselves and gave some information about SSMC. Then, the parents were asked to form groups according to the age of the children for whom they had been worried (preschool children, elementary school children, adolescents, mixed ages.) At least two SSMC members took over the coordination of each group.

Next, we asked the parents to answer a few written questions: How many members does your family have? Which child is worrying you the most? How would you explain your worries? Which are the best characteristics of the child who worries you? Have there been any big changes in your family life during the two last years (e.g. illness, birth, death, divorce, unemployment, imprisonment etc.)? In fact, the parents were very willing to write down (anonymously) their answers.

Next, in each group, the SSMC members classified the written answers according to the parents' worries (e.g. behavioural, existential, moral dilemmas etc.) and started a reflective dialogue between themselves in front of the parents, about the classified information at hand.

Fotini: Very interesting! Carry on!

Efrossini: As in all reflective/dialogic conversations, at first, there was: listening to what each one of us had to say, acceptance of his/her point of view, debate and finally some common understanding. So, as the dialogue went on, our thoughts, coming from different points of view, were in agreement or in disagreement and transformed via the dialogical process.

Finally, the conversation opened up to include the parents. In a very natural, spontaneous way, a conversation started developing between the parents and us. At times, we went back to our own reflective dialogue for a while and then back again to the wider dialogue with the parents.

In the end, people were invited to share their impressions about the whole dialogic experience.

Fotini: Well, I must say, that is quite an impressive dialogic process you co-created there!!

Efrossini: Absolutely! There was a strong involvement and a real wealth of ideas and suggestions coming mainly from the parents themselves.

Fotini: How did they actually evaluate their experience?

Efrossini: They talked about it as an unprecedented and very satisfying experience. Most of their comments showed that they had started to think differently, not only about their children but also about themselves and to take into consideration a lot of parameters, one of which was their own behaviour. At the general meeting at the end, they said that it was the communal struggle against the Gold Mining Company that had changed them and made them able to participate and appreciate a discussion like that. They thought that if the struggle had not begun it would have been impossible for them to participate.

Fotini: And the participant SSMC members? How did they feel?

Efrossini: We were all feeling content. We had met! That's what happened. But mostly, we were pleasantly surprised by the possibilities of this dialogicality – especially by the sense of equality... Personally, I think it was one of the most extraordinary experiences of my working life.

Dimitra: I feel it was such a valuable experience because you had contributed to a unique and fulfilling dialogical event!

Fotini: I feel the same. Which part of this process, would you say, was the most difficult for you?

Efrossini: Well, nothing seemed to be difficult in this operation. The whole experience had a kind of lightness and was full of good spirit. We paid special attention and discussed a lot about some issues posed by the parents. You see, a lot of these villagers, being leaders in the local protests against gold excavation, had suffered indictments, oppression, violence by the state, the justice, the police because of their intense opposition to the government at the time, which supported the gold company. So, their main questions were:

- What can we say to our children about Justice, the Government, the Police, since all of the latter support the Company and act violently against us? Instead of protecting us, they protect the Company's interests!
- In which way should we talk to our children, without risking enraging them and pushing them to extreme actions?
- How to deal with our children's anxiety about our own physical integrity if we participated in relevant protest campaigns?

Fotini: How moving! And how about SSMC, how did the rest of its members feel about this event?

Efrossini: Later on, we had a review meeting with our colleagues in the SSMC. Out of that discussion a lot of possible contributing factors emerged. One or two of them stood out, e.g. the fact that we participated in a collective of solidarity by default had put us on the same level with the resisting community. Both the parents and the SSMC members acknowledged that although group action might restrain individual agency in some ways, at the same time it multiplies individual and collective potentials and choices. This common ground, then, coupled with the process of discussion somehow absorbed all "expertise" and "clientele" façades...

One of the conclusions we reached was that our preliminary discussion, before meeting the parents, had been very useful particularly in helping us to keep in mind, during the process, who we were, who they were and within which social context all of us were embedded.

Dimitra: In the end, the SSMC members were satisfied, I think, because they felt that the chosen dialogical process communicated very well a way of thinking and conversing on equal terms, instead of separating opinions and having monologues...

Efrossini: The bottom line of all this, I think, is that all participants experienced this dialogic, giving meaning process as a useful way of co-understanding with others and dealing with anxieties, in large groups of people and communities.

Fotini: It seems to me that this way of "languaging" (Maturana 1988) expresses very suitably the SSMC's ideology...

Electra: ... which is nicely worded by Massimo De Angelis:

> "It becomes easier for people to participate in a new approach, when they understand that this has already been a part of what they are doing..." (2000)

Fotini: Back to the Solidarity Social Medical Centre, then! A last word?

Electra: Two basic elements of common goods (commons) there are that they belong to all citizens and that they are matters of life. All Social Medical Centres in Greece take action around a common good, Health, in a critical historical moment when the whole public access to Health has broken down.

We could see that the direct democratic way, in which SSMC of Thessaloniki has been organised (around Health), is a way of re-activation of common action (commoning) that aims at proposing an alternative to status quo arrangements according to which common goods are either privatised or nationalised.

A final word, then, could be: *Our attempt to get organised around Health, is a social-political praxis, the vision of which would be the viability of SSMC, beyond the State and the Market –to get, that is, Health in our hands, not as consumers but as active collective subjects.*

Fotini: I am not sure if a final word is needed after such a strong political statement! Still...

> "... The wind has its reasons. We just don't notice as we go about our lives. But then, at some point, we are made to notice. The wind envelops you with a certain purpose in mind, and it rocks you. The wind knows everything that's inside you. And not just the wind. Everything, including a stone. They all know us very well. From top to bottom. It only occurs to us at certain times. And all we can do is go with those things. As we take them in, we survive, and deepen."
>
> Haruki Murakami, *Hear the Wind Sing* 1979

Acknowledgements

Special thanks to the MD Maria Dragasaki, family doctor, (currently the main collaborator of Dimitra Pouliopoulou in the joint sessions), for her contribution in the writing of this text.

Many thanks also to this book's editors for their invaluable comments and suggestions on earlier versions of this "dialogue".

References

Andersen, Tom (Ed.) (1991). *The Reflecting Team: Dialogues and Dialogues About the Dialogues.* London: W. W. Norton.

Anderson, Harlene & Gehart, Diane (Eds.) (2007). *Collaborative Therapy. Relationships and Conversations That Make a Difference.* London: Routledge.

Asen, Eia; Tomson, Dave; Tomson, Peter and Young, Venetia (2004). *Ten minutes for the family. Systemic interventions on primary care.* Routledge.

Bateson, Gregory (1980). *Mind and Nature: A Necessary Unity.* London: Fontana.

Boscolo, Luigi; Cecchin, Gianfranco; Hoffman, Lynn & Penn, Peggy (1987). *Milan Systemic Family Therapy. Conversations in Theory and Practice.* New York: Basic Books.

Cecchin, Gianfranco (1992). Constructing Therapeutic Possibilities. In S. McNamee & K. J. Gergen (Eds.), *Therapy as Social Construction.* London: Sage.

Cecchin, Gianfranco (1992). *The Irreverent Therapist as a Social Constructionist.* Keynote Speech, 1st International Family Therapy Congress, EFTA, Sorrento, Italy.

De Angelis, M. (2000). Globalization, New Internationalism and the Zapatistas, *Capital & Class,* Spring, 24, 9-35. http://cnc.sagepub.com/content/24/1.toc

Maturana, Humberto R. (1988). The Search for Objectivity or the Quest for a Compelling Argument, *The Irish Journal of Psychology,* 9(1), 25-82.

Mayo Clinic Book of Alternative Medicine, Integrating the Best Natural Therapies with Conventional Medicine, 2nd Edition, (Ed. B. Bauer), Mayo Clinic Health Solutions, https://store.mayoclinic.com/products/books/details.cfm?mpid

Milorad Pavic (1994, Greek edition). *The Inner Side of the Wind, or The Novel of Hero and Leander,* trans. Christina Pribicevic-Zoric. New York: Knopf.

Murakami, Haruki (1987 [1973]). *Hear the Wind Sing.* Kodansha International Ltd.

Seikkula, Jaakko & Arnkil, Tom E. (2006). *Dialogical Meetings in Social Networks (Systemic Thinking and Practice Series).* London: Karnac Books.

Stephenson, Anne (Ed.) (2004). *A Textbook of General Practice.* 2nd Edition. Hodder Arnold Publication. CRC Press.

A 'Fifth Wave' Systemic Practice Punctuating Liberation
Reflective practice and collective social action

3

Taiwo Afuape

Introduction

During my clinical psychology training in the late 1990s, I facilitated a group with Cathy Thorley (a clinical specialist occupational therapist and systemic therapist) for survivors of sexual abuse, four White British working class women aged between twenty four and sixty one ("Lee", "Libby", "Leslie" and "Lucy"), who had mild to moderate learning difficulties. Given our interest we designed the group based on a multi-systemic model (Boyd-Franklin 2003) utilising systemic techniques (Donigian & Malnati 2005) as well as social constructionist (Simon & Whitfield 2000) and narrative approaches (White 2011) which made links between individual experience and social context.

The qualitative analysis of group sessions and post group interviews suggested the development of "voice-in-relation" (Afuape 2002): developing their voice within the group and reflecting on the position of women in society gave the women the confidence to challenge significant people and structures to gain greater agency in their relationships. For instance, if told not to smoke by staff in her home, Leslie (who was an elective mute) was saying "It's my right to have a cigarette in *my* house", which perturbed staff who described her as "less aggressive" post the group, but "too assertive". Given systemic consequences of Leslie's assertiveness, systemic consultation was offered to staff in order to encourage a shift in focus from Leslie's "anger care plan" to changes in the system that supported her "voice". As a result, Leslie asked for more activities outside the house and a forum to describe her experiences of injustice. The women's reflections in their post group interviews highlighted the importance of actual increases in power and changes in life circumstances, as opposed to just changes in their sense *of themselves* in relation to the world. This got me thinking about whether social action was an intrinsic possibility in all groups, if "liberation" rather than amelioration was punctuated (where a punctuation is a snapshot that captures aspects of our experience in order to make sense of what is happening (Burnham 1986)). I later trained as a systemic therapist given its radical departure from an individualistic, apolitical and decontextualised approach to wellbeing. However, despite the inspiring social justice agendas of the Just Therapy Group in New Zealand (Waldegrave et al 2003) and the Fifth Province Associates in Ireland (McCarthy & O'Reilly Byrne 2007) the opportunities I had as a systemic therapist in London to engage in interventions that went beyond the family, were limited.

I am a Nigerian British-born woman of working class origin who trained as a clinical psychologist and systemic therapist in institutions that emphasised the social construction of reality. As an undergraduate psychology student I learnt about Solomon Asch's conformity studies (in which participants' responses in a perception task were influenced by those of a majority group who were giving obviously wrong answers), Phil Zimbardo's Stanford Prison experiments (where participants were split into prisoners and prison guards, which although "pretend" brought forth abusive behaviour in those labelled guards) and Stanley Milgram's obedience to authority studies (where participants were tricked into believing they were administering shocks to other participants in response to an authority figure). I do not remember the emphasis being on the rebellion of the Stanford "prisoners" or how the "guards" used divide and rule to squash the solidarity of the prisoners that had made the rebellion possible. The emphasis was on the twenty six participants in Milgram's experiment who administered what they believed to be 450 volts; not the fourteen who refused to. The emphasis on conformity erased the presence of resistance. Later, Irvin Janis wondered if something happens in groups ("some kind of psychological contagion") that interferes with members' "mental alertness" (Janis 1982, p.vii), where they become "more concerned with retaining the approval of the fellow members of their group than with coming up with good solutions to the tasks at hand", "particularly when a 'we-feeling' of solidarity is running high" (p.vii). Solidarity was associated with a worrying "we-ness" called "groupthink" that turns us into mindless sheep. The destructive potential of groups, the tendency of individuals to uphold rather than challenge the status quo, and the value-less way psychology was taught, did not inspire me. I later discovered liberation psychology (Martín Baró 1994).

In this chapter I reflect on the waves that have taken place within the systemic field and argue for a fifth wave, which draws more explicitly from liberation approaches – a broad term I use to describe the related fields of liberation theology, liberation psychology, community psychology

A 'Fifth Wave' Systemic Practice Punctuating Liberation

and just therapy. In particular, I explore how punctuating liberation in group work releases the group's potential for collective social action. To do this I describe anonymised composite case examples that are based on my work as a systemic therapist, consultant, supervisor and trainer.

Waves in systemic theory and practice

The fifth wave

The systemic field has been influenced by four waves based on different philosophical and political ideas about reality, power and knowledge, moving the field from a focus on families as the target of intervention, to a focus on systems. The *first (positivist) wave* saw individuals and systems in fixed, structural terms, as defined by the expert therapist. The *second (constructivist) wave* understood that there are as many versions of reality as there are observers to view it. The *third (social constructionist) wave* was mindful of the relationship between power and knowledge, and centralised reflexivity. Gerald Monk (1996) described the *fourth wave* as the narrative approach to systemic therapy, which reflects more explicitly on social power, as well as people's various forms of resistance (Wade 2005). A *fifth wave* would centralise collective social action (Ratts 2009). Although ideas about social justice are already present (Waldegrave et al 2003; Hernandez-Wolfe et al 2005; Almeida et al 2008; Brown 2008; McGoldrick & Hardy 2008; Garcia & McDowell 2010; McDowell et al 2012; McDowell 2015), a "wave" would sweep across the field, rather than being dotted around it, giving liberation approaches even more fluidity, breadth and influence.

A 'recurring wave'

Early liberation ideas are often missed out when describing the various influences that set the scene for the developments in systemic therapy, truncating history and making it seem as though liberation ideas are a post-modern invention. Although Salvador Minuchin, an Argentinian Jewish Family Therapist, developed a structural approach to family problems (perhaps influenced by his "hierarchical family"), he "felt deeply the plight of the poor" and viewed structural family therapy as "a political intervention" (2006). Minuchin's work in poor areas of the US, such as the *Wiltwyck School for Delinquent Boys* led to his first book, *Families of the Slums* (1967), at a time when psychoanalytic therapy and its focus on individual psyches, reined. For some, this was revolutionary in that Minuchin "brought those families into the range of view of people in the field who had ignored them completely" (2006). In the context of civil rights movements in the US and UK, many people were arguing that interventions should challenge the social environmental causes of distress such as critical psychiatrist R. D. Laing (1967) and pioneering clinical psychologist George Albee (1990). Community organiser Saul Alinksy's ideas were used by poor communities for radical social action. His daughter-in-law Joanne Linowes Alinksy (2009) argued that Saul's approach moved people from complaint to action.

A liberation approach

Liberation approaches start with the assumption that collective social action is the most effective way to prevent and address distress. They are based on theories of protest as well as prevention, and have tended to be developed by oppressed communities themselves (read W.E.B. DuBois, Paulo Freire, Ignacio Martín Baró, Geraldine Moane, Frantz Fanon, Steven Biko, J Deotis Roberts, bell hooks, Just therapy Team, Fifth Province Associates and Vikki Reynolds). Despite family therapy's radical roots and its movement towards an exogenic emphasis on the social construction of reality, family-based interventions do not necessarily challenge the oppressive social structures of society. For example, the Department for Communities and Local Government "Troubled Families" programme, launched in response to the August 2011 riots in England, sought to "turn around" the lives of 120,000 "troubled families" in the country, by the end of the coalition's term in 2015. This so called "no nonsense" and "common sense" approach (DCLG 2012), psychologised social abuse by locating the source of social problems inside people and families. In addition, Minuchin's structural family therapy as "political intervention" demonstrated the ways in which having a social justice agenda does not necessarily concur with a liberation approach. As such, liberation approaches are bold and likely to be controversial. In 2001 Scott Johnson wrote an article about the "Messianic tendencies" within Family Therapy in which therapists fancifully believe that they and their field can and should be the world's salvation (Johnson 2001). In response, Monica McGoldrick, Kenneth Hardy and Carlos Sluzki re-iterated and underscored their unashamed liberation agenda, calling on the profession to directly challenge forms of social abuse that impact on our lives (Hardy 2001; McGoldrick 2001; Sluzki 2001).

Jesuit priest, psychologist, philosopher and activist, Ignacio Martín Baró (1994) is most commonly associated with liberation approaches. Martín Baró argued that there were three important tasks inherent in this approach: 1. The recovery of historical memory, 2. De-ideologising everyday experience and 3. Utilising the people's virtues. To recover historical memory means to discover through social, interpersonal and collective memory, those elements of the past which prove useful in challenging oppression and facilitating liberation today. To "de-ideologise" meant to make direct links between emotional distress and social circumstances, given that oppression operates by concealing these links and creating fictions that justify it. People's virtues (such as resilience and hope) are not individual characteristics and feelings but relational processes and activities performed in collective action with others (Flaskas et al 2007). Martín Baró based his theories on the work of seminal educator and philosopher Paulo Freire, who coined the term *conscientizacao* or "conscientisation" to describe learning to perceive social, political and economic oppression, and taking action against it (Freire 2004). Freire believed this process was fuelled by what he termed "praxis" or "true dialogue".

True dialogue, true word and praxis

"Communication" and "conversation" are not quite the same as "dialogue". "Communication" comes from the Latin *commun* and the suffix "ie" which means "to make or to do". So one meaning of "to communicate" is "to make something common" or "to do something common" (Bohm 2014). When I think of my mum and her best friend, who sometimes talk over each other when they communicate and yet experience intimacy in their relationship, "to make common" does not necessarily mean to make knowledge and information common, but might mean to engage in interactions that each participant values. What my mum and her friend are creating together is an embodied experience rather than a purely linguist one. They sit close to each other, sharing physical affection, laughter and mutual respect. But dialogue is still more than communication. Based on Russian philosopher and literary critic Mikhail Bakhtin's work, Finnish clinical psychologist and family therapist, Jaakko Seikkula, along with his colleague Dr. Mary Olson attempt to delineate the special features of dialogue in their approach to working with people with severe and enduring mental health problems, called Open Dialogue. Dialogue from this perspective is about listening carefully to what people say so that they feel heard, respected, and validated. Everything said or done is a response to what has been said or done before. Talk, here, is not defined by what is said "about" the person, but a way of "being with" the person and living through the situation together (Seikkula 2011). Similarly Shotter (2011) refers to a *withness* rather than an *aboutness* approach to dialogue.

Seikkula's approach was influenced by the Finnish Need-Adapted approach of Yrjö Alanen and his team, which emphasised strength-based and family-centred interventions that are flexibly and individually tailored to the specific needs of clients (Alanen 2009). In both approaches "open meetings" involved service users and their family discussing relevant issues, from the start, such that all plans and decisions were made with everyone present. Seikkula and his colleagues propose that dialogue that is transparent, heterarchical, hopeful and responsive is central to wellbeing. Open Dialogue improves services for those having a severe crisis by allowing *relational expression* rather than *individual expression* because it leads to social action. Whereas liberation approaches regard the "what" in dialogue as important, with respect to the difference between dialoguing about "mental insight" versus dialoguing about "social outsight" (Smail 2005). Liberation approaches do not see the family as the most important system of intervention, and acknowledges the power abuses and inequalities that can exist in families.

Any description of dialogue can only "punctuate" certain aspects of this complex phenomenon in order to "punctuate" a certain metaphor of humanness, relationship and wellness. Whereas Open Dialogue "punctuates" responsivity, Freirean dialogue punctuates "liberation". Freirean dialogue is not just meaningful and responsive reflection but transformative action (Freire 2004). Freire (2004) argued that dialogue or "true" words involve both action and reflection "in such radical interaction that if one is sacrificed –even in part –the other immediately suffers" (p.87) and society is not transformed. Thus, without action, words are "idle chatter", what Freire termed "verbalism", and without reflection words are action for action's sake or "activism". "Praxis" was Freire's term for the linking of action and reflection, practice and theory (Freire 2004, p.87). Praxis creates true words and true words create "true dialogue", which leads to *conscientizacao* and social action.

Collective social action – the place of group work

As described above, my education in psychology focused on the human propensity to conform, as well as evaluating groups in terms of collective "rationality". Janis' book is littered with such references, with respect to "distortions of thinking" and "short comings in information-processing" that lead to "human error" and "temporary states ... that reduce a person's mental efficiency" (Janis 1982, p.2). General systems theory studied how groups of objects, component parts or systems were interconnected and work together to produce a result (Bertalanffy 1969). Rather than viewing group members as having fixed qualities and roles, systems placed each member (including the group facilitator) and the

A 'Fifth Wave' Systemic Practice Punctuating Liberation

group itself, within social, cultural and political context, and saw behaviour as interactional, relational and fluid. In addition, systemic concepts – such as circularity, multiple perspectives, curiosity, reflecting processes and reflecting on power and context – supported the group process. It is clear that groups can bring out the worst as well as the best in individuals. The group can close down into itself, in individual as well as group ways, or the group can be an opportunity to reach out into the world. The group's ability to reflect on its relationship to the social, cultural, political and historical milieu seems to be the key to its potential for social transformation.

Group work as a conduit for collective social action

Figure 1. Social action psychotherapy

I. Patient on Pills ⟶	II. Individual Psychotherapy
At this stage people are "patients" who endorse the dominant view of them as ill. As a result they join people in passively treating their problems with psychotropic medication, as though there is something wrong inside of them, and accept the diagnosis assigned to them.	This stage represents the first alternative to the medicalised treatment of emotional distress, which is talk therapy. People who are "clients" relate to people who are "therapists", and together they explore the meaning of the client's difficulties and potential causes.
IV. Taking Action ⟵	III. Talking in Groups ⟵
The person moves from "patient", to "client", to "group member" and finally becomes an "activist" challenging the social structures underlying oppression. However, some people may be "content ... with the relief from symptoms ... therapy gives them" (Holland 1992, p.73).	Becoming a "group member" means the person is able to move past the personal challenges acknowledged and addressed in psychotherapy and discover their challenges are universal amongst similarly marginalised individuals. Solidarity is built for the collective good.

A liberation perspective on group work goes beyond the common sense understanding that "three heads are better than one" and "a problem shared is a problem halved". The long history of social action group work in the social work field (Vinik & Levin 2010; Singh & Salazar 2011) was popularised within the mental health arena, when Sue Holland developed the "social action psychotherapy" model, as a result of working with a group of women in West London (Holland 1992). Her work which is frequently cited as influential by community psychologists drew on both psychoanalytic theory and the concept of *conscientizacao* (Freire 2004). Holland (1992) argued that group work was a stage in the process of moving from "psychic space" through "social space" and then into "political space", as depicted in the diagram above adapted from Holland (1992).

This model corresponds to Freire's notion of *conscientizacao* being the movement from "naïve" to "critical" consciousness (Freire 2004). Systemic theory further elaborates the recursive relationship between action and meaning. For example, in Coordinated Management of Meaning (CMM), the stories we tell about our experiences ("stories told") will inform our future actions ("stories lived") and vice versa. We are always both trying to make meaning and coordinate our actions with others. In addition, "mystery" describes the magical non-rational aspects of communication (Pearce 2007). Holmes (2010) has depicted the different stages of Holland's model with respect to whether the main focus for the person seeking help is change (action) or understanding (reflection), in the individual or the social sphere. In the social action process, focus shifts from *changing the individual* (with medication), to understanding the individual (with psychotherapy), to *understanding the social context* (in group work) to *changing the social context* (with social action) (Holmes 2010). By integrating self with society and understanding with action, "true dialogue" in groups brings subtler aspects of experience from the shadows into full and collective view; giving form to that which might otherwise stay vague and formless if left to languish within monologues.

A group based on "true dialogue" has an exogenic focus rather than an endogenic one. Members and facilitators work collaboratively and expertise belongs to everyday knowledge and personal experience rather than "professional" understanding and pre-existing theories. For example, my colleague Gillian Hughes and I worked with young people who were "gang affected". That is, they were affected by the use of the widespread term "gang", involved in actual "gang" activity, at risk of being involved in "gangs" or had something to say about the range of positive and negative experiences of being part of groupings and crews. However, the focus of intervention was not on changing their behaviour or the impact of trauma, but on coming together to use creative means of directly influencing policies created about them and the ideas floating around in their communities about young people. The focus of the group was not on

A 'Fifth Wave' Systemic Practice Punctuating Liberation

treating mental health problems but on building on their values, skills, hopes and forms of resistance (Hughes & Afuape 2015). In their creative pieces the young people explored and shared their experiences through diverse forms such as poetry, theatre and film. It was clear that they had been connoisseurs of resistance, survival mavens in their everyday lives, refusing to be content, being assertive, joining collectives/"gangs", doing well in school, dropping out of school, getting into fights, disconnecting from adults who did not understand them and so on. And yet, they expressed dissatisfaction with some of these forms of resistance, as well as with the social circumstances they were responding to. Their self-inspired resistance did not always feel liberating. However, coming together to work creatively with their peers highlighted the ways in which they were not yet done with resistance; their collective resistance reignited their imaginations and gave fuel to their creativity. The group context was like oxygen enabling their resistance to breathe and thrive. They described their collective and creative forms of resistance as satisfying in ways that they had not experienced when their resistance was confined to the privacy of their mind and their personal experience.

Dialogue in a group is a special type of coming together and becoming, that is about not being done yet. It reminds us that there is always more to us in our becoming; more work to do to resist oppression/adversity and live well with each other. But simply coming together is not enough. The concept of "true dialogue" reminds us that how we approach our coming together, our communication, and our coordination impacts on what can emerge from it. Far from being a simplistic process moving people towards positive social experiences such as "solidarity", "true dialogue" has to be able to hold the tensions between disparate aspects of reality, such as cooperation and conflict, coherence and contradiction. Movement through the social action stages is often not linear, straightforward and progressive. It is far more likely that "true dialogue" involves back and forth, fluid and organic movement between understanding and change, reflecting on self and reflecting on society.

During my systemic training, as I drew the genogram of a survivor of sexual abuse and despite believing I was doing it collaboratively and respectfully, I was moved when she told me that looking at all the zigzagging lines coming at her from all directions (depicting violence, harm and abuse) as well as going to and from other members of her family across three generations, made her feel sad and ashamed. She taught me about the power of the stories we help people tell and how important it is to enquire about and respect the stories that people *want* to tell about their lives. It also made me wonder if the aims of individual therapy, or insight-based group work, was to encourage individuals to reflect on issues that seem to be in the realm of their influence (their personal experience in interaction with their immediate environment) so as not to engender powerlessness. Contrary to that belief, I believe that group work that punctuates liberation might highlight the distal forces impacting on us whilst possibilities for influencing those forces might be brought closer to group members' grasp. Given that what we can achieve together is generally more than what we can achieve alone, groups have the potential to make us more powerful.

With a movement towards a social focus comes a concern with privilege and inequity. Liberation-focused group work requires an exploration of how power, privilege and marginalisation shape group facilitators and members, especially in the context of solidarity, and given that every person will have a "privileged" social status, even while being a member of an oppressed group. We might argue that group work punctuating liberation is a "two-fold unveiling" (Freire 1998); we unearth social justice issues outside the group whilst attending to them inside the group.

Reflecting on power and privilege within the group
A focus on content in social action groups needs to accompany a reflection on addressing the processes within it. For example, a group of adults coming together to challenge mainstream psychiatry may need to attend to the ways in which differences in skin colour and ethnicity impact on members' experiences. Any one of us at any given time might resist some oppressive social stories whilst conforming to others. Those who stand side by side in "solidarity" may still experience the constraints of power and privilege impacting on their interaction. The action continuum (Adams et al 2007) describes eight stages in the movement between actively participating in oppression, and initiating social changes. It demarcates the different stages individuals and groups might find themselves at, from no reflection/no action to some reflection/no action and reflection and action combined, leading to collective social action. We may go back and forth through the stages at different times, with respect to different levels of context and different social issues related to Gender, Religion, Age, Ability, Class/caste, Culture, Colour (skin), Ethnicity, Education, Sexuality, Spirituality (social GRAACCCEESS – Roper-Hall 1998).

> While teaching about social action group work some students listened but remained silent. A student raised the issue of "silence"

and asked what a systemic and liberation approach to "uncooperative", "silent" group members would be. I asked what ideas the group had about silence. Those who spoke had only negative things to say, feeling that silent members were not contributing. I began to talk about silence having many meanings other than lack of engagement, lack of reflection, lack of knowledge and lack of disagreement. I invited the group to critically reflect on traditional group theory which fixed group members in particular roles ("blocker", "initiator", "aggressor", "gatekeeper" and so on), with respect to the systemic view of positions as contextual, relational and social. I shared my own personal experience of being silent in groups and how it related to racism, sexism, and classism as well as being largely an introverted person. I also shared my sense of relief when I read the book Quiet by Susan Cain (2013) as it reflected on the underestimated benefits of being quiet in a world "that can't stop talking". Only at this point, previously silent members began to talk, about silence as a response to oppression, such as racialisation, and silence as liberation, with respect to the affordances of a listening position. We explored the learning they could take into their own group work by reflecting on their experiences of being in a group.

Talking about power and privilege can be anxiety provoking and difficult, partly because people do not always feel powerful or privileged and thus their social position may be at odds with how they view their personal experience. For example, Black group members who are beset by constant disqualifications of their experiences of racism may find it undermining to explore their privilege in a racially mixed group. As a Black woman identified as heterosexual, I try to talk about my experiences of both discrimination and of privilege. Talking about privilege might also accompany feelings of shame and/or defensiveness because people in positions of privilege benefit from it. For example, many white students have expressed confusing and conflicting feelings when asked to explore their "invisible knapsack" of privilege (McIntosh 1988). The systemic idea of "talking about talking" (Burnham 2005) is a helpful way to reflect with the group on their readiness to dialogue about oppression and privilege. This might involve questions such as, "how well does this group talk about the impact of skin colour and class on the interactions within it?" "What are the benefits of talking about these issues?" "What are your concerns about it?" "How might it inform your wider aims of challenging oppression outside the group?" If discussion becomes competitive in relation to an invisible hierarchy of oppression,

I try to invite the group to reflect on what we might learn from different forms of oppression as a resource for our personal and collective liberation. With respect to challenging my own prejudices and the limitations they impose on my thinking I have utilised Vikki Reynolds' ideas about bringing "solidarity teams" into our work (Reynolds 2011).

During work with a group of teenagers who had been excluded from school, I noticed a growing prejudice within me about teachers. In my attempt to humanise the pupils, I was developing an image of them as embodiments of resistance and teachers as pawns and puppets of an oppressive education system. I was denying teachers their complex subjectivities with respect to their own experiences of oppression and resistance. I decided to dialogue with my friends who were teachers about their views and experience. The picture began to change to one of overworked, committed and often stressed adults, who liked young people. I started bringing them to mind as a "solidarity team" in my work with excluded pupils; reminding myself that Freire had been an educator. Despite my "team" being invisible and unspoken, the young people began to talk about creating dialogical spaces between young people and significant adults in their community – including teachers.

***

Working with a mixed gender group of Black African teenagers, who were all mental health service users meeting to challenge the links between racism and mental health problems, a group member started to talk about homophobia "in the Black community" and how widespread it was. Another group member challenged this view saying that he felt that the assumption that Black people were more homophobic than White people was another way of casting Black Africans as inferior. A group member made references to the importance of respecting people's "religious beliefs" about sexuality. Another group member challenged this view but said that we had to focus on "our own cause first and let other people focus on theirs". I asked the group if they had heard of Baynard Rustin, James Baldwin, Audre Lorde and Langston Hughes, who were pivotal figures in the fight against racism and also gay, and they had not.

Reflecting on this discussion in the next session some group members drew on religious views to justify heterosexist and homophobic ideas. I checked in with the group about how they were feeling given disagreement and difference of views and shared my dilemma about wanting to respect everyone's beliefs but also wanting to be true to mine. The group showed curiosity about my position and I told them that most of my friends are gay and that I felt that my daughter being surrounded by gay people, gay history and gay culture was liberating for us both, given that my daughter would grow up with a deeper, more inclusive and kind view of her own sexuality and humanity as well as the humanity of others. I felt that challenging homophobia and heterosexism would support my daughter to be included, inclusive and just; other people's liberation is essentially ours.

This led to a discussion about the sensationalist headlines used to condemn a whole continent, widespread poverty and corruption in Africa that Britain is complicit in, the anti-gay laws in Africa introduced by colonialists and the influence of North American fundamentalist evangelical Christians, that encourage and support a culture of intolerance which had not existed in many parts of Africa, preceding the brutality of empire. Some group members felt challenged by exploring their "invisible knapsack" (McIntosh 1988) of heterosexual privilege. Other group members discussed the ways that any form of prejudice, discrimination and oppression challenge our ability to have authentic relationships with each other and ourselves, where we are fully seen and fully see the other. In doing so they made links between their aims of challenging racism and challenging homophobia and heteronormativity, drawing on the African liberation theology of Desmond Tutu, as a prolific, well-known and outspoken religious advocate of LGBTQQ human rights.

I have found groups can be stressful encounters but there is also the opportunity to challenge the emotional, intellectual and physical distance that people from different social groups can have. Reflecting on the complexity of power and privilege also supports richer, more varied and deeper forms of social action based on a greater understanding of different types of oppression.

A group of women had set up a mental health community resource service to support women and challenge sexism. The group were concerned about gender, but there were tensions related to "race", as Black and other ethnic minority women often felt dismissed, talked over or undermined. In consultation with them, group members began to talk about unhelpful responses from men when they tried to discuss sexism. They described their hopes that men in their lives and men they encountered through their activism would "become allies". I shared with the group Anne Bishop's description of three common responses to her, as a White woman conducting "unlearning racism" seminars with her African Nova Scotian colleague: 1 the "backlashers", who deny the existence of racism, express outrage that they are forced to discuss it and take too little responsibility 2 the "guilty", who personalise the issues explored and become defensive and paralysed because they do not see the social aspects of oppression and take too much personal responsibility and 3 the "allies", who use any opportunity to learn more about the social structures that underlie oppression and then act on what they learn (Bishop 2002, p.109). Some of the White group members reflected on these descriptions as helpful and continued to talk about them with respect to gender. I reflected that the group was similar in terms of gender but different from each other in other ways such as skin colour. I wondered if looking at a "social GRACE" other than gender, would add something to their understanding of oppression, privilege and becoming an ally. It did not feel safe to have an open-ended discussion so the group decided to get into three sub-groups that discussed one of the three positions presented by Bishop. Each group was mixed in terms of ethnicity. Questions to aid the discussion were generated by the group and included: "what maintains this position, with respect to personal, interpersonal, familial, community, social and political levels of context?" "What might challenge this position, with respect to personal, interpersonal, familial, community, social and political levels of context?" When feeding back as a larger group, it was clear that for the people in the "backlashers" group the dialogue about racism had been tense. The group members reflected that the dialogue became tense the further away from social context the group members went. The more they personalised their responses or the views of others, the more likely they were to be dismissive, defensive and attacking of each other. They were able to reflect on the ways in which White group members did not personally invent racism, but good intentions were not enough to prevent some of them at times enacting it. By reflecting on "race" and racism the women came to realise that ally positions are not that common precisely because there is a powerful social context socialising us to ignore the cruelty of oppression and rest within the false peace of privilege. In future sessions the women were able to apply this learning to their anti-sexism activism, as well as to their relationships within the group. They better understood that power works by concealing itself inside our "normal". Unearthing power and calling it out became a source of strength rather than a source of anger and pain; a beacon of hope, rather than a baton of shame.

Concluding reflections

Liberation approaches aim to make visible and explicit the "natural" and taken for granted social order and locate distress in its social context, thereby reducing individuals' sense of personal failure, shame and isolation. Punctuating liberation changes the types of interventions we engage in as well as how we see our role; potentially shifting from therapist to "social change agent, activist, consultant, and social advocate" (Smith et al. 2009, p.165). It might also require that we re-introduce into our training, skills in intervening at "meso" levels of context, such as in homes, schools, GP surgeries, community centres and work places, as well as "macro" levels of context, with respect to policy, legislation and laws, rather than just thinking "family". A liberation perspective reminds us of the need to reflect on the ways in which resistance to oppression may at times lack sufficient influence if it stays confined to the privacy of individual experience, or even, to the "privacy" of the family context. Any form of cruelty breeds more of it somewhere on the globe. It is therefore my personal view that the "fragmentation of suffering" (Prilleltensky 2003) that happens when social movements focus all their energies on the cause of their reference group, potentially colludes with the oppressive tendency of "identity" to link us to some "others" whilst disconnecting us from other "others".

Punctuating liberation in groups creates space for the emergence of critical consciousness. "Critical" consciousness, in my experience, is rarely far from the surface, hence the enormous work oppressive systems have to do in order to keep this consciousness from emerging (for example, the media consistently describes rape and sexualised violence as a "*sex* crime" or "*sex* offence". Portrayals of Black men and women in popular dramas tell a highly limited and negative story of what it means to "be Black"; celebrities, particularly if they are women, are treated as though their bodies belong to the scrutinising gaze of the masses and so on). Praxis makes it incumbent on liberation group work to reflect and act within their groups as much as without. In a group context that punctuates liberation collective resistance encourages the creativity of an imagination previously confined to dreaming of that which is, and not that which is possible.

References

Adams, Maurianne; Bell, Lee Anne & Griffin, Pat (Eds.) (2007). *Teaching for Diversity and Social Justice.* (2nd Edn.) New York: Routledge.

Afuape, Taiwo (2002). *The Development of "Voice-in-Relation": A multi-systemic approach to empowerment of women in a group for survivors of sexual abuse with learning difficulties.* Unpublished University of East London Research Thesis.

Alanen, Yrjö (2009). Towards more Humanistic Psychiatry: Development of need-adapted treatment of schizophrenia group psychoses. *Psychosis,* 1, pp.156–66.

Albee, George Wilson (1990). The Futility of Psychotherapy. *Mind & Behavior,* 11(3/4), pp.369–84.

Alinksy, Joanne Linowes (2009). Letter: The organiser's organiser. *The New York Times.* www.nytimes.com August 26th 2009.

Almeida, Rhea V.; Dolan-Del Vecchio, Kenneth & Parker, Lynn (2008). *Transformative Family Therapy: Just families in a just society.* Boston, MA: Pearson Education.

Bertalanffy, Karl Ludwig von (1969). *General System Theory.* New York: George Brazillier.

Bishop, Anne (2002). *Becoming an Ally: Breaking the cycle of oppression in people.* (2nd ed.) London: Zed Books.

Bohm, David (1996). Foreword to the Routledge Great Minds edition. *On Dialogue.* London: Routledge.

Boyd-Franklin, Nancy (2003). *Black Families in Therapy: A multi-systems approach.* (2nd ed.) New York: Guilford Press.

Brown, Andraé L. (2008). I Too am Feminist: The journey of a Black male transformative feminist family therapist. *Journal of Feminist Family Therapy,* 20(1), pp.1-20.

Burnham, John (1986). *Family Therapy: First steps towards a systemic approach.* London: Tavistock Publications.

Burnham, John (2005). Relational Reflexivity: A tool for socially constructing therapeutic relationships. In Carmel Flaskas, Barry Mason & Amaryll Perlesz (Eds.), *The Space Between: Experience, context and process in the therapeutic relationship* (1–17). London: Karnac Books.

Cain, Susan (2013). *Quiet: The power of introverts in a world that can't stop talking.* London: Penguin Books.

Department for Communities and Local Government (DCLG) (2012). *The Troubled Families programme: Financial framework for the payment-by-results scheme for local authorities.* London: DCLG.

Donigian, Jeremiah & Malnati, Richard (2005). *Systemic Group Therapy: A triadic model.* Andover: Cengage Learning.

Flaskas, Carmel; McCarthy, Imelda & Sheehan, Jim (Eds.) (2007). *Hope and Despair in Narrative and Family Therapy: Adversity, Forgiveness and Reconciliation.* Hove: Brunner-Routledge.

Freire, Paulo (1998). Cultural Action and Conscientization (reprint). *Harvard Educational Review*, 68(4), pp.499–521.
Freire, Paulo (2004). *Pedagogy of the Oppressed*, 30th Anniversary Edition. New York: Continuum.
Garcia, Marisol & McDowell, Teresa (2010). Mapping Social Capital: A Critical Contextual Approach for Working with Low-Status Families. *Journal of Marital and Family Therapy*, 36(1), pp.96–107.
Hardy, Kenneth (2001). Healing the World in Fifty-minute Intervals: A response to "Family Therapy Saves the Planet". *Journal of Marital and Family Therapy*, 27(1), pp.19–22.
Johnson, Scott (2001). Family Therapy Saves the Planet: Messianic tendencies in the family systems literature. *Journal of Marital and Family Therapy*, 27(1), pp.3–11.
Hernandez-Wolfe, Pilar; Almeida, Rhea V. & Dolan-Del Vecchio, Kenneth (2005). Critical Consciousness, Accountability, and Empowerment: Key processes for helping families heal. *Family Process*, 44(1), pp.105–19.
Holland, Sue (1992). From Social Abuse to Social Action: A neighbourhood psychotherapy and social action project for women. In Jane Ussher and Paula Nicholson (Eds.), *Gender Issues in Clinical Psychology*. (pp.68–77) London: Routledge.
Holmes, Guy (2010). *Psychology in the Real World: Community-based group work*. Hertfordshire: PCCS Books.
Hughes, Gillian & Afuape, Taiwo (2015). What's Our Story: Centralising young people's experiences of gangs, crews, and collectives, to develop services that promote wellbeing. In Taiwo Afuape & Gillian Hughes (Eds.), *Liberation Practices: Towards Emotional Wellbeing Through Dialogue*. London: Routledge.
Janis, Irvin L. (1982). *Groupthink: Psychological studies of policy decisions and fiascoes*. Boston: Houghton, Mifflin.
Laing, Ronald David (1967). *The Politics of Experience and the Bird of Paradise*. Harmondsworth: Penguin.
Martín Baró, Ignacio (1994). *Writings for a Liberation Psychology*. New York: Harvard University Press.
McCarthy, Imelda & O'Reilly Byrne, Nollaig (2007). A Fifth Province Approach to Intra-Cultural Issues in an Irish Context: Marginal illuminations. In Monica McGoldrick & Kenneth V. Hardy (Eds.), *Revisioning Family Therapy: Race, Class, Culture, and Gender in Clinical Practice*. (2nd ed.) New York: Guilford Press.
McDowell, Teresa (2015). *Applying Critical Social Theories to Family Therapy Practice*. AFTA SpringerBriefs in Family Therapy series. New York: Springer.
McDowell, Teresa; Libal, Kathryn & Brown, Andraé L. (2012). Family Therapy and Human Rights: Domestic violence as a case in point. *Journal of Feminist Family Therapy*, 24, pp.1–23.

McGoldrick, Monica & Hardy, Kenneth V. (2008). *Re-visioning Family Therapy: Race, Culture, and Gender in Clinical Practice.* (2nd ed.) New York: Guilford Press.

McGoldrick, Monica (2001). Response to "Family Therapy Saves the Planet." *Journal of Marital and Family Therapy*, 27(1), 17–8.

Minuchin, Salvador; Montalvo, Braulio; Guerney, Bernard G. Jr.; Rosman, Bernice L. & Schumer, Florence (1967). *Families of The Slums: An exploration of their structure and treatment.* Wiltwyck School for Boys, New York: Basic Books.

Minuchin, Salvador (2006). *Inviting the Family Dance.* London: Association for Family Therapy.

Monk, Gerald (1996). Narrative Approaches to Therapy: The "fourth wave" in family therapy. *Guidance & Counselling*, 1(2), 41–7.

Pearce, W. Barnett (2007). *Making Social Worlds: A communication perspective.* Oxford, UK: Blackwell.

Prilleltensky, Isaac (2003). Commentary – Understanding, Resisting, and Overcoming Oppression: Toward Psychopolitical Validity. *American Journal of Community Psychology*, 31(1/2), pp.195–201.

Ratts, Manivong J. (2009). Social Justice Counseling: Toward the development of a fifth force among counseling paradigms. *The Journal of Humanistic Counseling, Education and Development*, 48(2), pp.160–72.

Reynolds, Vikki (2011). Supervision of Solidarity Practices: Solidarity teams and people-ing-the-room. *Context*, 116, pp.4-7.

Roper-Hall, Alison (1998). Working Systemically with Older People and Their Families Who Have "Come to Grief". In Pauline Sutcliffe, Guinevere Tufnell & Ursula Cornish (Eds.), *Working with the Dying and Bereaved: Systemic approaches to therapeutic work.* (pp.177–206) London: MacMillan Press.

Seikkula, Jaakko (2011). Becoming Dialogical: Psychotherapy or a Way of Life? *The Australian & New Zealand Journal of Family Therapy*, 32(3), pp.179–93.

Shotter, John (2010). *Social Construction on the Edge: "Withness"-Thinking and Embodiment.* Ohio: Taos Institute Publications.

Simon, Gail & Whitfield, Gwyn (2000). Systemic and Social Constructionist Therapy. In Dominic Davies & Charles Neal (Eds.), *Pink Therapy*, Vol. 2. London: Open University Press.

Singh, Anneliese A. & Salazar, Carmen F. (Eds.) (2011). *Social Justice in Group Work: Practical Interventions for Change.* Oxon: Routledge.

Sluzki, Carlos E. (2001). All Those in Favor of Saving the Planet, Please Raise Your Hand: A Comment about "Family Therapy Saves the Planet." *Journal of Marital & Family Therapy*, 27(1), pp.13–5.

Smail, David (2005). *Power, Interest and Psychology. Elements of a Social Materialist Understanding of Distress.* Ross on Wye: PCCS Books.

Smith, Shannon D.; Reynolds, Cynthia A. & Rovnak, Amanda (2009). A Critical Analysis of the Social Advocacy Movement in Counselling. *Journal of Counselling and Development*, 87, pp.483–91.

Vinik, Abe & Levin, Morris (Eds.) (2010). *Social Action in Group Work*. Oxon: Routledge.

Wade, Allan (2005). *Honouring Resistance: A response-based approach to counselling*. Vancouver, British Columbia: Viewers Guide Stepping Stone Productions.

Waldegrave, Charles; Tamasese, Kiwi; Tuhaka, Flora & Campbell, Warihi (2003). *Just Therapy – a Journey: A collection of papers from the Just Therapy team, New Zealand*. Adelaide: Dulwich Centre Publications.

White, Michael (2011). *Narrative Practice: Continuing the conversations*. New York: WW Norton & Company.

4

Fourfold Vision and Cybernetic Unity
Therapist as scientist, theorist, humanist and artist

Hugh Palmer

> *May God us keep*
> *From Single vision & Newton's sleep*
> William Blake 1802

When I was a child in the 1960s I was very fond of an elderly relative, Uncle Wilf, who to me was a source of wonder and fascination. He used to take me to local nature reserves and teach me to observe and appreciate the world around me. I learnt about different birds and mammals and how they fitted into ecological systems such as woodlands or estuaries. My uncle, E.W. Taylor CBE, like Gregory Bateson, died in 1980, and by that time, I understood that he was a Fellow of the Royal Society, had an honorary doctorate for his work in optics and was a founder of the Yorkshire Wildlife Trust. He had been involved in work with other scientists during the second world war exploring early cybernetic systems to enable searchlights to converge on a single spot thousands of feet above the earth and worked with Barnes Wallis of Dambusters *fame, developing sighting instruments.*

As I reflect upon the life and work of my uncle, I appreciate that he was able to span both scientific thought and wider ecological issues, as well as being a particularly kind and humble man; all attributes that I associate with Bateson, too.

This chapter revisits the legacy of Gregory Bateson, whose influence upon the field of systemic therapy was significant, particularly in the earlier years. It could be argued that some of his thinking was wilfully or erroneously misinterpreted by others; in an impoverished understanding of Bateson's epistemology. Bateson (1991) was critical of action orientated people who would take ideas onto the wards without attempting to understand the ideas behind the theory, and perhaps this very hurry to implement his ideas has left therapeutic practitioners with poor models of therapy that continue to conceptualise and treat relationships and systems as "things" rather than ideas. For example, Bateson was

Fourfold Vision and Cybernetic Unity

clearly frustrated that the double bind theory he co-developed about communication was re-presented by his co-workers as a causative model of schizophrenia. The reification of this idea led to families being blamed by professionals who did not fully understand the theory with the consequence of impeding the progress of systemic family approaches to severe mental illness by many years. Being known for embracing Bateson's ideas, systemic therapy was blamed by other professionals for blaming mothers. Bateson's exasperation at his ideas not being understood became apparent with his disagreement with Jay Haley regarding the concept of "power". This issue will be explored in some detail to offer a perspective on Bateson's epistemology that might be helpful for therapists. As I have grown older and begun to more fully appreciate how the things I learnt from my uncle led to an affinity with the work of Gregory Bateson, so too, it seems natural for me to attempt to work and think about therapy in a way that reflects their wisdom, humility and passion.

It is worth noting that Bradford Keeney, whose 1983 book *Aesthetics of Change* was an attempt to bring the wisdom of Gregory Bateson to working with families and other interactional systems, wrote more recently about the lack of systemic thinking in systemic therapy; complaining that

> *the postmodern advocates of higher order cybernetics never embodied its circularity, but favored non-circular interpretive discourse that highlighted endless commentary, reflection, conversation, and description of observations and observations of observations.*
>
> (Keeney & Keeney 2012, p.26)

It could be argued that whilst berating postmodern approaches, Keeney and Keeney have not appreciated how these very approaches have attempted to aesthetically and respectfully incorporate circularity, and these have been necessary steps towards an approach that can also include the self of the therapist in a more dynamic way. Later in this chapter, further issues raised by Keeney and Keeney will be identified and addressed in relation to the "Fourfold Vision" model which I propose.

Bateson was primarily known as a scientist although he actually considered himself foremost a biologist. He was precise and loathed "muddled" thinking, something he frequently made clear in both writing and lectures. Bateson also advocated being human with patients. Bateson, as a researcher, actively treated patients as part of Macy Foundation funded research projects that he led between 1948 and 1963 and part of what he attempted was to help them find valuable patterns in their lives.

Bateson was able to incorporate both the precision of being "scientific" and the empathy and intuition of "being human" in his interactions with others, including patients with schizophrenia and their families. It could be argued that he considered that the field of psychology was broadly evolving in two similar directions: the consciously scientific "circularist" and the more intuitively based "humanist" (Charlton 2008).

Many readers will be familiar with talk of the "art and science" of practices such as medicine, nursing or therapy, where art and science are seen as forming separate domains, parallel but differentiated and not necessarily proportionate with each other. Later in this chapter, I will outline an approach to therapy, influenced by Bateson, that eschews the idea of separate domains; integrating the scientific and aesthetic, the circularist and humanist as processes.

Bateson as therapist

Many commentators were struck by the wisdom and compassion evident in Bateson's interactions with others, and Lipset's (1980) biography reveals that this was also the case with his work with patients. The following transcript of a 1958 patient interview (Bateson, cited in Lipset, 1980, p.220-221) illustrates the disarmingly open way Bateson connected with the family of a young man diagnosed with schizophrenia in a conversation about why a family moved location so often:

Bateson:	I agree with much of what you say.
Mother:	Moving is just for the birds
Bateson:	Having been an old –
Father:	(laughing)
Mother:	And even birds stay in the same nest (laughs).
Bateson:	– been an old mover myself. I spend time in New Guinea, in the Dutch East Indies, and God knows what else.
Mother:	Well –
Bateson:	But –
Mother:	It's all right if you're built that way. I mean each person has to do –

Fourfold Vision and Cybernetic Unity

Father: No.

Bateson: I don't know.

Mother: The reasons have to be voluntary. Mine are involuntary, I know –

Bateson: I was frankly running away from all sorts of things.

It is apparent that Bateson felt comfortable in disclosing personal information about himself and in admitting his vulnerability or weakness. Perhaps Bateson was in tune with writers who – nearly half a century later – advocate a degree of transparency in their interactions, although it takes little effort to imagine some modern readers will recoil from the idea of admitting to their clients that they were "running away from all sorts of things". I believe that Bateson's position here was not merely an ethical stance, but a reflection of a man being wholly consistent with his epistemology.

Jay Haley, in a personal letter to Lipset, suggested that Bateson would "...stay up all night with alcoholics, to get them through...He felt that being human with people was good for them" (Lipset 1980, p.215). R.D. Laing, who observed Bateson in 1962, considered that, like some of the best therapists, Bateson didn't regard himself as a "therapist", going on to add "....If I was the patient in the session, I certainly wouldn't have felt there was anything to be frightened of...he never indicated that he thought in terms of actually actively adopting strategic, practical means to use to pry people out of the entanglement they were in..." (Lipset 1980, p.220)

William Fry, another of Bateson's colleagues, suggested that Bateson was like an anthropologist with families, more of an observer than clinician or therapist, and would "...switch between that role and a sort of friendly mother's brother...raising tantalising and significant issues... They were very intuitive and hit the nail on the head, and would do all sorts of terrible things...creating insights and stirring family patterns up". (Lipset 1980, p.219)

From these observations of Bateson's clinical practice which spanned more than ten years, two broad themes become apparent: i) he showed compassion and intuition in his interactions, and he emphasised the importance of therapists and doctors "being human" with their patients (Bateson 1961); ii) he was however also able to take on a more "scientific observer" position too and seemed to be able to shift between these different positions.

Bateson, disillusioned with psychotherapy – partly because of Haley's inability to understand fully the epistemological issues, particularly with regard to power – left the Palo Alto group to study dolphins. The thorny issue of power was never fully resolved. Nevertheless, his position on power reveals a vigorously ethical stance with regards to being in relation with others; a position echoed by more recent authors who, whilst they may not overtly discuss "power", advocate a non-expert, collaborative and non-directive approach that echoes aspects of Bateson's approach. Like Guddemi (2006), I see Bateson's position on power as placing us in a double bind – a bind that encourages creativity and offers a route towards thinking more wisely about how Bateson's legacy can inform and shape therapeutic practice.

The problem of power: a double bind that leads to creativity

Bateson offered us an epistemology of unity and through the use of various metaphors and descriptions he offered glimpses of a universe that is complex and interrelated beyond our perceptual abilities and comprehension. Therefore any attempts to create boundaries or to selectively take only piecemeal bits and pieces of his epistemology would not only be an error, it would represent a gross misunderstanding of what he was attempting to convey.

Bateson's view that power is a myth insofar as relationships are concerned is central to his epistemology, for his world was one of "ideas" not "things"; a world where power simply cannot exist in the realm of mental process – it based on a fiction of unilateral control. Guddemi (2006) notes that Bateson's distaste for power as explanation was aesthetic and moral as well as scientific.

Bateson makes his position on power clear in several passages (for example, in collections of essays published in 1972 and 1991) and this quote from "Angels Fear" is typical:

> *Consider on the other hand the popular verbal cliché —the power of mind over matter. This little monster contains three combined concepts, "power", "mind", and "matter"' But power is a notion derived from the word of engineers and physicists. It is of the same world*

> as the notions of energy or matter. It would therefore be quite consistent and sensible to speak, say, of the power of a magnet over a piece of iron. All three items – the magnet, the iron, and the power – come out of the same universe of discourse. The magnet and the iron and the power can meet each other in the same statement. But mind, since Descartes split the universe in two, does not belong in that world. So in order to give physical power to mind, we must give it materialistic existence.
>
> (G. Bateson & M. C. Bateson 1987, p.60)

There is no mistaking Gregory Bateson's position: thinking in terms of power with regard to mental process and relationship is lunacy. Haley, in a personal letter to Lipset, elaborated on this position with specific reference to therapy;

> *Bateson didn't like power. He didn't even like the word...anyone who said "I'm going to change this person". If they said "I will offer this person some ideas, and if they change, it's up to them," then Gregory would have no trouble with them. But if you take responsibility for changing people, then you would have a problem...Any influence outside the person's range is odious to him. Any indirect manipulation is [also] out of the question.*
>
> (Lipset, 1982, p.226)

While Bateson did agree with Haley that power is a central human concern, he wished that we humans would stop believing in power because the pursuit of power entails the epistemologically erroneous thinking that always causes trouble, for example the idea that "bigger (or more) is better".

Guddemi (2008) notes that, despite interpretations of many writers regarding his discourse about power, the view of Michel Foucault is surprisingly close to that held by Bateson and Guddemi cites what I believe to be an important observation by Foucault:

> *The exercise of power is not simply a relationship between partners, individual or collective; it is a way in which certain actions modify others. Which is to say, of course, that something called Power, with or without a capital letter, which is assumed to exist universally in a concentrated or diffused form, does not exist.*
>
> (1982, p.788)

Since Bateson originally challenged the concept of power, some authors (for example, Harries-Jones 1995 and Dell 1989) have offered ways out of the double bind he left us with, and the following section will outline two attempts to wriggle free: one considering power in wider contexts, the other considering the problem of power as confusion between different domains. I will argue for a third way out of the double bind: a path that leads to a cybernetic approach to working with others that is very much in keeping with Bateson's epistemology.

Wider contexts

Traditional linear views of power rend to conceptualise one party having power over another, and first order cybernetic views tend to view both parties having some kind of complementary relationship where the "powerless" party in some way requires the other party to have power over it and vice versa. The difficulty with both these views is that they de-contextualize the relationship, thus ignoring, for example historical, cultural and gender aspects.

Harries-Jones (1995) suggests that, instead of thinking of power in human relationships, we would be better served by reflexive dialogue about the "metaphor of power", and see ourselves as simply parts of a larger situation. This does indeed offer a partial resolution to the problem, and if we widen the context, then the relationships may be seen as part of wider circuits. Simply focussing on individual injustices risks ignoring the wider, cultural injustices in which the actions are located, so by broadening the focus, the "power" of one person over another person may be seen to take place within wider patterns of human domination and violence towards others, of patriarchal societies, of international conflict, of elites and the arms trade and so on. However, simply shifting our focus to a wider context is not adequate; to have a greater understanding of the relationship, we need to shift focus between contexts, to move from detail to context and back again.

Different domains for understanding power

Dell (1989) attempted to explain the problem of power as a confusion between two profoundly different and separate domains, suggesting that Bateson talks of power and lineal control in the domain of scientific explanation, whereas, as therapists, when we talk of "power," we are speaking in the humanist domains of experience and description. Whilst this may appear on the surface to be an attractive resolution to the double bind, thinking of "domains" suggests separateness, and this is antithetical to Bateson's epistemology of unity, so it is not an adequate solution.

Fourfold Vision and Cybernetic Unity

What is required is a means of thinking that respects Bateson's concept of unity and recognises the importance of shifting focus between contexts, and this, in part, is what I hope to address.

Steps towards unity

Consideration of power as an issue that relates to either context or different domains is inadequate, although both positions have value. A third way of conceptualising the problem of power would be to consider it as being a problem of both context and domains. A clue to another way forward is to be found in Charlton's (2008) discussion of Bateson in which he proposes that Bateson considered psychology to be evolving in two directions, "humanist" and "circularist". The humanist way of working with clients could be considered as one human being interacting with another; the practitioner intuitively responds from personal emotional resources to act spontaneously out of his or her own integrity. The "circularistic" approach would be characterised by practitioners being consciously scientific, articulate about methods and results, aiming for predictability and logical coherence. Charlton (2008) suggests that Bateson saw the way forward as being a compromise: a working together of both types of practice, between intuition and examination/description, each informing the other. Charlton also acknowledged other aspects that might be important: "Humanist, scientist, artist and theoretician are all needed to form the cybernetic unity of healing" (Charlton 2008, p.94).

Towards a Fourfold Vision

Following on from this discussion I would propose that a therapy truly influenced by Bateson would involve moving between all four positions identified by Charlton (humanist, scientist, artist and theoretician) and having the wisdom to value them all.

A way of conceptualising these positions that also offers a means of being able to shift focus from detail to context and avoids separate "domains" was offered over two hundred years ago by William Blake:

> *Now I a fourfold vision see,*
> *And a fourfold vision is given to me;*
> *Tis fourfold in my supreme delight,*

> *And threefold in soft Beulah's night,*
> *And twofold Always. May God us keep*
> *From Single vision & Newton's sleep.*
> (William Blake, Letter to Thomas Butt, 22 November 1802)

Blake's Fourfold Vision has been discussed by literary scholars, including Northrop Frye (1947) and later by Rose who recognised the unity that is inherent within Blake's concept of Fourfold Vision: "That is, four is really one all the time, but in order to describe unlimited perception, a paradox is stated" (Rose 1962, p.173). The following is a necessarily simplified overview of the four types of vision Blake offers us.

A version of Fourfold Vision for therapists

I have linked Blake's four types of vision to Charlton's four positions of scientist, theorist, humanist and artist and relate these to therapeutic practice. Whilst reading these, it is important to appreciate that although they are presented as separate entities, and bear in mind these are descriptions of iterative processes, not of separate domains.

Single Vision – therapist as scientist

Single Vision is concerned with observational skills and the ability to focus on detail. This incorporates being able to make linear descriptions of the client (s) and what they present, including:

- What is the issue?
- Who is involved?
- When does it happen?
- Where does it happen?

As part of the focus and attention to detail, I would also give due consideration to the possibilities of alternative explanations for the presenting issues. A simple example of this might be someone who presents as depressed, but has an underlying thyroid disorder. Single vision is the domain of evidence. However, as Bateson & McCarthy (2013 p.5) warn, our professional practices can become deformed in the tick-boxes of diagnostic categories divorced from relational contexts, and this is why it is necessary to consider the other types of vision.

Twofold Vision – therapist as theorist

Twofold Vision moves the focus from specific details to more relational aspects of interest and would incorporate consciously scientific obser-

Fourfold Vision and Cybernetic Unity

vation of patterns within the family system. Internal systemic relationships, including first order cybernetic patterns, such as circular causality, would be an obvious consideration, although I would also include within this focus thinking about second order patterns that would include the new unit of clients plus therapist(s). This links in with Bateson's aphorism about "the difference that makes a difference" where multiple versions of "Single Vision", along with the consideration of relational aspects of the clients' lives can contribute to a sense of a greater unity. This is analogous to the theory of Humberto Maturana (2005) that human experience takes place in the relational space of conversation.

Threefold Vision – therapist as humanist

This focus of attention is around the human aspects of therapy, where the therapist might make connection with their personal experiences and be mindful of any intuitions they might have in relation to the therapy or the clients. Within this focus, other important aspects of the self of the therapist will be acknowledged and considered, including embodied aspects of practice and empathy. How these will be used in

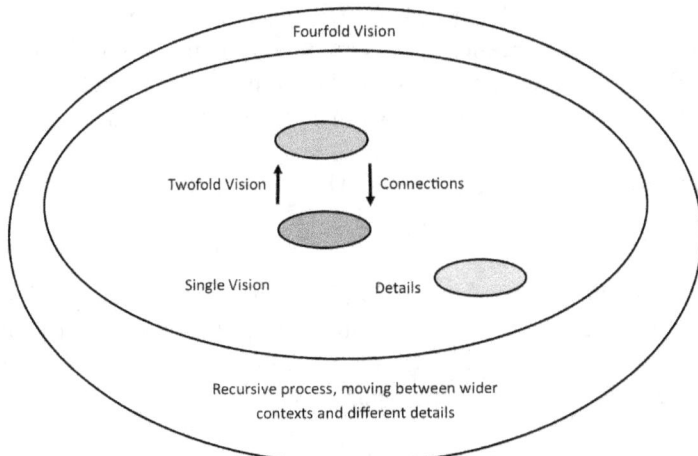

terms of reflexivity and disclosure and transparency will depend on the preferences and constraints of the therapist and agency. A further but important consideration, is to consider how the self of the therapist is also open to change and learning from the clients.

Fourfold Vision – therapist as artist

Similar to Blake's sentiment, Fourfold Vision could be thought of as the aesthetic delight of working with and between single, twofold and threefold visioning. Fourfold Vision is akin to the phenomenological notion of the hermeneutic circle, although the scope of attention is variable – moving between detail and wider contexts. The attention of the therapist moves reflexively between levels of detail, relationship and broader context; the process is not static, and the focusing reflexively on particular details, widening the context, and then focussing again, perhaps on different details. Nora Bateson (2012) uses the helpful analogy of a telephoto lens in this context, and calls the process of shifting between detail and wider context "zooming in" and "zooming out". Focussing in on a detail and then "zooming out" to a wider context permits the viewer to reflect upon where to next "zoom in". In this process, the therapist and the family are located and theorised in wider and wider contexts, including the ethical (Lang & McAdam 1995). The personal, reflexive aspect of Threefold Vision provides both direction and meaning to the process of exploring Single and Twofold Vision. Whilst there are links between Fourfold Vision and Lang, Little & Cronen's (1990) domain of aesthetics (Fourfold Vision incorporates working ethically, elegantly and gracefully) it is important to stress that in this approach, the aesthetic element is found within the evolving, ever shifting Fourfold Vision that movies between single, twofold and threefold visioning. This is where "sparkling moments" or the emergence of deep connection and empathy can occur, which, along with an appreciation of the wider connections that hint at a greater unity; the unity which Bateson considered to be sacred.

The problem of 'power' from the perspective of Fourfold Vision

Bateson's denial of power was simply an aspect of his rejection of a non-relational, one dimensional epistemology. Power is not the problem; rather it is how we think about our relationships with each other (and the environment) that is the problem.

To begin to think of power from Bateson's epistemology, it might help if, as an example, we explore violence and think about how violence is used at all levels of society in attempts to exert control; whether individuals using their fists or nations using bombs and un-manned drones. We can consider the economics of international arms trade, appreciate that weapons used to kill and maim women and children may be manufactured in your country, perhaps even making your neighbourhood more affluent. We can wonder if bombing a population makes them more or less inclined to conform, and how useful violence is in changing people's minds or having any long-term influence in controlling others. Moving

Fourfold Vision and Cybernetic Unity

back to Single and Twofold Vision, we can look at, and locate local episodes of violence and attempts to control as being part of a wider problem.

As Bateson suggests, the myth of power is self-validating, and this is evident within all levels of society; through the behaviour of individuals or groups of people through to nation states. People continue to attempt to exert power over others, because it seems to be effective. To begin to shift towards Bateson's epistemology, whilst we might condemn the individual perpetrator of violence, we must also condemn the patriarchal structures, many of which are born from violence, where individual acts take place – the very structures that we are part of.

Fourfold Vision: nested, not separate domains

What has been presented here is analogous to the hermeneutic circle familiar to those who use phenomenological approaches. However, in Fourfold Vision the therapist (or observer-participant) continuously moves between detail and wider, relational contexts, whilst simultaneously reflecting on the process, allowing personal intuitions and embodied sensations to create shifts in attention, so different details and contexts continuously move in and out of the frame.

Whilst it may be convenient to think of Fourfold Vision as a means of describing what might be happening in therapeutic practice, I have also been exploring how to use it to guide my own practice and as a concept to help clients in their thinking too. An obvious example of this is where a client who focuses on minutiae and details to the detriment of seeing the bigger picture (or vice versa) is invited to shift the focus whilst supporting a reflection upon the process, including noticing and exploring differences in feelings as the focus moves around.

The following section is an attempt to illustrate the process used when working with an extremely traumatised client, who is here called A.K. She has experienced multiple difficulties in her life. A.K. has agreed to share her story with us and she chose the pseudonym for me to use.

Working with Fourfold Vision: the descent into hell

A.K. is 32, and has been "clean" for five years. Previously she worked as a prostitute and was addicted to alcohol and other drugs, including cocaine. In the four years preceding this, she had been kept as a sex slave, locked in a room and routinely tortured and degraded by her male partner who regularly "pimped" her out to groups of men.

A.K. identified that there were many cruel and terrifying incidents that she wanted to surface and speak about, yet all of these incidents blurred together. She was not sure of the timescales as many of the ordeals were similar in nature and she would often black out or dissociate from her body during these episodes.

Working with Fourfold Vision: making (some) sense of it all

We needed to find a way for A.K. to begin to talk about these events, and for the talking to have some meaning. She found it easier for me to not look at her during times she spoke of her memories, and together we devised a process where I would look away from her, and ask questions that might prompt particular memories and then, still not looking at her, respond to what I heard. She would find a way into telling me about an episode of terrible violence against her in the slowed down time of trauma. After she had finished the telling, I then retold her story and described my experience of listening to her account, about how distressing it was to hear, and articulated connections I made. Some of this was with links to my own experiences, with theory, for example, Foucault's (1975) notions of gaze, and of Dante's Inferno, with the descriptions of descent through the nine circles of hell. A.K. described how helpful it was to hear my retelling of her story; how it felt as though she was no longer on her own in that particular memory. This became an on-going process, with much work being done by both of us to encourage the surfacing and telling of stories, sometimes hampered by the nature of what she called "disassociation", but A.K. was been able to express that she felt we made significant progress.

Working with A.K., as with most clients, the aspect of Single Vision (Therapist as Scientist) is pretty much self-evident; the initial focus is upon her story, and the meanings she has made. In A.K.'s situation, Single Vision would also take into consideration explanations such as "Post Traumatic Stress Disorder" and "Dissociation" that might account for her difficulties; for example, how ordinary, everyday physical sensations can precipitate overwhelming emotional responses. At the same time, it was important to be consciously aware of the particular details that attention was being given to, with some reflexivity regarding the rationale for these choices and decisions.

Fourfold Vision and Cybernetic Unity

Twofold Vision (Therapist as Theorist) in the case of working with A.K. incorporated showing an interest in her relationships with others, including family members and her abusive boyfriend. Exploring patterns in relationships was helpful, and we explored her experience of feeling invalidated by different men in her life. However, a significant element of the focus of Twofold Vision is also the therapeutic relationship between A.K. and I; we thought together about how the relationship emerged, and how we managed and discussed issues like gender, age or spirituality. Regarding the relationship, it may be helpful at this point to share A.K.'s own (2012) words:

> "I needed someone who knew me, to whom I wasn't anonymous, to see at first hand the different heads, the frozenness, to spend time with me and get to know me so that they could understand me and what it's like to be me, and help me to move forward. The last 6 months have seen that change. You listen rather than telling me how it is, you check out if you are getting things right and I find myself able to trust you."

A.K. noted that I was compassionate but constructive, I listened and had a better understanding of her than anyone she had seen for therapy before.

The significance of Threefold Vision (Therapist as Humanist) emerged in the process of therapy. Whilst listening to A.K. giving an account of a particular experience, I found that, while I was not looking directly at her, I would be much more aware of my inner experiences as I reflected upon what I was hearing. Rather like listening to a (horrifying) radio drama, I constructed images of what I imagined to be happening; trying to feel what it would be like to be so vulnerable, exposed and naked, punched, spat at and penetrated so violently by groups of faceless, laughing men. The process of listening and responding was slow, difficult and very moving, for both A.K and I. Keeney & Keeney (2012, p.33) suggest that:

> "The liberated from-models therapist isn't holding on to a list of therapeutic taboos or a code of banned, blacklisted forms of therapeutic understanding and action. Here you are free to be moved by whatever the client presents. The embodied circular loop of improvisation is the most respectful relationship possible with a client for it utilizes whatever the client and therapist bring and then utilizes what happens next in the interaction. We call this 'circular therapeutics' and regard it as the key to bringing a healing heart to therapy."

Being open to improvisation during the process of therapy, for example in developing a process that enabled A.K. to speak without my gaze, enabled her to share with me experiences that she had never spoken about before, but also led to significant shifts in my position regarding pornography, the objectification of women and feminism, which links very much with the concept of Fourfold Vision (Therapist as Artist); as well as being beneficial for the client, the process has changed me, too. I can shift between compassion and empathy to outrage about living in a society that implicitly privileges the objectification of women that creates the context for the sort of abuse A.K. experienced. The work we did changed both of us; my understanding of the impact of trafficking, prostitution and pornography on both women and men has led me to becoming involved in campaigning work to oppose the trafficking of women into prostitution. A.K. now has a partner and a son. She still has flashbacks, but is much happier with her life.

Conclusion: Fourfold Vision is only a map

Fourfold Vision encourages a move towards thinking in terms of the reflexive shifting of focus within a greater unity rather than thinking in terms of separate domains. To separate things into domains, categories or groups may be convenient but it is not systemic, and is certainly antithetical to Bateson's thinking. More important than breaking free of limiting, boundaried domains, this approach offers a means for systemic therapists to become more flexible and to improvise. It meets the challenge presented by Keeney & Keeney (2012 p.32) who noted that first-order cybernetics resulted in therapists taking responsibility for changing the client, but that "second-order cybernetics ups the ethical imperative by asking us to change ourselves in order to foster change in others". Further, this model allows for a "both/and" approach of taking account of the value of evidence and data collection (Therapist as Scientist) whilst at the same time providing for a relational focus (Therapist as Theorist) and personal elements (Therapist as Humanist).

The concept of Fourfold Vision offered in this chapter is an attempt to articulate and share a way of thinking about our work with clients and families that is respectful of Bateson's cybernetic epistemology. The experience of fourfold vision is to move gracefully between detail and relationships, between theory and data, whilst simultaneously allowing your own inner experiences and intuitions to inform your attention and to allow the possibility of being open to change oneself. It is not a prescription, but an invitation.

Acknowledgments

to "A. K." and Nora Bateson

References

"A.K." (2012). Personal communication.
Bateson, Gregory (1961). *Perceval's Narrative: A Patient's Account of His Psychosis, 1830–1832*. New York: William Morrow and Company.
Bateson, Gregory (1972). *Steps to an Ecology of Mind: Collected Essays in Anthropology, Psychiatry, Evolution, and Epistemology*. Chicago: The University of Chicago Press.
Bateson, Gregory & Bateson, Mary Catherine (1987). *Angels Fear: Towards an Epistemology of the Sacred*. New York: Macmillan.
Bateson, Gregory (1991). *Sacred Unity: Further steps to an ecology of mind*. New York: A Cornelia & Michael Bessie Books.
Bateson, Nora (2012). Personal communication.
Bateson, Nora & McCarthy, Imelda (2013). An Ecology of Mind: Family therapy in the face of new emerging conditions. *Human Systems. Journal of Systemic Consultation and Management*, 24, 4–16.
Charlton, Noel (2008). *Understanding Gregory Bateson: Mind, Beauty and the Sacred Earth*. New York: SUNY Press.
Dell, Paul (1989). Violence and the Systemic View: The problem of power. *Family Process*, 28(1), 1–14.
Foucault, Michel (1975). *Discipline and Punish: The Birth of the Prison*. New York: Random House.
Foucault, Michel (1982). The Subject and Power. *Critical Enquiry*. 8(4), 777–795. http://www.unisa.edu.au/Global/EASS/HRI/foucault_-_the_subject_and_power.pdf
Frye, Northrop (1947). *Fearful Symmetry: A Study of William Blake*. Princeton: Princeton University Press.
Guddemi, Phillip (2006). Breaking the Concept of Power (and Redescribing its Domain): Batesonian and autopoietic perspectives. *Cybernetics and Human Knowing*. 13(3–4), 58–73.
Guddemi, Phillip (2008). "You Are Adapting More to me Than I am Adapting to You" (But What Does More Mean?): Cybernetic and Foucaultian explorations of the domain of power. *Proceedings of the 52nd Annual Meeting of the ISSS. University of Wisconsin*, Madison, Wisconsin. http://journals.isss.org/index.php/proceedings52nd/article/view/939
Harries-Jones, Peter (1995). *A Recursive Vision: Ecological Understanding and Gregory Bateson*. Toronto: University of Toronto Press.
Keeney, Bradford (1983). *Aesthetics of Change*. New York: The Guilford Press.

Keeney, Bradford & Keeney, Hillary (2012). What is Systemic About Systemic Therapy? Therapy Models Muddle Embodied Systemic Practice. *Journal of Systemic Therapies,* 31(1), 22–37.

Lang, Peter, Little, Martin & Cronen, Vernon. (1990). The Systemic Professional: Domains of action and the question of neutrality. *Human Systems: The Journal of Systemic Consultation & Management.* 1, 39–54.

Lang, Peter & McAdam, Elspeth (1996). *Referrals, Referrers and the System of Concern.* Unpublished manuscript, Kensington Consultation Centre.

Lipsett, David. (1980). *Gregory Bateson, the Legacy of a Scientist.* Boston: Beacon Press.

Maturana, Humberto. (2005). The Origin and Conservation of Self-consciousness: Reflections on four questions by Heinz von Foerster. *Kybernetes,* 34(1/2), 54-88.

Rose, Edward (1964). "Mental Forms Creating": "Fourfold Vision" and the poet as prophet in Blake's designs and verse. *The Journal of Aesthetics and Art Criticism,* 23(2), 173–183.

The Event. On experimenting with complex systems

5

Christopher J. Kinman

(The artist)... like you, has been brought,
unasked, in this world of variety,
and where, like you,
he must find his way...

Paul Klee 1949, p.11

Event I

A Beginning Thought

Nothing truly begins
Abbotsford, British Columbia

Unceded Sto:lo Nation Territory – 2015

My purpose in this chapter is not to instruct on how to intervene in the workings of complex systems with the goal of producing pre-determined results. Gregory Bateson, back in 1968, ended any hope that conscious purpose, and the interventions it produces, might be helpful in our interactions with ecological systems (If one wishes, read, The Effects of Conscious Purpose on Human Adaptation, in Bateson, 1972). But, this does not mean that we have no part to play. On the contrary, from in the midst of relational worlds, we do have an influence – not an interventionist's control, but an influence none-the-less.

In this chapter we move through influences and possibilities that might come to play as we participate in worlds of complex systems.

Event II

Watcher and Watcher

"*Poets, you know, are always ahead of science.*"
(Oscar Wilde, from his memorial in Dublin, Ireland).

We start beside a river – always a good place to start.

The Harrison River
Sts'ailes First Nation Territory – 2008

This is a poem I wrote after a brief encounter with a seal.

Watcher and Watcher

A seal emerges in the river
Oversized eyes
Wary of my presence
We are in relationship
Watcher and watcher
Fear, curiosity
Even delight

He and I
Have some things in common
We both survive
As eaters of the salmon

We do find comfort
By the river

The complex system – perhaps there are no other kinds. For, as we encounter a river, a seal, the salmon, a comfort, a much wider world converges upon us. In the midst of the encounter, relations always are expanding beyond what is previously given.

This is what Gilles Deleuze (2004) would call "the event".

The event, and the expansion of relations that accompanies it, particularly comes to life in response to the poetic assemblage. In fact, expanding relations are perhaps always waiting, poised to emerge into life, with most of the arts. Many academic traditions, the strategising of institutions, as well as much therapeutic practice, reduces life to scales amenable to measurement and management. The gift of art, as with the event, tends to shun such simplifications. Instead a proliferation of relations is more likely to be experienced. But, such a proliferation does not obscure and confuse, as some might imagine, rather it creates and opens up a renewed and renewing world of possibilities and hope.

The Event. On experimenting with complex systems

According to Deleuze and Parnet (1987), the event is not concerned with the static and reductive language of TO BE, but rather with the conjunctive, with worlds composed of... and... and... and...

And... in connection with the event of the previous poem, *Watcher and Watcher*, an assemblage of bourgeoning relations is ready to come to life. Rivers, seals, salmon, and so much more, are set to overflow the banks of that initial poetic moment.

An event-assemblage experiment

And... whether in fact, in art, or in imagination, other seals enter the flow; as do other creatures, including people, with whom we have shared important moments of encounter... And... there are movements of ecologies to which we, the seal, and all the others that assemble around this event are inextricably connected... And... we come face to face with ideas – ideas associated with complexity, ideas connected with living beings, relations, systems, nature, families, art, and beyond. Ideas are never absent from events and ecologies... And... people come forward, students of relations, practitioners of relations: Gregory Bateson, Gilles Deleuze, Felix Guattari, Claire Parnet, Lynn Hoffman, Rachel Carson, Bruce Alexander, Paul Klee, Nora Bateson, Imelda McCarthy, Harlene Anderson, Mary Olson, and on and on (for those I missed – please forgive me)... And... we find First Peoples moving upon this scene – people who have lived for millennia with these ecologies, with salmon and seals, eagles and ravens, with the cedar, with the creation of images, with songs and dancing, with the winter smokehouse – today they continue to move upon these lands and waters... And... political stirrings impinge upon the event – some fishermen complain about the seal, for the seal eats salmon... And... a seal is shot... a chief is shot... disputes between competing fisheries leave little room for another living creature who eats salmon... And... seal and salmon repeatedly caught in life/death complexities with human realms... And... events and chemicals travel – flows from industry and agriculture seep into waters through the soils, drainage ditches and canals, streams and rivers; they pass through gills of salmon and digestive systems of seals... And... all of us – we are caught in the double-binds of the political... And... events... traveling and expanding through images and words – poetic words, among others... And... the seal and I together become watcher and watcher of complex worlds in movement – differing perspectives, but together we watch... And...

these worlds are ever expanding – trickling, flowing, crashing, quaking, turning, drifting, withering, reviving, wandering... ever outward... And... and... and...

And, this – which is just a beginning... and just one possible trajectory – is what an assemblage might look like.

All of this in response to an event, a poetic event, a river event. And... there is no end... just further flows.

> (I)t is a world of exteriority, a world in which thought itself exists in a fundamental relationship with the Outside... a world in which the conjunction "and" dethrones the interiority of the verb "is"; a harlequin world of multicolored patterns and non-totalizable fragments where communication takes place through external relations.
> (Gilles Deleuze 2004, p.38)

More thinking on how to think of an event

Events are not internal to a soul or a body, certainly not internal to an individual brain or neural chemistry. Rather, events are geologies and geographies, ever close to the quakes, shifts, flows and languages of land, water and air. In unpredictable ways events are always journeying – like spilled-milk, travelling the surfaces, expanding their distributions.

With the event, concepts of health and illness are shaken; they become something other. Try it – imagine that which we call "mental health" as a geography, as an event-assemblage. How might such a change in thought and talk also change our engagements?

Events are occupied by nomads who are never limited by striated boundaries and imposed categories. These nomads are always roaming toward and through diverse territories. These nomads are human, they are animal, plant, bacteria, fungus, virus, ideas, creations of art, combinations of all this variety, living assemblages which we have yet to name. Such nomads do not just travel over pre-given geographies, they also alter all they touch. Amidst their movements and interactions new ecological and geographical territories are born.

> (T)o remove essences and to substitute events in their place...
> (Gilles Deleuze 2004, p.64)

And... always with company...

The Event. On experimenting with complex systems

In this chapter I am particularly engaging with the thinking and work of several relational experimenters: Gregory Bateson (1972, 1979, 1991) – cybernetician, biologist, anthropologist; Gilles Deleuze (2004; Deleuze & Guattari 1983, 1987; Deleuze & Parnet, 1987) – philosopher, student of the event; and Lynn Hoffman (1981, 1993, 2002, 2012) – family therapy pioneer, iconoclastic experimenter.

Moving beyond identities and commodities...

Joining with these four experimenters, we put aside the all-too-common idea that a "complex system" can be a known as bounded *thing* or *commodity*. That is, a kind of entity which:

- can somehow be distinguished as separate from the ecologies and relations that give it life;
- (in accordance with this separation from relations) can also be assigned a clear, designated identity, and organised in accordance with previously determined categories;
- can be stopped in its movements and fixed in time;
- can be accurately measured;
- can be replicated, packaged, marketed, and made ready for the shelves of modern capitalist institutions;
- and... can be readied for the filing/organising systems, and the strategic change schemes of modern managerial and educational processes.

Along with these thinkers/experimenters, I perceive worlds of relations as never pinned down into such commodified forms. This shift of perception and language is a political act, an environmental act, and a therapeutic act.

Instead, complex systems are imagined as event-assemblages, coagulations in the flows of time, knots of relations entangled in movements of life. Coming together, coming apart, reassembling – the living and dying of all organic life.

Towards the beautiful...

Rather than just explaining an event, we invite an entering into the event.

This chapter is arranged as a sequence of event-assemblages – we are already in the midst of them. By engaging with such events, and many other possible events that may be evoked, we come to further appreciate the unceasing complexities and possibilities that move through our own lives and work. For it is in such movements where the beautiful, the hopeful, the imaginable and unimaginable, and the enchanted can come to life before us.

> *What is individual is the relation, it is the soul and not the ego... Stop thinking of yourself as an ego in order to live as a flow, a set of flows in relation with other flows, outside of oneself and within oneself.*
> (Gilles Deleuze 1998, p.51)

Event III

The Wing of a Gull

Vancouver, BC, Canada

Unceded Musqueam, Squamish and Tsleil-Waututh Territories – 2008

And now, another way of looking at the event.

The utter complexity of the mundane

One day I found myself taken by the wing of a gull. The bird flew by, resolute toward some destination of which I knew nothing. But gulls are always flying by. They are, as they say, a dime-a-dozen, nothing special. This was not a rare bird, nothing unusual in its flight. The same silver-grey wing, the same bend in the wrist, the same lines and movements as I can see every day. Yet, today, for just a moment, I was stopped in its elegance.

Thinking of two economies

Yes, in response, I think of two economies!

One, an economy of restriction (see Stephen David Ross, 1996). Value rising with rarity, with inaccessibility. Value in Vancouver real estate, in gold. Value which arrives when something is seen to be uncommon and/or extraordinary. Value which emerges through an exception-to, a break in the ordinary movements of time and place.

Much of that which we associate with economy is built upon such assumptions. Empires are made upon such assumptions. And, we are all

The Event. On experimenting with complex systems

inescapably tied to the exchanges of these restricted economies, whether we like it or not.

Something such as a glimpse at the wing of a gull is lost, transcended, made irrelevant in such an economy.

Yet there is another form of exchange – often called the economy of gift (again, see Stephen David Ross, 1996). In this economy (if we choose to call it economy) value rises with plenty and regularity. In an economy of gift, an over-abundance doesn't drive values down, rather value and significance escalates as goods multiply in a repetition of exchanges. Value and significance increases in expanding circles with lines shooting-off toward untravelled realms. Yet these values have almost nothing in common with the numerical valuations of the restricted economy. Rather there is a kind of valuation built upon the continuous multiplication and movement of goods flowing from point to point, as gifts exchanged. Such valuations are produced by means of calculations far beyond numbers, computations emerging from and entering into something more akin to the mystical – the spiritual – the ancestral.

Complex systems...as ongoing and multiple exchanges of gifts

In the part of the world in which I live, the value at one time was seen as residing with the salmon, with the cedar, with the endless winter rains replenishing the mountains, with the expanses of the sea, with the sheer volume and power surging through the rivers, and with the relations of people that have historically lived with these abundances. These very things which for thousands of years were identified as images of health and prosperity now seem cheapened through the mechanisms of a restricted economy. The value of these goods is lessened precisely because of their very abundance. And, what is particularly disturbing, the value only increases as the abundance itself is diminished. It seems the limiting of abundance is built right into the processes of the restricted economy.

Back to the wing of the gull

Explore a gull's wing. Make an event out of your exploration. Explore each feather as if an unknown geography. Explore the gull in flight, the intricate movements of the bird herself. Explore a flock of gulls (for they always come in multiples); examine the coordinations of many wings taking to the air together. Explore a flock of gulls in swirling wind, co-ordinating with air and water, responding to the fish of the sea or the food-laden human beings below. A cacophonous, symphonic event comes to life.

Nothing of a naïve, reductive, managerial world emerges in response to the movement of a gull's wing.

Events of complexity moving amidst the simplest of moments

This simple event, a repeated and even mundane event, becoming a moment of intensity where something approaching the mystic moves around souls and bodies. For in this gull's wing, so easy to ignore, so easily obscured in its very commonality, beauty emerges, and, for a sliver in time, this beauty arrests me. A bend in a feather, a bend in the wing – as occurs endless times each hour – can turn the eyes to a world of gifts cascading through the everyday and the ordinary.

> *We show that we have attained maturity of understanding when we no longer go where rare flowers lurk under the thorniest hedges of knowledge, but are satisfied with gardens, forests, meadows, and ploughlands, remembering that life is too short for the rare and the uncommon.*
>
> (Friedrich Nietzsche 2006)

Event IV

On Becoming Snake

> *Is it an encounter with someone, or with the animals who come to populate you, or with the ideas which take you over, the movements which move you, the sounds which run through you? And how do you separate these things?*
>
> (Gilles Deleuze & Claire Parnet 1987, p.11)

An event – a sudden explosion – not seen coming

Sts'ailes Nation – 2007

One day I was working at a First Nation's school, while there I met with this particular boy. I asked him to draw something for me, anything whatsoever. I gave him a drawing pad. He quickly drew a pattern, then he stopped, looked at it, and was about to turn the page. He seemed to want to flee that very page, as if a mistake had been made, as if another educational inadequacy had just been created by his hand. I stopped him and said that this was a beautiful pattern. I told him that I really liked it. He looked again at the image. Then he put his face down near the paper, as if breathing life into that very point where pencil meets paper. He drew a small squiggle just beyond the previous pattern. He looked at me with light beaming from his eyes, saying, while pointing at the little squiggle, "This is a snake," then pointing to the larger pattern, "and he is breathing fire." The squiggle became a snake, and the larger pattern above became fire bursting from the snake's mouth.

Prepare... to be singed

This drawing was no longer a pattern and a squiggle, it became what Deleuze and Guattari (1987) call a becoming-animal, more specifically, a becoming-snake – and, one that breathes beautiful patterns of fire.

In this moment I had to put aside much that defines a professional's work. For, I asked nothing of hidden meanings, nothing of theories which I should apply. I did not want to join in throwing some opaque paint of supposed professional knowledge and practice upon the child and his creation. I did not want to make invisible his unique ways of seeing, hearing and moving through his world. I did not ask the transcendent question of what this pattern meant.

Instead I went with the boy to a becoming-snake that was bursting from the page, a becoming-snake slithering and constricting and breathing fire from the boy's living relations with eyes, hands, paper, pencil and world. And, the snake also becomes in my eyes, and is still becoming. Together we entered a world with snakes coming forth from paper and pencil, a world where enemies are in danger of catching ablaze, and the unsuspecting who happen to be in the vicinity might just become frightened out of his skin. For this snake breathes fire. Who would have thought?

I am a richer man – a bit singed and surprised, perhaps, but most certainly, a richer man.

Let's celebrate this becoming fire-breaking snake! Let's celebrate with the boy, with his family, with his community, with...

A world explodes forward around two squiggles on paper.

> *There is no work of art, that does not call on a people who do not yet exist.*
>
> (Gilles Deleuze 2006, p.324)

Event V

A Meal of Crabs and Clams

Northampton, Massachusetts – 2012

Family therapist, Lynn Hoffman, has for years now been experimenting with thinking and practice related to events and assemblages. The event, as both Deleuze and Hoffman imagine it, is always a web of relations – inclusive of the human and otherwise – that is always in movement.

> *Things that are in relation with each other are always changing and moving. If you pin something down – as a cat or a dog or a table or a chair – they can't move. But now we have a picture of a web, like the internet, all of a sudden it seems that static objects, names of objects, are no longer sufficient to present these ideas we want to get across about human living. A body, or a self – these concise words that describe almost a biological entity for the persons we are and the actions we perform – they don't really exist and are not useful if they do.*
>
> (Lynn Hoffman 2012c, p.7)

Porto, Portugal – 2008

Such a shifting complexity was beautifully evidenced at a family therapy conference in Europe which both Hoffman and I attended.

> *Lynn was the keynote presenter at a large, international conference. I followed her presentation with a presentation of my own. When I was finished, Lynn and I connected on the stage for a reflecting conversation. We talked together about what touched us in response to the event so far. Then we invited others to also share in the exchange. A growing conversation began to form. Lynn asked each person who wanted to share to come up to the stage with us, and to bring the chair he or she was sitting on. Many came and shared their thoughts, conversations emerged and spread like lines of flight. Everyone who came stayed with us on the stage. It was truly an event, and a visual event at that, for what began with just*

The Event. On experimenting with complex systems

> two in conversation grew and grew till the stage was overwhelmed with bodies. People had to repeatedly move and adjust their chairs to make room for others. It was a surging, sinuous, somewhat clumsy, movement-entity coming into life. And, during this event, a people were created – not an institution, not a prescribed or intentional community, but a people who were previously unknown and undefined, an event, an ecology that congealed and became populated at a specific moment in time.
>
> The event then dissolved, but I am certain it did not disappear; rather it flowed to other places, to other continents, in other languages, into contexts far away and near. New events, of which we are not aware, and of which we have no direct influence, are now moving upon the surfaces of this world.

An event like this one is not pre-given, it cannot be planned or predicted. Rather, Hoffman invites us to enter into the ecologies that surround us, to find ourselves part of these complexities and responsive to them. From within these ecologies we give witness to and are at play with the new creations that come forth.

> (The artist says of the world): "In its present shape it is not the only possible world.' The deeper he looks... the more deeply he is impressed by the one essential image of creation itself, as Genesis, rather than by the image of nature, the finished product."
>
> (Paul Klee 1949, p.45)

Hoffman's world is replete with such creation eliciting event-assemblages. They all involve a people who are created and a people who, in turn, are creating. She was captured by this form of entity.

We go on a trek with Lynn Hoffman

The Columbia River, USA – 2008

A number of years ago now I went for a drive with Lynn Hoffman in the Pacific Northwest of the USA. Beginning in Portland Oregon we followed the Columbia River to the West Coast. When we arrived at the small town of Astoria, Oregon – at the very location where the flows of the Columbia River enter into the North Pacific – we decided to stop for lunch.

Some weeks after that journey I wrote a poem reflecting upon that day, and particularly upon the meal we shared together.

A Meal of Crabs and Clams

The years gather together
In a dizzying lucidity
So much
Such a long time
Now merging into one
Unfinished conversation

Bits and pieces

Perhaps the sacred
Can be made of nothing else

A life is shared
A whole life
Yet
Never all of it

And it comes to be
As do
Our crabs and clams
From local abundances

Still after all this time
Local abundances

We sit together
A plastic table cloth
There is no way to eat this and be clean
So life is devoured
In its messiness

Perhaps all these movements
These comings
These goings
These glories
These tired bones
These spirits
Still soaring with the seagulls
And this spattering crab nectar

The Event. On experimenting with complex systems

It all comes together
In a local eatery
Amidst a buttery
Clutter of
Sacrificed crustaceans
And the charm
Of a local hospitality

And it is never finished
For there remains
Always
A pile of
Broken shells
Arguably
Not a sacrifice at all
But a return

From calcium to calcium

Perhaps the sacred
Can be made of nothing else

The *event* marks movements of time that emerge even *before* the celebrated moment. For this poem is composed, in part, of previous intents and wishes, including an enduring and percolating desire to honour the life and work of a friend and mentor, Lynn Hoffman.

The time of events and complex systems, is never bound by a unidirectional arrow of time. Past, present, and future – in the event – become unrequired fictions.

Event VI

A Conclusion — Perhaps

Returning Home

Abbotsford, British Columbia – Unceded Sto:lo Nation Territory – 2015

Nothing that is worth knowing can be taught.
    (Oscar Wilde, from his memorial in Dublin, Ireland)

As we end this chapter, I turn to the ending of Lynn Hoffman's 1980 book, *Foundations of Family Therapy*. There she focuses upon the ideas of Paul Klee. As Klee talks of his work, Hoffman sees him opening up complex systemic worlds. Let's listen to Hoffman's words as she reflects upon Klee – for maybe, just perhaps, these words might even now describe something of our own words, our own lives and practice.

> *The epistemology of this passage is circular not linear. It is multifaceted and therefore systemic. It sets no part over any other part, so it is not dualistic. It does not chop the ecology to pieces, so it is holistic. It links the viewer of one period to the viewer of another, so it is recursive. And it is evolutionary because it highlights a shift toward greater complexity between these different times.*
> (Lynn Hoffman 1980, p.349)

And now, to end the ending, a few thoughts I wish to offer to you, the reader, before you move to another chapter, or another book, or one of the other many tasks of life. Not instructions here... just thoughts. If they fit – that's good. If they don't – there are many more thoughts within this book.

In work and life (as if they can be divided) look for events, assemblages, webs of relation – not individual entities – for it is (perhaps) there that we discover life.

Move with events, dance with them, play with them; but don't stop a living world through unreflective productions of cold and motionless identities and categories.

Imagine life and work as acts of withness, as ecological bonds, always composed of many relations... many nomads, ideas, causes (if you need causes – have many), many gifts, possibilities. Never the separations and withdrawals of an icy, objective and objectifying aboutness (withness and aboutness are concepts developed by John Shotter – 2005, and often discussed by Lynn Hoffman – 2012).

Events – find them, create them, join them, and make them always a multiplicity... a withness.

> *(The) EVENT. It is a question of life...*
> (Gilles Deleuze and Claire Parnet 1987, p.93)

> *Well, I hope that may have given you some entertainment, something to think about, and I hope it may have done something to set*

The Event. On experimenting with complex systems

you free from thinking in material and logical terms, in the syntax and terminology of mechanics, when you are in fact trying to think about living things.

That's all.

(Gregory Bateson 1991, p.242)

References

Bateson, Gregory (1972). *Steps to an Ecology of Mind: Collected Essays in Anthropology, Psychiatry, Evolution, and Epistemology.* New York: Ballantine.

Bateson, Gregory (1979). *Mind and Mature: A Necessary Unity.* New York: Bantam.

Bateson, Gregory (1991). *A Sacred Unity: Further Steps to an Ecology of Mind.* New York: Harper Colins.

Deleuze, Gilles (1998). *Essays Clinical and Critical.* New York: Verso.

Deleuze, Gilles (2004). *The Logic of Sense.* New York: Continuum.

Deleuze, Gilles (2006). *Two Regimes of Madness.* Cambridge, Mass: Semiotext(e).

Deleuze, Gilles & Felix Guattari (1983). *Anti-Oedipus: Capitalism and Schizophrenia.* Minneapolis: University of Minnesota.

Deleuze, Gilles & Felix Guattari (1987). *A Thousand Plateaus: Capitalism and Schizophrenia.* Minneapolis: University of Minneapolis Press.

Deleuze, Gilles & Claire Parnet (1987). *Dialogues.* New York: Columbia University Press.

Hoffman, Lynn (1981). *Foundations of Family Therapy: A Conceptual Framework for Systems Change.* New York: Basic Books.

Hoffman, Lynn (1993). *Exchanging Voices: A Collaborative Approach to Family Therapy.* London: Karnac.

Hoffman, Lynn (2002). *Family Therapy: An Intimate History.* New York: Norton.

Hoffman, Lynn. Participant (2012). *All Manner of Poetic Disobedience: Lynn Hoffman and the Rhizome Century.* Documentary Film. Vancouver: Christopher Kinman.

Hume, Mark (2010, March 11). Ugly Incident Yields Peaceful Coexistence on Fraser River. *Globe and Mail.* http://www.theglobeandmail.com/news/british-columbia/ugly-incident-yields-peaceful-co-existence-on-fraser-river/article4252828/

Klee, Paul (1948). *On Modern Art.* London: Faber and Faber.

Nietzsche, Friedrich (2006). *The Gay Science.* Minola, New York: Dover.

Ross, Stephen David (1996). *The Gift of Beauty: The Good as Art.* New York: State University of New York.

Shotter, John (2005). *Janus Head*, 8(1), 132–158. Amherst, NY: Trivium Publications.

6

Looking for a Home
An exploration of Jacques Derrida's notion of hospitality in family therapy practice with refugees

Lucia De Haene & Peter Rober

At the time of writing this contribution, thousands of refugees are leaving their home countries and attempting to cross the borders of European countries in search of a home, encountering both practices of welcoming and refusal. In this chapter, we aim to develop a reflection on our ongoing work within a refugee family therapy service at our Faculty's clinical centre, through connecting it to the work of French philosopher Jacques Derrida on the encounter with the stranger and his call of welcoming and hospitality.

Erdal has been referred to our psychotherapy service for refugee families by a community-based organisation. Erdal is a Kurdish asylum-seeker, resettled and employed in Belgium. For 11 years now, his asylum application has been pending, leaving Erdal without any response. The only element that was communicated during his application before the Refugee Board, indicated that his engagement in his home country's armed struggle was labelled by some states as an involvement in terrorist activities and that this would severely complicate the procedure of being granted protection as a refugee.

In our first meeting together with an interpreter (a member of the Belgian Kurdish community), Erdal recounts fragments of his story as a refugee. Throughout his young adulthood, Erdal was a member of the Kurdistan Workers' Party and its armed struggle for Kurdish cultural and political rights. As a son of an important community leader, he played a key role in the autonomy struggle, taking part in paramilitary acts and being involved in the development of political theory on societal justice and redistribution. After many years of political and military engagement, the imprisonment of his Party's leader invoked Erdal's decision to withdraw from membership of the Party and his escape to Belgium. In therapy, Erdal talks about his sense of living in a space of insecurity, ambiguity, and meaninglessness. He feels unable to project his life into new future perspectives.

Erdal's story is an account of suffering on being denied hospitality when asking for a safe home to stay. It provides a window into the profound suffering that is invoked by the lack of a welcoming climate in a host country in which discourses on security and social integration legitimise harsh asylum and migration policies. His story accounts for the lived experience of many refugees who seek protection within the borders of western societies but who find themselves within a host society climate in which distrust prevails (Kirmayer 2007). Even for those refugees who receive resident permits, experiences of discrimination and marginalisation are very often part of their resettlement process (e.g., Carswell et al 2011), invoking refugees' encounter with a lack of hospitable social practices in exile. In his writings on hospitality, Jacques Derrida used the figure of the stranger, a refugee, as a starting point to reflect on the encounter with the other and the radical obligation of hospitality that is provoked by it (Derrida 1999, 2001; Derrida & Dufourmantelle 2000). These writings on hospitality have inspired several authors in the field of family therapy, who have engaged with Derrida's philosophical work in describing the therapeutic relationship as a space of welcoming clients' voices of otherness (Anderson 2012; Larner 2004; Paré & Larner 2004). In this chapter, we aim at a further engagement with Derrida's original work on hospitality, with a particular focus on transcultural psychotherapeutic work with refugees. Throughout this exploration, we further reflect on the evolving case story of Erdal, as a narrative account (with all identifying details omitted) of our encounter based on written notes made following sessions.

Derrida on hospitality

The ethics of welcoming the foreigner
In his thinking on hospitality, Derrida takes as a starting point the sudden appearance of the stranger at the doorstep. Derrida identifies this moment as an ethical moment: the arrival of the stranger resonates the absolute ethical imperative of hospitality, an obligation of hospitality without restrictions, "without asking of them either reciprocity (entering into a pact) or even their names" (Derrida 2000, p.25). Here, the foreigner's call for a home confronts us with the imperative to respond, to open our world, to welcome, and to give a place to the one who is unknown. In response to this ethical imperative, the host has to engage in a concrete practice of hospitality. Here, Derrida emphasises that every response to the ethical call of the stranger, any performance of hospitality cannot but fall short of the imperative of an absolute hospitality. As reflected in Erdal's story, it is clear that western societies'

reception of refugees is bound by such failure in relation to the ethics of hospitality: current practices of dealing with the influx of refugees arriving on boats or trying to cross wired borders show a decline of a shared sense of solidarity (Fekete 2005). Equally, western asylum policies are permeated by a discourse of suspicion, viewing refugees as potentially submitting illegitimate asylum claims and vectors of violence. Interestingly, Derrida reflects on the way nation-states, in their response to the arrival of strangers, develop specific migration policies that necessarily translate the unlimited ethical imperative to practices of conditional hospitality that fall short to this imperative: "the necessity, for the host [...] of choosing, electing, filtering, selecting their invitees, visitors, or guests, those to whom they decide to grant [...] hospitality" (Derrida 2000, p.55).

While Derrida's emphasis on the ethical obligation of unconditional hospitality invoked by the arrival of the stranger is easily understood and fitting our liberal politically correct agenda, his writing becomes unsettling when he articulates this kind of selecting or filtering of guests as unavoidable in the practice of hospitality. Derrida emphasises the paradox of "no hospitality without sovereignty of oneself in one's home": in order to be hospitable, one has to declare oneself sovereign owner.

> "To dare to say welcome is perhaps to insinuate that one is at home here, that one knows what it means to be at home, and that at home one receives, invites, or offers hospitality, thus appropriating a space for oneself, a space to welcome [accueillir] the other."
> (Derrida 1999, p.15–16)

Here, the host doesn't only appropriate the identity of the host, he also exercises the host's power. At this point, Derrida explicitly links the practice of hospitality with violence: "[..] sovereignty can only be exercised by [..] excluding and doing violence" (Derrida 2000, p.55). In its inherent conditionality of practice, every act of hospitality becomes an act of violence.

Violence and hospitality
The word "violence" holds an important place in Derrida's vocabulary, as it highlights the ethical dimension of the conditionality of hospitality: in his response to the arrival of the stranger, the host's concrete act of hospitality is necessarily limited, re-appropriating the intruded home as a space of one's own sovereignty and hereby failing to respond to the imperative of unconditional hospitality. In Derrida's perspective, violence

does not exclusively refer to explicit physical brutality and cruelty, nor to the person's explicit intention. Here, Žižek's reflections may clarify Derrida's understanding of violence (Žižek 2009). Žižek identifies systemic violence as opposed to subjective violence. While subjective violence is explicit and brutal as it is measured against the background of peace and understanding, systemic violence is subtle and fitting with the social context. It is not attributable to concrete individuals, but rather it is "objective, systemic, anonymous" (Žižek 2009, p.9), a by-product of social and economic processes. Hence, when Derrida describes violence as a necessary and often unintended part of any practice of hospitality, he aims to indicate these subtle processes of systemic violence. Yet, this does not invoke Derrida's insistence on accepting violence. On the contrary, Derrida precisely intends to emphasise how failures of hospitality should be continuously remembered.

Furthermore, Derrida does not exclusively situate the violence of hospitality in the position of the host, but also in the figure of the guest. The arrival of the foreigner is an invasive moment of a stranger entering your life, in search for a place to stay. Derrida emphasises the intrusive, disruptive nature of the foreigner's arrival: "The guest (...) traumatizes," he writes (Derrida 2000, p.78). Indeed, the arrival of refugees like Erdal consists of an intrusion of distant echoes of violence, breaking the shell of safety and mastery we have built around our world. Erdal's story embodies our fears of uprootedness and the fragility of community (Bauman 2002). By invading the security of our home and depriving us of our authority of this safe haven, the other distorts our world in its peaceful order. Derrida emphasises how, in this intrusive moment, the guest becomes host and the host becomes his hostage: "the inviting host [..] becomes the hostage [..] (and) the guest [..] becomes the one who invites the one who invites [..], (t)he guest becomes the host's host". (Derrida 2000, p.125). This perspective of the host becoming the guest's hostage enables an understanding of host societies' fears and defensiveness towards refugees. Host societies build barbed wire, fences, walls, and adhere to strict migration laws, as if walls and regulations could protect them from the ethical call of refugees' despair.

The aporia of welcoming
The inevitable presence of violence in the concrete hospitable relationship in essence refers to the translation of the unconditional law of hospitality into concrete laws and regulations of hospitality: "In order to be what it is, the law thus needs the laws, which, however, deny it, or at any rate threaten it, sometimes corrupt or pervert it" (Derrida 2000,

p.79). The ethical law of unconditional welcoming necessitates its performance in concrete acts of hospitality, while at the same time these conditional performances of hospitality are continuously drawn towards the ethical imperative. However, they are in constant tension as they imply and exclude each other: "They incorporate one another at the moment of excluding one another, they are dissociated at the moment of enveloping one another" (Derrida 2000, p.81) This paradox of hospitality, of being at the same time the unconditional law (singular) and the conditional laws (plural) of hospitality, cannot be resolved, as there remains a constant tension between the imperative and hospitality in practice. According to Derrida, this is the core of concrete practices of hospitality: the host's response to the foreigner's call precisely resides within the tension between the ethical law and the actual laws. This is why Derrida conceptualises hospitality as an *aporia* (ancient Greek: ἀπορία: *impasse; doubt; confusion*). Acts of pure, absolute hospitality are impossible: they are situated within the paradoxical tension of being conditional while carrying the ethical imperative of unconditionality. Here, a shadow of violence is cast over all acts of hospitality.

The subject's encounter with alterity
Derrida's writing on hospitality fundamentally aims to articulate the subject's encounter with alterity: the foreigner's arrival in essence refers to the encounter with otherness in the other. The experience with radical alterity, evoked by another human being, distorts the subject's understanding of his world. In this disruptive experience with otherness, the order of the subject's universe is criticised in what it is unable to speak about, the diversity of meaning it fails to account for: "the primary haunting of a subject prevented by alterity from closing itself off in its peacefulness" (Derrida 2000, p.4).

This intrusive questioning of the subject evokes a fundamental responsibility to speak out in the world about otherness and difference. Here, the ethical imperative of hospitality becomes the subject's obligation of an unconditional responsibility to give voice to the other, to the otherness that is not accounted for in the subject's meaning-making or that is silenced in the social world. But also this unconditional responsibility is an impossibility, as it is tainted by violence. Any presence with and speaking to the other always falls short of doing justice to the other's radical alterity, as it is inherently grasping and defining the other: "a form of mastery, bringing the unknown back to the known, breaking up its mystery to possess it, shed light on it, name it" (Derrida 2000, p.28). Our positioning towards the other, while invoked by otherness and trying to speak of it, inherently fails to do justice to this otherness and in essence incorporates difference into sameness, into what is defined within the horizon of our understanding. Our acts and words in response to the other become marked by the impossibility to give voice to alterity, to "try to come close to a silence around which discourse is ordered, but always pulls back from unveiling in the very moment of speech" (Derrida 2000, p.2). Inevitably, the subject's response operates in the aporetic space of giving voice to the other and incorporating the other at the same time: words and acts become an appropriating act of violence, but are at the same time continuously drawn towards the echo of otherness that initiated this response.

Hospitality in the therapeutic relationship – the therapeutic position as carrier of healing and violence

In recent years, several authors in the family therapy field have referred to Derrida's hospitality to address the therapeutic position of welcoming openness (Anderson 2012; Larner 2004; Paré & Larner 2004). Paré and Larner (2004) write about an ethic of hospitality in the therapeutic space involving openness and an exchange among diverse ways of knowing. As ways of ensuring the therapist's openness to clients' voices, Anderson (2012) emphasises the importance of being courteous, sensitive to the uneasiness of our clients, and careful not to intrude. Hence, these authors have provided a perspective on the role of a welcoming therapeutic position, a continuous hospitality to clients' alterity. In what follows, we aim to build on the work of these authors through engaging with Derrida's view of hospitality as an invitation to reflect on the way in which the therapist's welcoming openness simultaneously involves healing and violence. Indeed, a thorough articulation of the therapist's presence from the perspective of Derrida's figure of the host implies an understanding of the therapeutic position as an aporetic space between an unlimited responsibility for clients' unique otherness and the inherent conditionality of the encounter.

Inspired by Derrida's work, we come to understand how the conditionality of the therapeutic response inevitably implies violence: in meeting with clients and provoked by the client's call for unconditional hospitality, the therapist's response can only fall short of this absolute hospitality. Notwithstanding our best intentions, we will inevitably be violent in some way and fail to attain absolute hospitality. Our unintended violence can present itself in different forms: in our use of hurtful words or intrusive questions, our use of classifications or our refusal to classify, our labelling of suffering, our intervention as well as in our passivity in dealing with issues we choose to ignore, our pushing for disclosure, the hubris of our understanding, our speaking of words borrowed from a professional ideology with its dominant view on normalcy and pathology. Our violence as therapists is, at least in part, systemic in Žižek's sense, as it will be seen as part of the normal state of practices and discourses. Indeed, Žižek's concept invites us to understand that our words and acts within the therapeutic space echo the social context in which we live: in using words and acts that borrow their meaning from a society that is structured around inequality, language becomes an agent in reifying social systems' invisible, systemic violence that define borders of normality and legitimacy.

Derrida's emphasis on violence as inherent part of hospitality is not evident to accept, as being a vehicle of violence does not seem to correspond to our best intentions and professional commitment. Yet, Derrida's work invites us to understand how our responsibility precisely involves a willingness to reflect on our welcoming from the continuous question of where we fail to welcome. Here, the ethical responsibility of the therapist becomes more fundamental than the mere orientation on welcoming openness, as it requires a continuous monitoring of moments in therapeutic dialogue that resonate our implicit, unintended violence. This involves a permanent reflection on those aspects of hospitable presence that reflect its conditionality and its appropriation of the other. Such monitoring is not necessarily an inner monitoring, but it is also attentiveness to explicit or subtler signs of discomfort in the client in reaction to the therapist's words and actions. Here, we can try to support clients to protect themselves to our unintended violence by inviting them to set limits and say "no" to the way we offer hospitality. The client's "no" is often veiled in hesitations or polite objections, but it seems important that we understand that it may be a way of the clients of protecting themselves against our inevitable misunderstanding. Hospitality in practice implies our active interest in the client's otherness and the continued commitment to creating a dialogical space in which the client feels legitimated to set limits. It is important that we value our client's feedback and criticism, and use it to guide our actions in therapy.

> *In subsequent individual sessions with Erdal, we talk about the way his becoming disconnected from his political engagement in fighting for Kurdish autonomy provoked a strong sense of personal loss. I invite Erdal to seek words in his mother tongue that could account for his sense of mourning a meaningful life course. He writes down*

> the Kurdish words for "meaninglessness", "responsibility" and "guilt" on the large blackboard in between us. While writing down the words, Erdal talks about his strong sense of purpose during his political involvement in his home country, and his sense of responsibility for his community. "This is a loyalty," he explains, "pertaining to my group's cultural identity". Here, I try to relate these words to his precarious position in our host society and express my understanding of how his current experience of social disconnection may strengthen his sense of loss of meaning. Erdal recounts how he deeply mourns the strong sense of family and community cohesion in which he was raised, and how his social isolation in our host society echoes a life futile to others. When I ask him to address the word "guilt", Erdal remains silent and I join in his silence. After a while, he whispers he doesn't want to elaborate on this word: "This is very much present, but too difficult to speak about". When I ask Erdal whether the word should remain on the blackboard, he says it should.

Erdal's story involved the experience of the arrival of otherness, seeking a home. His narrative is imbued with multiple layers of otherness, revolving around cultural difference, uprootedness, and distant noises of atrocity from a space beyond humanity. As an interruption of the therapists' protected world of social order, Erdal's story invited meanings that revolve around the precariousness of community, connectedness, morality, and humanity itself (De Haene et al 2012; Rousseau 2003). Each of these dimensions of alterity invoked a strong moral appeal, a request to be welcomed. Erdal's lived experience of not being welcomed in the broader social fabric only exacerbated the sense of a therapeutic relationship filled with a request for a space of hospitality, as if our encounter became a social space that could reverse the larger society's pervasive silencing of his predicament.

In her search for a hospitable presence to Erdal's story, the therapist attempted to engage in a joint exploration of a language that is able to hold his suffering. Here, the therapist aimed to provide a space of shared understanding, moving beyond the use of fixed diagnostic entities to account for Erdal's suffering. Erdal was invited to seek his words to express his lived experience. In Erdal's silence when he was invited to talk about the word "guilt", it becomes clear how the therapist's question was an intrusive intervention, even though it was aimed being a hospitable act welcoming his lived experiences revolving around his previous involvement in violence. Erdal's response however indicated that he did not wish to talk about this layer of suffering. Here, his insistence on keeping the word "guilt" on the blackboard, suggests Erdal's wish to remain present around the theme of guilt in a shared silence, a silence that could hold his lived experience of unspeakable pain (Uehara et al 2001). Erdal's hesitation to talk about guilt was accepted by the therapist, showing Erdal that the therapist was committed to respect his feedback and use it as a guide in the process of therapy.

> In a later session, we gather around the written words on the blackboard again and explore the imprint of the past and present political context on these words of "meaninglessness", "responsibility" and "guilt". Erdal talks about the sense of loss of purpose after his party leader was imprisoned and advocated to stop any form of armed struggle. He recounts how this novel orientation in his Party invoked strong doubts on the meaning of his long-term engagement. He did not disagree with the change of policy that was advocated within his Party, but the change evoked his questioning of the necessity of what he had done. He wonders "what was the meaning of the blood", and then abruptly stops talking. The interpreter silently cries, and I wonder how this seems to touch upon her experience as member of the Kurdish community. I look at Erdal who is sitting in front of me. I'm silent too. I sense how the space between us resonates echoes of violence and atrocity. I feel his sadness, and remember that in one of the previous sessions he did not want to speak about "guilt". I sense how this encounter with Erdal and his struggling with intricate moral questions deeply moves me. It invokes an experience of a strong sense of connection, a connection to a shared humanity, to those complex human life trajectories as carrier of both good and harm.

Erdal's "no" to addressing "guilt" in one of the previous sessions was strongly present in the therapist's inner dialogue that followed Erdal's abrupt silence when he briefly referred to the meaning of the bloodshed he was involved in. Here, joining in the silence, exploring its meanings, and remaining present to the complex questions of moral responsibility that resonated within this silence enabled a careful witnessing of echoes of atrocity and complex moral questions of responsibility and guilt filling the therapeutic space. This complex bearing of an encounter with another human being who was an active perpetrator of violence in the political struggle for his community invoked a strong experience of a shared humanity (Rober & De Haene 2014), an understanding of violence as an integral part of the human condition. Here, the therapist may have engaged in a shared silence that operated as a space of hospitality to the suffering Erdal wished to voice.

Hospitality in mental health care institutions — moving suffering and healing into social worlds

In this paragraph, we focus on exploring the role of the mental health institution as both the context and host of clients' alterity. In our societal climate of overregulation (Keith 2013), mental health care discourses seem preoccupied with efficient production, evidence-based perspectives, diagnostic nosology and treatment protocols. The clinical encounter has become heavily imbued with the imperative of effectiveness, leading to a strong focus on measuring and evaluating the effectivity of treatment protocols (Tilbury 2004). Indeed, in many mental health organisations, therapeutic practice is actually governed by the language of economy and administration. These discourses of managed care and protocolled treatment strongly reflect a predominant medical model, in which the diagnostic identification of a fixed construct of psychic morbidity leads to a clearly defined treatment plan. Here, we want to address how these institutional discourses may create organisational contexts that fail to operate as spaces of hospitality in which clients' voices are welcomed, listened to, and explored as valid expressions of suffering and hope. Indeed, current discourses on efficacy, protocol, and managed care may invoke a dominant focus on categorisation, exclusion, and control, defining borders of normality and pathology and hereby reducing voices of alterity into a monolithic understanding of suffering and healing (McCarthy, 2011). In such a climate, it is difficult for therapists to be hospitable as the institution in which the therapist works may not be oriented on hospitality and welcoming the alterity of clients' voices.

Here, we argue that assuming the responsibility of hospitality within current institutional discourses may involve a twofold orientation. First, a commitment to being responsible for the clients' wellbeing; rather than being accountable towards the institution's directives. This includes the therapist's continuous focus on minimising violence within micro-processes of the therapeutic relationship, and protecting clients' institutional trajectories against systemic violence of the institution one works for. Often, a focus on the client's wellbeing is not contradictory to adhering to the institution's directives, but in case of such tension the therapist seems invited to act as a rebel in radically opting for hospitality towards the client, while being as loyal as possible towards the institution. This could imply, for instance, a moving beyond the language of medicalisation, objectifying definitions of pathology, and predetermined vocabulary of treatment protocols within the therapeutic encounter. Through sharing in those stories through which clients express their worlds and engaging with a multiplicity of voices and resources in dealing with suffering (De Haene et al 2012; Rober & Seltzer 2010), the therapist may resist a purely interventionist concept of therapeutic positioning and, hereby, reduce the disempowering effect of directive expertise that may deprive clients from expressing their voices. This might equally entail a questioning of how the medicalising language invokes an individualising understanding of clients' pain that emphasises individual distress rather than an account of a suffering that carries the imprint of societal injustices or disruptions in social relationships (Kleinman & Lock 1997). Here, in orienting therapeutic dialogue towards the explicit inclusion of cultural and social meanings of suffering and healing, both therapist and clients become involved in reflexive practices of resisting and subverting broader institutional discourses. Such reflexivity equally requires a careful monitoring of how bringing in cultural and societal voices could carry the risk of an appropriation by these institutional practices and therefore invites a continuous imagination of potential, novel ways of speaking and acting within mental health care (Kirmayer, 2011).

Second, an orientation on hospitality within clients' institutional trajectories equally involves moving towards broader public spaces, to question the violence of current practices of mental health care and to promote more humane and less violent alternatives. Here, the orientation on hospitality invites the therapist to speak within the broader organisational and political realm, assuming responsibility for addressing the violent implications of current societal and institutional context within public spaces. While being respectful of the fear of unsettling voices that may underpin current institutional discourses of categorisation and control, therapists have an important voice in challenging reductive or disempowering practices of diagnosis and treatment and contributing to the humanising of mental health care.

Hence, we argue minimising implicit forms of violence invoked by societal and institutional practices involve practices at both the level of the therapeutic relationship as well as in political spaces of public discussion and action. Yet, such orientation on reducing violent practices on both levels runs the risk of the therapist's understanding of the therapeutic relationships as a hospitable encounter within a non-hospitable organisation or exclusive societal context. Here, Derrida's aporia as interconnected poles of violence and hospitality may become polarised in such a way that the therapist assumes the comfortable role of the hospitable, benevolent host, while exclusively locating violence in reductive institutional discourses or social inequalities, outside of the warm intimacy of the therapeutic room. In therapeutic work with refugees, this disconnecting of violence and hospitality may be exacerbated by clients' experiences of pervasive marginalisation in their host societies, invoking the therapist's understanding of the therapeutic relationship as a necessary space of healing within an unjust societal climate. At this point, a Derridaian inspiration invites us not to exclusively locate violence and the lack of hospitality within the broader institution or social fabric, but, on the contrary, to accept complicity of the therapeutic position with this social or institutional context. Derrida's notion of the aporia of hospitality invites us to engage in a continuous and careful reflection on how our own therapeutic position may unwillingly take part in practices of categorisation and exclusion.

In listening to Erdal's account of his lived experience of loss of a meaningful life perspective, I wonder whether the lack of recognition in Belgium might exacerbate Erdal's strong sense of loss. I see Erdal's silent tears, and I feel responsible for my society's silencing of Erdal's suffering. This strengthens my orientation towards providing a space of welcome in our encounter. I reflect that it could be supportive for Erdal to connect to other members in his cultural community that maybe share his experience or that could provide a source of recognition for his earlier engagement. When I express my thoughts, Erdal remains silent. I sense the weight of the silence between us, as well as between Erdal and the interpreter who has now bent her head down.

Erdal says: "No, that is not possible. I cannot talk about this with Kurdish people living here". He adds that those members of the Party who withdrew their membership now face isolation and exclusion from their community. The interpreter keeps her head bent down. I sense Erdal's account moves her.

"Can you help us understand this, Erdal?" I ask.

"They reject me, because I withdrew from the Kurdish fight," he responds.

I feel how the space between us resonates his isolation. I suddenly wonder whether Erdal faces being represented as a betrayer within his community. I hesitate to express my thoughts, fearful the word betrayal may be hard to hear for someone who so deeply expressed his loyalty to his community.

Trying to find the right balance between my hesitation and my wish to join in Erdal's pain, I ask: "May I think that members of your community think of you as a betrayer, Erdal? Would that be the right word?"

The interpreter looks up at Erdal. Erdal bends his head down.

Following a brief silence, he whispers: "That is not the right word, but it is the word they use." Erdal starts to cry, and I notice that the interpreter starts to cry as well.

After a while, I say: "That must be difficult for you to bear, Erdal. It must not feel as the right word, in your life story in which you so strongly felt the responsibility for your community". The interpreter apologises for her tears and says: "It is what we do in our community."

They sit together and both cry silently.

I feel strongly moved by what I feel is happening between Erdal and the interpreter, a sharing of the pain that is lived in apparently opposing parts of their communities, a presence to the complexity of moral meanings, a holding of the pain in both parts and, through that holding, a crossing of borders. After I while, I say how I wish to thank them for how they remained present together in a shared suffering, a mourning of the fragmentation and division of their community provoked by long-term violent conflict, and I express how I feel both of them engaged in a brief fragment of restoration.

These fragments of therapeutic dialogue with Erdal and the interpreter indicates the therapist's ongoing search for language to express Erdal's lived experience, without medicalising and individualising his story, exploring to locate suffering and healing within broader social worlds. Here, this attempt to move beyond a language of individualisation also clearly involves a complex intersection between hospitality and violence, rather than a shift towards a mere hospitable relationship. The therapist's lived experience of responsibility in listening to Erdal's story that is silenced within the society indeed betrays a sense of a certain complicity with this societal lack of willingness to listen. In the therapist's inner voices, this experience of becoming a representative of an exclusive society invokes an intricate sense of how the therapeutic encounter itself may resonate or reactivate the societal marginalisation of Erdal's story, for example through failing to give voice to Erdal's "no" or through locking Erdal's story within the walls of the therapeutic encounter and within the limits of the psychological language as if it does not bear on broader societal processes of exclusion and declining solidarity.

Furthermore, the attempt to move beyond a therapeutic position of expertise and directive intervention equally involved a shifting of the therapeutic position towards an active inclusion of the interpreter as conversational partner. Here, inviting the interpreter as member of the client's cultural community to step in as a conversational partner equally indicates a process of decentring in the clinician's position (Rousseau 1998), an enlargement of the clinical space that seeks to invite a plurality of social and cultural voices within an often monolithic institutional discourse. In the case of working with clients from diverse cultural communities, such decentring entails the explicit invitation of a multiplicity of cultural meaning and knowledge systems at stake in clients' realities. Through explicitly exploring cultural understandings in clients' stories and through involving members of clients' cultural or religious communities, the therapeutic space may become a vehicle of hospitality in which different ways of understanding and performing illness, suffering and healing can circulate, exchanged and negotiated as valid universes of meaning and action (De Haene et al 2012), or even lead to novel forms of healing and coping.

Equally, the active involvement of the interpreter as member of Erdal's community in exile enabled an articulation of his suffering as both a personal and collective story, an account of the both intimate, social and political meanings shaping his story of isolation and disconnection (Kirmayer 2011). Here, a purely diagnostic or protocolled therapeutic language that would fail to articulate suffering at this intersection between individual and collective meanings may precisely aggravate the fragmentation of social connectedness in clients' worlds. In this case story, this developing understanding of Erdal's disconnection as carrying the imprint of a larger destruction of social connectedness within his community equally initiated an engagement in a process of restoration between Erdal and the interpreter, belonging to conflicting groups in their cultural community. Here, the therapeutic space might have carried a fragment of healing that crossed the border of the mental health care institution and created a moment of hospitality within the larger social fabric, a space of welcoming and holding divergent stories of suffering in a community divided by a shared history of violent conflict.

Conclusion

In this chapter, we aimed at furthering the engagement with Derrida's notion of hospitality in the family therapy field. We explored how Derrida's work on hospitality invites us to view clients as others in search for a welcoming place in which their voices of hope and despair can be shared, highlighting the fundamental experience of being placed in responsibility in the face of clients' suffering as well as the disruptive experience of clients' otherness. At the same time, it invites clinicians to identify how precisely this responsibility involves a reflection on the way the therapeutic position intricately intertwines healing and violence. Such understanding clearly moves beyond the emphasis on establishing a non-hierarchical, collaborative therapeutic relationship, and it even denies that such a therapeutic relationship would in practice be possible. Instead, Derrida's concept of hospitality calls on therapists to accept the complexity of therapeutic responsibility as a form of supportive, healing presence that necessarily and simultaneously involves violence, appropriation, and inequality, inviting clinicians to find an inner space in which one can bear to be a violent healer and to negotiate a therapeutic space that opens up spaces to address those relational processes of balancing healing and violence. This orientation on shaping hospitality as balancing movement between welcoming and appropriation invites clinicians to actively contain those fragments of implicit violence, the invisible parts of violence evoked by the clinician's reductive diagnostic notions, push towards disclosure, or appropriating language and amplified by the therapist's powerful position as a representative of the broader society that takes part in normalising institutional practices of diagnosis or the imposition of predefined treatment strategies. Through remaining present to these voices of violence, we may accept the relational resonating of coercion and inequality and hear how these voices may aggravate clients' isolation and disconnection from self and others. Through actively accepting these voices of violence, we may keep engaging in seeking a therapeutic space that is able to provide a home for failure and injustice as part of human encounters, and precisely because of this home, urges to never stop broadening our imagination of humanity and the human condition.

References

Anderson, Harlene (2012). Collaborative Relationships and Dialogic Conversations: Ideas for a relationally responsive practice. *Family Process*, 51, 8–24.

Bauman, Zygmunt (2002). Society under siege. Cambridge: Blackwell.

De Haene, Lucia; Rober, Peter; Adriaenssens, Peter & Verschueren, Karine (2012). Voices of Dialogue and Directivity in Family Therapy with Refugees: Evolving ideas about dialogical refugee care. *Family Process*, 51, 391-404.

Derrida, Jacques (1999). *Adieu to Emmanuel Levinas* (translated by Pascale-Anne Brault & Michael Naas). Stanford, CA: Stanford University Press.

Derrida, Jacques (2001). *On Cosmopolitanism and Forgiveness* (translated by Mark Dooley & Michael Hughes). London: Routledge.

Derrida, Jacques & Dufourmantelle, Anne (2000). *Of Hospitality*. Stanford, CA: Stanford University Press.

Fekete, Liz (2005). The Deportation Machine: Europe, asylum and human rights. *Race & Class*, 47, 64–91.

Keith, David (2013). The Self of the Therapist in the Empire of Overregulation. In: Baldwin, M. (Ed.). *The Use of Self in Therapy* (3rd ed.). New York: Routledge.

Kirmayer, Laurence (2007). Refugees and Forced Migration: Hardening the arteries in the global reign of insecurity. *Transcultural Psychiatry*, 44, 307–310.

Kirmayer, Laurence (2011). Les politiques de l'altérité dans la rencontre clinique. *L'Autre: Cliniques, Cultures et Sociétés*, 12, 16–29.

Kleinman, Arthur & Lock, Margaret (1997). *Social Suffering*. Berkeley: University of California.

Larner, Glenn (2004). Levinas: Therapy as Discourse Ethics. In Strong, Tom & Paré, David (Eds.). *Furthering Talk: Advances in Discursive Therapies* (15–32). New York: Kluwer Academic/Plenum Publishers.

McCarthy, Imelda (2011). Abusing Norms: Welfare families and a fifth province stance. *Human Systems Journal of Systemic Consultation and Management*, 22, 339–350.

Paré, David & Larner, Glenn (2004). Towards an Ethic of Hospitality. In Paré, David & Larner, Glenn. (Eds.). *Collaborative Practice in Psychology and Therapy*. Binghamton, NY: Haworth Press.

Rober, Peter & De Haene, Lucia (2014). Intercultural Therapy and the Limitations of a Cultural Competency Framework: About cultural differences, universalities and the unresolvable tensions between them. *Journal of Family Therapy*, 36, art.nr. 10.1111/1467-6427.12009, 3–20.

Rober, Peter & Seltzer, Michael (2010). Avoiding Colonizer Positions in the Therapy Room: Some ideas about the challenges of dealing with the dialectic of misery and resources in families. *Family Process*, 49, 123–137.

Rousseau, Cécile (1993). L'horreur et l'humanité. *Frontières*, 15, 60–62.

Rousseau, Cécile (1998). Se décentrer pour cerner l'univers du possible: Penser de l'intervention en psychiatrie transculturelle. *P.R.I.S.M.E.*, 8, 20–36.

Tilbury, Clare (2004). The Influence of Performance Measurement on Child Welfare Policy and Practice. *British Journal of Social Work*, 34, 225–241.

Uehara, Edwina; Farris, Martha; Morelli, Paula & Ishisaka, Anthony (2001). "Eloquent Chaos" in the Oral Discourse of Killing Fields Survivors: An exploration of atrocity and narrativization. *Culture, Medicine and Psychiatry*, 25, 29–61.

Žižek, Slavoj. (2009). *Violence*. London: Profile Books.

A Systemic-Dialogical Perspective for Dealing with Cultural Differences in Psychotherapy

7

Andrea Davolo & Laura Fruggeri

In the systemic family therapy field, dealing with cultural differences has been an important issue. Working with families from different backgrounds has been considered a great challenge. Reflecting on one's own cultural bias and developing cultural competence has been a goal for family therapists to assist them in overcoming ethnocentric ideas and practices (Falicov 1995; Di Nicola 1997). When working with refugees, another "must" is added: the consideration of trauma. Putting the two aspects together, many psychotherapeutic interventions take into account the cultural context of the suffered trauma (Nicholl & Thompson 2004).

Moving forward from this tradition, in this chapter, we will not talk about therapists' cultural prejudices or competencies; nor we will talk about clients' trauma. Rather, we will focus on the potentials of the systemic approach in developing a dialogical psychotherapeutic perspective on culture. We will specifically illustrate some methodological principles of the systemic therapeutic practice that can engage clients who are refugees – thus "foreigners"to therapists and "marginalised" in society – into a conversation that opens space for their point of view; a practice that legitimises their perspective and trusts them to be reliable in handling their own life. We will focus on a systemic therapy that addresses, instead of reducing, the social tensions generated between people from different cultures (Rober & De Haene 2014). We will reflect on how history, politics and geography are social dimensions that contribute to structure the "self", and how systemic therapists should have knowledge of such dimensions (Falicov 2007; McGoldrick & Hardy 2008). We will describe a practice that considers "culture" as what we do together, not as a category that labels people (Cole 1996).

There are three guidelines that inform our therapeutic practice with refugees: the notion of *irreverence/curiosity* (Cecchin et al. 1992), the acknowledgement of *clients' competence* (Fruggeri 2012), and the interconnection of *socio-political dimensions* and personal psychological processes (Sironi 2007). The first two guidelines underline that intercultural therapy is a dialogue of living persons, as any other kind of systemic therapy (Rober & De Haene 2014); the third is specific of the work with migrants and especially with refugees.

Three methodological guidelines

The Health Centre for Immigrants (HCI) is a polyclinic that is part of the Italian National Health Service. The Centre offers social and health support to the newly arrived migrants and works in connection with the Refugee Protection Programme. In this space, we met Fatna, Mahmud, and Larysa whose stories we want to share with you. All names are invented and the cases are narrated in a way to protect their privacy, yet we would like to underline that all three of them were more than happy to let their story be told, and you will understand why, reading Larysa's story.

Fatna, Mahmud and Larysa will help us illustrate the three guidelines listed above.

Fatna: the inspiring notion of irreverence/curiosity

Fatna, 28 and Idriss, 34, are married. They arrived in Italy from an African country involved in a civil war. They have two children: Susheta, a girl of 6 years, and Hassan, a boy born in Europe a year ago. Fatna contacted HCI showing a court order imposing the separation of the children from their parents. The reason for the order was that Fatna, while pregnant of her second child, had interrupted her participation in the Refugees Protection Programme, escaping abroad with Susheta. In the European country to which she had escaped, Fatna gave birth to Hassan. Few months later, the local authorities communicated to Fatna that, according to the Dublin Regulation, she and her children had to go back to Italy, the country in which she had started the procedure for asylum. Fatna returned to Italy and dutifully contacted the local police. The sudden and inexplicable departure of Fatna with Susheta, and her determination to avoid any explanation, worried the court to the point of ordering the social services to host Fatna and her children in a shelter while observing and supporting Fatna's parental skills. Meanwhile, Idriss was living with friends. While at the shelter, Fatna proved to be an adequate mother to her children, yet she attempted to leave twice. For this reason, the court decreed that the children should be separated from their parents and demanded an assessment of Fatna's and Idriss' personalities. It is at this point that Fatna got in touch with HCI seeking help. During the consultation with the psychologist, Fatna appeared not to realise how potentially dangerous the situation was for the children.

A Systemic-Dialogical Perspective

She minimised the episodes, gave incoherent explanations for her decisions, rejected any responsibility, and attributed a deliberate intention to harm her by the social workers. The situation appeared incomprehensible to the psychologist who wondered, "Why does Fatna persist in running away from situations that are thought to be protective for her and her family?"

This question might have a different answer within a universalist or a relativist vision of culture. From a universalist stance, the reason for Fatna's behaviour is expected to be found in some pathological mechanism like a cognitive deficit or a personality disorder. The universalist perspective relies on a definition of "good parenthood" that is expressed through the behaviours defined by western expectations of "what a good parent should do" regardless of the context. According to this definition, Fatna's behaviours appear senseless. The limit of the universalist perspective is exactly this: it uses psychological categories as if they had the same meaning everywhere. Conversely, attributing Fatna's behaviours simply to a cultural belief (the relativist perspective) could lead to thinking that a parent who belongs to a different cultural group cannot be evaluated, helped, or supported by a western professional. The relativist hypothesis would, in fact, imply that even if the professionals identified a potentially dangerous situation for a child of an immigrant family, they should not intervene due to respect for the parents' cultural belonging, paradoxically generating a situation of less protection for the immigrant parents and their children.

As elegantly discussed by Rober and De Haene (2014), both the universalist and the relativist perspectives are restricted visions. The universalist stance psychologises and individualises social responses; the relativist perspective justifies any behaviour as driven by cultural beliefs. Within both perspectives, the client-therapist relationship is conceived as asymmetrical. The universalist position imposes a worldview; the relativist viewpoint leads to the ambiguous position of tolerance that while "understanding" reaffirms the superiority of the culture of those who consider themselves "tolerant".

Systemic therapists have been dealing with the issue of multiculturalism for years, and a lot has been accomplished to overcome the limits (technical, ethical, political) of a universalistic approach. We take here a stance also in favour of overcoming the relativistic/ethnographic/external vision of culture, a vision that looks for stable and shared characteristics and values of the different cultural communities, and consequently ends up stereotyping the members of those communities while also defining the diagnostic and therapeutic categories according to one cultural group or the other.

We claim that in systemic therapy practice with people coming from different cultural backgrounds and experiences, a binocular perspective is needed (Bateson 1979): a perspective that legitimises and celebrates relations of differences; a perspective that, instead of asking therapists to choose between their own culture and clients', relies on the power of dialogue between different stances in generating new and shared frameworks. As Barnett Pearce (1989) wrote, in what he refers to as multicultural cosmopolitan communication, people "put their resources at risk"; in other words, they are open to change through the encounter with "the otherness", thus underlying that change is the result of a relational process, not of an aprioristic cognitive individualistic decision. People inevitably engage in communication exchanges from their own specific position of culturally situated individuals. The difference pertains whether they respond to cultural heterogeneity with respect and curiosity or not. In the first case, the exchange becomes a dialogic experience that can generate new ways of seeing and doing in the world; in the second, the exchange becomes an exercise of power on behalf of a member of the dominant group on others.

We are aware of the power issue that is at stake in the relationship between a therapist and a refugee. Therapists are representatives of the dominant culture and they cannot escape from that. An effective way to address the power issue without either denying or mystifying it, is to give equal legitimation to all viewpoints. In this sense, working with clients coming from different cultural backgrounds implies dealing with the constant tension between diversity and equality. Diversity refers to the idiosyncratic culturally and socially situated positions of each individual; equality refers to the acknowledgement of the equal value of all positions.

Gianfranco Cecchin's invitation to irreverence and curiosity is the methodological guideline for embracing a dialogic practice that, in its attempt to legitimise all different viewpoints, makes these viewpoints communicate, connect and generate new visions (Cecchin et al., 1992). Cecchin invites therapists to become irreverent with respect to their comprehension of the situation and to take a curious position with respect to what others understand. It is an invitation to raise questions before coming to a conclusion, to develop an interest in how people make sense of their experiences. Curiosity towards others' ways of making sense of the world

A Systemic-Dialogical Perspective

is sustained by questions such as: In which context would this behaviour make sense? Questions like this place therapists in a dialogical position that invites the interlocutors to participate in a shared relational process.

Starting from these reflections, the initial question, "Why does Fatna persist in running away from situations that are thought to be protective for her and her family?" was reframed as, "From which viewpoint is escaping from the Protection Refugees Programme a way for Fatna to protect her children?" Both questions are centred on the shared value that children need to be protected. But the first one implies that there is only one way to protect: that of the dominant culture (the social services, the Refugees Programme, the court). The second question implies that there are different ways to protect, and that Fatna was protecting her children according to assumptions that the professionals simply ignored or of which they were ignorant. With this question in mind, the therapist invited both partners for a meeting during which the story of their family, the reasons of their travelling, their hopes and fears could be explored.

After marriage, Fatna and Idriss escaped from their country because the government persecuted them. Fatna had to hide from a totalitarian state since her childhood: many of her relatives had been tortured and killed by the police. In the African country where they moved, they could live a quiet life for some years. The little Susheta was born there. The blow up of a new war forced them to escape once more. They arrived in Italy and were included in the Refugees Protection Programme. As refugees, they had to refer to the Social Services for any need. Yet, Fatna and Idriss were obsessed by the amount of time that the procedure for their asylum was taking. Since they didn't have a residency permit, they couldn't work. In face of Fatna's second pregnancy, they wondered with worry how they could rear two children without working.

At this point of the session, the therapist asked, "What happens in your village at home when parents cannot raise their children?" Idriss answered that the parents would entrust their children to a member of the larger clan chosen by the elders in the father's family. So the conversation continued:

Therapist:	Do you have relatives in Italy?
Fatna:	No.
Therapist:	So ... the children...
Idriss:	Children here belong to the State.

Therapist:	What do you mean?
Idriss:	If you don't have a job, Social Services decide.
Therapist:	Did the social worker tell you this?
Fatna:	No, a mediator told us that it could happen.

This is how Idriss and Fatna made sense of the situation and acted accordingly. They had interpreted the meetings with the social worker as "warnings" that, in case they didn't prove to be able to solve their problems, the children would have been taken away. To avoid this, Fatna escaped. When she was sent back to Italy, she forcedly had to contact the police authorities, which in her experience are not seen as reliable since, in her life to date, she always had to escape from state authorities. After her placement, with her children, in the shelter, Fatna started to think that the social services were deliberately planning to harm her and her family. This piece of conversation highlighted two "blind spots" that prevented the development of a shared vision in the relationship between Fatna and the professionals. For the parents, *"the children of troubled parents belong to the clan"* translated in the migratory context as *"the children of troubled parents belong to the state"*, which for Fatna assumed a tragic meaning since for her *"the state is a prosecutor"*. On the other side, the professionals assumed that *"a meaningless behaviour is a symptom"* and *"a mother who exposes her children to risky situations, cannot be a good mother"*. These parallel visions acted in a self-referential way in this situation, yet confirming each other, thus generating a recursive spiral headed toward the worst outcome. The curiosity of the psychologist toward Fatna's viewpoint led to an understanding of all enacted behaviours. He then wrote to the social workers in charge of the case and offered his interconnected description of the situation, suggesting that he work with the couple in a way that possibilities might emerge for a third shared perspective from which it would be possible to co-construct Idriss and Fatna's "parenting in a context of forced migration".

The idea of irreverence fits very well with the notion of "culture as something that people do together" (Cole 1996) and with the idea of "putting one's own resources at risk" (Pearce 1989). The therapist involved in an intercultural dialogue does not know beforehand the perspective from which the others behave. The meanings of people's behaviours are not predefined, written in the genetic code of their culture. Meanings are generated in the encounters that people happen to live and experience. Fatna did not escape from the protection programme and fear the social

A Systemic-Dialogical Perspective

services because of her culture. Fatna's behaviours followed from how she was making sense of the situations she had to deal with coming to Italy with her family as a refugee. This is how the idea of irreverence can be helpful. Irreverence is an invitation to approach others' behaviours considering that we still do not see the perspective from which their behaviours make sense. The concept of irreverence tells us that even if we knew everything of Fatna's culture, we still should not take for granted our understanding of Fatna's behaviours. Her belonging to a specific cultural background and her position as refugee are, of course, important elements to consider in the reconstruction of the meanings of Fatna's behaviours and of her feelings. Yet if they were not combined with the personal experiences that she lived, they could objectify Fatna as a member of a group. Practising irreverence toward one's own premises leads to a genuine curiosity toward others' epistemology, that is, a curiosity toward the viewpoint that makes their story sensible.

Mahmud: clients are the experts of their life story

The acknowledgment of clients' competence is embedded in the systemic perspective above illustrated. From a systemic point of view, the process of change is rooted in the difference emerging from the relationship between therapist and client. The client, in such a relationship, is as competent as the therapist, even if in a different way: systemic therapists are trained to analyse relationships and processes, clients are experts of themselves and their context (Fruggeri 2012). In systemic practice, clients are considered a trustful source with respect to themselves and the context of which they are a part. Therapists rely on the fact that clients are competent in telling their story, in connecting emotions and meanings to the events they experience.

Mahmud's story helps us to illustrate how therapists themselves grow in expertise when they trust the client's competence to provide clues for the understanding of their own story.

When Mahmud contacted HCI, he was 23 years old. The staff of the Refugees Protection Programme referred him for a psychological consultation because he reported frequent severe backaches that seemed to have no organic cause. He also suffered from insomnia and was deeply depressed. Mahmud comes from an African country that he had to leave because of the chaotic and violent situation that was starving the people. In his country, Mahmud was a soldier-boy. One day he was involved in a gunfight and was seriously wounded. Once discharged from the hospital, he decided to escape. He organised his journey toward another

African country, where he, though, was put in prison as a "clandestine person". Mahmud reports the tortures he suffered there: he was beaten with iron bars, electric cable and was shocked with Taser guns. Once freed, he reached Italy.

The narration of Mahmud's migratory story fits very well the trauma theory that western professionals have in their "toolbox". In fact, the psychiatrist of the HCI pointed out two moments that were possibly connected to his pains: the episode of the gunfight (pre-migratory trauma) and the tortures suffered in prison (migratory trauma). A diagnosis of post-traumatic stress disorder was made and an anti-depressive drug was prescribed. But, as time passed, the therapy proved not to be effective. Mahmud continued to be in pain and depressed. So he was referred to the psychologist of the HCI, who also collected his migratory story, but differently from the psychiatrist, the psychologist thought that the idea of a trauma following the experiences of the war and tortures didn't really make sense of Mahmud's suffering. In fact, Mahmud had provided significant information: the pain came and went, he experienced the pain in different situations, the pain was not connected to physical damage. The psychologist decided to ask Mahmud some questions aimed at emphasising these clues.

Therapist: How do you explain that you have felt the backache in X (the first camp in Africa after he escaped his home country) and in Italy, and not in Y (his home country) even if you almost died in the gunfight?

Mahmud: In Y, I felt strong.... Here, no.

Therapist: What made you feel strong in Y?

Mahmud: ...My family. Here nobody shoots and kills, but I am alone.

Therapist: When the pain disappeared after the release, didn't you feel alone then?

Mahmud: ...but I was free

Therapist: Did you lose your freedom in Italy?

Mahmud: No, but they made me take a medicine and they didn't explain why.

Therapist: What happens if one takes a medicine without knowing why?

Mahmud: It means that... maybe I am crazy. Isn't that why I am here?

A Systemic-Dialogical Perspective

Was it really so simple? Would Mahmud feel better if someone explained to him why a medication was prescribed? Was it really only a matter of clear communication? The therapist decided that he wanted to know more about Mahmud's understanding of the events he had gone through. Considering the focus made by Mahmud on medications, the psychologist wondered: What is the meaning of drugs in his cultural experience? Who prescribes drugs and when? Asking these questions, the following scenario took shape. In his home country, clinics and hospitals handled by the NGO take care of organic diseases; the "care of the spirit" sometimes possessed by the djin, the white demons responsible of the madness of humans and animals, is left to the Koranic Healers who prescribe herbal compounds often administered by relatives against the patient's will. This framework shed light on Mahmud's story. In the process of trying to make sense of the discomfort and disorientation felt during the convulsive events experienced in Africa and in Italy, he had relied on the explanation made available by his culture: "a medication is administered against your will when you are mad." The psychiatrist's disregard for Mahmud's meanings made him blind to the fact that he was confirming, in a iatrogenic way, the explanation upon which Mahmud relied to make sense of his situation: "they gave me a medication because they think I am mad and since they keep giving me a medication, they confirm I am still mad."

After this reflection, the dialogue went on to explore new connections between the experiences lived by Mahmud as they were emerging in his narration.

Therapist: In Italy doctors gave you medicine without you knowing why... Also in prison in X, the guards beat you up without you understanding the reason of the beating.
Mahmud: It's true.

The therapist's comment connecting the "incomprehensible" prescription of the drug to the "incomprehensible" tortures suffered in jail opened a new path of exploration and introduced the possibility of a different narrative where the theme was not Mahmud's backache, or the prescribed medications, not even the traumatic events he had lived. The topic of the conversations became his agency, his comprehension of the painful events lived.

Therapists need to explore clients' stories, but even more important is to explore *clients' viewpoint on their own stories*. This is what it means to explore a story relying on the client's competence. The reconstruction of the cultural origin of Mahmud's interpretation of the situation was just the place to start in reconstructing the sense of a chain of events, emotions and encounters whose meanings had gone lost in the alienating experiences lived by him. To us, this is a lesson learned from Cecchin's work: reach the clients where they are, and from where they can start a new journey to some other "place" where new meanings can give sense to new stories (Fruggeri 2005). The psychologist, in collaboration with the staff of the Protection Refugee Programme, started then to construct with Mahmud a new project in which he could actively overcome his distressing experiences, through the process aimed at obtaining political asylum.

Larysa: when psychology, culture, history and politics intertwine

Cultural belonging, political story, and psychological status, are intertwined (McCarthy & Byrne 2008). Therapists cannot address the psychological status of clients, who are migrants or refugees, without taking a dialogical attitude toward the cultural and political dimensions of the clients' experiences. In this section we will address this particular aspect of working with people who have been the victims of collective violence.

In the perspective of Geo Political Clinical Psychology, the victims of intentional collective violence do not suffer from intra-psychological disorders; their suffering is due to socio-political constructions (Sironi 2007).

Victims of collective violence often suffer disavowal. They have often experienced more than one episode of subjection aimed at offending and demolishing their cultural belonging, thus their identity (Sironi 2007; Nathan & Zajde 2012). The perpetrators of collective violence have the deliberate political goal to "de-acculturate the individual". In these cases, the cultural and personal psychological processes intertwine with Geo-Political dimensions; thus the therapists have to add a new competence to their background. Psychotherapeutic knowledge is not enough; even the respect for differences and self-reflexivity concerning one's prejudices are not enough in dealing with victims of collective violence. Awareness of political, historical, economic and legal international events has to be part of the therapist's cultural knowledge.

When working therapeutically with victims of collective violence, it is important to support them in the acknowledgement of the political goals and responsibilities of their aggressors, as a way to regain their lost identity; but it is also important for the victims to recuperate a sense of self

A Systemic-Dialogical Perspective

as active subjects able to respond to and resist the consequences of the aggression. In this perspective, the approach known as *Response-based therapy* (Todd & Wade 2003) can integrate into the therapeutic practice proposed by *Geo-political clinical psychology* very well. Combining the two approaches, the therapeutic session develops through the description of the suffered violence, the clarification of the responsibilities and intentions of the aggressor, the identification of response and resistance to violence, together with the analysis of the social response that could have mitigated the aggressor's responsibility and blamed the victim.

The case of Larisa will help us to develop these ideas.

Larysa is a young woman of 28 years from Ukraine. She contacts HCI together with her mother Olga who worries because Larysa has frequent episodes of uncontrolled anxiety that follow sudden flashbacks recalling traumatic situations experienced few weeks before meeting with HCI. Larysa reached her mother (already in Italy for many years) after escaping the violent civil war that is taking place in the Donbass region of Ukraine. Larysa decided to leave her country because the bombing of the Ukraine Air Force and the guerrilla actions on the ground had become unbearable. Before going to Italy, Larysa lived in Lugansk with her father. Larysa's father is not a supporter of the central government established in Kiev, yet he decided not to take part in the Resistance either, since he disagrees with the separatist option. Larysa shares her father's political positions. Before deciding to escape to Italy, Larysa moved from Lugansk to Kiev. Having a good professional curriculum, she thought she could easily find a job. Unfortunately, events took another direction; she got a lot of negative responses and, as "a woman from Donbass", she often had to deal with discriminatory and abusive attitudes. Larysa decided to join her mother. Once in Italy she had an alienating experience. At that time in Italy the mass media did not report any news about the tragedy of Donbass, and people seemed not to be interested in what was happening in that area. Larysa did not identify herself with anything and anyone, and she was not acknowledged by anyone. Larysa did not identify with the Resistance of the population of Donbass. She did not identify with the Ukraine Central Government either. She was refused and expelled from Kiev, no one acknowledged her condition of exile in Italy. She came to Italy looking for refuge, protection and recognition. Instead, she found herself immersed in a social and political reality that made her re-live the experience of alienation, the contempt for her story and the denial of her identity.

Larysa's therapist decided he could not avoid taking a political stance. He studied in order to become knowledgeable of the Ukrainian crisis and be able to engage with Larysa in discussions in which she was the expert of the history and of the actuality of her country, and he was a curious and prepared interlocutor. Then the therapist asked Larysa to bring articles from Italian and Ukrainian newspapers, and texts downloaded from blogs or social forum. These materials have been used to analyse and deconstruct the linguistic categories and the rhetorical devices used either to blame the populations of east Ukraine (when the authors were pro-government Ukrainian journalists or Italian ones) or to present them as acquiescent (when it was someone from the Resistance to write about their compatriots who had refused the separatist option). Sometimes, the therapeutic sessions sounded like dissertations about the geography or the history of Ukraine and Russia. Sometimes like debates about the political situation of those states and of Europe.

Through this type of intervention, Larysa regained her sense of belonging to a collective identity. In fact, after several sessions of this type, Larysa said she was feeling better and optimistic about the international attention paid to her country in the future. But overall she felt that she herself could do something for this cause. In the last session, she read to the therapist the letter that she meant to send to the local newspapers telling her story as a refugee from Donbass.

Conclusions

Systemic therapists have been dealing with the issue of multiculturalism for years, and a lot has been done in overcoming the limits (technical, ethical, political) of a universalistic approach. As stated at the outset of this chapter, we take a stance also in favour of overcoming the relativistic/ethnographic/external vision of culture. From the dialogic perspective proposed in this chapter, culture is not in the mind of people. It is conceived as a process generating meanings and constructing realities through the participation of people in joint actions with others and in relation to the available artefacts. From this viewpoint, the behaviours or the psychological states of persons coming from different backgrounds are not simply determined by the values, rules, and traditions of the context of origin. Rather, they emerge from the sense they make of the events through the encounters they experience once they have departed from their cultural context. The reconstruction of the chain of events-encounters-meanings is the result of a therapeutic relationship, which, in

A Systemic-Dialogical Perspective

turn, is a ring of the chain. It is a process that, starting from specific cultural/semantic devices, generates new cultural/semantic devices.

It is in the relationship between therapist and Mahmud, that what had been senseless became comprehensible. It is through their dialogue that the meaning of Mahmud's pain emerged as a result of a chain of events (escape from the war, tortures in prison and encounters with the western medicine) in which his agency was more and more diminished to the point of loosing his sense of self ("if they give me medicine I am mad"). It is in the relationship of Fatna, Idriss and the psychologist that Fatna experienced the accountability of the institutions. It is in their conversations that the cultural-political-personal devices for making sense of the events lived by Fatna's family became clear. It is in the reconstruction of the socio-political context, made through the conversations of Larysa with her therapist, that she could regain a sense of self.

The systemic dialogic approach refers to an exchange among people that implies that the therapist adopt an attitude that legitimises and values others' points of view and acknowledges the multi-layered complexity of working with people whose different background puts them in the position of minorities struggling for recognition.

References

Bateson, Gregory (1979). *Mind and Nature*. New York: Bantam Books.
Cecchin, Gianfranco; Lane, Gerry & Ray, Wendel, A. (1992). *Irreverence: A Strategy for Therapists' Survival*. London: Karnac Books.
Cole, Michael (1996). *Cultural Psychology*. Boston: Harvard University Press.
Di Nicola, Vincenzo (1997). *A Stranger in the Family. Culture, Families and Therapy*. New York: Norton.
Falicov, Celia (1995). Training to Think Culturally: A multidimensional comparative framework. *Family Process*, 34(4), 373–388.
Falicov, Celia (2007). Working with Transnational Immigrants: Expanding meanings of family, community, and culture. *Family Process*, 46(2), 157–171.
Fruggeri, Laura (2012). Different Levels of Psychotherapeutic Competence. *Journal of Family Therapy*, 34, 91–105.
Fruggeri, Laura (2005). Making Sense: Lessons from Gianfranco Cecchin's work. *Human Systems Journal of Consultation and Management*, 16, 27–30.
McCarthy, Imelda & Byrne, Nollaig (2008). A Fifth Province Approach to Intra-Cultural Issues in an Irish Context: Marginal illuminations. In Monica McGoldrick & Ken Hardy (Eds.) *Re-visioning Family*

Therapy: Race, Class, Culture, and Gender in Clinical Practice, 2nd Edition. New York: Guilford Press.

McGoldrick, Monica & Hardy, Kenneth (Eds.) (2008). *Re-Visioning Family Therapy. Race, Culture, and Gender in Clinical Practice*, 2nd ed. New York: Guilford Press.

Nathan, Tobie & Zajde, Nathalie (2012). *Psychotérapie démocratique*. Paris: Odile Jacob.

Nicholl, Catherine & Thompson, Andrew (2004). The Psychological Treatment of Post Traumatic Stress Disorder (PTSD) in Adult Refugees: A review of the current state of psychological therapies. *Journal of Mental Health*, 13(4), 351–362.

Pearce, W. Barnett (1989). *Communication and the Human Condition*. Chicago: Southern Illinois University Press.

Rober, Peter & De Haene, Lucia (2014). Intercultural Therapy and the Limitations of a Cultural Competency Framework: About cultural differences, universalities and the unresolvable tensions between them. *Journal of Family Therapy*, 36(1), 3–20.

Sironi, Francoise (2007). Psychopathologie des violence collectives. *Essai de Psychologie géopolitique clinique*. Paris: Odile Jacobs.

Todd, Nick & Wade, Allan (2003). Coming to Terms with Violence and Resistance: From a language of effects to a language of responses. In Tom Strong & David Pare (Eds.), *Furthering Talk: Advances in the Discursive Therapies*. New York: Kluwer Academic Plenum.

Living Supervision in Practice
Structuring accountability with men therapists working alongside women and gender-variant persons with precarious lives

8

Vikki Reynolds & Andrew Larcombe

Introduction

This writing illustrates the practice of Living Supervision Interviews (Reynolds 2014a), which is one of many Supervision of Solidarity (Reynolds 2010a) practices that follow from our commitments to an ethical stance of justice-doing in supervision, therapy, and community work. This stance aims to support practice that is both decolonising and resists replicating oppression and dominance (Reynolds & polanco 2012). We outline the theoretical understandings and ethical positioning that have evoked the Living Supervision Interview, which is informed by activist practices of witnessing, intersectionality, anti-racist feminism, queer theory, social construction approaches to language, and systemic, collaborative, and narrative therapies. Some of the purposes this practice can serve in supervision are offered. We also include a fictionalised re-telling of a compilation of Living Supervision Interviews to evoke the spirit of the practice.

The experiences of Living Supervision we are illustrating are situated at the intersections of gender accountability with women and gender variant clients who are marginalised in relation to poverty, survival sex work, men's violence, substance misuse, and precarious housing. We will be writing from our locations as supervisor and therapist in these conversations, and will make public our intentions and experiences of the practice.

Despite our best intentions and commitment to training, we learn our work on the backs of clients. Our most trustworthy and useful "supervision" comes from our clients. Living Supervision aims to centre the client as the expert on the therapeutic relationship, and, in this work context, to provide one structure of accountability for men therapists working with women and gender variant clients who have experienced men's violence. The witnessing supervisor attends to two co-existing ethical centres for this practice, meaning that they hold the client at the centre, but are also simultaneously responsible to hold space for the care and mentoring of the therapist.

Notes on inclusivity

We embrace inclusive queer-informed language that contests the gender binary of he/she, because language that reinforces gender binaries renders transgender and gender variant people invisible (Butler 1990). We therefore use "they", "their", and "them" in both the third person singular and plural throughout this writing, unless a specific person's preferred pronoun is known. This is a resistance against the erasure (Namaste 2000) of subordinated identities and knowledges. In an effort to not replicate a binary of transgender and cisgender as two categories of women, in this writing we do not differentiate or name if women are gender variant or cisgender, as all involved self-identified as women.

A supervision of solidarity & hopeful scepticism

A Supervision of Solidarity evolved in response to the contexts of injustice and marginalisation in which Vikki was supervising therapists and community workers. A Supervision of Solidarity speaks to an ethical positioning for justice-doing in therapeutic supervision informed by activism, and thus is profoundly collaborative. Vikki supervises therapists who work amidst structures of injustice where death is ever-near, alongside people whose experiences of marginalisation are extreme, and whose suffering is unconscionable. In these contexts of structural oppression, scarce resources, and abundant need, workers struggle to practice in line with their ethics, and to respond to the suffering of clients. Losing clients to suicide and violent death is a reality, and experiences of being overwhelmed are common. As the supervisor she needed to respond to the desperation, risk, and isolation experienced by clients, as well as the spiritual pain held by therapists who can experience working in contexts of injustice as shovelling water. The creation of the Living Supervision Interview was Vikki's response to these reflexive supervision questions:

- How can I help therapists be more accompanied and less alone when working with clients who have a finger-hold on dignity, and are suffering experiences of social and political injustice and exploitation?

- How can I make myself more available to therapists struggling with despair, paralysis, or feelings of incompetence, in the face of grave problems?

- How can I assist therapists to create a sense of belonging within a community of others who work in accord with our collective ethics, embrace a spirit of solidarity, and see our collective work as justice-doing?

Living Supervision Interviews are one of a number of practices that emerged from the ethics of a Supervision of Solidarity. Living Supervision is a response to the ethical requirement for accountable supervision informed by a stance for hopeful scepticism in supervision. While the supervisor is hopeful the therapist is enacting their collective ethics for justice-doing in practice, they are also sceptical. This stance of hopeful scepticism is informed by Kvale (1996) and Ricoeur's (1970) hermeneutics of suspicion. The Living Supervision Interview is a way of doing supervision in which the supervisor is invited into the therapeutic relationship of the client and therapist. This practice is connected to a rich history of innovative supervisory practices that bring families and professionals together, beginning with the Milan Team in Italy (Boscolo et al, 1987), and including Andersen (1991) in Norway, also Madigan (1991) in Canada, amongst others (Anderson & Jensen 2007; Reynolds 2010a).

Living Supervision allows the supervisor to witness the therapist's actual work, and not rely solely on self-reports, which allows confidence that the supervisor has a more embodied understanding of the therapist's capacities, skills, and struggles. By their nature, gaps in the work cannot be seen, and the practice of Living Supervision aims to reveal and repair what is unattended to, mis-taken (McCarthy & Byrne 1988), ineffective, harmful, or frankly unethical in the therapist's practice. This articulation of the Living Supervision interview is informed by the writings on "living practice" of Gail Simon (2010) who describes herself as a UK-based lesbian systemic supervisor:

> *I have noticed the amazement and confusion for trainees, supervisees and other systemically inclined colleagues as they explore the spontaneous and innovative practices arising out of systemic therapy. Through supervision, people seem to become more curious as to what the relationship is between dominant organisational values and systemic practice and between systemic and other therapeutic ways of working...My own experiences of belonging to oppressed and marginalised groups, theoretically, professionally and politically, have influenced my inclination to work with people to create theory out of their lived experiences and develop theory-in-the-moment as a transient, living way of being.*
> (Simon 2010, p.309)

Living supervision interview practice examples

The following two examples of the Living Supervision Interview involve counsellors working on a team in a multidisciplinary primary health care clinic located in the Downtown Eastside of Vancouver, the poorest off-reserve area in Canada. Clients struggle against multiple oppressions including, homelessness, colonisation and racism, the criminalisation of poverty and suffering, and struggles with substance misuse and mental wellness (Boyd & Kerr 2015). This stance for supervision is informed by inclusive feminism (hooks 2000). This writing draws on examples of this supervision practice that centre accountability for two men therapists, Andrew Larcombe and Dale Wagner, working ostensibly as Addiction and Mental Health Counsellors with women and transgender clients who have experienced men's violence.

The names of clients have been changed and identifying details have been obscured in the following composite re-tellings to serve confidentiality and to structure safety. We acknowledge the ethical messiness of obscuring the names and identities of clients who helped shape this work, while naming the practitioners involved. This speaks to the lack of safety for clients and the mechanisms that elevate practitioners as the knowledge holders and creators while silencing and subsuming the contributions of clients. A consistent use of pseudonyms would smooth over this discomfort, but would also mask important differences in access to power that were made public by engaging messy practice (Reynolds 2014b).

In this context of Living Supervision the supervisor has a conversation with the man therapist, and the client, the woman, who has suffered men's violence. The man therapist is in a listening position and the supervisor interviews the woman client. We are inquiring about the therapeutic relationship, and the supervisor asks how the therapeutic relationship has been useful, the ways it has not been useful, and what qualities the therapist brings to the work that the woman speaks of as useful to her. These questions inform this line of inquiry:

- Denise, has your work with Andrew been useful to you? In what ways? What do you think you have contributed to this usefulness? What has it taken for you to show up in these useful ways?

- How has Andrew been useful to you? Are there ways that Andrew could be more useful? Is there anything he has done that is less useful, maybe not useful?

- What has it taken for you as a woman who has experienced violence from men to be willing and able to enter into a helping relationship with a man? What does this willingness and these qualities say about you? Is this something you have known about yourself, or is this a new way of thinking of yourself? What is the history of these qualities? Where in your life did you learn these qualities?

- What are you having to resist in order to do this work with a man therapist? What might this resistance mean about you and how your life might be different?

- What difference might this respectful relationship you describe with a man make in your life? Is this a unique experience, or are there other men who might be part of a "culture of accountable men" (Reynolds 2002, 2014a) that you know? How might having these different relationships with men be useful to you in the future?

The woman client is asked to take a listening position, and the man therapist is then interviewed about the relationship, asking what the woman has brought to make it useful, acknowledging that our clients make us better therapists if we are open to listening to their responses in conversation. The therapist is asked about his hopes for the woman, and for any lived experience he has witnessed that shoulders up these hopes. The therapist is asked about his responses to the woman's conversation and what meaning it holds for him, allowing space for the therapist to acknowledge the "supervision", expertise and critique offered by the client. The inquiry might include these questions:

- Andrew, how has Denise contributed to the working relationship and what qualities has she brought to the work? Can you remember a specific time she was most useful, maybe helping you correct bad questions, or helping you pick up on the most useful pieces of the conversation?

- Denise described your relationship as respectful, and that this is a new experience for her with a man. Have you been intentionally trying to be respectful of Denise? What practices have you been doing to try to enact respect for her? Why?

- What do you think it takes for Denise, who has experienced violence from men, to work with a man therapist? What might this say about her? Have you witnessed any qualities or ways of being of Denise's that amplify your hope for her to make the changes she wants in her life?

- How can you invite Denise to let you know if you do anything she experiences as disrespectful? What can you do to let Denise know that you are open and willing to hear her critique and act upon it?
- Did you hear anything else from Denise in this conversation that is useful to you, or news to you? How will you take direction from Denise's conversation in the work ahead?

Andrew and Denise's Living Supervision Interview

Andrew is a mental health counsellor who has training as a psychiatric nurse and extensive experience in the Downtown Eastside. In our supervisory conversation, Andrew brought forward his concerns about the safety of a woman client. Denise spoke with Andrew of her ongoing struggles with cocaine, and of men who would buy her cocaine in exchange for sex. Andrew and Denise had created enough-safety (Bird, 2004, 2006; Reynolds 2010b) in their therapeutic relationship to address the exploitation and risk Denise suffers in her relationships with men. At this time Denise was in a relationship with an older man who had some money. Andrew was concerned about the exploitation and real danger that Denise was alluding to in her conversations with him. Andrew was consulting with Vikki, his therapeutic supervisor, to invite accountability and have someone standing alongside him as he and Denise navigated her difficult and potentially dangerous situation.

Vikki suggested that Andrew consult with Denise about the possibility of all three of them participating in a Living Supervision Interview. The purpose of the Living Supervision Interview was to have an inquiry into the relationship between Andrew and Denise, and to witness and promote the safety and usefulness of their work together with the purpose of trying to help them collaboratively address suffering and structure safety. While Andrew is at the centre of Vikki's supervision, care of Denise holds the centre for both Andrew and Vikki. Andrew spoke with Denise, who agreed to participate in the Living Supervision Interview. On several occasions Andrew introduced Vikki to Denise. There were some false starts, but Andrew and Vikki backed off and slowed down, wanting to move at Denise's pace. We were prepared to abandon the idea altogether if this was not of use for her.

The Living Supervision Interview began with Denise and Vikki in conversation, and with Andrew in a listening position. Denise and Vikki discussed risk and safety in relationship to men and cocaine, and brought forward much of her knowing of how to stay safe, which she had lost

Living Supervision in Practice

track of under the influence of cocaine. We made some plans for safety, including awareness of women shelters which Denise has accessed in the past. We also discussed fear as a resource. Being afraid in the moment or ahead of time was more useful to Denise than being afraid later. Denise brought forward stories of the usefulness of the counselling relationship with Andrew. When Vikki asked about Andrew's ways of being, Denise spoke animatedly and was specific about Andrew's compassion, his ability to be very present with her, and his ability to understand her. This was especially important because Denise carried many stories about being a person who did not make common sense.

Vikki then interviewed Andrew about the meanings he gave to witnessing Denise's conversation. Denise was in a listening position, situated as a witness to her own conversation. Andrew spoke of his respect for Denise and the lowering of his own anxiety as she spoke more about what she knew about her history of resistance, staying safe, and experiencing fear. Vikki asked Andrew what kept his hope alive for Denise and what kept him continually committed to his work alongside her. He spoke of her continued resistances and the many small successes in their work together. The asking of this question in Denise's presence created an opportunity for her to be witnessed by Andrew. Denise has extensive histories of suffering oppression and men's violence. Vikki's presence in the conversation, as a woman and as an ally, allowed Andrew to say things that he would not have said alone in a room with Denise. The presence of the supervisor allowed for enough-safety in the conversation for Andrew to be more of the counsellor that he aspires to be. The conversation also invited Vikki as the witnessing supervisor to be a witness to both Denise's life and Andrews's qualities as a counsellor.

The therapist's reflections
Andrew reflected in writing upon this re-telling, and has offered Vikki this response in his own voice:

> *The Living Supervision Interview allowed you to bring out into the open the strength of the relationship Denise and I have with each other. By witnessing Denise's experience of being in a non-oppressive relationship with a man, an exception to the many exploitative relationships that she has experienced, you enabled us both to openly acknowledge that we had a good working relationship based on trust. Without you as an interlocutor — and your gender was important here because as a woman in a patriarchal society you can speak to male oppression in a way that I can't — I don't*

think that I alone would've been able to examine the gendered dynamics of negotiating trust with Denise. Much of our conversation revolved around how negotiating boundaries has made our counselling relationship safe. Your line of questioning about safety and relationships with men brought some great moments where we were able to confirm Denise's acts of resistance (Wade, 1997; Reynolds, 2010b). We talked at length about boundary setting as an insurance policy in anticipation of risk, and as an act of resistance in situations of immediate threat.

The next week I asked you to join us again, without prior planning but with Denise's permission, because Denise reported a violent incident where she was the victim of a man. I remember feeling somewhat overwhelmed by her news and I felt a bit stuck as to what to suggest. You came in and your questions of me in front of Denise helped me get unstuck. I think that the issue of gender was important here too. She was fearful and I think that having another woman in the room was important for me, and hopefully for her, because it added an element of solidarity to the support that I was able to provide. By this I mean that as Denise was the victim of an act of male violence you were able to open up a conversation about safety that I alone might not have been able to.

Peace, Andrew

Dale and Shelley's Living Supervision Interview

Dale is an addictions counsellor on the same counselling team as Andrew in the Downtown Eastside clinic, and has extensive experience in residential treatment settings. In a supervision consultation, Dale spoke of his concerns about the ability of men counsellors working in the realm of substance misuse to work alongside women and gender variant persons who had experienced sexualised violence and oppression from men.

Like Dale, many of the men that Vikki supervises are concerned about their ability to be accountable-enough to work with women and gender variant persons who have experienced violence by men. We would be very discomforted if men counsellors were not concerned about their ability to be accountable-enough alongside women in these situations. We also believe that, at times, great opportunities could be lost if women clients are not given the opportunity to have a respectful and dignified relationship with a man counsellor. Men need to work hard to position

Living Supervision in Practice

themselves accountably in relationship to men's violence. However, we do not believe that any woman counsellor is necessarily better than any man counsellor. Humility and real-time feminist-informed supervision are extremely important across the spectrum of gender for the therapist and client. In particular, Dale was talking about his work with a woman client, Shelley, who had been brutalised by men both in the past and recently. Vikki felt there was a great resource available to Shelley in working alongside a man counsellor who held an intention of gender accountability. Part of the intention of this interview for Vikki as the witnessing supervisor was to place Dale's intention of accountability to women in front of a woman client (Reynolds, 2010c).

In our Living Supervision Interview, Vikki began by consulting with Shelley around her counselling relationship with Dale. Shelley spoke of the respect and dignity that she experienced. We had a rich conversation about the possibilities of Shelley being in one relationship with one specific man where she believed it was unlikely that she would be sexualised, propositioned, oppressed, subjected to a man's evaluation of her body, or disrespected in a gendered way. Shelley talked about this as being a very different experience from her life and let Vikki in on a thumbnail sketch of her previous experiences with men. This included both what she referred to as "sex work" and sexualised violence. When Vikki asked her what was present in her relationship with Dale, she spoke of respect and some new hope for her that there was a small possibility of some men behaving towards her in a different way than she had experienced in the past. We talked about her knowings in relationship with men and how she did not want to let go of any of that, while she also held onto the small hope that some things may be different in the future with some men.

Vikki then interviewed Dale about what he had witnessed in Shelley's interview, and Shelley was in a listening space. He spoke to Shelley holding on to hope of some future relationships with men that would be safe-enough, and the meaning that held for him. He spoke of the qualities that Shelley brought to their counselling relationship and her ability to trust him enough to even speak with him given that he is a man. When Vikki asked Dale what kept his hopes alive for Shelley, he recounted some profound stories of resistance. These stories spoke of her strength and her ability to stand up to men's power by using her intelligence and life experience.

In this Living Supervision Interview, Vikki declined the invitation to put Dale upon a pedestal for being an accountable man, which he did not want and would have been extremely discomforted by. Instead we witnessed Shelley's ability to work alongside a man given her wisdom about the way many men have been with her in her life. As the witnessing supervisor, Vikki was available as a witness to Shelley's ongoing resistance and wisdom. Dale was also witnessed as a safe-enough man at this time, in this particular counselling relationship with Shelley. The Living Supervision Interview provided a structure and some safety for this conversation to occur. Without this structure Dale would have been limited for being inside of the relationship and also for speaking the questions from his position as a man.

The therapist's reflections
Dale reflected on this re-telling of this Living Supervision Interview, and this is written in his voice:

> *The consideration of engaging in a Living Supervision Interview was initially a discomforting one, as I was hesitant to be so vulnerable. However, this was precisely where I needed help and why I had raised my concerns about my work with Shelley in our individual supervision. By participating in this process I sought to be less alone in the concerns that I held about my work with Shelley as she was a strong woman who had faced horrors that were foreign to my life's experience – mostly committed by people of my gender. She had developed ways of relating (particularly with men) that reflected this hard won wisdom. I was acutely aware of the need for our counselling relationship to be safe-enough. It was difficult to open up a dialogue with Shelley about our counselling relationship, particularly because it had the potential of replicating her previous negative experiences with men – namely that I would be seen as just another guy wanting something. The Living Supervision Interview allowed a safe means of putting our relationship on the table for discussion. In response, Shelley spoke positively about her experience of safety and being respected. While I didn't need to hear this to continue engaging in a respectful manner (although it was confirming), it seems that it gave Shelley explicit permission to talk about our relationship. More than permission, it gave Shelley an experience of doing so with my supervisor there to witness and affirm the value of her perspective.*
>
> *This reflection reminds me of the power of this experience and renews my desire to look for opportunities to offer the Living*

> Supervision Interview experience to my team, as I am now in a supervisor role.
>
> Cheers, Dale

Uses of the Living Supervision Interview

The Living Supervision Interview can be of use when the therapist is not sure how to respond, when the therapist wants to watch the supervisor conduct interviews in specific domains (such as responses to violence), or when individual supervision consultations reveal qualities and honouring of the client that they are not aware of, as these consultations occur in the absence of the client. This practice attempts to invite accountability as it allows the client's evaluation, critique, and concerns about the therapist's work to be heard and witnessed directly by the supervisor. The Living Supervision Interview has also been of use when the therapeutic relationship has turned a preferred corner, an obstacle has been overcome, or there are qualities of the client that the therapist hopes to amplify by inviting the supervisor to witness. This practice creates reflexive space (Burnham 1993) for the client to witness the supervisor witnessing them.

Preparation work: Fostering a culture of critique

Part of the preparation for the practice of the Living Supervision Interview is the co-creation of dignifying supervisory relationships and fostering a culture of critique (Reynolds, 2014c), in which hard questions and inconsistencies can be spoken. A Supervision of Solidarity resists smoothing over the spiritual pain that is experienced when our therapeutic practice is not in accord with our ethics for justice-doing. Rather it invites a solidarity that says, "I will walk alongside you as you struggle towards ethics, and I am also not perfect". This stance allows more vulnerability and invites accountability, rather than requiring therapists to continually present a fixed story of their competency.

Structuring safety for these relationships relies on pre-existing points of connection, solidarity, and ethical fit. The following questions aim to structure safety and create safe-enough relationships from which to build dignifying supervisory relationships that promote a culture of critique:

- What do I need to understand in order to respect you, make space for you, and not transgress against you in our supervisory relationship?

- What do you hold sacred, close to your heart, that it would be useful and important for me to know?

Supervisory relationships grounded in solidarity serve to dignify therapists and foster the moral courage required to be vulnerable, open to critique, and resist engaging in supervision with a static defence against negative judgments. Shouldering-up the dignity of the therapist resources the supervisory relationship to hold in a tension any transgression against ethics alongside the supervisor's witnessing across time of the therapist's relationship with competency.

These relationships of solidarity assist therapists to hold close the spiritual pain that reminds them of their ethical stance and commitments for social justice, and invites them to engage with discomfort as a useful and perhaps necessary (Kumashiro 2004) component of accountability.

Conclusions

These examples of the Living Supervision Interview have fluid structures and formations. Having a witness from outside visit and interview from a different location holds the relationship between client and therapist at the centre. Practitioners are invited to re-configure, re-theorise, and re-create this work in order for the practice to be of use in different contexts.

In the spirit of systemic practice, Living Supervision is an emergent practice evoked by enacting the ethics of a Supervision of Solidarity. Living Supervision is a response to the ethical requirement of the supervisor to enter the work of the practitioner, and not rely solely on therapists' self-reporting. In the context of this writing the practice was a response to our collective desire, as supervisor and therapists, to resist enacting dominance, and replicating oppression with women and gender variant persons struggling in the context of precarious lives (Butler 2004). We are committed to the ethical principle of autonomy, and activist traditions of critiquing and dismantling hierarchy and dominance in the delivery of therapy. These commitments invited us to look for practical, specific, and material ways to address power and centre the voices of women and gender variant clients, specifically in relation to their role in directing the kinds of service they want. In this understanding of voice we are informed by radical Brazilian educator, Paulo Freire (1970), who teaches that in liberatory dialogue the person's voice must not just be heard, but it must be responded to accountably, and not be dismissed.

Dedication

We learn our work off of the backs of clients: This writing is dedicated to these teachers.

This writing took place on Indigenous land which has never been surrendered.

Acknowledgments

Great appreciation to our clients, and the therapists and students we supervise for their generosity in sharing their experiences with Living Supervision Interviews, most especially Dale Wagner. Their critiques and reflections of our supervision practices and this writing have contributed much to its usefulness. Lorraine Grieves, Mary Marlow, Gail Simon, and Allan Wade offered useful critiques and ethical reflections. Appreciation to Coral Payne for her continued editorial expertise, and for making complex ideas understandable.

References

Andersen, Tom (1991). *The Reflecting Team: Dialogues and Dialogues about the Dialogues.* New York: Norton.

Anderson, Harlene & Jensen, Per (2007). *Innovations in the Reflecting Process.* London: Karnac Books.

Bird, Johnella (2004). *Talk That Sings: Therapy in a New Linguistic Key.* Auckland, New Zealand: Edge Press.

Bird, Johnella (2006). *Constructing the Narrative in Supervision.* Auckland, New Zealand: Edge Press.

Boscolo, Luigi; Cecchin, Gianfranco; Hoffman, Lynn & Penn, Peggy (1987). *Milan Systemic Family Therapy: Conversations in Theory and Practice.* New York: Basic Books.

Boyd, James & Kerr, Thomas (2015). Policing 'Vancouver's Mental Health Crisis': A Critical Discourse Analysis. *Critical Public Health*, (in publication). Retrieved from http://www.tandfonline.com/doi/full/10.1080/09581596.2015.1007923

Burnham, John. (1993) Systemic supervision: the evolution of reflexivity in the context of the supervisory relationship. *Human Systems: Journal of Systemic Consultation and Management*, 4: 349–381.

Butler, Judith (1990). *Gender Trouble: Feminism and the Subversion of Identity.* New York: Routledge.

Butler, Judith (2004). *Precarious Life: The Powers of Mourning and Violence.* London: Verso.

Freire, Paulo (1970). *Pedagogy of the Oppressed.* New York: Continuum.

hooks, bell (2000). *Feminism is for Everybody: Passionate Politics.* Cambridge: South End Press.

Kumashiro, Kevin (2004). *Against Commonsense: Teaching and Learning Towards Social Justice.* New York: Routledge.

Kvale, Steinar (1996). *Interviews: An Introduction to Qualitative Research Interviewing.* London: Sage.

Madigan, Stephen (1991). Discursive restraints in therapeutic practice: Situating therapists' questions in the presence of the family. *Postmodernism, Deconstruction and Therapy,* 3, pp.13-20.

McCarthy, Imelda & Byrne, Nollaig (1988). Mis-Taken Love: Conversations on the Problem of Incest in an Irish Context. *Family Process,* 27(2), 191–199.

Namaste, Viviane (2000). *Invisible Lives: The Erasure of Transsexual and Transgendered People.* Chicago: University of Chicago Press.

Reynolds, Vikki (2002). Weaving threads of belonging: Cultural witnessing groups. *Journal of Child and Youth Care,* 15(3), 89–105.

Reynolds, Vikki (2010a). A supervision of solidarity. *Canadian Journal of Counselling,* 44(3), 246–257.

Reynolds, Vikki (2010b). Doing justice: A witnessing stance in therapeutic work alongside survivors of torture and political violence. In Jonathan Raskin; Sara Bridges & Robert Neimeyer (Eds.), *Studies in Meaning 4: Constructivist Perspectives on Theory, Practice, and Social Justice.* New York: Pace University Press.

Reynolds, Vikki (2010c). Fluid and imperfect ally positioning: Some gifts of queer theory. *Context,* (October), 13–17.

Reynolds, Vikki (2014a). Resisting and transforming rape culture: An activist stance for therapeutic work with men who have used violence. *The No To Violence Journal,* Spring, 29–49.

Reynolds, Vikki (2014b). A Solidarity Approach: The Rhizome & Messy Inquiry. In Gail Simon & Alex Chard (Eds.), *Systemic Inquiry. Innovations in Reflexive Practice Research.* Farnhill: Everything Is Connected Books.

Reynolds, Vikki (2014c). Centering ethics in therapeutic supervision: Fostering cultures of critique and structuring safety. *The International Journal of Narrative Therapy and Community Work,* (1), 1–13.

Reynolds, Vikki & polanco, marela (2012). An ethical stance for justice-doing in community work and therapy. *Journal of Systemic Therapies,* 31(4), 18–33.

Ricoeur, Paul (1970). *Freud and Philosophy: An Essay on Interpretation.* New Haven, CT: Yale University Press.

Simon, Gail (2010). Self-supervision, surveillance and transgression. *Journal of Family Therapy,* 32, 308–325.

Wade, Allan (1997). Small acts of living: Everyday resistance to violence and other forms of oppression. *Journal of Contemporary Family Therapy,* 19(1), 23–40.

Family Therapy in an Emerging Professional Life
One story among stories

9

Therese Hegarty

Choosing a profession and a hope for influence

For those of us who enjoy the privilege of being able to choose the work we engage in, there is a sense of an emerging identity. Discourse, family expectations, prior experiences and economic contingency may all offer competing invitations to a young person making that choice.

As a middle class educated woman leaving second level school in Ireland at age 16 in 1972, I was no exception. The most common choices for young women seeking a professional career at that time were nursing and teaching. The nuns who had taught me, driven by an agenda of sending women to university, told me it was a disgrace if I did not study science, as my results were so good. My parents felt I was too young for University. All I really knew about was school and I was angry with school. I had achieved highly at a young age but there had been some punitive experiences along the way, a lot of streaming and segregating and far more attention given to my results than my well-being. I wanted to study education because I wanted to reform education.

I began my professional life in 1975 as a primary school teacher. From the outset, I found myself asking how, as a professional, I should respond to the specific needs of individual children. I embraced Froebel's child-centred pedagogy (Liebschner 2002) in which the teacher starts with the child's experience and builds a scaffold for learning on the basis of that knowledge.

Between 1978 and 1979, I spent a year in Abakaliki, Eastern Nigeria. The literacy programme I was sent out to support did not exist, nor did it seem a priority to the people. How should I respond in this situation? Steeped in the thinking of Paulo Freire (Friere 1970), who began his educational work with the concerns of the people, I began to listen to the priorities of the community and finally launched into rural health education work. The nurses were already operating clinics twelve hours a day and had no time for education. I studied the books, travelled each day to remote villages and began the teaching.

Responsibility for me had become a question of discernment about how I should respond to the context of the people and the challenges they faced. The Igbo people I worked with taught me much about resilience, celebration and community, which I had never learned in a western city environment. I, for my part, with no guiding documents, policy or protocols, learned to trust my initiative and try things which had not been tried before. This became something of a pattern in my career.

Finding new ways to respond within teaching

In 1980, I was appointed a senior teacher in a school in a suburb of Dublin which was designated disadvantaged. Many of the families had moved out from the city centre. In 1989, I was released from classroom duties and invited to develop a role which would support the children who were showing signs of social and emotional difficulties. As I developed the role, I committed to understanding the distress underpinning children's unacceptable behaviour. I organised breakfast clubs, social skills groups, individual playtime, and circle time (Mosely 1998).

I also started my own personal therapy and engaged in professional supervision with a Clinical Psychologist. I continued to develop new ways of working as, at the outset, there were no professional guiding documents for the role. My theoretical framework was Attachment Theory (Bowlby 1979). My hope was that school could become a "secure base" for children (Geddes 2006; Koplow 1998). Looking back on it now I see that what I developed was close to the Nurture Group model (Bennathan & Boxall 2000) in the UK in the but I had not heard of it. I was merely trusting my initiative again.

As the role developed, I worked less with children on their own and instead worked in a more systemic way involving children, parents and other professionals in their lives. Listening to the stories of the families, I could see a crying need for a local Family Therapy service which could be easily accessed, did not have long waiting lists and did not operate on a medical model. Some Department of Education inspectors were a little sceptical of my interest in the emotional lives of children. Others encouraged me to reflect and continue to use initiatives which addressed the local issues. Some understood my work as "going beyond my brief". It became too hard to maintain the innovation in the face of the educational discourse of the time. I needed to develop my ways of responding, new theory and new colleagues who could teach me.

Family therapy as a new way to respond

In 2000, I started a Masters in Family Therapy. At the same time, an external review of the local addiction agency close to the school suggested that they include Family Therapy in their services. I began to work for them as a student under supervision and was employed on a sessional basis when I qualified. Government funding has been erratic over the years as Ireland went through an economic boom and then a tough recession. I currently receive a small grant and see six families per week.

When I began work in the addiction centre, the coordinator and I both believed it should be a service for the whole community and not limited to families with addiction. We shared a conviction that Family Therapy involving children might reduce drug use further down the line. This continues to be the policy. Referrals now come from within the addiction centre itself, schools and other local agencies. As time goes on there are increasing numbers of self-referrals.

Unlike many of my colleagues providing Family Therapy in Ireland I do not work with a specific focus such as relationships, addictions, abuse, or domestic violence etc. This is a conscious choice as families are sometimes refused therapy by agencies in Ireland because they do not fit the criteria for that service. I prefer to fit the service to the families.

This choice of a community based practice where there is a great variety in the presenting issues poses challenges for me. I have to change age group and style of interaction somewhat several times in a day. The stories below reveal how I sometimes have a wish for more specific training. I sometimes work in parallel with mental health services or child protection services. I often engage in joint family-school work. I have also worked collaboratively with disability services. I regularly encourage clients to engage in education. Advocacy with other services is sometimes part of my work. This flexible and interagency approach to practice could be contested by those who advocate a strict adherence to boundaries in therapy. I take the position however, that when families have been very marginalised, they sometime need accompaniment when finding a place in society and when finding a voice. I often write down the exact words of clients and give them to them at the end of the session.

This has been useful for people facing any meeting where they have a fear of being silenced by professional discourses. Some of the families are living in or close to poverty. Only one of my clients at the time of writing is in third level education. Many are long-term unemployed. If marginalisation is part of the problem, I see therapy as a place where that can be named and resisted. It is important at this point to explain that my involvement with education did not end. I now work in initial teacher education, where I facilitate courses on care, identity and methodology. I am very involved in the revision of the programmes for initial teacher education to include such courses. So the vague hopes of the sixteen year old are coming to fruition even if it has taken four decades. My therapy and education work inform each other constantly.

Journaling to support responsibility

In accepting the invitation to write a chapter for this volume, I decided to keep a journal of my work for two months. I wanted to attend to my own practice which often challenges me. I wanted to make my intentions and actions clearer to myself.

Rather than share the stories of clients in depth, my hope is to share the story of the therapist's life during that time: decisions, struggles, and moments of joy. My hope is that some of this complexity will resonate with others in the field. My clients have seen what I have written and agreed to the work being shared. Names and other identifying information have been altered.

Mc Cormack (2010) describes well what I was seeking:

> "It (journaling) has allowed me to contain and work creatively with my own vulnerability and has provided me with a medium where I can accept, work with, and value my own vulnerability as a crucial resource in my work. When I can support myself to accept my vulnerability and to remain at my own cutting edge, I increase the chance of holding, supporting and challenging others at their growing edges. In my experience that acceptance and vulnerability is invariably the gateway to the kind of growth that emerges from the shared space of dialogue. In this way the revelatory power of the caring relationship can be held in a creative form" (p.35)

As a structure for the journal, I adapted the work of Korthagen and Vasalos (2005). In documenting my reflections, I was guided by the following questions:

Family Therapy in an Emerging Professional Life

What are my intentions for this session?
What do I encounter?
How do I behave?
What frames my response?
What perspective might be missing here?
How am I competent?
What models of Family Therapy do I use?
What do I believe?
Who am I?
How is this work linked to my purpose?

I committed to answering these questions after several sessions each day over two consecutive months. On a very busy day where this was not possible, I completed it at the end of the day in relation to my overall experience of the day. Both approaches proved valuable.

A reading of my journal three months later

Three months later, I read the journal to try to answer these questions. I noticed the patterns emerging. I tracked my answers over the two months to each of the questions. The words in italics below are direct quotes from my journal.

My intentions for the sessions
My first intention with a new family is to build relationship and collaboration:

To listen for their hopes for our work.

To really attend to this distress in its detail so that she feels heard.

To explore with them how we should proceed with involving the child.

Research suggests that there are four factors contributing to successful therapy: the strengths and resources clients bring, the therapeutic alliance, the capacity to hope for change and the specific therapeutic models and techniques (Hubble et al 1999).

I begin to work on a therapeutic alliance and to create a space when hope might be found. This involves a negotiation of the times that suit the family and a clear intention at the outset to hear their goals for therapy.

Michael White's description of therapy as "decentred and influential" has a resonance with my history of Froebelian pedagogy and Friere's community work.

> *"The notion 'decentred' does not refer to the intensity of the therapist's engagement (emotional or otherwise) with people seeking consultation, but to the therapist's achievement in according priority to the personal stories and to the knowledges and skills of these people. In regard to the personal stories of people's lives, in the context of this achievement, these people have a 'primary authorship' status, and the knowledges and skills that have been generated in the history of their lives are the principal considerations.*
>
> *"The therapist is influential not in the sense of imposing an agenda or in the sense of delivering interventions, but in the sense of building a scaffold, through questions and reflections, that makes it possible for people to: a) more richly describe the alternative stories of their lives, b) step into and to explore some of the neglected territories of their lives, and to c) become more significantly acquainted with the knowledges and skills of their lives that are relevant to addressing the concerns, predicaments and problems that are at hand."* (White 2005, p.9)

In terms of a specific approach, I often draw on Narrative Therapy to frame a way forward:

> *To create another unique outcome, a conversation free of conflict and shouting.*
>
> *To continue the work of externalising with more high level distancing questions.*
>
> *To listen for the tension between hope and despair as they pull this man's life in different directions, to look for exceptions, to highlight skills, to look for opportunities for a limited life to expand.*

Narrative Therapy is my preferred way of working and it supports confidence. I ask myself what stories the family members are telling about themselves and how these stories have been constructed. I look for skills and abilities. I seek alternatives to deficit descriptions (Winslade and Monk 1999). I seek out values, hopes and initiatives (White 2007).

There is sometimes a creative tension between the frame I plan for a session and the care of the relationship or "alliance" with the family. I try to follow the family's sense of what is important. For the most part this is a creative tension. It keeps us alive. On one day, I found the tension too much. Creativity got lost. I think I managed neither planning nor attending very well. I was tired. It was almost Christmas and I needed a holiday. I became acutely aware that I am limited in how much work I can do.

What did I encounter?
The two months of journaling invited me to attend to many stories in families: a "coming out" as gay, a traumatic bereavement, a man fearing he would go to prison, a man leaving prison, cancer, loss, household fights, loss of employment, and a relationship break up. Some weeks there is a lot of sadness or conflict and I am joined with these struggles as I join with the family.

What I encounter when a family arrives is not always what I expect. I can be challenged by "hopelessness", "antagonism", "an ostrich like engagement", but surprised by "a lot of energy and banter", "humour", "a willingness to be a team". I was really worried about one person but she arrived buoyant and I wrote:

> *Sometimes when you hang in with people at the really dark times and you feel it is all going nowhere, the simple act of accompanying of them has some impact you don't anticipate.*

One of the challenges for me is staying in the present with the person, listening regardless of outcomes. I do not think I will ever be satisfied with my listening but I have to trust it is "good enough" (Winnicott 1988). In this regard, I can recognise that my value on care and on the "secure base" still permeates my thinking.

I have a few long-term clients where my work is simply a "holding" of people living challenging lives, with ongoing challenges.

Teresa is rearing her granddaughters and she explains:

> *"I come here with my worries. I can trust here. I don't hide nothing. I see it as my time. It helps me get through day by day. I have been through a lot and this has helped me get back on track. I am a lot stronger. I am easy when I am here and I can focus. When the kids*

came I listened and understood what they were dealing with. I had to go to meetings with other agencies but my support was here. It's what gets me through. I think I will always have concerns with the girls like I did with my own children."

How do I behave? What frames my response?

Our minute-by-minute responses in therapy are always a choice framed by theory, prior experience, intentions and expectations (Schön 1983). I noticed that it was often the emotional cues in the room that altered the direction of my response. I had planned quite a playful session with one family but when they arrived, they seemed very discouraged. To continue as I planned might have left them feeling very unheard. In another session, a young child seemed to be staging a non-verbal protest so I came down to his level on the floor and coaxed some words from the child, words his mother was keen to understand.

My own history is always shaping what I attend to and what I miss:

> *Being an eldest child I did not pick up on this "second best" theme until late in the session and it was central.*
> *I want to stand up for the peacemaker. I feel for the man trapped between two women who have fallen out, a man who has empathy for both and is working on both relationships. I try to make space for his experience to be understood. I have been in places like this. I try to let my own experience inform what I ask but recognise his story is different. I keep the questions very tentative.*

I have sometimes found myself quite burdened or exhausted when cancer or fear of cancer is in the room. This was the case with two families in this period. My husband died from cancer and I sometimes find myself fearful and exhausted in these sessions. I have to censor my "internal voice" from jumping to negative conclusions. In one case, I linked with other key professionals to gain a wider frame of reference for work with the family, and to mitigate my own sense of isolation.

> *Looking back on it now, I see that I recruited a team.*

What perspective might be missing here?
> *There seems such a gap between this young person's intelligence and his educational achievement. As he speaks I am not impressed with the principal or the level of education he has received.*

In this case, I find myself thinking in a judgmental way and it is a "wake-up" call. I have to ask about other perspectives and my own bias.

I decide to organise a joint home-school session to hear the teachers' views. Schools are sites where stories, sometimes single stories, are produced. (Winslade and Monk 1999). To work with the young person I needed to know the stories shaping his identity in different contexts. The meeting re-established the relationship between teachers and parent and supported me in stepping out of judgment. The young man's schoolwork improved. As time went on, however, his mother wanted more for him, in terms of his happiness in school, as she had witnessed a very different engagement in youth leadership and political activism. As I complete this paper, the young man has changed schools and he explains: "I am really an active learner and I need a school which allows me to learn that way, just as my youth work has supported my learning."

Recently this pattern of dedicated mothers being taken for granted is cropping up a lot in sessions. I feel angry. A seventeen year old tells me that only four of the eighteen lads in his class live with their Dads. That if you make a new friend and assume his Dad is useless you are usually right. This is bleak but it is his lived experience.

Class and gender affect every client who comes into the room. I try to attend to how these and other socially constructed aspects of identity are playing out in their particular life. I attend carefully to including the men in therapy, in a context where men are not always fully present in families. Sometimes it is not possible.

Burnham (2011) invites us to consider how differences in age class, ethnicity, gender, sexual orientation might influence the stance, questions and disposition of the therapist. My clients during these months included people of European, Asian and African heritage, a gay client, a woman living with an intellectual disability, people of Christian, Muslim and others with no apparent religious faith.

I am a middle-class woman with considerable formal education. I see it as my responsibility to enter the world of my families and ask them to let me know if I misunderstand their meaning. I try to maintain a position of "not knowing" and ask questions such as "How does your Muslim faith influence the way you are trying to challenge these actions?" or "Is it your sense that this assault was racially motivated?" Clients sometimes correct me, telling me for example, that I am asking about the wrong kind of equality. I refocus and I am happy to create the context where I can be corrected like this.

How am I competent? What models of family therapy do I use?

I use the "maps" of Narrative Therapy. They open up spheres for enquiry but with the challenge for me to find the actual questions fitting the language of the client. White described his maps as like a map on a mountain, offering an overall vision of the terrain but allowing many directions from any point (White 2006a). This describes well how they offer me a platform for competence.

> *I use the externalising map. I explore how he has been recruited to disengaging with people and we find it very quickly in his history with men.*

> *I take care to ask what this means for the client rather than get hooked into a strong invitation to sharing my own thoughts. Narrative practice supports me in doing this as I focus on staying curious and decentred and work with the exact words of the client.*

> *I used the two chairs and asked Excited Susie to give advice to Worried Susie and documented it. I was prioritising her skills and knowledge and creating a permanent record of those skills and knowledges.*

However, other theories and models also come to mind as I make sense of what is happening in the room. Over the years, I have learned many theories and ways of working. Some come from a structuralist tradition. Ideas for directions in practice during a session can seem to "pop into my consciousness" like bubbles in boiling water. Whilst I hold none of them as implying "absolute truths" in relation to the problems being confronted by the families, these ideas can have a strong resonance with what is happening in a session. On one occasion as I listened to one client, I heard what Kübler-Ross might understand as a movement from shock to anger (Kübler-Ross 1969). This helped me map how the therapy is progressing, and to stay present to the experience of the client. I was struggling to build a therapeutic alliance with a young man who was told he had to attend therapy but then that mandate was dropped. He found therapy weird, yet he attended.

> *I think attachment theory is informing me here. I want to remain available to this young man while respecting his autonomy about*

coming or not coming to therapy. I want him to have power to choose but also to know he is very welcome. Both these invitations might challenge his internal working model.

Sometimes I believe that therapy is about willingness to stay with pain in the present and a belief in solidarity and witnessing.

I am not aware of what model I am using. This is a therapeutic alliance formed over many years. He is very scared. I give his own words, spoken over many years, back to him now in the hope of creating perspective... but mostly it is hanging on for now.

What do I believe?

When I look back at the beliefs that guided my work in each individual session I realise that I was continually contextualising.

I was mindful of the economic climate:

Despite her talents and passion it is going to be hard to find work. Am I setting her up for failure?

I was mindful of intergenerational patterns (Minuchin 1967):

I believe the distress is in the parental subsystem. I believe neither parent had consistent nurturing in childhood. I must explore what was good for them and what was difficult in their experience.

I am mindful of how mind and body influence each other (Kurtz 1990):

I believe that the trauma is still trapped in the body. I wish I was also trained in Hakomi.

I believe that our stories have a historical context, a local political context and can be experienced somatically. When I read the journal, I see that was constantly looking to the past, the present, the institutional, and the local and national context.

My work is not defined by postmodernism though I value it. I see postmodernism as a disposition, a commitment to question the taken for granted and to question what we do, to look for alternative perspectives, silenced perspectives and the particular perspectives of families. Most importantly, I see it as a tool to keep us vigilant about the possible consequences of our actions.

Who am I?

At the level of professional identity, I attend to my own experience, beliefs, hopes and intentions. In my journal, I describe myself as:

> *In for the long haul;*
>
> *motherly;*
>
> *a wanting to be redundant therapist playful yet serious;*
>
> *seeking accountability*
>
> *Like the Susan Sarandon character in Dead Man Walking – staying and not judging with not much optimism around.*

It is usually in the dilemmas that I find values competing and demanding a definition of what I stand for. The dilemmas during these two months often raised questions of boundaries and care.

> *Before Christmas, Brigid, who had been doing well, relapsed on drugs. As my two week Christmas break started I realised she was alone, very unstable and vulnerable, in conflict with most people in her life and reliant on new services which were operating on a reduced basis over the holidays. She was not eating and had run out of electricity at one point. I feared she might not survive. Should I maintain therapeutic boundaries? Should I maintain contact over my holidays? I decided to maintain some phone contact, to be at least a familiar voice, to be directive in relation to survival, to sound like a broken record about what was essential. Looking back I probably did no harm. I was thinking that maybe I did no good either but when stability returns, therapy is likely to return too and that would be good.*

Kaethe Weingarten claims that the challenge for the one who has been traumatised is to resist isolation and the challenge for the witness is to refuse indifference (2007, p.150). I had dreams about Brigid over Christmas. I was not detached. I was living the challenge that Weingarten describes and having her words gave me a way to name it.

My value on care came to the fore. The legacy of trauma in Brigid's life invited a refusal of indifference in my attitudes and actions. I consulted with a colleague about reasonable boundaries, and decided to act on my values. There was a cost to me involving an interrupted holiday. I decided that staying connected at that time was more important.

This woman is now off drugs and battling on a daily basis to create the life and family she wants. In her dealings with numerous agencies, she talks of the importance of the long-term link with me. I know her history and that allows her hold her own history with increasing coherence.

> *"I am emotional all the time." Dermot says, shaking. "The memories keep coming back. I am keeping active to cope with the stress. I have to talk regularly or I will flip. This is the only place I can talk safely." We decide to return to fortnightly sessions.*

> *I feel the weight of the decisions I have made in the setting up of this service. With Dermot what matters is the availability of this safe space as he negotiates fear and hope and traumatic memories, the consistency of a person who will be there long-term. This long-term work is not what my training taught me to offer. It is what my clients have taught me to offer. But again it raises questions of sustainability for me.*

My value on care demands a long-term involvement with people. A thirty-five year engagement with a community brings a lot of local knowledge. It sometimes brings exhaustion and a temporary losing of my nerve, but then I pick up again.

The journaling during those two months, supported a renewed valuing of the therapy work, the people I see, and myself. After the most demanding sessions, I found myself asking myself questions and finding more meaning in the work. I found that I was more present in the sessions than I had given myself credit for, except for one tired day. I witnessed a lot of suffering during those two months, which challenged me to care for myself. I will continue to journal not so much on a session-by-session basis but on my experience of each day.

How is this work linked to my purpose?
Family therapy emerged as a part of my journey when the school context limited the way I wanted to respond to children and their families. I believed in therapy. Twice in my life, I was overwhelmed and needed therapy myself and experienced a very safe and creative space. It was safe to tell the stories I could not tell elsewhere. I learned to trust my own experience and my own voice. I saw social and historical contexts and their influence. I came away every day with more compassion for myself and for others.

I wanted others to have that opportunity and I hope I have found a way to offer something like that experience to many families over the last fourteen years. Very few, if any of those families would have had the financial resources to pay for it. While I did not grow up in poverty, I am only one generation away from it and I like to think of my work as resisting inequality in a small way as I work to create an accessible service. When I least expect it I have moments of profound joy in the work when I would not swap it for the world.

The family come and the parents are a united caring team and tell the tragic story as clearly and gently as possible. It is their hands I will remember: mother and child holding hands, father and child, parents holding hands behind a child's back as I talk with him. We will meet soon again. I shed a tear after they leave. Unity, care and honesty in the wake of tragedy. I am humbled in the witnessing.

A few years ago I was at the hairdressers and the young man who washed my hair spoke to me. "Do you mind me asking you something?" he said. "You say your name is Hegarty. Should it not be Gibson?" I laughed. My married name was Gibson and it was the name I had used in school. "Do you not know me?" he asked. "I am Colm." I recognised him. The six-year-old was twenty. He was one of the children who had inspired my work in the school. "I remember you," he said, "Everyone who was in trouble went to you. You were like the Mother Goose of the school."

Perhaps it is still my purpose... in this community at least... for a little while more... to be a sort of Mother Goose.

References

Bennathan, Marion & Boxall, Marjorie (2000). *Effective Intervention in Primary Schools: Nurture groups*, (2nd ed.). Abingdon: David Fulton Publishers.

Bowlby, John (1979). *The Making and Breaking of Affectional Bonds*. London: Routledge.

Burnham, John (2011). Development in the Social GRRRAAACCEEESSS: Visible-invisible and voice-unvoiced. In Inga-Britt Krause (Ed.) *Culture and Reflexivity in Systemic Psychotherapy: Mutual Perspectives*. London: Karnac Books.

Freire, Paulo (1970). *Pedagogy of the Oppressed* (Myra Bergman Ramos, Translator). New York: Continuum.

Geddes, Heather (2006). *Attachment in the Classroom*. London: Worth Publishing.

Hubble, Mark A.; Duncan, Barry L., & Miller, Scott D. (Eds.) (1999). *The Heart and Soul of Change: What Works in Therapy*. Washington: American Psychological Association.

Koplow, Leslie (Ed.) (1996). *Unsmiling Faces: How Pre-schools Can Heal*. New York: Teachers College Press.

Korthagen, Fred A.J. & Vaselos, Angelo (2009). *From Reflection to Presence and Mindfulness: 30 years of development concerning the practice of reflection in teacher education*. Paper presented at the EARLI Conference Amsterdam 2009.

Kübler-Ross, Elisabeth (1969). *On Death & Dying. What the Dying Have to Teach Doctors, Nurses, Clergy & Their Own Families*. New York: Scribner.

Kurtz, Ron (1990). *Body-Centered Psychotherapy: The Hakomi Method: The Integrated Use of Mindfulness, Nonviolence, and the Body*. Mendicino California: LifeRhythm.

Liebschner, Joachim (2002). *A Child's Work: Freedom and Guidance in Froebel's Educational Theory and Practice*. London: Lutterworth Press.

McCormack, David (2010). The Transformative Power of Journaling: Reflective Practice as Self Supervision. In Benefiel, Margaret and Holton, Geraldine (Eds.) *The Soul of Supervision Integrating Theory and Practice*. New York: Morehouse Publishing.

Minuchin, Salvador (1967). *Families of the Slums*. New York: Basic Books.

Mosely, Jenny (1998). *Quality Circle Time in the Primary Classroom*. Cambridgeshire: LDA.

Schön, Donald (1983). *The Reflective Practitioner*. New York: Basic Books.

Weingarten, Kaethe (2007). Hope in a time of global despair. In Flaskas, Carmel; McCarthy, Imelda and Sheehan, Jim (Eds.), *Hope and Despair in Narrative and Family Therapy: Reflections on Adversity, Forgiveness and Reconciliation*. New York: Routledge.

White, Michael & Epston, David (1990). *Narrative Means to Therapeutic Ends*. New York: Norton.

White, Michael (2005). Workshop Notes. Retrieved from http://www.dulwichcentre.com.au/michael-white-workshop-notes.pdf

White, Michael (2006). Working with People who are Suffering the Consequence of Multiple Trauma: A narrative perspective. In Denborough, David [Ed.] *Trauma: Narrative Responses to Traumatic Experience*. Adelaide: Dulwich Centre Publications.

White, Michael (2006a). Workshop at the Glenroyal Hotel, Maynooth Ireland. June 19th 2006.

White, Michael (2007). *Maps of Narrative Practice*. New York: Norton.

Winnicott, Donald (1988). *Babies and their Mothers*. London: Free Association Books.

Winslade, John & Monk, Gerard (1999). *Narrative Counselling in Schools: Powerful and Brief*. Thousand Oaks California: Corwin Press.

10 Reflexive Processes in Higher Education
Systemic dilemmas in teaching research methodology by means of 'polyphonic dialogue'

Eleftheria Tseliou, Georgios Abakoumkin, Vicky Kokkini, Katerina Nanouri & Fani Valai

Introduction

Interesting phenomena occur when two or more rhythmic patterns are combined and these phenomena illustrate very aptly the enrichment of information that occurs when one description is combined with another.

Bateson 1979, p.91

Dear Reader,

In this chapter we aim to invite you along a journey which entails our efforts to face the challenge of introducing systemic and social constructionist ideas in the context of the everyday practice of academic lecturing in higher education. In particular, we will engage in a narrative of our attempts to introduce collaborative and reflexive practices on the basis of our inspiration by past and current theorising and practice in the field of systemic family therapy (Andersen 1987; Anderson 2012; Bateson 1972, 1979; Cecchin et al 1992; Maturana & Varela 1992; Seikkula 2003; von Foerster 1992).

So far, there is extensive theorising and practice in the field of education, which celebrates the use of collaborative and reflexive process in teaching, with extensive discussion of practices like co-teaching (Roth & Tobin 2004), peer tutoring (Colvin 2007) or peer mentoring (Terrion & Leonard 2007). Furthermore, there is a long-standing tradition of what has been termed as "engaged pedagogy" (e.g., hooks 1994), namely a preference for critical, creative and non-discriminatory pedagogical practice. In that sense, our proposal is not necessarily introducing something new. However, to a large extent, education overall and higher education still remain "plagued" with the dominance of linear, monologic learning processes which mostly reflect the idea that knowledge can be possessed by individual minds and simply transmitted within relation-

Reflexive Processes in Higher Education

ships of asymmetrical quality between "expert educators" and "ignorant learners" (Gergen & Wortham 2001).

In this text, we will share with you the particular story of an "experimentation", which reflects our effort to relate with our students from a standpoint of celebration of polyphony and collaboration. It is the story of inviting our postgraduate students as co-instructors, while struggling with the hurdles of teaching a research methodology module as part of a postgraduate course in an early childhood education department. This story will serve as the backcloth against which we aim to unravel our thinking about the ways that certain systemic and constructionist ideas can serve as fruitful resources of inspiration for transformations in academic tutoring, despite the difficulties inherent in such an endeavour.

Our text is a narrative of what we co-experienced with our students in the context of a non-systematic attempt to experiment with collaborative practices in higher education tutoring. We do not claim single authorship for either the experimentation or the narrative about it. Instead we think of both as the joint outcome of what Maturana & Varela (1992) might refer to as an act of co-ordination between "us", the tutors, and "them", the students. In that sense, this text is also the product of the juxtaposition of several voices, including those of the participant students but also of several authors whose voices have served as a source of inspiration. Of course, we cannot escape the conventions of writing a text, which include the choice of certain individuals as authors. Respectively, we cannot easily escape the unbalanced and unequal participation in the writing of this text between our students and ourselves. In order to partly deal with this, we have chosen to invite our students in a kind of co-authorship by asking them to contribute with their reflections about the narrated experience. We are thus grateful to Vicky Kokkini, Katerina Nanouri and Fani Valai who accepted our invitation to become co-instructors and co-authors in this joint endeavour for learning.

As a consequence, the authorship of our narrative will alternate between the singular and the plural person, as the voices of the different authors will be invited in the text in order to narrate different parts of our story. In this way, we hope to attend to Bateson's (1972) imperative for a fit between form and content, as hopefully this dialogic, polyphonic quality of our text will also reflect the actual dialogic and polyphonic space of our joint experience. Our hope is that this will also invite you as a participant into an imaginary dialogue, or – why not? – an actual one should you choose to contact us with your reflections about our story.

The story

A background and a beginning: setting a scene of celebration of difference by means of co-teaching

It is hard to decide upon the beginning of a story, should we espouse a systemic, recursive perspective about time, in which past, present and future intersect at any given point in time (Boscolo & Bertrando 1993). An arbitrary beginning of our story is our meeting (Eleftheria and Georgios) a few years ago, in the context of the two-year postgraduate course currently entitled *Educational Sciences: Educational Material and Pedagogical Toys* which is run by the Department of Early Childhood Education at the University of Thessaly, in Volos, Greece. At that time, I (Eleftheria) was appointed as an Assistant Professor in the Department with research methodology as my field of study, with a background in clinical psychology, systemic family therapy and training. Georgios, an Assistant Professor in social psychology, was the faculty member who had the responsibility for running research methodology modules at the department's postgraduate course.

My encounter with the system of higher education, felt like having to move to a different planet. Although I had previous experience with academic teaching I suddenly had to adjust myself to tutoring large audiences of students on my own as compared to training small groups of family therapy trainees mostly by means of reflexive and experiential processes, while working in a team setting. On top of that, I also faced the challenge introduced by teaching research methodology (Yates 1997) given that it is probably the least favoured module by students (Lei 2008). I was sceptical as to whether I would be able to find ways to reconcile my systemic, constructionist past with the present of what came across as a learning setting of monologic quality. The research methodology modules at the department's postgraduate course where I was asked to contribute seemed a fertile ground for this reconciliation, given the relatively small number of students (about 20) and the chance to work in a mode of co-teaching with Georgios.

Our joint, very first choice was to proceed with co-teaching by trying to turn our different backgrounds and epistemological perspectives into an asset. Of course, we do not claim authorship for the idea of co-teaching, which is widespread in the field of education (Roth & Tobin 2004) and to a smaller extend in higher education (Nevin et al. 2009). However, our main sources of inspiration were certain, well-known ideas from the field of systemic family therapy. First, we wanted to find a way to

Reflexive Processes in Higher Education

attend to Bateson's ideas about learning and its interdependence with interaction and the introduction of difference and change by operating as a "systemic mind" (Bateson 2000). By means of celebrating our own differences we hoped to create a learning context where "differences would hopefully make differences" (Bateson 1979, p.146) or generate double descriptions and thus changes in knowledge. Secondly, we also wanted to attend to von Foerster's ethical imperative of acting in ways, which increase the number of choices (von Foerster 1992). Thirdly, we also aimed at adhering to the celebration of polyphony and dialogue as opposed to monologue following ideas from Bahktin's (1984) dialogic approach to communication.

Our joint commitment to these ideas was reflected in a number of choices concerning both the content and the structure of the modules' lectures. First we decided to co-teach both of the two research methodology modules (winter and spring semester) although this would double the teaching workload for both of us. Georgios would retain responsibility for sharing his expertise in positivist research methodology and I would equally share my experience with hermeneutic, qualitative research methodologies. Both of us would be present in every lecture. Depending on its content, one would take the responsibility for it, whereas the other would act as a participant observer who could intervene at any point of time with his/her reflections. This often resembled a reflecting team (Andersen 1987) or even an open dialogue format (Seikkula 2003) in the sense that we would often engage into spontaneous discussions which often entailed debates or even disagreements while the students' actively listened by also participating with their voices.

Content-wise, in each module's first lecture we would introduce the various and contradicting epistemological perspectives, which inform choices in research methodology. This was meant to back up the idea that there are more ways than one for knowledge construction in the terrain of scientific inquiry, which despite their different access to power should be approached as equally valid (Gergen 1999). The total number of lectures was equally divided between quantitative and qualitative research in order to secure equal access to both perspectives.

In order to successfully complete the modules, the students had to design (winter semester) and conduct (spring semester) either a quantitative or a qualitative research study depending on their preference. They were asked to work in small research teams of three to five. During the lectures, we would insist on team-work as we would often invite them to engage in brief conversations in small teams about, e.g., a research paper they had been asked to study. The small group reflections would then be shared with the whole group. Following systemic imperatives (Bateson, 2000), our rationale was to foster connectedness and collaboration in knowledge construction by promoting a kind of networking but also a setting for "relational learning" (Anderson 2012; Wortham & Jackson 2012). Our choice seemed also in tune with long-standing arguments about the benefits of cooperative learning as well as peer-tutoring in higher education (Falchikov, 2001; Johnson & Johnson 2009; Topping 2005) which build on the theoretical legacy of Piaget (1971) and Vygotsky (1986).

From co-teaching to co-learning: inviting students as co-instructors
Despite our overt preference for co-teaching we were nevertheless aware of its limitations as concerns the remaining asymmetrical quality of our relationship with our students. Any choice about the module still remained a choice on one part of the student-instructor learning system, thus pointing to a remaining hierarchy in the place of our quest for heterarchy (Gergen & Wortham, 2001). We started wondering whether we could find ways to actively engage our students in the running of the module, by allowing space for their voices, in the sense that John Burnham (2011) has proposed in the context of GRRAAACCEEESS.

Past experience with attempts to involve learners in more collaborative and reflexive practices, had lead one of us (Eleftheria) towards the use of the polyphonic setting of reflexive team formats and their later developments (Tseliou 2007, 2010). In the one case (Tseliou 2007) the setting was again higher education, where I had experimented with engaging students in a reflexive team format in order to share social constructionist ideas about gender. The other (Tseliou 2010) included an attempt to experiment with an alternative approach to systemic family therapy trainees' evaluation which involved a polyphonic conversational context with the participation of both trainees and trainers. In both cases, I was inspired by Tom Andersen's (1987) innovative ideas about the use of reflecting teams and their later developments in the context of Jaakko Seikkula's and his colleagues' original proposal for the Open Dialogue Approach to the treatment of psychosis on the basis of Bakhtin's theorising (Seikkula 2003).

However, students' feedback to early invitations for a shared responsibility was not always encouraging. Our idea of assigning the responsibility for presenting and discussing academic texts about research methodology concepts to small groups was met with scepticism, doubt and unwillingness to let go the divide between the "expert tutor" and the "non-expert learner". This was possibly true on our behalf also, as we still retained the responsibility for structuring the lectures' format and content, despite our preference for Maturana and Varela's (1992) idea for the impossibility of instructive interaction.

Our choice to experiment with inviting our students as co-constructors sprung out following an inspiration by Anne Morrison's and Kristen Chorba's (2015) text about a social constructionist approach to peer mentoring in an academic setting in the context of their relational learning approach. We thought of inviting students who had successfully completed the modules to share with their new coming peers their experience and expertise in designing and conducting research studies. In a broad sense, this would position them both as "mentors" who share ideas and offer support but also as "tutors" who share expertise and knowledge. We thus invited two different groups who had experience with the running of quantitative and qualitative research studies respectively to run two three hour-long "lectures" in the winter semester module. Each group had the freedom to decide upon the content and the structure of the lecture. Our criteria for choosing the groups were for the students to have successfully completed the modules and for their research studies to fit with the modules' requirements.

Fortunately, both groups responded positively to our invitation. The invited students were on their second year of study, whereas the participant students were in the first year of their studies. The latter were informed about this different lecture in advance and we openly shared with them our thinking behind the invitation of ex-students as instructors. Vicky, Katerina and Fani also shared with us their ideas about how to proceed with the lecture. They had decided to split the lecture in two parts: in the first part they would present their research study by trying to stick to information, which would fit with the current students' familiarity with research methodology. In the second part, they would engage into a different, reflexive type of discourse, as they would narrate what they referred to as "the backstage experience" by focusing on issues they had to face and which they thought that the current students would also struggle with.

We were enthusiastic with their plan. During the "lecture" we both retained the stance of a participant observer by trying to let the interaction between past and current students evolve. At some points, students would invite us to join them in their conversation in order to clarify certain points. We tried to resist the challenge of taking the "expert" position as much as possible by stating that we would have the chance to clarify the content in subsequent lectures. At the end of the lecture, we invited the current students to reflect on their experience by responding anonymously to two questions, in the form of a written text. The questions were, "Describe your experience (what was the process like for you? How did you see you own participation in the process?)" and "Make suggestions for the next time we plan this". Also, we invited Vicky, Katerina and Fani to send us a written text with their reflections. Below we include part of these reflections, the choice of which was jointly decided. We also include part of the students' reflections. In both cases, we translated the selected extracts from Greek into English for the purposes of this text.

In search for a position: inviting the voices of Vicky, Katerina and Fani
Vicky:

> "If I attempted a reflection, I would necessarily need to define my position: Am I reflecting from the position of a student? Of a researcher? Or of a teacher?...I think that reflexivity does not fit so much with 'attempt' but rather fits with 'venture'...I participated in the process of this lecture from the position of an 'experienced colleague', avoiding any hint of adopting an axiomatic position and having accepted possible mistakes or wrong doings, in advance...this was possibly a fearful position for the undertaking of any responsibility ...thanks to this alibi, during the process of co-teaching there was no feeling of insecurity or inadequacy, at least on my side...another important aspect which was taken into consideration purposefully, was the one of the identification. One of the first criteria for designing the lecture was our effort to identify ourselves with the first year students...I believe without any doubt that the most important contribution to succeeding with group work which is worth-while has to do with the interpersonal communication and the constitution of the team. In an attempt to emphasize this psychosocial dimension we used the generated lecture atmosphere in order to trigger the students' interest for research.
>
> My sense is that at least from this point of view, this 'chemical reaction' was successful...yet I identified many variations between

the first year students and the previous year students' groups. The early stage at which the first year students were as concerns the design of a research study, as well as the lack of adequate study of the relevant literature made the communication of certain concepts pretty difficult, I think...In conclusion, I have to admit that the process of reflexivity was very difficult for me...When a created piece of work becomes the object of self-evaluation, any conclusion depends upon the position that his/her creator decides to undertake in this context. If he/she is part of the frame itself, then there is the danger that he/she cannot distinguish the bad shapes or the disproportions in the final creation....the whole process of such a lecture is, I think, revealing. In the same way as a depiction of multiple layers of distancing would be revealing. As an image placed within another image in the same way that the 'venture' of reflexivity' is revealing, after all."

Katerina:

"I reflect, I re-examine, I re-member, I re-study...Could reflexivity entail a suspicious intention? I am wondering. Could it, in fact, act as the perfect alibi?...My personal experience as the student who has had the experience of sitting on the student's chair but also happens to sit on the tutor's chair, I think it created a confusion in my thinking. This position, I am thinking now, requires the choice of an identity...To present a paper which was approved by the tutors could have functioned-and in fact it did- in a reassuring way. On the other hand the responsibility for the presentation, for exposing one's work, for exposing one's self, one's discourse, one's thinking in front of an audience, was for me a process which is not that easy...without this necessarily pointing to ignorance or anxiety. More than anything else, I would translate it as insecurity. And what about the authority and the power that the position of a speaker or a tutor entails?...inspiration. This started for me from our tutors, the way they approached the content of the module and the students...the issue of working in a group, when the group is inspiring like in my case, you know that this creates a safety net...I can say with certainty that I felt this safety net from both my group and my tutors...I am now discovering that the real researcher (and possibly the real educator) is constantly doubting his/her knowledge and is reconciled with his/her ignorance."

Fani:

> *"Reflecting on the novel experience that the research methodology course created for me when I was shifted from the role of a learner to the one of the 'tutor', I can say that my feelings are mixed, or to be more exact, contradictory. On the one hand I felt relieved because that was the end of a pending issue, which was particularly stressful for me and mostly because I felt that it went ok. On the other hand, after the first positive feeling, pretty quickly I entered a process of reflection trying to understand or better to make sure if and to what extend we met the expectations of our colleagues (students of the first semester) and of our tutors...various thoughts like these crossed my mind the days following the presentation which created a wave of insecurity as to if and to what extent we managed to meet the expectations of this novel role for me and for all of us.*
>
> *The feelings which predominated for me were anxiety and embarrassment. And this happened throughout the process: my anxiety prior to the presentation was if I would be good enough...if I would meet the expectations of my tutors and if I could 'prove' that they were right to trust me...my anxiety following the presentation was about whether our participation was satisfactory...during the last few days I started realizing the new dimensions of this experience...in this new context my classic role of the one who accepts the information from someone who 'knows better' than me who has the knowledge and the experience in an area where he/she will teach me about, seemed to become overturned. The sense that in this context, I would be the speaker, that is the one who 'knows more' and the one who could craft the others' opinion about how to go about with research felt like a big responsibility. Would I stand up to the facets of this role?...I was wondering, is this a role of 'power' against my colleagues?...What if I lead them to the wrong choices?"*

In the position of the "learner": inviting the voices of the rest of the group members

This part entails a non-inclusive selection of the students' reflections due to the lack of available space. Although we tried to include as much variation as possible, we chose not to intervene in any other way and in that sense, what we present is far from a systematic analysis of qualitative data. Inevitably, however, the act of selection is itself an "intervention" into the students' voices. Sixteen students attended the course on

Reflexive Processes in Higher Education

that day and gave their consent for the recording of the lecture and for its potential use for research purposes. Each student's feedback was not more than half a page long and there was also a blank paper handed in without any written feedback. S stands for Student, and the numbers indicate consecutive numbering of the students' responses:

> "This was a very informative presentation and as it proceeded queries that had never crossed my mind before started being created…" S2

> "This was a source of inspiration for continuing with passion something which I see (I still do!!) as being extremely difficult and (let me say this) boring…It was a taste in advance of what I will live, learn and get involved with…" S4

> "Some parts were difficult to follow because they have not yet been taught to us." S5

> "Very interesting presentation. The process seemed time-consuming to me, but it was worth-while…" S6

> "Excellent experience…we had the chance to discuss our concerns, our anxieties and to help each other from the position of those who are at stake…this strengthened our solidarity and the boundaries of cooperation were extended beyond the students of our own group. The only dark part…the anxiety and the insecurity for whether we will also manage this equally well." S7

> "Perhaps it might be better to present papers which had more problems, even if they were not excellent, because in this way the real effort and the progress are better shown and this can inspire the younger ones so that they will not get disappointed and they will go on or start with their own research." S8

> "I became pretty stressed, I saw our own mistakes as a team and overall I felt desperate…It would have been much more helpful for us if these presentations were done earlier so that we could get to know what each approach is like (quantitative and qualitative) in order to choose afterwards the type of research we want to do." S9

> "This was the most useful lecture. We saw in practice the course of doing a research study and the problems which may come up…

they talked not only about their paper but also about their own experiences and the ways they faced problems." S10

"Personally, I would have liked for these presentations to have happened a bit earlier...they would have helped us to avoid some mistakes at the stage where we are." S11

"...it is very useful and illuminating...it gives food for thought, inspiration and strength and courage to go on with the effort and to get away from the dead ends and the multiple obstacles which we find in front of us." S13

"...it was a process which removed part of the anxiety which I feel about the work I have to do and the way I have to do it...perhaps it would have been more right, although this requires more work, to adjust the presentation to what we already know at the stage we are." S16

An epilogue and some further reflections

Dear Reader,

In this text, our aim has been to share with you a story which reflects our effort to experiment with collaborative and reflexive processes in higher education. Our attempt has been to share a narrative of this story while including as many voices of the participants as possible. Our initial aim was to find a way to forward networking between past and present students in the context of a "learning system" where our voices would meet with the voices of our students in the context of a joint learning experience.

We openly admit to our prejudices which include a preference for collaborative and reflexive practices in the system of higher education and a belief to their merits. In retrospect, we also admit that our prejudices may have blinded us about issues like the stressful side of such an experience for the students who were assigned the role of a co-instructor. We are thus grateful to our co-authors who have highlighted this side in their reflections. We are now more aware of the challenges entailed in the struggle to decide upon a position in between the one of the tutor and the one of the student. Each choice implies a different membership and in that sense, a different belonging as well as competing loyalties. We were also blinded about the potential, difficult effects of this experience for the rest of the students. We now wonder whether the experience of meeting

Reflexive Processes in Higher Education

with students who had successfully completed the module early on could also have a counter-effect. Perhaps it might have introduced information which was difficult to follow and creatively process given the particular point of time. Current students were still struggling with the news of difference introduced by their encounter with research methodology. Tom Andersen (1995) has warned us against the practice of introducing too much of a difference in the context of a newly formed system.

In conclusion, although we share the enthusiasm with collaborative and reflexive practices in higher education we are now more sceptical about the often unacknowledged sides entailed in our attempts to overturn the existing power differentials. Our participation in this relational learning experience has sensitized us to the fact that perhaps our "good intentions" are not enough.

As a way forward, we think that more systematic ways of fostering such practices coupled with their systematic evaluation, e.g. in the context of research studies may shed further light to the nuances of the "here and now" of collaborative practices in higher education. Research has so far offered pertinent insight on the details or the contributions of peer-tutoring and mentoring practices (e.g., DeBacker et al.,2012; Heirdsfield et al. 2008; Roscoe & Chi 2007). However, little is so far known in a systematic way about the how and what of the everyday academic tutoring practice. Even less is systematically known about the ways that students experience and evaluate our "good intentions" for promoting less asymmetrical tutoring relationships.

Luckily, we are equipped with promising research methodologies from positivist and hermeneutic research. For example, discourse and conversation analysis could aid us in the effort to decode the detail of our everyday academic practices in the here and now of educational dialog and highlight the ways in which power is downplayed in the course of our discursive interactions (Tseliou 2015) in a similar way as in the case of the study of systemic family therapy process (Diorinou & Tseliou 2014; Tseliou 2013). One way or another, systematic research could help us de-mystify our "good intentions" and fruitfully reflect on our contributing part and thus on our prejudices in the sense that Cecchin has put it (Cecchin et al 1992), while experiencing educational collaborative endeavours.

Georgios: *"Well, this sounds as if we are speaking with one voice."*
Eleftheria: *"True. What has happened to our differences?"*

Georgios: *"Well, they are certainly there, no matter if we choose to obscure them like we did in this text or if we choose to speak them out."*

Eleftheria: *"Perhaps a synthesis can also be a difference, which can make a difference..."*

Acknowledgements

We are indebted to all our students who have decided to take the risk and follow us into this unknown territory of co-authoring the learning experience which we narrate in this text. We are also grateful to the anonymous students whose reflections are included in this text, upon consent. Finally, many thanks to our colleague Vasilis Strogilos who generously helped us by suggesting useful literature from his field of expertise.

References

Andersen, Tom (1987). The Reflecting Team: Dialogue and meta-dialogue in clinical work. *Family Process*, 26, 415–428.

Andersen, Tom (1995). Reflecting Processes; Acts of Informing and Forming: You can borrow my eyes, but you must not take them away from me! In: Steven Friedman (Ed.), *The Reflecting Team in Action: Collaborative Practice in Family Therapy*. New York: Guilford Press.

Anderson, Harlene (2012). Collaborative Relationships and Dialogic Conversations: Ideas for a relationally responsive practice. *Family Process*, 51, 8–24.

Bakhtin, Mikhail (1984 [original 1929]). *Problems of Dostojevsky's poetics* (C. Emerson, trans.). Minneapolis: University of Minnesota Press.

Bateson, Gregory (2000 [original 1972]). *Steps to an Ecology of Mind: Collected Essays in Anthropology, Psychiatry, Evolution, and Epistemology*. Chicago: University of Chicago Press.

Bateson, Gregory (1979). *Mind and Nature: A Necessary Unity*. Glasgow: Fontana/Collins.

Boscolo, Luigi & Bertrando Paolo (1993). *The Times of Time: A New Perspective in Systemic Consultation*. Scranton, Pennsylvania: W. W. Norton.

Burnham, John (2011). Developments in Social GRRAAACCEEESS: Visible and Invisible, Voiced and Unvoiced. In Britt Krause (Ed.), *Mutual Perspectives: Culture & Reflexivity in Systemic Psychotherapy*. London: Karnac Books.

Colvin, Janet W. (2007). Peer Tutoring and Social Dynamics in Higher Education. *Mentoring and Tutoring*, 15(2), 165–181.

Cecchin, Gianfranco, Lane, Gerry, & Ray, Wendel A. (1992). *The Cybernetics of Prejudices in the Practice of Psychotherapy.* London: Karnac.

DeBacker, Liesje, van Keer, Hilde & Valcke, Martin (2012). Exploring the Potential Impact of Reciprocal Peer Tutoring in Higher Education Students' Metacognitive Knowledge and Regulation. *Instructional Science*, 40(3), 559–586.

Diorinou, Maria & Tseliou, Eleftheria (2014). Studying circular questioning 'in situ': discourse analysis of a first systemic family therapy session. *Journal of Marital and Family Therapy*, 40, 106–121.

Falchikov, Nancy & Blythman Margo (2001). *Learning Together: Peer Tutoring in Higher Education.* London: Routledge.

Johnson, David W. & Johnson, Roger T. (2009). An Educational Psychology Success Story: Social Interdependence Theory and Cooperative Learning. *Educational Researcher*, 38(5), 365–379.

Gergen, Kenneth (1999). *An Invitation to Social Construction.* London: Sage.

Gergen, Kenneth, & Wortham, Stanton (2001). Social Construction and Pedagogical Practice. In K. Gergen (Ed.), *Social Construction in Practice.* London: Sage.

Heirdsfield, Anne M., Walker, Sue, Walsh, Kerryann, & Wilss, Lynn (2008). Peer Mentoring for First-Year Teacher Education Students: The mentoring experience. *Mentoring and Tutoring: Partnership in Learning*, 16(2), 109–124.

hooks, bell (1994). *Teaching to Transgress: Education as the Practice of Freedom.* London: Routledge.

Lei, Simon A. (2008). Factors Changing Attitudes of Graduate Cchool Students Toward an Introductory Research Methodology Course. *Education*, 128(4), 667–685.

Maturana, Humberto & Varela, Francisco (1992). *The Tree of Knowledge: The Biological Roots of Human Understanding.* Boston: Sambhala.

Morrison, Anne & Chorba, Kristen (2015). Relational Learning in Education. In Thalia Dragonas, Kenneth Gergen, Sheila McNamee & Eleftheria Tseliou (Eds.), *Education as Social Construction: Contributions in theory, research and practice.* Chagrin Falls, Ohio: Taos Institute Worldshare Books Publications. Retrieved from: http://www.taosinstitute.net/education-as-social-construction

Nevin, Ann I., Thousand, Jacqueline S., & Villa, Richard A. (2009). Collaborative Teaching for Teacher Educators – What does the Research Say? *Teaching and Teacher Education*, 25, 569–574.

Piaget, Jean (1971). *Biology and Knowledge.* Chicago: University of Chicago Press.

Roscoe, Rod D. & Chi, Michelene T. H. (2007). Understanding Tutor Learning: Knowledge-Building and Knowledge-Telling in Peer Tutors' Explanations and Questions. *Review of Educational Research*, 77(4), 534-574.

Roth, Wolff-Michael M. & Tobin, Kenneth (2004). Co-teaching: From Praxis to Theory. *Teachers and Teaching: Theory and Practice*, 10(2), 161–179.

Seikkula, Jaakko (2003). The Open Dialogue Approach to Acute Psychosis: Its Poetics and Micropolitics. *Family Process*, 42(3), 403-418.

Terrion, Jenepher Lennox, & Leonard, Dominique (2007). A Taxonomy of the Characteristics of Student Peer Mentors in Higher Education: Findings from a Literature Review. *Mentoring & Tutoring: Partnership in Learning*, 15(2), 149–164.

Topping, Keith J. (2005). Trends in Peer Learning. *Educational Psychology*, 25(6), 631–645.

Tseliou, Eleftheria (2007). "Polyphonic Dialogue" as a Means for Teaching Systemic and Social-Constructionist Ideas. *Journal of Family Therapy*, 29, 330–333.

Tseliou, Eleftheria (2010). From Feedback to Reflexivity: Inspirations by a "Polyphonic Dialogue" Methodology in Trainee's Evaluation. *Journal of Family Therapy*, 32, 334–337.

Tseliou, Eleftheria (2013). A Critical Methodological Review of Discourse and Conversation Analysis Studies of Family Therapy. *Family Process*, 52(4), 653–672.

Tseliou, Eleftheria (2015). Discourse Analysis and Educational Research: Challenge and Promise. In Thalia Dragonas, Kenneth Gergen, Sheila McNamee & Eleftheria Tseliou (Eds.), *Education as Social Construction: Contributions in theory, research and practice*. Taos Worldshare Books Publications.

von Foerster, Heinz (1992). Ethics and Second Order Cybernetics. *Cybernetics and Human Knowing*, 1(1), 9–19.

Vygotsky, Lev S. (1986 [original: 1934]). *Thought and Language* (A. Kozulin, Trans.). Cambridge: MIT Press.

Wortham, Stanton & Jackson, Kara (2012). Relational Education: Applying Gergen's work to educational research and practice. *Psychological Studies*, 57(2), 164–171.

Yates, Lyn (1997). Research Methodology, Education and Theoretical Fashions: Constructing a Methodology Course in an Era of Deconstruction. *International Journal of Qualitative Studies in Education*, 10(4), 487–498.

Systemic Practice as Systemic Inquiry as Transformative Research

11

Gail Simon

> *The Master's Tools Will Never Dismantle The Master's House*
> Audrey Lorde 1984

During this session with the final year trainees on the subject of systemic practice as a form of research, several of the trainees are looking very thoughtful. Lydia has something to say. She clears her throat as if she is creating an extra moment to work out how to formulate her thoughts. "I get it," she says. "I get that what we do in our practice is transformative. I get that what we do is a form of inquiry. I see that because I live it every day with people coming for therapy. It makes sense to me that this is a form of collaborative inquiry."

I notice several people in the group are nodding with some degree of gravitas. I want to feel relaxed as I feel something has been understood but I know something else, something important, is coming. I don't nod with the others. "But," continues Lydia, "my manager does not see this. She thinks research is not what we do or how we do it but how we measure what we do."

I feel a strong sense of responsibility. Guilt even. Should we really be encouraging therapists to present systemic practice methodology as a form of inquiry, generative of rich material, in a world in which systemic accounting is at odds with the dominant story of what counts as knowledge? I am reminded of the keynotes at therapy research conferences which urgently convey the message that we must sharpen our wits and prepare to defend the profession with instruments we are new to but must learn to use well – and quickly.

My thoughts are interrupted by Faizah.

"Our managers have changed tack. We still collect outcome measures but we have to produce case studies too – for the commissioners. They do read them because they sometimes ask our manager

questions about them. They say they want to hear the voices of real people."

"Well, in my centre," Imtiyaz joins in, "we don't just write case studies, we ask service users to write them. Sometimes people prefer to tell us their story of coming to the service while we write it down. Then we read it back to them and discuss their experience. It often turns into a review of the work we have done. Sometimes new things emerge that I had not understood."

"Isn't that just evaluation though?" asks Martin. "It's called feedback."

"Not if it happens while the work is going on," Imtiyaz responds, "It changes things. For everyone. I get a better understanding. The families learn more about each other. It becomes part of the process of the therapy. I asked one man how come he had not mentioned something before this research and he said he didn't think it was relevant to the work we were doing. His family were surprised – both by the story he told and that he didn't think there was a place for it to be told. So we discussed what makes a difference in our talk about what gets said and the work went on in quite a different way."

"We write parallel stories. The clients write one about the work we have been doing. The counsellor writes another – also about the work we are doing together. And then we discuss them. Yes, you're right, Imtiyaz, it does change things," says Faizah.

"So," suggests Martin "you are describing a feedback loop where the feedback is part of a constant movement. The feedback is not a thing separate from the doing of the work. It is the work." This time I allow myself to nod with some of the others.

People turn to Lydia who is holding out her hands as if waiting for the words to form so she can offer something to the group. She breathes in, holds her breath for a second and then speaks. "Yes, all this makes sense to me. But how do I sell it to my manager? Managers want to be assured therapy is improving lives. They want material to take as evidence to commissioners."

"My partner works as a commissioner of services," offers Faizah, "and she says they have loads of statistical evidence but that they want to understand why things work, how they make a difference and hear from people using the services. Sharing stories of how therapy has been a transformative process of collaborative inquiry with people makes a big impression on commissioners. They want to know that people are having a useful and ethical experience. Not just getting a tick in a box for having been offered any form of treatment."

Something has changed for me. I am feeling less worried. The anxious and protective voices of the dominant research discourse are receding as I hear the trainees' accounts of systemic therapy as a form of transformative inquiry. Several of the trainees really get the need to publicly recognise our work as research, as generative of transformation and new learning. They are using their course work to generate moving stories about moving processes for a wider audience than simply their assessors. They are experimenting with new ways of sharing knowledge, transparently and reflexively, about what is transformational with those who have decision making powers about services. In my mind's ear, I hear Jane Speedy telling a story at one of those anxious-protective conferences. A government minister has told her that most health commissioners have enough evidence at this stage about what works but, he said, it is the "killer case study" that they really want to hear.

Systemic practice as a form of inquiry

What we are doing in systemic therapy is already research. We are listening for information and reflecting on what think we have heard. We check on our first understanding – and our second, and our third. We wonder how the context is influencing the kind of talk and the information being created. We ask what makes a difference. We ask about our and others' participation in the process. We look out for feedback; we look out for our biases. We invite other perspectives. We experiment with wording *with* people. Relational ethics is at the forefront of everything we do. We negotiate with people, we are reflexive, we write reflexively (even when reporting the facts as we have heard them), we critically evaluate practices of power, we attend to internal and external dialogues. We make meaning and offer accounts. We review our theories. We have a history of asking questions with curiosity. These are practical and ethical activities that constitute an approach to research (Simon & Chard 2014).

My experience of teaching research to systemic trainees has been a rich opportunity for exploring narratives of permissions for speaking about systemic practice. Not only does talk about research allow us to journey into foreign lands and learn new languages and experience different paradigmatic cultures, it allows us to return to our own country of origin (systemic practice) and look afresh at what we are doing and how we learn from our practice, how we speak about and from within relational activity. But if we start by assuming others are more expert in researching (studying) therapeutic practice, several things happen. Firstly, we risk surrendering our own critically reflexive and contextually situated knowledge and ways of knowing (McNamee 1994). Secondly, we find ourselves entering into a dynamic long since critiqued within the field of systemic practice where the expertise is held in one party in the relationship and the other is positioned as passive learner in need of help. Thirdly, we re-engage with a reverence for modernist ways of producing knowledge separate from the knowers and the context in which it is produced (Tootell 2004).

There is something else. As the trainees are describing above, we are not simply collecting information and reflecting on how the context may influence whatever is generated. We are allowing ourselves to be changed at every stage of the dialogical process and at every level. We are questioning our hypotheses; we are hearing a tone in our voice, some choice of words and seeing how they are being received; we take back our words, ask our conversational partners for better words, check we are understood, and that we are understanding. We abandon the agenda when we suspect or know it to be inappropriate. Our in-the-moment knowing is a higher context of influence than a pre-scribed method of inquiry. We are not always leading so much as working out ways forward with our conversational partners. Systemic methods of inquiry are improvisational, relationally responsive, ethics led. The knowing emerges in and out of attempts to understand and behave with relational sensitivity to those in the room and at times, to those without.

Rather than think of ourselves as simply therapists we should think of ourselves as "practice researchers". There is a fantastic range of "research methods" available in the world but many, most perhaps, arise out of ideologies which subscribe to truth discourses, objectivity and de-contextualised knowledge. Systemic practitioners are critical thinkers. We are concerned

Systemic Practice as Systemic Inquiry as Transformative Research

not to transpose a particular way of working from one context to another without serious consideration of the potential advantages and disadvantages of a decontextualised approach for participants. We are well-placed to consider what we want to study, how, why and for whom. The "how" is perhaps the main focus of this chapter. So many brilliant and knowledgeable practitioners have been told that to *do research* involves learning another language called "research". This can tap into systemic humility where we are prepared to honour the knowledge of others and accept the limitations of our own knowledge base. The problem is really one of volume control. The sound of a method-led academy is often deafening. And undermining in its certain assertions about What Counts as Evidence and Tried and Tested methods for generating knowledge and know-how.

One of the gifts of systemic social construction is the reminder that all terminology, all theories, all methods have at some point been made up by someone for a particular purpose and in a particular context (Hosking & McNamee 2012). Language and ideas are always products of time, place, culture and power relations and, as such, are never innocent (McCarthy & Byrne 2007, p.330). Therapy and research are words which act as umbrella terms for an infinite number of varied practices. These practices arise out of different paradigms and are not simply ways of describing but are also ways of shaping our attempts to communicate and of framing of our noticings. A term can be useful to some people for some of the time – but not all of the time and not across all contexts or we start to restrict the learning and telling. John Shotter points out that "if our ways of talking are constrained in any way – if, for instance, only certain ways of talking are considered legitimate and not others – then our understanding, and apparently our experience of ourselves, *will be constrained also.*" (Shotter 1989, p.141).

It has been exciting and encouraging for me as a systemic practice-researcher to hear people from building design, musical instrument making, museum curation, education, business and so on share research on their own professional practice. Practice researchers in other professions have found ways of accounting for practice from within the daily doing of their work (Scott et al 2004). These studies value knowledge arising out of first person showcasing of reflexive ways of knowing. They demonstrate how much can be learned by really listening to what is happening in practice within their own unique contexts. The reflexive movements between relational co-ordinations, theories and values together act as a stimulus for shaping a methodological space which can then host a reflexively shaping process of knowledge and know-how.

What connects systemic practitioners with people from entirely different professions who are inquiring into their practice is the place of reflexivity in their inquiry and in their day to day practice (Finlay & Gough 2003; Hedges 2002; Burnham 2005; Simon 2012a, 2012b; Steier 1991). All activity is relational in some way whether people are working with different types of wood or with commissioners of services. We are all acting in to and out of feedback loops and expected to respond and adapt appropriately to this feedback. Systemic practitioners are committed to reflexivity-in-and-on-action to support ongoing care about ethical practice. Our preoccupation with relational ethics explains our commitment to adopt an enquiring stance. For example, we ask questions not simply to collect information but to orientate ourselves in response to it. We see connections between different parts of a systems and invite the whole system to become a reflexive observing system. This entwining of reflexivity and ethics provides strong and coherent conditions for first person practice inquiry.

The doing of practice can be understood as forms of action research or ethnography, storytelling or case study to name a few. These approaches invite reflection in and on the doing of practice (Schön 1983). Practitioners can do research from within "living moments" of relational activity rather than about them after the event (Shotter 1999, 2011). John Shotter distinguishes between "*monological-retrospective-objective* style of writing (about-ness writing)" and "*dialogical-prospective-relational* style of writing (or witness-writing)" (Shotter 1999). This allows practitioners to "try to write 'participatively,' i.e., *from within* an ongoing involvement within the activities in question, not as a detached outsider to them." (Shotter 1999).

By questioning the separate constructs of systemic therapy and research, not only can we continue to be the generators of knowledge about systems, ecologies, communication, change and human growth but also we can help to develop critically informed audiences who appreciate the kind of material and presentation of such that systemic practitioners are in a strong position to offer.

Transformative research

Not only do we have cousins in the arena of professional knowledge generation but there are other strong family resemblances within the playing fields of post-positivist qualitative research which is committed to research with a social justice agenda (Denzin and Lincoln 2014; Simon 2014a).

The term "post-positivist" is useful in the context of social constructionist systemic research as it is this that separates out some forms of knowing from others, not qualitative versus quantitative. Positivist qualitative and quantitative approaches subscribe to the idea that the researcher should stand well back from the research subject(s) and hold their breath while collecting the data so as to avoid contamination of the evidence and leave the scene of research as you found it, unchanged. Post-positivist research requires that you set out to change the site of inquiry through the doing of research. Post-positivist researchers not only declare their bias but put it to work and offer rich transparency as rationale, background and learning for the study. This is not simply a trend in research. It connects to concerns expressed by oppressed and colonised groups of people who have been researched and had all manner of falsehoods, intentional or otherwise written about them which have often led to the development of policies which have served to oppress these groups further (Clifford & Marcus 1986; McCarthy & Byrne 2007; Simon 1998; Visweswaran 1994).

Research is intended as a method of changing (meaning improving) the quality of life for participants in the study. This can range from something very local and immediate on a small scale to a wide ranging multi-actor project.

Several things lead me to describe systemic practice as action research and activist practice which I have described elsewhere as "Praction Research" (Simon 2012a).

i. Systemic practice is motivated by the desire to create political and social change or movement in communities.
ii. Systemic practice embraces perpetual reflexivity driven by the preoccupation with ethics-led practice and an openness to being moved by both the ordinary and the extraordinary (and understanding the ordinary as extraordinary).
iii. Systemic practice is committed to transparently stated recognition that some discourses dominate, discredit and silence others and being conscious that some voices carry more weight and meet the needs of the advantaged over the disadvantaged.
iv. Systemic practice is committed to dialogue in whatever form as transformative action.

I have been developing the terms *local reflexivity* and *global reflexivity* to make visible the i) power relationships, ii) relational movements and iii) transformative influences between the immediate and wider contexts in which practice is taking place. The focus of our work may be local but our work is inevitably influenced by, and influencing of, broader social and political environments in which we all work and live. Speaking about one's work involves finding ways of setting it in multiple contexts and describing the relationships between them.

Local reflexivity involves the practitioner-researcher:

- moving between the voices of their inner dialogue
- moving with their inner dialogue into outer dialogue
- moving in response to others and the polyvocality in outer conversation
- moving with emergent ideas and actions within the moment
- moving in response to reflections on the moment in the moment
- moving with a sensitivity and curiosity about the contexts one is acting into and out of

Global reflexivity involves the practitioner-researcher:

- moving in the process of reflecting on reflections on, in and after the moment
- finding something new to say about movement and transformation in practice
- finding ways of describing this movement and transformation to others
- using learning from practice to cha(lle)nge socio-economic power structures
- inquiring into what counts as professional practice and why and for whom
- addressing audiences with a mindfulness about relational communication choices and possible consequences of those choices for self and others
- stretching of the boundary of what counts as knowledge or knowing, practice and research across and beyond local and wider contexts

By connecting local and global reflexivity, we are staying alert to the limits, possibilities and responsibilities in co-creating transformative activities in specific and diverse contexts which have repercussions for the people with whom we are immediately working and the various communities in which we live.

Systemic Practice as Systemic Inquiry as Transformative Research

Approaches to systemic inquiry

So in addition to thinking of systemic practice as a form of inquiry and transformative inquiry, there are many punctuations of approaches – a word I prefer to methods so as to stay contextually responsive rather than understand procedure as the highest context – to how you might connect with a narrative of your positions in enquiring. We have many terms at our disposal. The question is not what does each of these terms mean but how might I utilise this expression to best describe to the work I am/we are doing? And, how am I going to take hold of this term and define it – with clarity and allowing space for fluidity? It is okay, ethical even, to say you have a preference. We just need to indicate what such a preference is about. In research supervision, I often advise people to let the methodology arise out of the practice, the participants, the subject. This is likely to create the conditions for curiosity to flourish and allow you to reflect on your interests, how they connect with what you have been doing and your own preferences in life. How might you speak from within the living moment to hear and honour the multiple voices with whom you are interacting in inner and outer dialogue?

These are not just voices or narratives. Neither are they only voices with narratives. These are voices which carry more or less sense of entitlement, which speak more or less loudly, which feel a greater or lesser expectation that they will be heard or acted on. Dialogue is not simply an exchange of views, of information. Dialogue is an enactment of power relations set within many overlapping cultural, social, political, economic contexts. So what might emerge if you connect these dialogues with the political contexts in which you and your conversational partners are living?

The systemic practitioner wishes to be aware of this, subscribing as we do to a conscious critique of power in relationships and institutional structures. When we reflect on dialogue within our work, we listen out for different voices at work and what they wish to say (Penn & Frankfurt 2004). We listen out for the power relations between the voices, sometimes personified in individuals or communities or policies, present or virtual.

There is so much noise in our heads, in our inner dialogue that we have to work hard to make sense of all those voices and their power relations. Part of our job is to be fair and recognise oppression whether in institutionalised or impromptu discourses and actions. While, at times, it may sound more like cacophony than organised conversation, we are incredibly skilled at responding with a fair degree of sensitivity to the context.

Human relations are difficult to study and many have challenged the idea that one should attempt to reduce lived experience through formal data analysis methods (Reynolds 2014). Law (2007) speaks of how "mess" in the social science research is inevitable and needs recognising as part of life, requiring new ways of telling rather than being treated as something that can always be formulated into structured and conclusive information. Organisational researcher and pianist and Frank Barrett (2012) encourages an interest in improvisation and discusses how coordination in jazz is a useful metaphor for appreciating that what might look like "mess" is careful, contextualised co-ordinations between people. What are likely to be the differences between an outside researcher studying improvisational jazz and a member of an improvisational jazz band making a study? Is one set of outputs more useful or might they have different consequences?

Systemic action research
Action research came about as an attempt to solve problems. Freire's idea was for a group of people, a community, for example, to come together and discuss a problem (Freire 1972). Then they would think together about how best to overcome the difficulties and agree a way forward to achieving their objective. So the method involved taking a first step, pausing to review and discuss whether the kind of action at this stage seemed to be going in the right direction. After some reflection, the participants would agree to either carry on as planned or do something different. They proceed according to their revised plan and then, at another stage, take another break, review and discuss revision and proceed towards a goal. Boal (1973) developed The Theatre of the Oppressed which has been used and developed within family therapy (Proctor et al 2008).

Action research originally was a form of grassroots activism (Freire 1973; Boal 1973). People collaborated to make changes, to overcome difficulties not solvable by existing methods. It was and is an experimental format. It has an in-built critique of power relations (Parker 2003). It is a highly reflexive process. It has a social responsibility or social justice agenda in that it aims to improve people's lives. It is collaborative and discursive.

Does this sound familiar to you? To me, it sounds like everyday systemic practice. Don't we start by setting a context with people, move on to try some kind of talk or other activity, then pause and review with our partners if this is working and decide how to move on – and then repeat this process at intervals? This is transformative action research.

Systemic Practice as Systemic Inquiry as Transformative Research

We have many systemic and non-systemic friends in the field of action research.

- Participatory Action Research has developed the work of Kurt Lewin to create a more politicised community of research practice with a social change agenda (Reason and Bradbury 2008).
- Dialogical Participatory Action Research has been developed for reflexive practitioners to be inclusive of all participants by encouraging practitioners into more of an inquiring stance within collaborative dialogue (Olsson 2011, 2014).
- Situated Dialogic Action Research focuses on studying mutual and spontaneous responsivity as generative of meaning and movement between people (Shotter 2008).
- Cooperative Inquiry promotes an inclusive research cycle which explores different types of knowledge to propose new ways of knowing and acting (Heron & Reason 2001).
- Praction Research understands systemic practice as reflection, in and as action with a view to social change and challenging unnegotiated practices of power (Simon 2012).
- The Rhizome Approach uses systemic ecology theory to challenge oppressive practices and collaborate on change in communities (Reynolds 2014; Kinman 2012).

These, like other approaches identified in this chapter, are not finalised or fixed methods. They are ways of being and knowing devised in response to a need for site specific transformation which take into account context, culture and agenda.

Critical ethnography

There are many forms of ethnography. Ethnography is a way of documenting and sharing what one notices from within a particular context. Often practitioners report noticing a trend in referrals or a theme running through their work, a change or contrast in dialogue, shifts in organisational policy or culture and how this is being played out across all areas of their work. Studying one's practice from within is what we already do but mostly in an informal way with colleagues.

Ethnography is a way of studying people and practices which has gone through many changes mainly as part of a post-positivist critique of what counts as knowledge production. Early anthropologists were pioneers in drawing attention to the importance of understanding meaning and practices in different cultures. They worked within the methods and philosophies available to them at the time including the belief that the observer and the observed occupied separate spaces with different levels of ability to observe. This has since been critiqued for its limited and unethical "aboutness" positioning (Shotter 2011) in which people were objectified as subject matter (Clifford & Marcus 1986). Kamala Visweswaran (1994) has described such observational practices and ideological bias from sociology and anthropology as demonstrating an undeclared extension of colonising practices in which the people being researched were oppressed by the descriptions of them developed by outsider researchers. Mary and Ken Gergen have re-framed ethnography as relational practice (Gergen & Gergen 2002). D. Soyini Madison (2011) encourages researchers to use their own life experience and challenge racist and colonising practices in the academy to generate more first person tellings and share the decision making about not only what to include but how to present people's lives. Despite the foregrounding of the voices of women affected by HIV and AIDS over those of the researchers, Patti Lather and Chris Smithies, the women participants were not happy with the editing choices made by the researchers (Lather 2007).

Ethnographic approaches to researching systemic practice have been developed by systemic practitioners.

- Embodied Dialogical Inquiry was created to study the complex movements in dialogical space between people and understand the co-construction of resonance in transformative conversations (Vedeler 2011).

- Relational Ethnography emphasises a relationally reflexive approach to writing from within one's own practice with special attention to relational ethics and relational aesthetics (Simon 2012b). It elaborates on writing as a form of inquiry (Richardson 1994) and autoethnography (Bailey 2005; Ellis 2004, 2008; Reed-Danahay 1997).

- Performance ethnography is becoming popular in therapeutic groups as a form of social action to make public private or hidden stories with a view to inviting witnesses, audiences to be moved into heightened consciousness about the experience of others (Denzin 2003; Spry 2001).

- Reflecting team work, definitional ceremonies and outsider witness groups (Andersen 1987, 1997; Speedy 2004; White 1995) offer similar opportunities for synthesis between communal participation, social action and therapy.

Systemic Practice as Systemic Inquiry as Transformative Research

Case study research

A snippet from a supervision conversation:

Supervisor: That's such a moving story. I feel like I have learned so much from what you and the client talked about. And from how you have just reflected on the conversation. It makes me think how other systemic therapists would love to hear that and feel the benefit for their own practice.

Supervisee: I thought about writing it up. But then...

Supervisor: But then...? What?

Supervisee: I think who would read it? Who would publish it?

Supervisor: Who published Freud and the other writers of case studies?

Supervisee: Aren't case studies criticised though for being too subjective?

Supervisor: They can be, but usually in cases where the writer has not owned up to their subjectivity and written about their work without the participation, or even permission, of the clients. There is now much case study research by psychotherapists but produced more ethically.

Supervisee: Yes, I would worry about objectifying my client. Stealing their story. That wouldn't be in the spirit of the work. Or my ethics.

Supervisor: So if you were to write with your client, or at least include them in some ways, how would you do it?

This is a case study of a discussion about case study as a method of inquiry. Systemic inquiry positions all participants in a study of practice within the frame of the research. In addition, there is so much more one can include – not illustrated in this example above – about breathing, bodily movements, intonation and timings to name just a few parts of the process. Of course, the most significant information missing from traditional research methods is that of the researcher's inner dialogue, reflexive noticings and embodied responses. Our noticing activities are the core of what we rely on in everyday practice. We have all kinds of ways of knowing how to go on in conversation. To focus exclusively on the spoken word removes many intrinsic layers of context which inform the process. A transcription of the spoken words will not, on their own, describe transformational work except perhaps at a limited cognitive level. Such a study removes extraordinary complex relationally situated ways of being and knowing.

Case studies can have an ethnographic element. But they can also be fictionalised tellings of real life situations in the interest of telling true stories using real or composite people or events. Carolyn Ellis writes what she calls a methodological novel from within her teaching a class autoethnography (Ellis 2004). She uses real and composite characters to allow some difficult positions or opinions to be expressed without being located in one or more real people. This allows for true stories to be told but relocated into safer ways of sharing them. In her book, *Becoming a Reflexive Researcher*, Kim Etherington (2004) shows how she uses herself when sharing case examples from her counselling practice. She discusses reflexivity as an approach to researching her work as a counsellor and group facilitator. Case studies can be written in ways which foreground participants' words alongside the reflexive responses of the researcher written both from within and without the conversations as demonstrated by the detailed account of a consultation process by Lisen Kebbe of her work with a family going through a family business succession (Kebbe 2011).

Storytelling as a form of inquiry
Storytelling is a form of inquiry through people telling detailed and engaging stories of complexity. It could be a telling of a story from within therapy performed by the client as storyteller or by a whole family or therapist, or members of a reflecting team (Andersen 1987). It could involve the performing of a story which has been heard not written. Of course, stories don't just exist. They come into being through the presence of an actual or imagined audience. Storytelling is a relational art in which writers imagine their readers or audience (including all those involved in the story) and anticipate their responses. This guides the shaping of how a story develops, how it is told.

Storytelling is a dialogical exchange. Writing stories and oral story telling is a performative activity in that it always takes place in a relational space. Stories are intended to be told and heard and experienced. They are invitations to reflexivity. There is a saying in the field of qualitative inquiry, that good, ethical research shows, not tells, the reader what is happening to leave enough space for readers to make their own reflexive meanings from the story. Storytelling relies on literary devices and creates many permissions for therapists practising in ways closer to the arts than the sciences.

Systemic Practice as Systemic Inquiry as Transformative Research

Storytelling transforms private experience into public sharings and authorises the experiences of people who have been expected to, for example, keep secret aspects of their lives for safety reasons. Some practitioners write from within the living moment of relational practice, in the first person. Other practice researchers have imagined the other and enabled the story to be told in ethical ways using ventriloquation (Bakhtin 1986; Simon 2014b; Tannen 2009) or ghostwriting (Rhodes 2000; Simon 2014b).

More punctuations of systemic inquiry

There are many more ways of framing systemic practice as a form of transformative inquiry.

- Collaborative Inquiry (Anderson 2007, 2014) is a form of joint-action (Shotter 1984) which many therapists understand as the model for the doing of therapy.
- Coordinated Management of Meaning is both a way of discussing episodes, influence and transformation and developing accounts of transformation within the work as well as for public sharing (Cronen 2004; Pearce 1989, 2004; Pearce & Walters 1996; Oliver 2005).
- Research as Daily Practice (RDP) shows how reflexive tellings can generate rich learning for practitioners (St George and Wulff 2014).
- Pragmatic Inquiry involves a joint inquiry into the systemic practices of developing ways of going forward and finding solutions to problems (Cronen 2006; Juhl 2014)
- Performative writing and methodology in family therapy address the relational elements of research (Bava 2005, 2014).
- Documentary (Bateson 2010; Kinman 2012); sculpting; improvisational drama.
- Writing as a form of inquiry (Richardson 1994, 2005): scriptwriting, poetry; fiction, life story research, for example, and like storytelling are relational activities with social consequences. Each approach allows for different kinds of punctuations and tellings and responding.

As I am wondering how to close this chapter, I hear voices from a conversation between the same trainees debating another topic which echoes so many conversations I have had. Yes, I will include it here...

Martin has been looking thoughtful for a while and then finds a space in the conversation. "So how do you analyse the data when you do something like a collaborative inquiry?" This is a common question. People are keen to conceptualise a whole process and want to be properly informed. But this is also a received idea from another discourse about what one can do with "information".

"What do you mean when you say 'analyse'?" I ask.

"Well," Martin responds, "you have your stories which you have co-written with the clients. Then what? How do you find out what the stories really tell you?"

Faizah jumps in. "The telling of the story of the work is a process of meaning-making. Not just reporting." This is not a satisfying answer for Martin. "But where is the data?"

Faizah is leaning forward to see Martin while she is speaking. "The story is the data. The whole story. The process of the work we have done together is the data. The reflecting on the process and how we happened upon things and how we asked and responded to each other. All that." She sits back in her chair. Martin looks a little unsure. "I thought you had to analyse it," he says, "run the material through a process. My friend analysed his research using a method for breaking it all down into categories. He kept going over and over it. It took him forever."

Faizah, still leaning back in her chair as if a little tired says, "Patti Lather didn't do that exactly but she was unsettled by how upset her research participants were when they found out she and her co-researcher had chosen to use only some parts of what they had said when they thought they were telling the whole story so others could learn from their experiences."

Imtiyaz is nodding. "Yeah, I think it's ethical not to mess with people's stories."

Faizah leans forward again this time to look towards Imtiyaz. "Whose stories are you talking about now?"

"Well, I had in mind clients' stories. But that's maybe when we need stories for commissioners. When we are researching our own practice, I guess it is a collaborative inquiry because I am checking out my understanding with the people with whom I am working. So it should be 'our' stories." Imtiyaz picks up a pen and starts writing something. I am both relieved to hear the debate and unsettled by the speed with which some people are taking a position. I ask "What about the parts of the work where you have been thinking things that you don't want to share with your clients?" Let's get some more context on these choices.

Imtiyaz takes a quick position. "I am fine about sharing anything." I am preparing a response and worried about my voice being allied too quickly with a single ethical position but Lydia comes in and I am pleased as she has not spoken for a while and I have been worried she could be experiencing too much difference between the course culture and her work context.

"Well not everybody might be fine about sharing everything. I wouldn't want someone to know I found them boring, for example," Lydia offers, with a nervous giggle.

Faizah comes in again. "But there may be a story behind that. I could tell a story about someone I found boring but when I tried to orientate myself to a more appreciative stance I noticed other things of interest and I asked about them and it turned things around."

"Yes. Okay," Lydia caries on, "But what about echoes of personal experiences that the client might find a burden to hear?"

"Oh we are back to transparency..." laughs Faizah.

"And use of self," says Imtiyaz.

"And boundaries..."

"And the specific needs of each situation..."

I am smiling and hear myself say "I love this complexity of overlapping theory and ethics you are connecting to."

"So," Martin is back in the conversation, "wouldn't it then be best to sidestep all this and not research our own practice?"

I am not sure if what I am about to say is the best thing to do in case it could sound like a critique of Martin's ideas but then we are meant to be critical thinkers and I do have an opinion. And suddenly I hear an impatient part of me address the liberal systemic part of me. "It is not just an opinion as if we each have our own view! Systemic practitioners need permission to speak with their knowledge and know-how, to find ways of articulating stories which, as Michael White would have said, are present but not yet told or heard or acted on! Stories people are not encouraged to tell. Stories about practice which are being systematically devalued by modernist accounting practices! This is a political issue. Not just your personal preference like wanting a window seat on the train!"

Only a second has passed. A rather stimulating second in which I wobbled and rebalanced my many selves. As I breathe out I hear myself say, "Well, we also need to develop learning about how we are working, about what sorts of talk or ways of being are transformative and use that first person experience..." My calm talk is interrupted by Faizah, who is animated.

"I want to write from within therapeutic conversation. When I write, I understand more. When I read it back, I find something new and I start to see a whole. Not a finished whole. A whole for now. And reading what I have written changes me. Other people reading what I have written and responding transforms of my thinking which transforms my practice."

I feel we are just beginning to get to the heart of the matter but then someone points out we have run over time and someone has a bus to catch and the conversation falls away as the group packs up. I am reminded that there is something isomorphic here. We are struggling with the task of studying and developing accounts of systemic practice. Our accounts have no objective start or ending. We choose where to start and where to end the telling. Our studies of our work, like the work itself, are inevitably incomplete. We use time as a frame to create a sense of completeness yet transformations start and carry on way beyond the activities we call therapy. Unfinalisable descriptions of unfinalised processes, and still I hear myself think "We will get there next time we meet."

References

Andersen, Tom (1987). The Reflective Team: Dialogue and meta-dialogue in clinical work. *Family Process*, 26, 415–427.

Andersen, Tom (1997). Researching Client-therapist Relationships: A collaborative study for informing therapy. *Journal of Systemic Therapies*, 16(2), 125–133.

Anderson, Harlene & Goolishian, Harold (1992). The Client is the Expert: A not-knowing approach to therapy. In Sheila McNamee and Kenneth Gergen (Eds.). *Therapy as Social Construction*. London: Sage.

Anderson, Harlene (2007). *Collaborative Therapy: Relationships and Conversations that make a Difference*. London: Routledge.

Anderson, Harlene (2014). Collaborative-Dialogue Based Research as Everyday Practice: Questioning our Myths. In Gail Simon & Alex Chard (Eds.) *Systemic Inquiry. Innovations in Systemic Practice Research*. Farnhill: Everything is Connected Press.

Bailey, Lucy E. (2005). When "The Research" is Me: Women's experiences as contingent instructors in the contemporary academy. *Thirdspace*, 4(2) 7–21.

Bakhtin, Mikhail (1986 [2007 reprint]). *Speech Genres and Other Late Essays*. Trans. V.W. McGee, Eds. C. Emerson & M. Holquist. Austin, Texas: University of Texas Press.

Barrett, Frank (2012). *Yes to the Mess. Surprising Leadership Lessons from Jazz*. Harvard Business Review Press.

Bateson, Nora (2010). *An Ecology of Mind. A Daughter's Portrait of Gregory Bateson*. Film. Written and directed by Nora Bateson. Bullfrog Films.

Bava, Saliha (2005). Performance Methodology: Constructing Discourses and Discursive Practices in Family Therapy Research. In Sprenkle, Douglas & Piercy, Fred, (Eds.), *Research Methods in Family Therapy*. [2nd ed.] 170–190. London: Guilford Press.

Bava, Saliha (2014). Performative Practices, Performative Relationships — in and as Emergent Research. In Gail Simon & Alex Chard (Eds.) *Systemic Inquiry. Innovations in Systemic Practice Research*. Farnhill: Everything is Connected Press.

Boal, Augusto (1973). *The Theatre of the Oppressed*. Abingdon: Routledge Press.

Boje, David M. (2001). *Narrative Methods for Organization Research and Communication Research*. London: Sage.

Burnham, John (2005). Relational Reflexivity: A tool for socially constructing therapeutic relationships In: Carmel Flaskas et al (Eds.) *The Space Between: Experience, Context and Process in the Therapeutic Relationship*. London: Karnac Books.

Clifford, James & Marcus, George E. (Eds.) (1986). *Writing Culture: The Poetics and Politics of Ethnography*. Berkley: University of California Press.

Cronen, Vernon (2004). Something Old, Something New: CMM and mass communication. *Human Systems: The Journal of Systemic Consultation & Management*, 15(3), 167–178.

Cronen, Vernon (2006). *Pragmatic Inquiry*. Working paper.

Denzin, Norman K. (2003). *Performance Ethnography: Critical pedagogy and the politics of culture*. London: Sage Publications.

Denzin, Norman K. and Lincoln, Yvonna S. (2014). *The Sage Handbook of Qualitative Research*. 4th ed. London: Sage Publications.

Ellis, Carolyn (2004). *The Ethnographic I: A methodological novel about autoethnography*. Walnut Creek: Alta Mira Press.

Ellis, Carolyn (2008). *Revision: Autoethnographic Reflections on Life and Work*. Left Coast Press.

Etherington, Kim (2004). *Becoming a Reflexive Researcher: Using Our Selves in Research*. Jessica Kingsley Publishers.

Finlay, Linda & Gough, Brendan (Eds.) (2003). *Reflexivity: A Practical Guide for Researchers in Health and Social Sciences*. Wiley-Blackwell.

Freire, Paulo (1972). *Pedagogy of the Oppressed*. Harmondsworth: Penguin.

Gergen, Kenneth. J. & Gergen, Mary (2002) Ethnography as Relationship. In Bochner, A. and Ellis, C. (Eds.) *Ethnographically Speaking. Autoethnography, Literature, and Aesthetics*. Oxford: AltaMira Press.

Hedges, Fran (2002). *Reflexivity in Therapeutic Practice*. London: Palgrave Macmillan.

Heron, John & Reason, Peter (2001).The Practice of Co-operative Inquiry: Research with people rather than on people. In *Systemic Practice and Action Research*, 15(3), 169–176.

Hosking, Dian Marie & McNamee, Sheila (2012). *Transforming Inquiry: A Relational Constructionist Approach*. Abingdon: Routledge.

Juhl, Andreas (2014). Pragmatic Inquiry. A research method for knowledge creation in organisations. In Gail Simon & Alex Chard (Eds.) *Systemic Inquiry. Innovations in Systemic Practice Research*. Farnhill: Everything is Connected Press.

Kebbe, Lisen (2014). Writing Essays as Dialogical Inquiry. In Gail Simon & Alex Chard (Eds.) *Systemic Inquiry. Innovations in Systemic Practice Research*. Farnhill: Everything is Connected Press.

Kinman, Christopher (2012). *All Manner of Poetic Disobedience: Lynn Hoffmann and the Rhizome Century*. Film. Directed by Christopher Kinman and Lars Meyer.

Lather, Patti (2007). *Getting Lost: Feminist Efforts Towards a Double(d) Science*. New York: State University of New York Press.

Law, John (2007). *After Method: Mess in Social Science Research*. Abingdon: Routledge.

Lorde, Audrey (2013 [1984]). "The Master's Tools Will Never Dismantle The Master's House". In *Sister Outsider*. New York: Ten Speed Press.

Madison, D. Soyini (2011). *Critical Ethnography. Method, Ethics and Performance*. London: Sage Publications.

McCarthy, Imelda Colgan and O'Reilly Byrne, Nollaig (2007). A Fifth Province Approach to Intra-Cultural Issues in an Irish Context: Marginal Illuminations. In Monica McGoldrick & Ken Hardy (Eds.). *Revisioning Family Therapy: Race, Class, Culture, and Gender in Clinical Practice*. 2nd ed. New York: Guilford Press.

McNamee, Sheila (1994). Research as Relationally Situated Activity: Ethical implications. *Journal of Feminist Family Therapy*, 6 (3), 69–83.

McNamee, Sheila (2014). Research as Relational Practice: Exploring Modes of Inquiry. In Gail Simon & Alex Chard (Eds.) *Systemic Inquiry. Innovations in Systemic Practice Research*. Farnhill: Everything is Connected Press.

Oliver, Christine (2005). *Reflexive Inquiry: A Framework for Consultancy Practice*. London: Karnac Books.

Olsson, Ann-Margreth (2014). The Impact of Dialogical Participatory Action Research (DPAR). Riding in the peloton of dialogical collaboration. In Gail Simon & Alex Chard (Eds.) *Systemic Inquiry. Innovations in Systemic Practice Research*. Farnhill: Everything is Connected Press.

Parker, Ian (2005). *Qualitative Psychology: Introducing Radical Research*. Milton Keynes: Open University Press.

Pearce, W. Barnett (1989). *Communication and the Human Condition*. Carbondale, Illinois: Illinois University Press.

Pearce, W. Barnett & Walters, Kim A. (1996). *Research Methods: A Systemic Communications Approach*. Draft. Pearce Walters Inc.

Pearce Associates (2004 [1999]) Using CMM. http://www.pearceassociates.com/essays/cmm_seminar.pdf

Penn, Peggy & Frankfurt, Marylin (2004) Creating a Participant Text: Writing, Multiple Voices, Narrative Multiplicity. *Family Process*, 33(3), 217–231.

Proctor, Kerry; Perlesz, Amaryll; Maloney, Banu; McIlwaine & O'Neill, Imogen (2008). Exploring Theatre of the Oppressed in Family Therapy Clinical Work and Supervision. *Counselling and Psychotherapy Research Journal*, 8(1), 43–52.

Reason, Peter and Bradbury, Hilary (Eds.) (2008). *The Sage Handbook of Action Research: Participative Inquiry and Practice*. London: Sage Publications.

Reed-Danahay, Deborah (1997). *Auto/Ethnography: Rewriting the Self and the Social*. Oxford: Berg Publishers.

Reynolds, Vikki (2010). Fluid and Imperfect Ally Positioning: Some Gifts of Queer Theory. *Context*. October 2010. Association for Family and Systemic Therapy, UK, 13–17.

Reynolds, Vikki (2014). A Solidarity Approach: The Rhizome & Messy Inquiry. In Gail Simon & Alex Chard (Eds.) *Systemic Inquiry. Innovations in Systemic Practice Research*. Farnhill: Everything is Connected Press.

Rhodes, Carl (2000). Ghostwriting Research: Positioning the Researcher in the Interview Text. *Qualitative Inquiry*, 6(4), 511–525.

Richardson, Laurel (1994). Writing: A Method of Inquiry. In Denzin, Norman K. and Lincoln, Yvonna S. (Eds.). *The SAGE Handbook of Qualitative Research*. London: Sage Publications.

Richardson, Laurel & St Pierre, Elizabeth (2005). Writing: A Method of Inquiry. In Denzin, Norman K. and Lincoln, Yvonna S. (Eds.). *The SAGE Handbook of Qualitative Research*. 3rd ed. London: Sage Publications.

Scott, D., Brown, A., Lunt, I., & Thorne, L., (2004). *Professional Doctorates: Integrating Professional and Academic Knowledge*. Milton Keynes: Open University Press.

Shotter, John (1984). *Social Accountability and Selfhood*. Oxford: Blackwell.

Shotter, John & Gergen, Kenneth (Eds.) (1989). *Texts of Identity*. London: Sage.

Shotter, John (1989). Social accountability and the social construction of "you". In Shotter, John & Gergen, Kenneth (Eds.) *Texts of Identity*. London: Sage.

Shotter, John (1999). *Writing from Within "Living Moments:" "Withness-writing" rather than "aboutness-writing"*. Paper written for Fourth National Writing Across the Curriculum Conference: Multiple Intelligences. Cornell, June 3rd–5th, 1999.

Shotter, John (2008). *Situated Dialogic Action Research*. Qualitative Research in Management and Organization Conference, March 11–13, 2008. Anderson Schools of Management, University of New Mexico, Albuquerque, New Mexico.

Shotter, John (2011). *Getting It: With-ness Thinking and the Dialogical... in Practice*. New York: Hampton Press.

Simon, Gail (1998). Incitement to Riot? Individual Identity and Group Membership: Some reflections on the politics of a post-modernist therapy. *Human Systems: Journal of Systemic Consultation and Management*, 9(1), 33–49.

Simon, Gail (2012a). Praction Research: A Model of Systemic Inquiry. *Human Systems Journal of Systemic Consultation and Management*, 23(1), 103–124. https://docs.google.com/file/d/0B5TWuGoJVPe_UDNYdGJ5NXl1dGs/edit?pli=1

Simon, Gail (2012b). Relational Ethnography: Writing and reading in and about research relationships. *Forum Qualitative Sozialforschung*

/ Forum: Qualitative Social Research. http://www.qualitative-research.net/index.php/fqs/article/view/1735

Simon, Gail (2014a). Systemic Inquiry as a Form of Qualitative Inquiry. In Gail Simon & Alex Chard (Eds.) *Systemic Inquiry. Innovations in Systemic Practice Research*. Farnhill: Everything is Connected Press.

Simon, Gail (2014b). *Ventriloquation and Ghost Writing as Responses to Oppression*. Paper presented at 15th International Bakhtin Conference, Royal Art Academy, Stockholm. 23–27 July 2014.

Simon, Gail & Chard, Alex (Eds.) (2014). *Systemic Inquiry. Innovations in Systemic Practice Research*. Farnhill: Everything is Connected Press.

Speedy, Jane (2004). Living a more peopled life: Definitional ceremony as inquiry into psychotherapy "outcomes". *The International Journal of Narrative Therapy and Community Work*, 3, 43–53.

Spry, Tami (2001). Performing Autoethnography: An Embodied Methodological Praxis. *Qualitative Inquiry*, 7, 706–732.

St George, Sally & Wulff, Dan (2014). Research as Daily Practice. In Gail Simon & Alex Chard (Eds.) *Systemic Inquiry. Innovations in Systemic Practice Research*. Farnhill: Everything is Connected Press.

Steier, Frederick (1991). Research and Reflexivity. London: Sage Publications.

Stronach, Ian, Garratt, D., Pearce, C. and Piper, H. (2007) Reflexivity, The Picturing of Selves, The Forging of Method. *Qualitative Inquiry* March 2007, Vol. 13, no. 2, 179–203.

Tannen, Deborah (2009). A*bduction, Dialogicality and Prior Text: The Taking on of Voices in Conversational Discourse*. Plenary address presented at the 84th annual meeting of the Linguistic Society of America, Baltimore, MD, January 8, 2009. Georgetown University.

Tootell, Andrew (2004). Decentring Research Practice. *The International Journal of Narrative Therapy and Community Work*, 2004, 3 Dulwich Centre Publications.

White, Michael (1990) Story, Knowledge and Power. In M. White and D. Epston (Eds.) *Narrative Means to Therapeutic Ends*. London: W. W. Norton.

White, Michael (1992). Deconstruction and Therapy. In *Experience, Contradiction, Narrative, & Imagination: Selected papers of David Epston and Michael White, 1989–1991*. Adelaide, Australia: Dulwich Centre Publications.

White, Michael (1995). Reflecting Teamwork as Definitional Ceremony. In *Re-authoring Lives: Interviews and Essays*. Adelaide: Dulwich Centre Publications.

Visweswaran, Kamala (1994). *Fictions of Feminist Ethnography*. University of Minnesota Press.

12 Framing the Symmetry
Nora Bateson

If you look out the front window of your home you will see something very different than if you look out the back window. It is not our doors which hold us in our trenches, not the gates or walls, but instead it is the windows. The frames through which we perceive limit and define what we can see. I am not so sure, on some days that humans are worth saving. They are reckless and mean, destructive and greedy, they are careless and self-centred. Human beings can and do intentionally harm children. Is there anything worse? They abuse sentient animals, pollute, lie, steal, betray...

At this juncture every country on earth is living with pathologies compounded upon pathologies. With so little time left to tend to the rivers, forests, children, oceans, air cleanliness and refugees, and so few moments remaining to reverse the unravelling of the natural systems of our world, I realise the impossibility of shifting our course. The trenches are deep. It is not, after all, in the monetary interest or the political interest of our existing institutions to come together and alter the patterns of our living, as we must. It is not our job, nor our nations' responsibilities to take up the task of a total system change. Anyway, we are too late, we say, the tipping point has come and gone. Sometimes it seems that humanity is hopeless.

But then, there is art.

The way we think has everything to do with the way we perceive. While our logical, rational frames of reference can only see small pieces of the larger patterns of our world, art provides leverage in our powers of perception by stretching us into new territories of knowing. There are levels of communication that only art can reach. For me, this is where hope waits and where faith can be found and created in the moments of our greatest fears about our world disappearing.

Unlike either religion or science, art does not offer explanation. Through subjectivity, art brews the healing salve of multiplicity. It plunges us into a realm where there are more than one and also more than two versions of truth. We know there is no singular interpretation of a poem, or a sculpture, but we do not know and cannot know what all of the interpretations will be.

Framing the Symmetry

I found this paragraph in a letter written by William Bateson (WB), my grandfather, to Gregory Bateson (GB), my father. It was written in an effort to console Gregory after his brother, Martin had committed suicide. In these few lines of fatherly advice, I see the map of the unique commitment that the generations of Batesons have had toward the study of life.

> *"The faith in great work is the nearest to religion that I have ever got, and it supplies what religious people get from superstition. There is also this difference, that the man of science very rarely hears the tempting voices and very seldom needs a stimulant at all, whereas the common man craves it all the time. Of course there is great work that is not science — great art, for instance, is perhaps greater still, but that is for the rarest and is scarcely in the reach of people like ourselves. Science, I am certain, comes next and that is well within our reach — at least I am sure that it is well within yours...To set oneself to find out something, even a little bit, of the structure and order of the natural world is, and will be for you I dare foresee, a splendid and purifying purpose, into which you can always withdraw in the periods of suffering that everyman must pass through. If you keep your eyes on that, the other things in life look so poor and small and temporary that the pain they give can be forgotten in the greater emotion."*
> (Letter to Gregory after Martin's death, 1922, pp.555–561)

In this letter I can see the passion, and the loneliness, of science as a path alongside an esteem of the arts that is nearly untouchable. The distancing from religion is in contrast to the "purifying purpose" of the pursuit, to "find out something, even a little bit of the structure and the order of the natural world". Without question the embracing of this infinite study of life is in its own, atheistic, way a practice of both care and curiosity. This great work is not a job, it is not a way to gain prestige, or a book deal – it is a way of staving off the pain and suffering that comes with being human. It is learning to learn, both within and about the systems that are inside and outside ourselves, micro, macro, biological and social. More importantly, it is a way of seeing, a way of living.

Gregory's father William used to say that genius can only be found in two places: in art and in nature. He went on to add that while science would never actually achieve "genius" – it should always be inspired by it. As a film student, I was riddled with guilt for not having followed in my family lineage of science, and I found solace in this statement of William's. It vindicated me, or so I thought. It has taken me years to unravel it. And as I have begun to understand what he meant, I am starting to think that it might have been easier to be a scientist than an artist.

Why? What is he saying? It has to do with the idea of understanding how this pursuit of structure and order in the natural world has everything to do with context. The tricky part is that both WB and GB were familiar with the scintillating paradox of the idea of "structure and order", both of which sound acceptable enough to an untrained ear; but if you know Bateson, you will know that the notions of "structure", "order" and "natural world" together equal a massive process made up of smaller processes of communication and relation that occur at multiple levels and through time. In short, "structure and order" as such are only solid at the level of "eternal verities". Since not many of us have figured out what those are – the quest continues.

Eternal verities provide paradoxes too. Because if there are no eternal verities then that is a verity – and if there are eternal verities then they can only really be eternal if they are all about change, complexity, unpredictability, interaction, confusion, distortion, and so on. They seem to require a necessary flexibility in order to hold "truth" from so many perspectives as the world presents. "Structure and order" in Batesonian vernacular are meta-terms. We will get further in our understanding if we think about them like this: the structure of structure, and the order of order. After working with GB and WB's ideas for several years I have become increasing aware of the interrelated vital processes that they refer to as *context*. Sometimes we call that context "the system", or we label it more specifically as a kind of system; the body, language, culture, politics, the university, the forest, the globe.

Co-evolutionary contexts

The "order" and "structure" was a scaffolding of patterns around which other patterns might form and shift. "Evolution," they both said, "is in the context". Organisms learn and develop in an environment that influences their genotypic evolution, as well as somatic evolution. The evolution of one species is inherently tied to that of other species it shares life with. In the century since WB first began his studies of contextual inheritance, science has begun to embrace this multifaceted approach to the study of genetics. The branches of science which first came close to aligning with this holistic search were cybernetics and its subsequently articulated cousin, systems theory. Later developments have reshaped these studies into complexity theory. While there are important differences in these fields there is much that they share in terms of discovering the dynamic processes of how ecological contexts, or living systems, function. In fact I would say that without these additions to science, (cybernetics, systems theory, and complexity theory), our universities and research institutions would have virtually no capacity for studying either the philosophy or the operations of interrelating patterns in life. Collectively, this work has pushed the need for interdisciplinary thinking into the fore, and generated entire schools of thinking around psychotherapy, ecology, information technology, management, personal development and more.

However, the project of defining systems science has been through the gauntlet of trends in academic and pop culture, and it has been dented here and there along the way. It is, I believe, still the best option for preparing for the changes we are facing globally, but I would caution that care is needed now, as the word "system" itself has gathered meanings that are distracting. Before we get lost down the rabbit holes of what has become " cybernetics, systems theory and complexity theory," I would like to address the way in which I am inspired by my ancestry's common thread of attraction to and appreciation of art, toward a new version of contextual research. As I see it, art allows us to perceive from multiple perspectives simultaneously. In order for science to really work with complexity we need art to help inform science on the approach to perceiving. I maintain that although Gregory's work was seminal in the formation of cybernetics, systems theory and complexity, there are departure points that significantly change the tone of his work from that of his colleagues. One such departure point is the way that art and poetry has informed the scientific inquiry that both William and Gregory explored. For Gregory, the process through which art might expand and integrate the many parts of the mind was an explicit element of his thinking. While, for William, his inspirations were kept closer to the chest. Nevertheless, William inspired Gregory with his love of art and appreciation of poetry, especially the art and poetry of William Blake.

In *Steps to An Ecology of Mind*, Gregory addresses the way in which art brings multiple aspects of communication and culture together to integrate the conscious and unconscious sense making of our world. In the chapter, "Style, Grace, and Information in Primitive Art," he courageously assigns art to the task of doing that which science cannot, namely, to pervade our knowledge with what he calls "grace". Gregory opens the chapter with a reference to Aldous Huxley's take on "grace":

> "Aldous Huxley used to say that the central problem for humanity is the quest for grace.... He argued – like Walt Whitman—that the communication and behavior of animals has a naiveté, a simplicity, which man has lost. Man's behavior is corrupted by self-deceit, by purpose and by self-consciousness."
>
> (Gregory Bateson 1972, p.128)

He goes on to say,

> "I shall argue that the problem of grace is fundamentally a problem of integration and that what is to be integrated is the diverse parts of the mind."
>
> (Gregory Bateson 1972, p.129)

It is interesting to notice that Blake, like the Batesons, was captivated by an urge to study the structure and the order of life. The insight Blake had into the systems and interrelatedness of life – especially in the tension between man and nature – was a poignant compass in our household, which has informed my work at every level.

Keeping William's letter in mind, as a plea for his son's pursuit of pure purpose in the scientific search for the order of life, I am reminded of the famous poem of William Blake's, *The Tyger*. Blake asks, "What immortal hand or eye could frame thy fearful symmetry"? The poem seems to me to be a forerunner to the questions that Gregory spent his life asking. What is pattern? Not because there was or is an answer, but because the question brought both rigour and imagination into the inquiry. The noticing, of each aspect of the symmetry and grace of the tiger, is an invitation to another kind of empathy. Who has the right to say how the tiger was made? Who can claim truth over this magnificent collection of ideas, and processes? Blake's poetic portrait of the tiger burns with the impossibility of knowing what made this Tyger, what forged its remarkable integrations of the brain, the feet, and the heart. Then there is the lamb to consider which is of course part of the tiger's set of relationships as well. This is a call to the humility of biology; it is about culture, it is about ecology, it is about psychology, it is about information and communication, it is about behaviour, it is about science in its glory, and its failings. The poem brings in many relationships, those within the tiger, those of the reader's relationship to nature and science, and the double reflexive relationship of both to God.

Framing the Symmetry 197

Science and religion have always flanked the path of knowledge. So, the quest for structure and order requires careful attention. To study the workings of life through inquiry places one on a path in which religion is one side, proclaiming the mystery; and mechanistic application is on the other side, with blueprints. On one side the high priest is ready to save souls and on the other is the eager engineer. Without this tension the field is numb. The contrasting polarities are two ends of the same rope, as they say. Between the two exaggerations are multitudes of great minds, with breaking hearts and good ideas to play with.

Systems thinking on the wire

Framing the structure of life is not for the greedy: neither in religion, nor in science. Rather, the starting place is to find the edges of our epistemological window frame, and play with it. To bring the arts into the process of describing living systems is to embrace a questioning about how we think. When we start to study one aspect of life, the complexity will expand the scope of our vision to include much more. I have seen letters in the Library of Congress where GB is referring to "systems" as early as 1929. He offers a clear definition. The idea of "systems" began to get traction in the 1950s when cybernetics emerged through the Macy Conferences. The Macy Conferences were an important event in the 20th century in which artists, scientists, philosophers, mathematicians and others came together and found a new way to discuss the processes of observation and the patterns in which complex systems are organised. Observations of life! Cybernetics emerged as a new way to bring together the sciences. Though heavily entrenched in the metaphor of the machine, Cybernetics also gave way to new fields of psychology, communication, biology, medicine, and more. Cybernetics brought the much needed insight of interconnectedness, but, we have now arrived at a moment in the development of these ideas where they find themselves face to face with the polarities of our culture.

Back to the window. I am acutely aware when using the world "systems" in this era that it has meanings that tag into a number of trendy furnishings in the popularised culture of both science and spirituality. The lens through which we see "systems theory or cybernetics or complexity... will influence what we do with them. Since our culture has a penchant for mechanism, it will seek mechanistic versions of "systems thinking" And conversely, since our culture seeks to fill the hole that science dug up where religion used to hold its soil in place, un-rigorous forms of systems thinking will provide explanation through mystery. In both cases what is lost is the ability to stretch across the disciplines. The "system sciences" are probably our best chance at adding depth to our understanding of life. And to think that there is such a misplaced mechanistic metaphor positioned in the centre of the field is indeed a challenge to take to heart. In fact, if you Google the word systems, and select "Google images," you will see only a rather bizarre collection of abstract models and diagrams, with boxes and arrows in varying layouts and primary colours. Not a single living thing has been selected by Google to represent the input of "systems." I think that is frightening. I have a bias against those models. I will admit it. I see in them the traps of lineal and causal thinking, the notions of control, and the repeated mechanistic approach to life that is evident in all aspects of our culture. Perhaps as intellectual crutches they are fleetingly useful, but only if they are then thrown away. Why? Because, life does not work that way.

The larger conversation that forms an ecology, includes all of the organisms interacting and learning. My father once said: "Every feather is, as it were, a flag whose shape and coloring denote the values of determining variables at the point and time of its growth." (Bateson 1972, p.383) Understanding how living systems function and learn is not mappable. I will probably get in trouble for saying that. But, the processes are taking place at multiple levels and between multiple parts of a system, and within those parts of systems there are more systems with parts… and all the parts are in communication… and, communication is not the same thing as a script. One example I like to use is this: imagine you are going to a party, and you want to enjoy meeting other people, so in preparation you study, memorise and practice every line of Hamlet, right down to the emotional expressions and body movements. You will find that your contribution to the conversation is out of sync, unintelligible, perhaps absurd, and meaningless. I am a great fan of Hamlet – it is a script, which says important things about life – but living people, living organisms, and living systems do not communicate in scripts. The maps are scripts.

Systems theory is struggling inside a system that doesn't accommodate it

In scientific circles the systems sciences have become a haven for a modelling and explanatory language for how to deal with complex problems. This would be ok, except that the linearity and the mechanistic principles of reductionism in our western cultures have wormed their way into the systems vocabulary. The result is that we get strategic methodologies

Framing the Symmetry

and defined models for fixing isolated issues within complex living interactions that have a living context. To put it more bluntly, the old way, of addressing problems by defining causality and applying predetermined formulised "actions" to "solve" the problem defined, has gotten itself painted into the terms and language of the new systems and complexity disciplines. The vocabulary has changed, but the thinking remains the same. "Recursive" becomes a word that brings to mind a series of boxes connected by arrows and decoupling seems to now refer to a mechanistic split in systems linkages. Something is getting lost. But it seems to get lost in the ether of new age oneness, or it slips down the other side of the cliff into engineering. This is rigour and imagination, yet it is all out of balance and distributed weirdly across our epistemological horizon.

Interconnection

There is a sort of fashionable movement right now toward popularising "systems thinking", made popular with the thrust of ecology celebrities looking for a way to make more palatable the bad news about the ecosystem, and how we can respond to it. It has a crossed into the genre that includes the western misunderstanding of "interconnectedness." You might hear something like the cry for unity in our world and ecosystem in the slogan "we are one with the planet." This has by all accounts a benevolent intent to improve the sickness in thinking that we are NOT one with our planet. It is an improvement, I hope. But it is an improvement that is coming at a high cost. Perhaps, the cost is indeed too high. The concept of "interconnectivity" has become a sloppy way of addressing the vast tangle of interactions in a living system. The very idea of interconnectedness has allowed lazy lines to be drawn between nodes or parts of the whole system. The world may be able to use the terms of systems, but some of the thinking has lost its real value, and become muddled into something more akin to "oneness".

The deepening of our understanding of how the vast variables and interactions in the natural world are functioning will inform our actions, it will inform our ethics, our choices, and our epistemological frame. Take out the vast variables and replace them with oneness, and you lose the differences, the information, the aesthetics of interaction, the evolution, the complexity, the life. Unity is not about oneness. Gregory's concept of "the difference that makes a difference" requires that the relationships inside a system be communications of contrast. The gecko that catches its food by seeing the insect's movement is an example of a pattern of cognition and evolution that exists between species. Yes, they are interconnected. No, they are not in a big oneness. The differences are beautiful, and they matter. In the study of structure and order of life, as WB refers to above, these are the rich co-evolutionary forms that offer insight into all sorts of other systems. In this sense the idea that systems thinking can offer a scientific overtone to a spiritual movement is making a mess of the possibilities that a more rigorous intellectual pursuit of the ideas will deliver. It's a rip off. In fact, the beauty and awe that can be generated by seeing the world as a nest of millions, billions, and trillions of interdependencies interacting with each other across time and geography is profound. But, it is not a profundity that asks for vacant surrender; instead it beckons for study, for art, for active learning.

Uncertainty

Then there is uncertainty. Another curse and blessing brought by the realm of systems and complexity thinkers. Without doubt the tone of our studies becomes poisoned with hubris. This is evident in the application of most scientific discoveries. Whether it be medicine, space travel, or technology, we are too often sure that we have cracked the code of nature and found the answers we need, and that is usually the moment at which we brazenly commit the most destruction. So, uncertainty is healthy. It can change the tone of our approach, make us humble, give a bit of pause, and cool off the arrogance that comes with the "solutions." We cannot know all the millions of relational interactions in our own digestive process, let alone the larger ecology we are disrupting with the genetic modification of our food. We should take that uncertainty seriously. We do not know why two people fall in love or fall out of it – and we should take that seriously too. In this form uncertainty is good.

Uncertainty has also become a sort of island of intellectual excuses for deferring deeper study. The problem with making a place for mystery is that it so easily gets co-opted into an eddy, where ideas go in easy circles instead of lending themselves to the movement of a wider stream. While there is a kind of sweetness and beauty to this deferral, it is also an entry point to binary thinking. There soon exists in that epistemology, two categories, that which we know, and that which we do not. This is a divide that later gains potency and can contaminate our work. Both in terms of what we feel we can understand, which gets a more rigid and possibly arrogant form, and that which we can't, which turns to fluff and blows away in the wind. I would suggest a more modest motivation, which is neither to "completely understand" nor to label as mystery, but to simply deepen our understanding. The deepening is not finding the answer, not looking for a final truth, but becoming increasingly familiar with the many complexities that surround all that we study. We will never understand it completely, but we can continue (endlessly) to increase our comprehension of the variables at play. As William said, "to find out something, even a little bit, of the structure and order of the natural world…".

Integration of many levels

Art and nature share the genius of contextualising multiple levels of relatedness and communication at the same time, and across time. A painting is a study of relationships of colour, of culture, of subject, of framing, of light, of concepts, and of perspective. The meaning that is found in the visual metaphor today will, and can, change in ten minutes – and in a hundred years. The meanings change between people and across cultural references. Likewise, a pond is a study of all the relationships that make it; the water, the algae, the fish, the bacteria, the insects, the birds, the micro-organisms, the leaves on the shore, and the animals that drink and feed from it – now, a hundred years from now, and a hundred years ago. So, where is the art? Where is the pond? They are in the relationships.

In contrast, the planned and strategised cultural mandates of our social norms do not give voice to the multiple threads of information needed to make decisions. Nor does our daily professional vernacular communicate the unseen interruptions that are made in our haste to solve problems. Like the horse with blinders on, or the pointed focus of a camera lens, we have the unspoken agreement that we will not blur the interactions of specific issues. The professional adult tone of respectability and credibility is monotone and singular. It says, "I am not capricious, and won't be fooled by the flim-flam of 'complexity'", I can be objective and level headed about what needs to be done. But subjectivity is gone, purposefully stamped out. Professionalism and authority demand a tone and an approach that is unswayable. Of course, the evidence is in our back pocket, the facts, the statistics, the graphs, and indicators all point to one simple truth, and that is what we will clearly and wilfully state. But is that possible? Is it a cultivated lie? The subjectivity of our perspectives gives depth and information to everything we see. Information is lost in the masking of subjectivity. Interactions are lost.

I am remembering a time when I was asked by the Saybrook Institute, located in San Francisco, to come teach a workshop on complexity. I was thrilled to join their classroom of graduate students who were studying the noble material on complexity, but when I read the sheet that described my contribution, I blanched. It said something like this: Nora Bateson will join us for a workshop in which she will present a feminine perspective on complexity. "What? What is that?" I thought. I have certainly studied my share of feminism, and that was fine. And I have certainly studied my share of complexity, and that was fine... but what in the world is a feminine perspective on complexity?

I arrived at the class, a wonderful group of about thirty bright and eager students, all poised and ready to receive this illumination, and promptly asked them: "Does anyone here have any idea what a feminine perspective on complexity is?" They were unsure for a moment if they had been either sold a faulty teacher, or if there was a trick. Of course, neither was the case. With absolute honesty I found I had to describe my predicament. You see, I am a woman, yes, and I can only speak as a woman. I cannot remove the woman-ness from who I am. But I am also a filmmaker, and I cannot remove that either. I am also a traveller, a daughter, a mother, a friend, a partner, a student, a teacher, an artist, a writer, an American, a resident of Sweden, and I cannot surgically or otherwise remove any of those influences or experiences from who I am at any given moment. I am complex. We all are.

One student pointed out that, with the addition of more versions of herself in her work, she was freed from the obligation of representing a particular cultural or disciplinary perspective. With her newfound subjectivity she could employ a much richer perspective on her work. She could present herself as more than her race, more than her gender, more than her religion and so on. There is no room for racism, or religious discrimination, or professional insult, if we can begin to see each other and our selves as multifaceted in their complexity. Our subjectivity then offers a voice uniquely ours to speak from. The epistemological frame through which I and you, and the rest of the world's population, see the world is a living invocation of all of our experiences and reflections, mixed into memory and learning. The subjectivity of our perspectives is what gives depth and information to everything we see. We can pretend to remove those voices, but we can never do so. They are there in everything we say and do. In the way we listen, in the way we watch, in the way we touch, and receive touch.

Art informs knowledge

Art lets us be subjective without asking us to commit medieval surgery on the vocabulary of our impressions.

Art asks us to meet it with our particular-ness exposed and open.

Art changes. It cannot be pinned down. It is un-located. Unreasoned. Unproven.

Meanings change when we receive them through different lenses. Ask any room of people to describe what a Magritte painting means to them and each person will have a different take. Start back at the beginning and yet another set of meaningful observations will arise. We are allowed to move in art. The ecology of our ideas and epistemological limitations is permitted another sort of oxygen altogether when art is the subject. Art is free to move through culture and time, to reverberate the outlines of a particular moment in history against others that are unmentioned. Art pulls the differences between light, notes, colour, subjects, framings, ideas, emotions, and stories. Art speaks in relationships. It is relationships. And we are in relationship to it and each other. All this relatedness is a mess of entangled shifting impressions and associations. It is, in that sense, alive, much like a pond or a forest. Art is a system of systems, which we enter with our additional systems – our perceptions, our sense, our thoughts and histories, our personal injuries, our educations, our willingness, and maybe our sense of humour. Art is un-located, and it un-locates us. We are not exactly sure where the art is. Is the music in the notes, or the rhythm, or the musicians, or the audience, or the era? Is the painting in the colours, in the artist, in the subject, in the viewer? Is the poem in the words or between them? Is it in the poet's head or is it in ours? Where is the art? It is in the relationships, and in our relationship to it. It is in the subjectivity of the observer, and the subjectivity of the artists, and the very capacity to explore all the levels of information that those realms unleash. Art is unreasoned. It does not apologise. My father, once said, "Poetry is not a sort of distorted and decorated prose, but rather prose is poetry which has been stripped down and pinned to a Procrustean bed of logic." (Bateson 1972, p.136)

You may remember that Procrustes was a Greek god whose job it was make sure people who were entering Athens were fit to be allowed in. He measured their fit-ability by placing them in his iron bed and either trimming or stretching them to fit Athenian requirements. Art does not fit in this Procrustean way. But instead, there is a constant shifting and fitting of a different kind, in the minds and hearts of the both the artists and the audience of art. Each space left free, each metaphor opened, is fitting to those who come in contact. It is there for the subjective perceptions of each individual to form ideas and memories around, to make sense of in their own way. Combined with skill, talent, imagination and a whole collection of other lifelong practices, art digs below the surface of our conscious planning.

But most importantly, in this moment, art can teach us the value of information that does not demand proofs. Art offers a compliment to the realm of science in this capacity. Bravely, Gregory said,

> *"Not only can we not predict into the next instant of the future, but, more profoundly, we cannot predict into the next dimension of the microscopic, the astronomically distant, or the geologically ancient. As a method of perception, – and that is all that science can claim to be – science like all other methods of perception is limited in its ability to collect the outward and visible signs of whatever may be truth. Science probes, it does not prove."*
> (Gregory Bateson 1979, p.27)

We live in a world of evidence. Our cities' infrastructures and our environmental planning, our school curricula and our economic predictions, are all filtered through the funnel of data that compiles mechanisms of "science." Fair enough. We need to KNOW what the new bridge will cost, or how many chemo treatments the patient can withstand; we need to calculate and measure the success of our work. But, it is clear, that we have made some serious miscalculations in the last 100 years. All the proof in the world did not provide the information that we need to see the complexity of the world we live in. We do not understand it. We make decisions that unfold into wild and unforeseen consequences. The proof was not enough. We needed the pattern. Art, does not ask for proof, it directs us to look for pattern.

Strung between the chords of a flamenco song is the empathy of a thousand years of love and pain. In the gestures of a contemporary dancer we can remember all that we have never imagined, and follow the form of the body into an unknown dictionary of emotions. In the strokes of colour on a wall in London, we find the humour and irony of our own mistakes. On a canvas, in a photo, up on the screen we see ourselves seeing the world. We see it, we see us, we take in the cockeyed framing that tilts our heads and rests our status quo on its ear. The poetry is there, un-killable. And, each of the 8 billion of us is an artist, dabbing in rhythms, colours, metaphors, and harmonies into our moments.

While abstract concepts may rollercoaster through us in art we don't understand, the metaphors still enter us, and one day, maybe years into the future they will speak to us. In the gruesomeness of art we find we are vulnerable, and that we bleed. I have a small poster of Picasso's "Woman Weeping" on my dresser to remind me that to be a student of LIFE is to be willing to be shattered. The darkness in art gives us a visceral experience of being dug up, emptied of the seeds of trust, and carved into the anger or jealousy that has overtaken us. There are things to be angry about in life, and art lets us explore the community of that experience. Through the breaking, tingling, crackling, smoothing, and opening we are in art, with unnamed resonances coursing through us. We are pulled from our illusion that we can watch life from our safe place at the window. We are participants in the process.

In all forms, art can offer an experience of integration that calls upon our cultural language of symbols, our imagination, our history, our intellect and our emotions. While we often portray the importance of "creative expression", it is perhaps more vital at this moment in our history to explore what art offers toward the possibility that our perception itself can be brought into larger circuits of cognition through metaphor. Appreciation of a piece of art can be seen as recognition of the pattern that connects. As I see it, art allows us to perceive from multiple perspectives simultaneously. In order for science to really work with complexity, we need art to help inform scientists toward a more developed ability for perceiving context, that includes all the disciplines, emotions, cultural symbols, and personal memories.

> "A tear is an intellectual thing."
>
> (William Blake)

References

Bateson, Gregory (1972). *Steps to an Ecology of Mind: Collected Essays in Anthropology, Psychiatry, Evolution, and Epistemology.* New York: Ballantine Books.

Bateson, Gregory (1979). *Mind and Nature.* Cresskill, NJ: Hampton Press.

Blake, William (1985 [1794]). The Tyger. In Notebook after *Blake Complete Writings*, Ed. Geoffrey Keynes. Oxford: Oxford University Press.

Forsdyke, Donald R & Cock, Alan G. (2008). *Treasure Your Exceptions: The Science and Life of William Bateson.* New York: Springer Press.

Transformative Conversations II

Community Work and Psychotherapy as Two Sides of the Same Cooperative Practice

13

Umberta Telfener

There are these two young fish swimming along and they happen to meet an older fish swimming the other way, who nods at them and says "Morning, boys. How's the water?" And the two young fish swim on for a bit, and then eventually one of them looks over at the other and goes "What the hell is water?"

David Foster Wallace, 2009

I believe that systemic thinking and practice still have much to teach us and continue to be very useful frames within which to include narratives and dialogical dimensions. As a teacher in the tradition of the Milan school I continue to think that the systemic model is the most interesting when dealing with complexity, whatever the context. Respecting complexity is a necessity but it is not always easy to do. This is true for at least three main reasons: (i) all the problems we deal with involve many different professionals but they are not always connected in a network nor do they share a common hypothesis; (ii) institutions answer complex issues in a "simple" linear way; (iii) professionals tend to work by linearly summing up interventions (1 + 1 + 1) rather than by organising a coherent inclusive proposal that considers the "problem determined system" as a shared management of narratives (Anderson & Goolishian 1988).

Until the 1990s, professional were hired by institutions, and they could at that point expect to follow their career paths and stay there until retirement. Nowadays, psychologists and psychiatrists, nurses, social workers, pedagogues and doctors set themselves up as self-employed teams and organise joint practices; they work as consultants on different projects for different institutions. They propose interventions which change over time, following deadlines based on the mandate. They must be prepared to change plans and strategies, to design proposals in accordance with the ever-changing needs of the context (an institution, a mental health clinic, an organisation, a hospital). They are confronted with constantly mutating demands that oblige them to operate in a highly focused way. This can also become a source of anxiety. In fact the current financial crisis and lack of funding has forced us to offer more focused practices. At this point in time, mental care professionals need to operate like lasers, proposing interventions sustained by good strategies, clear thinking and a good rapport between costs and benefits.

In this chapter, I intend to state very strongly that the systemic model constitutes one of the most useful frames both for the interpretations of the problems and for possible solutions. I will explain that systemic interventions in larger contexts and psychotherapy imply similar transversal operations in both public institutions and private practice. In both community work and psychotherapy, relationships become units of observation that include multiple social groups.

I strongly believe that psychotherapy (the second order narrative process which implies reflection on the part of the practitioner) is one of the many possibilities within a systemic frame and that too often we limit our opportunities to just this option, constricting ourselves and withdrawing in the four walls of our office.

Interventions in the mental health field start always with a reading of the context, followed by the necessity of defining what we are called in for (by whom, when and to do what) in order to organise the most coherent way to intervene, to choose a path (Telfener 2011). We have the choice of following a "first stage modality" – community work – where we operate with a group of people and their problems, involving the entire staff of the institution. In this case we allow the institution to become the holder of the healing process, where professionals can also rotate without creating a fracture in the evolving care. We can also intervene in a "second stage modality" – psychotherapy – which implies a specialised intervention, a contract, at least one referring agent and one or more clients who look for help. Naturally we need to distinguish these two types of intervention and to clarify for ourselves and for our clients our intentions: how we act is a result of our decisions as to what to do in each context.

In both cases – whether a community intervention or a psychotherapy setting – we analyse the context, its needs and resources; we bring forth relational aspects; we hypothesise a possible path and reflect on the ongoing process. For our work to be effective, we need: (i) to operate at our best in an emotional dialogue with the others; (ii) to share a common co-responsibility; (iii) to imagine a future.

I have learned through my supervising practice that institutions can become the best context for professionals to learn cooperative practice. In our work we can all "naturally" become educated to contexts – as Bateson

Community Work and Psychotherapy

would say – if we take the chance to reflect collectively and individually on what we do, on the lens we use to produce transformative actions.

Organising a reflexive process

Within the frame of second-order cybernetics and constructionism, we are given back the freedom to define each happening together with others and to consider any ensuing problematic event. Confronted with a problem, whoever has brought it to our attention, forces us to: (i) analyse the referral (who called us in), differentiating the commissioner from the clients and from the referring agent; (ii) analyse the expectations and re-define them; (iii) respond according to the mandate; (iv) engage without accepting the proxy (institutions and individuals very frequently like to give others responsibility for their problems and tend to delegate possible solutions to professionals); (v) build an intervention following the request received; (vi) start co-creating possibilities for narratives to emerge.

To assume a reflexive positioning (Bateson 1972) means to do all the above actions while reflecting on the lens used, on what has been accomplished and on what has emerged. In order to maintain one's perturbative attitude, professionals are invited to question themselves. In this, they need to reflect on which operations made the reality they are dealing with emerge. This reflexive stance allows them to favour curiosity, sharing and resilience.

The ability to reflect on one's own premises and actions is fundamental. This is because the interventions we carry out are not objective procedures but emerge from the dance between ourselves and others. The dialogue and the actions we then take, need also to become the object of our observation. I am referring to a recursive second-order systemic/cybernetic process that produces a world of meanings. Information does not arise from an outside "reality" but results from the shared "dance" and from the process that emerges from the therapeutic system just formed. It springs from assembling the professional and the insider knowledge in an imbricated, meaningful plot.

Shared actions, coherent to many settings

Working in different contexts is very stimulating, but at the same time it implies a great responsibility. I will describe in this section some actions that are needed in both the psychotherapy setting as well when intervening in community work in larger contexts. All professionals' outcomes emerge from the dance which includes all those working on any situation – even those we would prefer to discard because they appear peripheral but which in my experience must be taken into consideration. Interventions are a dance where everyone participates with their own premises, experiences, beliefs and emotions. It is the collaboration of heads/hearts/ human becomings (Buber 1923) who act together on living material, endlessly rewritten and transformed. What the professional tries to understand does not exist before the encounter and emerges from the common involvement. The characteristics of the therapeutic process come to life within the common story and are not foreseen in advance. It involves the experiences, ideas, actions and emotions of all the participants.

I will organise my thoughts around the description of two different requests I received. One from Paul whose family called me in for therapy at my office in Rome; the other came from the mayor of a small island who wanted to organise an intervention to get citizens to participate more actively in the public sphere. I decided to discuss the two different narratives together here in order to show very clearly how even two different contexts involve the same pragmatic moves from the professional.

> **Paul** *is a 30 year old young man who lives with his father, mother and his dog. At the age of 20 he had a very severe manic episode and was hospitalised and put on heavy medication for the "rest of his life". They went through family therapy years ago; at the outset of my intervention, Paul's father was not very supportive of psychotherapy while his mother was eager to "give it a try". I saw the three of them for two sessions during which they expressed their negative and hopeless feelings about the whole situation. Their main focus was Paul and his symptoms. We came to an agreement to try and negotiate a reduction in Paul's medication and decided that Paul would see me individually, as I felt I could have more leverage with him alone.*

> **The small island of V.** *has approximately 700 inhabitants. It has always been a tourist attraction with a very different quality of life in summer and in winter, when many citizens leave for the mainland until the island comes to life again in the spring. The mayor was concerned because the population remaining on the island withdraws into themselves and there is a lot of alcohol and drug abuse. Advised by the director of health from his Region, he called me in my capacity as adjunct professor of a post graduate course in health psychology at the University of Roma where I work with a team of psychologists in training.*

Analysing the client's expectations and the request for help

In order to create a new therapeutic system, it becomes necessary to create a bond between the professional/s and the new system and to decide how to intervene. In order to organise the intervention, it becomes necessary to create this connecting pattern (Ugazio 1989), to create an observing system (von Foerster 1990). The analysis of the client's request for help (who calls, who is informed, what are the dynamics of the request and the referral, what have they tried previously, why are they calling now, what are the resources they can employ, what are their motivations, who wants to come and who does not) becomes an intervention in its own right. It is a useful way to analyse expectations, to investigate the complexity of explicit and implicit demands that are brought to the professional, and to connect the people who before did not know each other. It implies the co-construction of a pluralistic collaboration, based on the request itself and on the negotiation that follows. I strongly believe in shared work and constantly see the advantages of more minds reflecting together, creating a cybernetic brain which allows complexity to survive and perturbation to happen. Analysis of the request for me implies in itself a reflexive collaborative stance.

We can never work without an explicit request, as it provides the professional with clues about the various interactive aspects: the pattern formed by the problem, desires and expectations concerning the future. We always have to be aware that the request for help will emerge from the negotiation processes that leads to the construction of a shared frame. I consider it an essential start. In constructing a shared narrative, each participant will enhance certain specific information, stress some aspects, underline and extract others; they will make hypotheses and form opinions. They will attribute roles and values to actions, relationships and meaningful people, including themselves. Each participant will fashion his or her own interpretation of the therapeutic system that has just been formed. What does it mean for a professional to take into account such differences? It means being able to consider plurality as a resource, a cultural enrichment and not – from a dichotomous viewpoint – an obstacle. It means accepting the inevitable presence of more than one culture, that meanings and beliefs are constantly evolving, and that they are far from being a static and coherent homogenous image.

> ***In Paul's situation*** *I carried out this analysis of the request twice, the first with the family as a whole when I saw them in the*

first session, the second time with Paul alone. Here are some of the questions I began to ask of myself and them: Why had the family decided to come now, after 10 years of heavy medication? What had they tried in the meantime? How did they explain what had happened and what was their current emotional state? What were their expectations for the future? My questions in relation to Paul were as follows: what were reasonable hopes for his daily life, what were his interests and passions? What was Paul ready to give up of his life and what was absolutely untouchable?

In a specific encounter that took place before accepting and signing the contract, in **the situation of the island** *I analysed the request for help issued by the mayor and his staff. What were their expectations and fantasies about the possible outcome? What did they want to obtain; why now and why us, were some of my main curiosities? What kind of processes did they imagine building with the citizens, how had they tried before to obtain their goals? What resources could they put in and what did they think the participants would oppose and propose? After three encounters with the major and his staff, we decided to go and interview the inhabitants and check into the possibility of a shared encounter in the near future. We explored how the inhabitants were describing life on the island in winter, what their needs and their complaints were, how they could participate in a better life. Bars and squares become the informal meeting points for these conversations on the island, in a friendly mode. We then had to make sure that people were committed and would come to the meeting; we did this by involving key personalities of the island.*

Choosing a positioning

The role I occupy determines my position within the system and what will emerge from the shared dialogue. The positioning (Campbell & Groenbaek 2006) we assume in front of the other is not given in advance and declared once and for all. Our positioning determines our leeway, the creativity and the possibility to explore options instead of repeating the same moves. The information we obtain depends on the role we share in the "new" system, on our relationship with our colleagues, on the freedom to move in and out of discourses. Clients can then become our favourite colleagues, the most authoritative people to ask about the topics they desire to deal with. To pick a respectful and equal stance means to collaborate as two scientists who work on a common project. Also clients take a position and similarly assign us one and together we both need to adapt in order to enhance collaborative possibilities. To begin with, we are equal but asymmetrical since we have different responsibilities: we are social agents and are "paid" to bring about change, they are responsible for their family context and the interactions shared in their lives.

Deciding how to act with a group member who becomes irreverent or a client who leaves the room abruptly during a session is part of positioning, as is the choice of the fee and of setting policies. There are no universal rules, every set-up calls for specific decisions that are related to what is occurring. No actions we take are neutral and free of meaning. Everything is part of a process, even when we think we are acting instinctively.

> ***In the individual setting***: *my positioning was authoritative as I had been called in by Paul's psychiatrist who probably could see no future with this family. He had told them I was their "last chance" and that I was very effective with "desperate cases". He then had sent me Paul and his family without any pharmacological reduction and I needed to analyse the psychiatrist's request and negotiate a drug reduction, which he was very reluctant to grant me. I needed to "fight" for my position, to be able to make decisions and not just "obey" the referring psychiatrist. I needed to check his expectations and verify whether he could support my plan as it unfolded. Should he fail to support my position, I would not have been able to take on the family as the medication was keeping Paul in a "dormative" state.*

> ***The community setting***: *In the encounter in the main piazza, I needed to negotiate our engagement and mutual relationship. We decided that the University team would act as their consultant with a privileged stance, since we could observe from an external position. We agreed on some rules for our time together. We decided that we would use an informal stance ("tu" in Italian) and that we would create an experimental setting where we could all brainstorm without judging. We started again with questions: what did they think were the aims in organising this encounter, what did they want to obtain? How could we know that the meeting had been useful, behaviourally and emotionally what should have happened?*

Looking for the coherence between the problem and the system

In systemic practice we are mostly interested in the multiple reasons as to why a particular story has emerged and we search for the adaptive meaning of what is happening. It is useful to question what keeps people where they are together with which presuppositions and relationships enhance the problems we face. It is also important to understand what the meaning is of the presented problem and its "aim" in the history of the observed system. In our work we need to help others overcome their usual script, in order to consider a broader design that includes more generations, many narratives, multiple descriptions and the possibility of making the future present. In order to live a better "here and now" we need to hypothesise possible adaptive meanings for what is happening. We can do this by reflecting on and questioning around the presentation. For example, we can wonder, in what ways can we describe the presented story as adaptive? What has it allowed to happen? What explanations are there for its duration? To look for this coherence in possible patterns means also that we can distance ourselves from a judgmental attitude, refusing to believe in what is right or wrong and trying to break the usual pattern by which we continue doing something because we have already done it before. It is the projection into the future that allows us to describe what is happening here and now: what is keeping the problem stable; which premises and behaviours prevent change. Is the symptom a useful response to a previous problem, an answer that now has become the trouble or problem?

> **Paul and his family**: *I asked myself which was the adaptive meaning of Paul's problem and how it had been useful both to him and to his family. Since his mother had left his father when Paul was 10, we reflected on the possibility that Paul's hospitalisation has brought them back together again. We hypothesised that he could think he needed to continue being "sick" in order for them to want to be together. His brothers received more benefits than he (an apartment, expenses paid by the father), could it be that Paul need to act "crazy" in order not to be totally forgotten? Since he had lost a lot of time being "sick", there could be someone who thought it was too late to start a new life: who though that way, we asked ourselves. I questioned my own premises, if I was able to consider a future for him and how not to become a participant in the failure of this delicate process.*

> **The island**: *I questioned the island inhabitants, myself and my students regarding the connection between the narratives they presented about their lifestyles and the organisational life of the island's government. We reflected on the possibility that their habits seemed unchangeable because they matched their shared premises that "who remained on the island in winter was a failed person". We speculated on the future and on how these premises should*

Community Work and Psychotherapy

change in order to introduce the desired frames of mind and consequent new actions towards a more dynamic style of life.

Looking for resources

"Competency is within people", says Eia Asen (2001), "and our task is that of creating contexts where it becomes possible to enable competency to emerge." This statement implies the need to look for and use available resources within systems, both in the open social setting and in the therapeutic room. We need to pay attention to situational strengths. In order to do this, it is useful to become aware of the potentials of both the individual and of the system, not expecting them to be strong and optimistic at all costs, but rather accepting both their shortcomings and their aptitudes. The Milan School is famous for the faith it has in the capacities of its clients, and in general in the human becomings to adapt and constantly evolve (Boscolo & Cecchin 1982). We also need to have trust in the perturbing capacities of the just formed therapeutic system, in the evolution of the dialogical narratives and in the possibility of using the relationship as a primary tool in our work. If we relate to the others as subjects, we will be able to enter together into the relationship as subjects; this will allow all of us to grasp the emerging qualities of the people involved, including ourselves.

The professionals' attention to resources coupled with the narratives that emerge from all the people actively involved (individual/family, other workers in the larger context) together form a morphogenetic field (Sheldrake 1995) with shared memories and a common evolutive attitude. Mutual trust can thus be actively constructed and will show its advantages.

> **Paul**: *Paul is a handsome young man, although he is overweight due to the medication and no exercise. We wondered together where his interests lay, if he could give up sleeping late and sitting in front of the TV, only hoping for the day to pass. I asked him if he could commit to one movie per week that I would discuss with him; whether once he was off medication he might be eager to start a course. I noted his fine sense of humour and tried to play with it.*

> **On the island**: *interesting people attended the meeting in the main piazza. From the discussion it emerged that there were exciting activities to be organised in winter: kite building and flying, cultivating lentils, upgrading the vineyards, preparing for the summer. A writer living on the island all year round proposed*

shared readings once a week, a restaurant owner planned some cooking classes, the priest said he would open the sacristy in the afternoons...

Investing in the future

The systemic model assumes that each system can know and act only within the constraints put forward by the specific organisation by which it is ruled. It may change only in the manner in which it is organised. This aspect emphasises the autonomy of systems. Individuals, families and larger systems, may be considered as non-trivial machines that function in an unpredictable way (von Foerster 1990). This stance precludes the ability to anticipate which specific solutions the system will find, since it will find them in an autonomous unforeseen manner.

To organise interventions doesn't mean knowing where to go step by step, or having a prejudged and specific idea of how the situation should evolve. To imagine a future means establishing oneself as a constant: we need to acquire a certain "weight" so that we are not pulled to where the system is, so that we are not "bought" by its premises. In order to maintain a perturbative force, it is important that we have an evolutive idea of the whole therapeutic system we have just formed with our clients, and that potentially we can imagine its evolution. Together we need to visualise virtuous circles that emerge from the dance we dance together, as it will be clear in the situations you are following. Even singularly, professionals tend to lose their efficiency within an organisation where there is no future planning and where there is no felt need to imagine how the system might proceed.

> ***Paul***: *in order to imagine Paul's way forward I needed to cast myself into the future. I had no plans for him, except to imagine a more dynamic life: he could start with an activity, then become more autonomous, find a job, travel. The day his father called me at dawn shouting that Paul was a "bloody psychotic out of control" I scheduled a session for the family group and before they came I told myself not to fall into this "trap". I did so, remembering all the qualities Paul had, the construction we had built together and our common evolving plan for his life.*
>
> ***The island***: *at the end of the meeting we set together few clear goals: to enhance the collaboration among those who remained on the island and to create new stimulating plans that might even bring some tourists in winter. I would help them to enhance their planning*

Community Work and Psychotherapy

and to maintain their energy levels in order to achieve their goals. Together we initiated virtual circles reinforcing their sense of pride.

Beware unintended outcomes

Successes and failures do not depend unilaterally on the client or the professional but emerge from the history of their reciprocal encounter. Good results are not guaranteed by theories or techniques nor by their correct application. The dance may be smooth or may create unintended outcomes (McAdam & Lang 2009). The risk is not due to the gravity of the situation itself, but rather to how processes are dealt with. Unintended outcomes can even emerge from an intervention that has been well coordinated and carried out by the people involved.

What are the possible negative unintended outcomes? I am not speaking about mistakes, since within a cybernetic framework, these are signals that can help clinicians to correct their path and are usually within a behavioural domain. Whereas, unintended outcomes emerge in those circumstances where we are not aware that we do not see, where the discourse is too close to us, too delicate, sensitive, taboo or emotional. They are useless and harmful interventions, at times iatrogenic (Anderson 1990; Bianciardi & Telfener 1995). Over the years in my practice I have encountered various such outcomes: (i) *Resonance* (Elkaim 2008) is often inevitable and occurs when the clinician becomes blind to certain themes and processes. (ii) *Normative interventions* reduce complexity, tend to normalise, to respond to the request as it was made, without redefining it. (iii) *Collusion* (Laing 1972) connects the clinician too closely to the clients, "buying" into their rules/premises and therefore contributing in maintaining the status quo. It places clinicians in the position of "doctor homeostat" (Hoffman 1985). (iv) *Chronicity* involves re-enforcing the pathology and being organised by it. In chronicity we reify the problem and its severity by creating an invisible bond between all the professionals involved, all sharing the belief that there is no solution. All the above traps are overcome by team work, super-vision and shared reflexion.

> *Thinking about unintended outcomes we might ask ourselves if a client needs to double the number of sessions when s/he gets worse. Should the intervention in the island be abandoned because the Mayor becomes discouraged? How often do we passively accept the decisions of others (clients, customers, politicians) answering with "obedience". To those reporting a worsening of their condition after a session, Gianfranco Cecchin would propose a longer lapse between sessions. "If someone feels worse after a session, it could mean that*

the encounters are too perturbative and we need to increase the lapse between sessions," he would teach us. The relational meaning of this move is quite clear: avoid slipping into the logic of pathology; continue to have faith in the client and his/her capacity to cope with even greater anxiety; do not allow symptoms to blackmail us.

Conclusions

I would like to end my reasoning by referring to the attitude of the professional in bringing forth the desired work. It is necessary that we perform network connections also when we are alone in our psychotherapy room; that we propose an attitude of respect, which means equity and equality. Over time, I have learned that people who work together share a common dignity; I learned to share concrete and interesting narratives with my clients who were the experts on their lives, whilst we professionals are the experts in change processes. Further, I learned that working in a team becomes a guarantee for respecting complexity, an antidote to the risk of both oversimplifying and of becoming homeostatic.

The ethical stance we need to assume finds expression in responsibility, which is mandatorily built with all the others involved. Clinical interventions emerge from a shared reality, within a collaborative, co-responsible and dialogical context. Responsibility implies interventions that either favour or hinder the construction of shared meanings. The professional's responsibility is not to take charge of knowing in a foreseen way and of acting according to predefined protocols of action. Responsibility implies assuming onus for ones' attitude and for ones' choices, in a constant becoming. Thus, we may speak of responsibility of our responsibility as the awareness of acting in the domains of aesthetics, explanations and production (Maturana 1988) for which we have already assumed responsibility. This is a second order operation that brings about a second order accountability: the modalities by which we mean our professional responsibility plus the co-responsibility which we share with all the people who work with us, clients included.

References

Andersson, Mia (1990). Paper presented at the First World Conference of Family Therapy, Dublin, Ireland.
Anderson, Harlene & Goolishian, Harold. A. (1988). Human Systems as Linguistic Systems. *Family Process*, 27, 371–394.
Asen, Eia (2001). *Multiple Family Therapy*. London: Karnac.

Bateson, Gregory (1972). *Steps to an Ecology of Mind: Collected Essays in Anthropology, Psychiatry, Evolution, and Epistemology.* New York: Ballantine Books.
Bianciardi, Marco & Telfener, Umberta (1995). *Ammalarsi di psicoterapia.* Milano: Franco Angeli.
Bianciardi, Marco & Telfener, Umberta (2014). *La psicoterapia come pratica ricorsiva.* Torino: Bollati Boringhieri.
Boscolo, Luigi & Cecchin, Gianfranco (1982). Training in Systemic Therapy at the Milan Center. In *Family Therapy Supervision: Recent Developments in Practice.* London: Academy Press.
Buber, Martin (1937 [1923]). *I and Thou.* New York: Charles Scribner's Sons.
Campbell, David & Groenbaek, Marianne (2006). *Taking Positions in the Organization.* London: Karnac Books.
Cecchin, Gianfranco; Lane, Gary & Ray, Wendel, A. (1992). *Irreverence: A Strategy for Therapists' Survival.* London: Karnac Books.
Cecchin, Gianfranco; Lane, Gary & Ray, Wendel, A. (1994). *The Cybernetics of Prejudices in the Practice of Psychotherapy.* London: Karnac Books.
Elkaim, Mony (2008). Resonance in Supervision and Training. *Human Systems, Journal of Systemic Consultation and Management,* 19, 1–3, 16–25.
Foerster, Heinz (Von) (1990). "Ethics and Second Order Cybernetics", International Conference Systems & Family Therapy, Ethics, Epistemology, New Methods. Paris 4–6 October, 1990.
Foster Wallace, David (2009). *This is Water: Some Thoughts, Delivered on a Significant Occasion, About Living a Compassionate Life.* New York: Little Brown.
Hoffman, Lynn (1985). Beyond Power and Control. *Family Systems Medicine,* 3, 381–396.
Laing, Ronald (1971). *The Politics of the Family.* New York: McGraw Hill.
Maturana, Humberto (1988). The Biological Foundation of Self Consciousness and the Physical Domain of Existence. *Conference Workbook: Texts in Cybernetics.* American Society For Cybernetics Conference, Felton, CA. 18–23 October, 1988.
McAdam, Elspeth & Lang, Peter (2009). *Appreciative Work in Schools. Generating Future Communities.* West Sussex: Kingsham Press.
Sheldrake, Rupert (1995). *Seven Experiments that Could Change the World.* Rochester, VT: Park Street Press.
Spencer-Brown, George (1969). *Laws of Form.* London: Allen & Unwin.
Telfener, Umberta (2011). *Apprendere i contesti.* Milano: Cortina Editore.
Telfener, Umberta & Casadio, Luca (Eds.) (2003). *Sistemica. Voci e percorsi nella complessità.* Torino: Bollati Boringhieri.
Ugazio, Valeria (1998). *Semantic Polarities and Psychopathologies in The Family: Permitted and Forbidden Stories.* London: Routledge.

14 The Aesthetics of Interruption:
Points of entry in systemic therapy

Ged Smith

"Once upon a time, New York City had a sixth borough."
"What's a borough?"
"That's what I call an interruption."
"I know, but the story won't make any sense to me if I don't know what a borough is."

Jonathan Safran Foer 2005, p.217

As a systemic practitioner and family therapist I am constantly balancing the tension between attempting to facilitate sessions collaboratively and being mindful of my own power on the one hand, while being somewhat directive and having my own agenda on the other. I value the importance of listening and providing the core conditions of warmth, transparency and authenticity. However, a regular feature of my work involves interrupting people, in several different meanings of this word as I will make clear. And yet, an important part of my role as therapist is to facilitate polyphonic communications – and do it well! A paradox is that interrupting is a necessity in family therapy in order to enable space for other people's contributions. We stop some voices in order to hear other voices; we interrupt in order to prevent interruptions. An interruption is often understood as a violation of speaking rights but in family therapy terms an interruption can be made to protect others' speaking rights. This paradox can be tackled collaboratively, even with advance notice and agreement.

Mother:	Ok, well, we're all here now, and it's important we all speak without being interrupted.
Ged:	Yes, let's try to do that, but I can't promise not to interrupt…
Mother:	What do you mean?
Ged:	Well, in family therapy often the conversations can become quite heated and people have a lot to say, which is very important. But I find that I have to interrupt sometimes so that no single person dominates, and so that everyone has a chance to be heard.
Mother:	Ok, that sounds good actually.

The Aesthetics of Interruption

This example shows an enhancement of the speech flow or chain (Bakhtin 1986) referred to by linguists, and enhances the important therapeutic concept of attunement. We speak in anticipation of the other's response, and our words are co-shaped within conversations so that we achieve shared understandings and coherency. This can be embodied and thus felt within family members just as it is within us as we facilitate sessions. As therapists we listen in order to understand not in order to reply, and so if our replies are slower then so be it, as long as we have a better understanding. This active listening may also act as modelling for families. It may also be that we have to be more active in our interrupting than we wish to be but some family members need to understand what we are doing rather than us constantly preventing their contributions:

> *Ged: I'm sorry Julie, I know I keep interrupting you but it's really important that I hear from the others on this important matter. How would it be if I ask you to just listen for about five minutes and then I promise I'll come back to you and I'd be really interested to hear what you think?*

Seikkula said "We must become aware of what is occurring within us before we give words to it." (Seikkula 2011). I would like to enhance this idea, also spoken of by Tom Andersen, (1995) another "embodying therapist" who stresses the importance of being aware of bodily as well as emotional reactions. *Mouthfeel* is a concept well known amongst wine connoisseurs whereby you know a good wine by the feeling you have in your mouth as you experience it. I propose "mouthfeel" as a concept for psychotherapy where you know a helpful comment or question as it is formed in your mouth, about to make its entry into the room. Of course language is formed in your head not your mouth, and develops with co-conversationalists, but I know that when I pause and deliberate, when I shape an idea in my mind, it can be located in my mouth as I shape my tongue around the sound I might start with, ranging from M to O to L, all of which make my mouth do different things. The mouthfeel changes and can struggle to find comfort. This happens relationally, again according to co-conversationalists who can help with the (dis) comfort.

Ged: I notice when you talk it's like erm, like you erm, like you slur your words. Do you know what I mean?

Jane: Slur? What do you mean? No, that makes me sound drunk!

Ged:	No sorry, it's not slur, it's erm......I don't know the word, it's like you talk slow and sometimes not quite clear. And I don't know what to make of it. It's erm...
Jane:	Dampened? Like my words are dampened?
Ged:	Yes, that's it. I knew slur was the wrong word but I couldn't think of a better way to....yes it's dampened. That's much better.

This was me achieving a better mouthfeel with Jane's help. She was taking 60 painkiller tablets a day and recognised her dampened speech, but not slurred speech which she did not like the idea of. We roll ideas around to see how they fit and hope they will become "internally persuasive" (Bakhtin 1981). It may also follow that we would be moved to question a context which prescribes 60 painkillers a day to a person, part of the effects of which can be to deform the process of languaging, as well as deforming the body in creating further patterns of disease within the whole body.

Language in therapy can be co-constructed and is all the better for it. It is also collaborative practice in action. We can search and think out loud and this struggle can be helpful in the therapeutic process by demystifying, equalising, and inviting mutual engagement. When we have a good therapeutic alliance with people we can do this with more ease, and be more open to taking risks, knowing that mistakes will more likely be understood in this way rather than diminishing the work we are embarked on together. I have written about this elsewhere (Smith 2011a) and continue to be intrigued with language, risks and relationships in therapy and supervision. In this chapter I write about these concepts, and the processes of talking with people who seek our help in an attempt to move forward with these ideas and continue our explorations in communication; always travelling, never arriving. As a therapist I believe that I have licence to ask questions and explore personal areas which in any other context would be unacceptable. We must however be aware of how this is a socially constructed position and as such can be contested so that what constitutes a "therapeutic conversation" is always open to challenge.

Silence

To a large extent language is all we have, notwithstanding the myriad non-verbal encounters present in therapy, most of which we ignore or are not aware of. We privilege language so much that we call what we do *the talking therapies*. We also regard silence as a problem, and something

The Aesthetics of Interruption

to be overcome. Silence is often viewed as problematic, especially in a talking milieu, and it can be seen negatively or mistaken for passivity or an absence of something. Whatever silence is however, it is not nothing. Silence can be eloquent or dignified, and it can be precisely the right response in some circumstances. The problem with silence is usually for others, not for the keeper of silence. The famous dictum that we cannot not communicate (variously attributed to Bateson or Watzlawick) applies very strongly to silence. Jack Bilmes however expresses this more forcefully for our purposes: "Where the rule is "Speak", not speaking is communicative." (Bilmes 1994). Playwright Samuel Beckett portrays the deeper meanings of silence in several of his plays, but perhaps Israeli poet Avi Geffen (2013) expresses the idea most powerfully with his line "My silence is my scream." Silence is much written about in individual therapy but less so in family therapy where it is more likely to be children who prefer not to speak, and for these instances again we have to balance respect for the individual with encouragement to verbalise in ways that we hope will be of benefit for them once they have found their voice or overcome resistance, fear, mistrust, or whatever it is that feeds the reluctance to speak. Unlike the police, we do not declare that people have the right to remain silent, but therapists must not adopt the belief of the Roman Senate; *qui tacet consentire videtur* – he who keeps silent is presumed to consent. Inviting younger children to play whilst listening and to join in or comment if they wish to enables a way forward I have found useful. Asking circular questions (Selvini Palazolli et al 1980) of others where older children's silence is being considered can also help, while returning to the keeper of silence to remind them that they can agree or disagree at any time, or they can choose to remain silent. This also raises the philosophical question of whether it is possible to interrupt silence.

In Herman Melville's 1853 short story "Bartleby the Scrivener", the eponymous Bartleby is a character employed at the narrator's law firm and after a brief period of good work eventually refuses to do anything, or respond to requests in any way other than by saying "I would prefer not to." This causes great consternation to his employer and colleagues, some of whom want to beat him up, but he is allowed to stay despite constantly refusing to do anything. He persists in replying politely and consistently with "I would prefer not to", and occasionally in response to questions about his behaviour with "I would prefer not to answer". Characters in the story question Bartleby's mental health and the boss considers his options but for his own reasons keeps him on despite him doing no work at all, constantly preferring not to. Most critics have analysed Bartleby and what his stance might mean, raising philosophical questions of determinism and free will. The story also raises systemic interest for us however, about the boss's reactions, and we may view him as generous, sympathetic, naïve, timid, caring, conflict-avoidant, or any number of possible interpretations. It also points to communication, and while Bartleby is not silent, his repeated responses might be seen as a near-equivalent to it. In family therapy we often meet with people who do not want to be there, especially children, and while I have never met with a Bartleby-like response (which would be very disconcerting), most of us will have met with people who would prefer not to engage, answer, or even be there. Sometimes we meet with silence, and while family members usually do their best to encourage engagement or responses we will often be more interested in the process of persuasion. Silence has a bad name in the history of human communication. It is something to be "broken", often to help us feel more comfortable or help us know what is going on with other people as the "not-knowing" can be intolerable.

Knowing, not-knowing and interrupting expectations

"Not-knowing" (Anderson and Goolishian 1992) is a popular approach in contemporary family therapy, which could be defined as not assuming to know in advance, despite the familiarity of the presenting problem. Recently, I had occasion to take the experience of not-knowing to new lengths in a case which involved silence, interruption, second-order cybernetics, and issues of power and expertise.

Hannah and Jason (not their real names) brought their 13 year old daughter Aimee to family therapy because she was having sex with her 14 year old boyfriend and they wanted her to stop having sex with him. Jason was particularly incensed by this. He was refusing to allow the boyfriend near the house and was constantly angry with Aimee. Hannah took a more diplomatic and understanding approach. She worked hard to prevent Jason from permanently grounding Aimee and, instead, was hoping to communicate with Aimee's boyfriend to resolve matters but this had not happened as Hannah was being prevented from doing so by her husband. The parents had involved Social Services and the police to no avail. The family was at a total impasse when they came to us. After telling us the background to what had been happening, they sat quietly as if they felt they had handed matters over to us and were saying, "Tell us what to do!" I had no idea what to do and explained that I understood their difficulties, and could imagine feeling similarly if my daughter had been in this position. Diplomatically, but honestly, I explained how I would probably feel much like Jason does, but also agreed with some of what Hannah does. I also tried to imagine what Aimee was feeling listening to all of this. She remained silent throughout. I spoke of the power of young love, even invoking the story of the similarly aged Romeo and Juliet. But in the end, I did not know what to do and that is all I could say. When the reflecting team came in they gave a similar message. To my surprise, the parents found this very helpful, commenting that it was good to hear professionals did not have the answers and were equally perplexed. They had been fearing that there was an obvious solution that they were not seeing, or that it was somehow their fault, or they had created this. They also came to therapy with the expectation that therapists would tell them what to do. With their fears unrealised however, having a not-knowing position was acceptable and was an interruption to their expectation and beliefs about therapy. This episode also acted as an interruption to similar expectations of trainee psychiatrists behind the screen observing family therapy and seeing that omniscience and answers were not always necessary or possible. This example illustrates issues of power within therapy and how second order cybernetics theory within family therapy (Atkinson and Heath 1990) assist us in avoiding a didactic or psycho-educational approach. The second order approach (contrary to the therapist-as-expert approach espoused in the first order approach) saw a shift in the role of the therapist towards one who explored meanings, beliefs and explanations collaboratively with families. This approach critiqued the idea of "objectivity", instead encouraging reflexive exploration of issues in ways that for families and therapists alike can only be subjective. On the other hand, sometimes knowing from an "expert" position can have a place in family therapy and this may be an interruption of others' strongly held views.

Hazel brought her 14 year old son David to therapy because she could not get on with him, found herself disliking him for his behaviours and his seemingly wilful refusal to eat. She also commented that he was insincere and that she could not believe what he said and that she caught him out lying several times. I found David to be a timid little boy, acting much younger than his years and somewhat startled by the whole experience. My attempts at safe engaging questions about school, football or other interests were met with a strange hesitation as if he was carefully measuring his answers. Hazel was quite vociferous in her dislike of her son, explaining how, compared to her other two sons, he was by far her least favoured and she didn't even think she loved him. David heard all of this. At one point David answered my question about whether or not he agreed with something his mother said by clearly nodding and shaking his head at the same time in a way that meant both yes and no.

Ged:	Is that a yes or a no, David?
David:	[Nods and shakes his head again] Erm....Yes. No.
Ged:	Did you see what happened then Hazel?
Hazel:	Yes, that's what I'm telling you, you never know where you are with him. He doesn't answer questions or say what he thinks, he drives me mad.
Ged:	Why do you think he might do that?
Hazel:	I've no idea, you tell me. His brothers don't do that, I don't know what's wrong with him.
Ged:	Do you want to say anything about this David?
David:	[Silent, tearful]
Ged:	If David could speak up, say what he's really thinking, or doing, what do you think he'd say?
Hazel:	I told you, I've no idea. You tell me.
Ged:	Ok, I don't know, but I can tell you what I think?
Hazel:	Go on...
Ged:	Well I notice that throughout this session David hasn't been telling us what he really thinks, just like you said. But I don't think that's because he's insincere, or playing some wilful game. I wonder if it's more because he doesn't feel safe to say what he thinks because he wants to please you, because he wants you to love him, and he knows you don't love him because you've said that here today. So David might be trapped, wanting to say the right thing, but not knowing what that is.
Hazel:	[Pause] Oh my god, I've done all this haven't I? This is my fault. [Crying]

Following this I was clear to explain that this was not her fault but that we are all at the mercy of our childhoods and as parents we all struggle sometimes. Neither fault nor blame would be of interest to us, but we could work together with the family in interrupting the belief that David was wilful or insincere. Rather, there were alternative understandings which can free them both from guilt and work together towards something more healthy.

Being interrupted

The experience of being interrupted as a therapist is something we will all be familiar with and is part of everyday conversational practices as

The Aesthetics of Interruption

we co-construct meaning and dialogue. There is a difference however when we assume a particular position within that discourse as therapists usually do, one of being a facilitator of the talking and as such, a holder of some power. How might this affect the ways in which talking is done in therapy, and how might we avoid the position (if we wish to avoid it) of "It's ok for me to interrupt you but not for you to interrupt me". My own approach to this is not to assume that I have greater access to the truth which must be listened to, but that as facilitator I will sometimes need to create talking and listening space for everyone present and that this will involve me being directive and interruptive at times in order to do this. It can be done with humility as referred to in the little scenario later, or with some authority if the need to interrupt dominance is identified. There may also be times when we find ourselves interrupted in full flow and, depending on the relationship, humour is often useful.

Mother:	So before we go, we've told you all this, can I ask you what you think?
Ged:	Well, you can ask yes, and I can give you some thoughts if you'd like, although that doesn't mean that this is the absolute truth. So......what strikes me is that what you and Mary have said today reveals something really important and telling about why John might have behaved as he did, because when John was 12 and you left the family home for a few weeks.....
Mary:	Mum, can I go to Kate's tonight?
Ged:	Hang on, I'm in the middle of my big speech here! Tsk!
Mother and Mary:	[laughter]

More interruptions

In her *Journal of Family Therapy* article, Jacqueline Stratford (1998) makes the point of therapist power, whereby we may be seen as conversational experts with some obligation to ensure that things get talked about. As therapists, we "ask most of the questions, select most of the topics, and are therefore largely in control of the conversational floor. Thus therapists have more power than clients to speak about a topic of their choice or to select another speaker or topic". (Stratford 1988 p.388) This by necessity will involve some level of interruption at some point, and she goes on to caution,

> "High levels of interruption by the therapist may be experienced by clients as an appropriate use of their expertise, to helpfully alter the direction or content of the therapeutic conversation, or be seen as a culturally legitimate means of responding to families, or fitting in with the families' own particular style of communication. On the other hand, irrespective of whether family members are consciously aware of being interrupted by the therapist, they may be left feeling angry, disqualified, not listened to, or believe themselves to have little to contribute to the therapeutic conversation and be disadvantaged as a result."
>
> (Stratford 1998, p.388)

It is the job of the therapist then to ensure that family members do not feel disqualified or disadvantaged. As with my earlier example of explaining to families that interruptions will be a part of family therapy, this may require more explicit explaining, such as "I'm sorry, I need to interrupt you now John as I can see that Lisa has something to say and we haven't heard from her for some time. Is this ok, and I can come back to you later?" Even on the rare occasions when the speaker insists on finishing a point they will understand the need to conclude and that other voices are competing for space. This facilitation by the therapist relates to the therapeutic relationship which has been hugely researched and is almost universally agreed upon as being a crucial factor in good therapeutic outcome. There may be times however when we are more suspicious of a dominant family member such as one who seems to be controlling the flow of information or keeping others silent by their very presence. The above pointers are still indicated, perhaps along with a transparent inquiry about people's sense of openness and exposure to questions, always bearing in mind people's safety. I have discussed elsewhere how to challenge masculinity within family therapy settings (Smith 2011b).

Timing of interruptions and sharing responsibility

After some time into a first session Margaret was talking a great deal without pause and with little opportunity for me to engage in dialogue or ask questions. At a rare intake of breath I jumped in and apologised for interrupting and said I would like to ask her if she had told her story to many people before, and if so, to whom and when. I then asked her how she could tell it to me today in a way that would be helpful to her, given that she already knows the story. She replied,

The Aesthetics of Interruption

Margaret: Well, I thought you'd want to know all this.

Ged: I do, I want to know what you think I should know, but sometimes people think that in therapy you can only be helped if your therapist knows everything, and that's not really true. I have a sense of your story from what you've told me already, and also from the referral that your psychiatrist sent us. What do you think it would be really important for me to know so that I might be able to help you?

Margaret: [Answers with some brief details about abuse and neglect in her life]

Ged: Ok, I can see how that is so important. And in telling me about this, would it be ok if I interrupt you occasionally to ask questions, so I can understand better how we can make this therapy different for you; different from the therapies you've already had that you've told me haven't helped?

In declaring my own position with Margaret, and agreeing this with her I wanted to achieve two things. The first was a message that informing me of every detail, uninterrupted was not only unnecessary but also potentially unhelpful to her. The second was to invite her to join me in taking responsibility for the therapeutic process we were both part of, and that this endeavour needed dialogue to optimise its benefits.

If family members feel that the therapist is authentic and empathic, that any interruptions are made with good intentions and for the greater engagement of all, then the therapist will be freer to make such challenges and have them understood. This engagement takes time and so excessive interruption early on is not advised. It is also important to consider the many diverse and intersecting factors within therapy relating to ourselves and the family members with whom we are working. By this I am suggesting we take account of how it might be experienced for a black woman, a Muslim father, or an elderly grandparent to be interrupted by a white male therapist (in my case) or by any professional in order to make space for another family member to speak. Once again, there is very little that a good therapeutic relationship cannot allow, or rectify if offence is caused. This speaks to our own humility and transparency, creating a context where people are free to question us about what we are doing and thinking, and us responding with respect if asked. The culture of there being an openness to challenge for all participants is part of good therapy, as is openness to change if what we are doing is not helping or going anywhere useful. In this respect we can be seen as interrupting ourselves, that is, interrupting our journey to improve it by taking feedback seriously. And so the concept of interrupting can take on wider meanings than violating a speaker's turn to talk. We can also interrupt not only ourselves and our approach, but also others' thoughts or beliefs as shared within therapy. This fits with systemic theory in that the process is co-constructed by all present; we influence family members and they influence us, such is the beauty of this work.

References

Andersen, Tom (1995). Personal communication. "Reflecting Practices in Action", Barnardo's Family Therapy Conference, Liverpool, UK.

Anderson, Harlene, & Goolishian, Harry (1992). The Client is the Expert: A not knowing approach to therapy. In S. McNamee & K. J. Gergen (Eds.), *Therapy as Social Construction* (Inquiries in Social Construction Series). London: Sage Publications.

Atkinson, Brent & Heath, Anthony (1990). Further Thoughts on Second-Order Family Therapy: This time it's personal. *Family Process*, 29, 119-130.

Bakhtin, Mikhail (1986). *Speech Genres and Other Late Essays*. Trans. by Vern W. McGee. Austin, Texas: University of Texas Press.

Bakhtin, Mikhail (1981). *The Dialogic Imagination: Four Essays*. Ed. Michael Holquist. Trans. Caryl Emerson and Michael Holquist. Austin: University of Texas Press.

Bilmes, Jack (1994). Constituting Silence: Life in the world of total meaning. *Semiotica* 98, 73–87.

Geffen, Avi (2013). "Silence" from the album *Aviv Geffen*. Mars Records.

Jonathan Safran Foer (2005). *Extremely Loud And Incredibly Close*. Boston, MA: Houghton Mifflin.

Selvini Palazolli, Mara; Boscolo, Luigi; Cecchin, Gianfranco & Prata, Giuliana. (1980). Hypothesizing-circularity-neutrality: Three guidelines for the conductor of the session. *Family Process*, 19, 3–12.

Seikkula, Jaakko (2011). Becoming Dialogical: Psychotherapy or a way of life? *The Australian and New Zealand Journal of Family Therapy*, 32: 179–193.

Stratford, Jacqueline (1998). Women and Men in Conversation: A consideration of therapists' interruptions in therapeutic discourse. *Journal of Family Therapy*, 20, 383–394

Smith, Ged (2011a). Cut the Crap: Language – Risks and Relationships in Systemic Therapy and Supervision. *The Australian and New Zealand Journal of Family Therapy*, 32(1), 58–69.

Smith, Ged (2011b). *Challenging Hegemonic Masculinity in Family Therapy*. Unpublished Doctoral Thesis, University of London, Birkbeck.

15

Restoring Communities for Children and Separated Parents Caught in Demonising Fights

Justine Van Lawick

Introduction: a network meeting

Manon, mother, 43, and Milan, father, 48, were asked to invite people from their network for the network evening. Manon arrives with her brother and sister, therapist, general practitioner, friends, niece and lawyer. Milan comes with his brother, friends, professional coach, and his lawyer. They have a son, Steven, 7 years old, who was born during their very short relationship. Having never married, they separated when Steven was three months after a year full of disputes and fights. They both have legal authority as a parent and both want to be with Steven as much as possible because they both love him so much and because they have a conviction: "I am the good parent and the other one is not." They do not trust each other at all and fight about everything one can think of: caring days and tasks, holidays, clothing, hairdresser, money issues, school, therapies for the child, appointments, sleeping times, food, family activities with grandparents and other family members and more. Therapists, child protection, mediators, lawyers, general practitioners, school, family, friends, everybody feels stuck in this endless relational war. They come to the network evening with much stress, distrust, despair but also hope.

One therapist, Erik, welcomes everybody and asks me (Justine) to start with an introduction:

> Three communities are here in the meeting. Mother Manon and her social network, father Milan and his social network and the community of therapists. All communities tend to share a strong conviction, a monologue.

> Mother is convinced that father is a dangerous parent, that he is mentally ill, that he probably is a psychopath. She is afraid nobody realises that and she has many examples that support her conviction. He went with the boy on a racing bike without protection, he isolates the boy, he goes abroad with the boy without her permission, he hides the boy and doesn't answer the phone and so on. He

also frustrates all her initiatives to get good help that the boy needs. She thinks the father needs serious investigation and therapy in a forensic setting. Until that time Manon thinks that Steven shouldn't go to his father. She does not understand that the well-known therapists do not agree with her, that they do not follow her path. The network of Manon will probably agree with her and support her in the conviction because they care for her and Steven and they believe her.

The monologue of father Milan is that the mother is a danger because she sees Steven as an object or a project that she can control; she is pathologising him all the time like she does with everybody. She sends him to many professionals to help him to move better, to sleep better, and to learn better in school. She wants him to take medicine. Milan wants to give his son the message that he is good as he is and is sure her behaviour is harming Steven. The people around him will probably share his convictions. The therapists also tend to share a conviction, a monologue: the main problem is the relational war between the parents, the demonisation, and the destructive patterns. So in order to get a better life for Steven, his parents and all involved should be able to stop the demonisation processes.

All that are present here tonight want the best for Steven; we have no doubt about that. But the problem of monological convictions is that through time they become more and more true. All information that fits our conviction will be taken in and will support what we already thought. Information that does not fit the frame of our conviction is not perceived or is ignored. If we keep being caught in the tunnel of our own convictions we cannot help Steven. So if we use the space in this meeting trying to convince the other two communities of the rightness of our own convictions we create a fight of three monologues that want to dominate each other. In this way we will add to the misery of Steven and we will do a very bad job.

We want to invite all of us into an open dialogue.

We want to open this dialogue by asking the people around Milan to tell us about father and son: what makes this father such a good father for Steven?

The people around father started to tell all kinds of wonderful stories about Steven and his father. How he always made a very cosy atmosphere in the house, how they like to visit father and Steven and take their children to play because Milan is such a good and attentive father, children want to be with him. One friend said how often she lets her children sleep over with Milan and Steven because she knows how much her children like that, she experiences Milan as a very safe father. Another friend talks about holidays together, building huts, playing football, laughing and romping. Milan's sister adds that he not only is a father that plays around, he also can be strict and is clear about rules. Meanwhile the network members of mother are exploding: "If he is such a safe father, how can he leave Steven alone in the street?!" We turn to the people around mother and ask them the same question: "Why is it such luck for Steven that he has Manon as his mother?" Then we listen to the stories of her family life. How she is always attentive with children, really with them, sitting on the ground, playing fantasy stories, how committed she is in following Steven in his development and supporting him wherever she can. One friend added, "And you can laugh with her so much!"

Reflecting on what the communities around Manon and Milan had to say I became aware of my own narrow perspective on this mother because I asked myself inside "Can you really laugh with this woman?!" And this helped me to broaden my perspective on the mother and see a richer image of her. Also the image of father became more colourful as a safe, playful but also strict father. I realised I had been affected by all the mother's worries about him.

With this opening of perspectives, the more of the attendees began to crawl out of their tunnels. A friend of Milan said: "I am starting to realise that I only hear the story from one side." The sister of Manon added: "I realise the same." These comments were followed by a friend of Manon. He said that he realised that he always speaks badly about the father and that he now understands that doesn't help Steven. He suggested to all involved to start to speak more positively about the other parent.

A lively dialogue then took place between all that were present with the leading question: "What does Steven need and how can we cooperate to help him out of the middle"? At the end of the evening people from the different networks exchanged mail addresses or telephone numbers and made plans to keep contact.

Four months later...

Four months later we had an evaluation session with Milan. He told us that the networks still were in contact, had organised Skype meetings and that the parents were now being guided by their networks. For instance, the father understood that he has to answer the phone to prevent Manon from panicking. "It's a small effort after all," he added.

No kids in the middle

The context of this network meeting is our project: *no kids in the middle* (Van Lawick & Visser 2014).

Working with separated parents who continue in bitter dispute for years is, for many experienced couple, child and family therapists, one of the most complicated areas of their practice. What is effective in therapy with families and children often seems not to work in these cases. Distrust, paranoia and the taking of a defensive stance, by one or both parents, frustrates the formation of a safe therapeutic relationship in which therapy might help. Ongoing legal fights or the threat of new legal proceedings along with the stress and financial consequences this imposes, complicate the dynamic.

Experienced couple and family therapists at the Lorentzhuis, a Dutch centre for systemic therapy, training and consultation, tried hard to promote a therapeutic dialogical space in which to create more safety for both family members and professionals. Sometimes they succeeded; however, there still remained a group of parents so caught up in their destructive fighting that they were unable to find the space to work together.

> *The Lorentzhuis therapists were increasingly concerned about the children of these parents and referrals were made to the* Kinder en Jeugd Trauma Centrum *(KJTC), a centre for treatment, training and consultation focussed on traumatised children and their families. However, the KJTC therapists had found that the help they were able to offer was of no benefit for the children as long as the main context of the child's problems remained the parental war. So they, in their turn, wished to refer back these cases to the Lorentzhuis! Ultimately both services needed each other. That is why the project "No kids in the middle" was developed by. Margreet Visser from the KJTC and me, Justine van Lawick, from the Lorentzhuis.*

In the *No kids in the middle* project we try to find new roads that create a context for movement out of deadlock for these families. We try to create a space where rigid, destructive and demonising processes (Alon & Omer 2006) can be made more flexible and dialogical for parents, children, their social network and the professionals who work with them.

To set the scene for the project it is important to understand the societal context. In order to avoid mirroring the demonising-corrective dynamic in society, families and networks we have to pay attention to this level of context.

Social political context

In the Netherlands, due to various reasons, the number of children caught up in the acrimonious divorce of their parents has grown (Spruijt & Kormos 2014). Since 1998, legal authority for children following divorce has been assigned to both parents rather than one parent. The emancipation of women has produced changes in patterns of childcare within families. Fathers have become more active in caring tasks and as a consequence, have legitimised their legal right to see their children. Mothers have also become legally obliged to cooperate with access arrangements. A successful political lobby by *Fathers4Justice* resulted in equal legal power for both parents after divorce in 1998 and in most other Western countries around that time. Most parents (around 70%) are able to divorce as partners and stay good enough parents for their children. (Spruijt & Kormos 2014).

The "two captains on a ship" model works for most families but a smaller group of parents are so caught up in their conflict that they become convinced they have to fight against the other parent for the sake of the children. Because they love their children they feel driven to rescue them from the other parent's damaging behaviour. Such long, fierce battles became a growing concern to many of the professionals confronted with the pain of children caught up in these situations and requests were made for the introduction of legislation to better protect children from their fighting parents. In 2009, the Netherlands introduced a new law that obliged parents to make a parental plan before being legally granted divorce. The unintended consequence of this legislation was that the relational war became situated even closer to the children. Research by van der Valk & Spruijt (2013) shows that this law aggravates the battles in high conflict divorces, the numbers went up: a clear example of a solution that creates a problem (Watzlawick et al. 1974).

So here the society, the state takes the colonising position (McCarthy 1995; Rober & Selzer 2010) that all parents have to form a good communicating parental team for the sake of their children. And many professionals feel the pressure to make this work. In this way we create professional illusions for clients and therapists, the illusion that we can bring families from the destructive life and bad parenthood to a more connected life, a parent team in collaboration and children that develop well again. We cannot. Bateson (1972) and Maturana & Varela (1988) explained already in the early years of systemic theory and practice that purposeful intervention and instructive interaction are ignoring circularity and can cause harm to relational systems. Professionals that try to change the clients according to personal or professional theories and ideas, can, without purpose or intention, add to escalations.

> *Iris: After mediation things got worse. We heard again and again that we can separate as parents but that we have to stay on good team as parents. We had to communicate better. We got all kind of assignments to communicate about arrangements. But I cannot stand him. I cannot be with him in one room. I am angered the moment I see him. He has done so many mean things. I cannot listen to him, I cannot think when I have to communicate directly with him. Sessions with the mediator always escalated. I never could remember what we talked about, I just was extremely tired and worn out.*

The mediator brought the image of what was needed: being a good team as parents, and that means to have more communication about arrangements, more contact. Although this seems very reasonable the voice and the perspective of the professional is dominant in the interactions and in the setting of goals. Voices that do not fit the therapeutic goals are rejected or silenced. Cottyn (2009) warns against romantic illusions of family therapists that expect all divorced parents to create a good functioning parental team. This colonising position is a burden for the therapist because it becomes her responsibility to bring the family to this "better" or "more civilised" or "child friendly" place. Often these images mirror dominant discourses in the social context. In the media and social media people speak badly about divorced parents that fight. "They should behave better! Poor children."

Therapeutic position

To escape the trap of colonisation we have to position ourselves as a curious and involved passer-by that like to reflect together with the parents, children and their network about a better place they want to be. Sometimes parents are able to team up more and communicate better when they have their child in mind but sometimes the differences or the hurts are so huge that the fighting can only stop if they take more distance and let the other parent do things his or her way without interfering. Cottyn (2009) calls this *parallel solo parenthood*. Quite often this parallel solo parenthood is a good outcome in our project.

Although we do not tell parents how they have to behave we are not neutral, our ethical standards are part of ourselves and play a role in all therapies. The need to create a context where parents are able to sense their children again and make a safer place for them is not optional. These situations demand a therapeutic presence. We, as human beings, as professionals, as a community, cannot accept that children are maltreated for years. We want to connect to the parents and accept them, but in the same time we are in contact with ourselves, rejecting their destructive behaviour. This positioning is related to the notion of "therapeutic presence" that many authors write about (Stern, 2004; McCarthy, 2010; Omer, 2010). Although differences are there all authors define presence as being open and available to the other and in contact with one self. Working with an open mind, with love and compassion and with an open end, not knowing the solution for the other. Presence also refers to being in the present moment (Stern, 2004), not obsessed about the past or worrying about the future. McCarthy formulates this beautifully as "we are present as presence in the present" (McCarthy 2010, p.9). Being *with* the parents in the present moment we find that trying to control the parents, or try to steer people in a certain direction by special interventions is unhelpful (Shotter, 2005).

This relates to systemic practice when constructivism and second order cybernetics entered the field of family therapy (Keeney 1983; Boscolo et al 1987). The basic assumption of second order cybernetics is the circularity between the observer and the observed. A person is inside the circularities of expressions in an ongoing stream of interactions. This means that in the cycle of interaction feedback loops are constantly influencing all expressions, verbal and non-verbal. Neither therapists nor clients can step out of this cycle of observation, reflection and interaction. Our interconnectedness is inseparable and can only be understood as a whole. As Keeney & Keeney put it "Second-order cybernetics doubles the notion of circularity, enabling cybernetics to emphasize the constant re-entries of the indicating cybernetician into the circularities that are of interest." (2012, p.27). This radical circular perspective acknowledges the autonomy of systems (Maturana &Varela, 1988), they cannot be changed from outside. Systemic therapists are thus *with* clients, interacting with them in a unpredictable way so that they can find their own, autonomous paths towards a better life. This interconnectedness not only refers to the smaller social systems of therapists and families, but also to the larger social systems in which we all are embedded.

These reflections about positioning and about circularity in and between larger and smaller systems resulted in the architecture of our *No kids in the middle* project. The main features are: working in groups of six families at a time, children in the centre of our attention, free space for interaction without therapists, communicating with the whole person, not only with words but also with the body, experiential exercises and artistic expression. Last but not least, we reach out to and work together with the networks around the families.

Working in groups

We work with groups of six families at a time. Twelve parents work with two therapists and, at the same time, all their children work with two therapists in a different room in the same building. Participants in both groups attend eight two-hour sessions, with a scheduled mid-session break. Group work with fighting parents creates more space for both the therapists and the parents. Ex-partners can observe other ex-partners fighting, whilst observing their own conflicts at the same time. This invites and encourages reflection, which is often missing in demonising fights. Therapists are also able to adopt a different position. Instead of a possible ally for two fighting parents, the therapist can become the involved and observing outsider who tries to create a safe therapeutic context where change becomes possible.

One could argue that the therapists function as a reflecting team (Andersen, 1990), reflecting together on what they hear, feel, think and what resonates in them while the parents are interacting together.

Erik: (therapist)	I hear so many complaints today from the mothers of being left alone, feeling so responsible because they have the feeling that the fathers are not really involved, not responding to their worries.

Justine (therapist)	Yes, I agree, but when I listen to the fathers I can feel their pain of feeling excluded, feeling marginalised by the mothers.
Cora (mother):	But what can we do when the men are not responding, stonewalling, what can I do?
Floris (father):	I hate this simple father–mother talk; I am the one that wants to talk, to communicate, she is not responding! What can I do?

From here a lively dialogue followed that created more flexibility in the views and convictions of the parents. Another entrance of understanding about what happens refers to Michael White's idea of the *outsider witness* position (White, 2007). In this process, the parents become outsider witnesses of the other parents in the group. They share frustrations and pain that they think other people cannot understand. But they accept reflections and feedback from the other parents in the group because they speak from similar experiences. In a group context, parents are able to help each other. They understand the entanglements of the other parents. When common conflicts emerge, around holidays for example, they can see possibilities where others get stuck. While helping the other members of the group, they help themselves to navigate similar problems and often become more flexible in their own efforts to negotiate conflict. This frees the therapists from the expectation that it is solely their role to help find solutions for the "insoluble" problems presented by members of the group. We position ourselves as in involved passers-by and put our expertise in facilitating the work that has to be done by the parents, and the parents are the experts on their own lives. In this way we co-create an observing system where members not only observe others but reflexively and simultaneously have the opportunity to observe themselves acting and interacting: an example of circularity in action.

Children in the centre

The parents and their networks are invited to see, empathise and connect with their children and act with their child in mind and body. The road to this end, and the steps that can be taken towards it, are open. As therapists we adopt a position of curiosity, irreverence and openness to the unexpected (Cecchin, 1987). We choose to focus on possibilities (Wilson, 2007). The parents with whom we work are involved in relational wars that have already lasted many years – some as long as 12 years – that are full of destructiveness, revenge, paranoia and demonisation. Some children can only remember fighting parents.

An example
In the first group session we ask the parents to introduce themselves as parents, to show pictures of their children and tell about a special and concrete memory of an experience together with that child. When there are 12 children of these 12 parents we listen together to 24 very short stories, full of relational experiencing and emotion. They can be very recent events or experiences of togetherness that come to mind in the here and now. Stories can be about baking cookies together, a talk at the bedside, laughing together, playing with a ball, helping each other. Anything meaningful will do. This exercise can be very painful for parents who have not seen their children, sometimes for years.

Tom:	I cannot tell you about a memory because I have not seen my daughter for four years now, because she [the other parent] has made me a monster in the eyes of Iris.
Therapist:	I hear you telling us that you have not seen your daughter for four years, and how painful that experience is for you. But maybe you can share with us a wonderful experience with Iris that occurred before that time?
Tom:	[silent for some time]: …I think of the day she was born, the best day of my life.
Floris (father):	I hate this simple father–mother talk; I am the one that wants to talk, to communicate, she is not responding! What can I do? [He bursts into tears.]

The whole group is touched by his sorrow. Even the mother of Iris seems to be confused.

This story raises the sense of warmth in the group. These emotional stories change the atmosphere in the room. We have the sense of being with twelve loving parents and their lovely children together. This raises a sense of hope and also sadness that so much love and connection has been overshadowed by all the conflicts and fighting. The children's group aims to give the children a voice. We aim not to problematise or pathologise their sometimes disturbing behaviour and to stimulate their resilience without being caught in the fights of their parents. The children are encouraged to make a theatre production or movie around their experiences being the child of fighting parents, or choose some other form of artistic expression. They are invited to enter the metaphorical world of their imagination. These artistic expressions are shown to all the parents and the therapists in a presentation ceremony in the sixth session.

Free space

For many families this is the first time in years that they are together. Group work creates the opportunity for parents to see the other parent interacting constructively with other group members and with the children. The room where the families come together without the presence of therapists turns out to be very important. Sometimes change starts to happen in this room and other areas away from the therapists, rather than in the therapy sessions. Children who have not seen one of the parents for some time (perhaps years) can mix with all the parents and children in the group, and are able to be in the same room as the alienated parent. For most children, this setting is the first time in years that they have seen both of their parents in the same room.

> *Mia, who didn't see her mother for a year, saw her mother interact with Susan, a girl from the group that she liked very much. She saw her mother laugh with Susan and this made her feel very sad and also jealous.*

> *Bob, who saw his ex-partner, Lisa, as a very disturbed person and a lousy mother who neglects the children now observed Lisa in interaction with other parents and children that apparently liked her.*

These happenings are shared with the therapists but there are also many transforming incidents that happen that we never hear of.

The whole person

We communicate with all our senses, mind and body. (Bakhtin 1981, Shotter 2007) Experiential exercises that invite people to enter the space of direct experiencing, feeling and acting were part of family therapy from the beginning on. One of the founding mothers of family therapy, Virginia Satir (1972) asked family members to play roles and interact from those roles. One of our founding fathers Salvador Minuchin (1974) asked family members to play together in the sessions, to re-enact a situation that was problematic at home or to enact different behaviour in a special interaction.

We continue this tradition in the group sessions by asking parents to re-enact their fights while other parents sit in small children's chairs to experience what the children might feel and think when the parents are fighting. Other parents are invited to be the buddy of the parents that fight about an issue, helping them to find a space (not always a solution) that is good enough for their children. All the parents are present with all their senses, while helping others they reflect about their own issues and crawl out of their tunnels; while sitting in the children's chairs they can feel the pain of their own children. Again an example of circularity in action.

Presentation ceremonies

Parents are given the assignment to prepare a presentation at home, together with involved people around them, about what they have learned in the group and what they wish for their children in the future.

In the sixth session we make space for the presentations of children (before the break) and parents (after the break). In this setting, everybody is vulnerable and feels a bit exposed. Because children are of different age groups their presentations can differ a lot. But almost always they share a message: please stop fighting! One small boy of five made a presentation without words of two cars bumping all the time and a very small car that got crashed in between. Another boy of 15 showed an image he found on the internet of two adults screaming to each other. He told his parents the following: "Mum, you think I suffer from the behaviour of dad and dad you are convinced that I suffer from the behaviour of mum. But I have to tell you: I suffer because you always blame each other, I get headaches from it, then I cannot sleep and then I cannot perform in school. And then you blame each other for being the cause of me not performing in school. It makes me crazy. STOP IT."

Angoly (9) wanted to show an incident where she felt happy. She made a small theatre performance with two other children from the group. Angoly went from her mother to her father, the parents were placed at a distance but friendly together, exchanged some words and some luggage and Angoly concluded: "This was very good, I feel happy and this way I do not suffer from the divorce of my parents".

After 9 groups (54 families), we have a huge and rich bunch of presentations of children that express their voices, with support from the other children. It is an empowering experience for them and helps them to move out from the middle between their parents. During the children's presentation, the parents are deeply affected by the effort the children have to put in the presentations. They are impressed and moved even if they often feel ashamed about their children's clear messages. After the break, the parents present what they prepared with their networks. We had parents with poems, singing, dancing, using creative symbols, making speeches, offering pictures, drawings, PowerPoint presentations and more.

One father, Hano, came with a big branch from a tree in a pot. He had all kind of pictures to hang on the tree, the tree of the life of his son Max (7). He brought pictures of his family, of his dog, of the family of the mother and even of the new partner of mother. Hano sat with Max on the ground and together they filled the tree with all the pictures, talking about a sense of belonging into the future and that he as a father wanted to support Max by making space for all the members of his tree. Sometimes the presentations are spontaneous speeches and sometimes these can also create some discomfort. One father used the space to tell his son that he understood that his parents should not use him again as a referee, and that he now expected his son to improve at school in order to have a successful and happy future and so on. These words were familiar to the son.

We have found that the children love the efforts that their parents make for them. The whole ritual is a powerful experience that creates space for a new dance.

Network meetings

We encountered difficulties after noticing that positive changes in the group had disappeared by the next session. We understood that the social network around each parent did not expect or understand the changes and reacted in a usual way that drew the situation back in the well-known old interactions. So we decided that it was also important to connect to the involved people around the families. We organised a network evening to be held before the first group session. Involved network members may include: grandparents, brothers and sisters, other family members, new partners, the family of the new partner, friends, neighbours, school/workmates, and professionals. These network members are very actively involved in the relational war. They tend to take sides with one of the parents whom they define to be the victim of the other one. They try to be a good ally but usually fail to improve the situation.

In this network evening parents can bring as many persons from their network as they want, on one occasion 70 persons attended. We make it clear that the evening is important as part of the preparation for the project and that it increases the likelihood of success. Attendance at the evening is anonymous, and its focus is to be informative. Only the therapists introduce themselves. At the network evening we present the project. We provide information about our basic principles and assumptions, how we work, and why we do what we do. We are as open as possible. People can ask questions; we are responsive.

A grandfather asked, "What do you do when one parent refuses to cooperate?"

A therapist answered, "I can imagine that you have lost hope over the years that positive change is possible. I think that many of you have. But we believe that it is possible. We have to, because we cannot give up on the children."

At the end of the evening all therapists line up before the public group and ask, "Please support us. Without your support we cannot make it work. Please help us in this work." Every time we organise this evening, many attendees thank us at the end; they wish us good luck and tell us they hope we will do well. "It has already taken much too long".

After the network evening, we continue to reach out to them during the project. We ask parents to share what we cover in the group with their network. We ask them to see movies together that address a relevant topic, and to reflect together on the movie. We send text messages for them to share with their networks. Sometimes we have sessions in-between with new partners or other network members. We try to be as responsive as we can because our experience is that this makes positive movement so much more possible. It also means that we need to create time in our agendas to be responsive.

Working with the networks means that we as therapists position ourselves as involved passers-by. We are committed to create a therapeutic context in which family members and other important persons can enter a space of reflective contemplation and movement out of dead lock. But we will never be part of their private lives, sit with them during celebrations, go with them on holidays or be present when they suffer at home. In that sense we are not important. The people from their network are much more important, they share their lives. We can only hope that our

Restoring Communities for Children and Separated Parents

therapeutic gatherings can help them to move into a better and connected life that suits them and where children can develop well.

In our work we have found potential that the network sometimes can act as judge. Jose and Mira and their eight year old son Juan participated in the project. They were absorbed in demonising fights that started already during pregnancy. They separated when Mira fell in love with another man. With this man she had another son, now five years old. Mira is convinced that living in the small family with his mother, stepfather and brother is a safe base for Juan. In this arrangement, Jose can be with his son only a few hours a week. Jose is furious about this as he feels he has very good hours with Juan and they need more. He says that Juan even tells him that he wants to live with his dad. Jose wants to have more time to go with Juan to his family and friends, to share his life, school, everything. They went to the court many times but although the court decided that Jose should see his son more, Mira refused to cooperate. In the group they made progress with positive exchanges. But when it came to a change in relation to the number of caring days the communication escalated and ended up in a dead lock. It was at this point that we decided to invite the networks of father and mother, but without the parents.

We started again with an introduction as explained at the beginning of this chapter. The friends and family of father could express many testimonies how committed father is with his son, what a good father he is. Also mothers parents, husband and friends could tell about her good motherhood, being, attentive, patient, clear, loving. Attendees from both networks checked out on different stories that they heard that they thought were harming Juan. They heard that Juan always has to change identity when leaving with his father. He has to change clothes in the car, they speak differently, he wants his son to grow his hair longer and tells him so. A friend of father is astonished. "They often come to me to play outdoors. I always ask them to put on old clothes because it gets dirty in my garden." They exchange many stories and try to understand what happens. Then they begin to find a better agenda for caring days and tasks. They all agree this fighting has to stop. The parents of Mira understand that the mother of Jose wants to have more contact with Juan because he is such a lovely boy. They come to an agreement of one long weekend (three nights) in two weeks and also whole holiday weeks. What they suggested was much more than the wish of Mira and much less than the wish of Jose. "And what if Mira doesn't agree?" asked her mother anxiously. "She just has to accept," Mira's friend said. The network agreed to coach the parents in this agenda and to keep contact.

Conclusions

Working from an individual or couple based perspective with high conflict divorces where children end up in the middle can add to the demonising dynamic. Therapists that try hard to reach the parents with the message they have to change towards better and more cooperative parenthood often recursively end up in the middle themselves. By creating communities of groups of children and parents and by cooperating with existing networks around children and parents new therapeutic spaces are opened. In this way of working therapists position themselves as involved and committed attendees that are active in facilitating a context where family members and children can work for a less demonising and more connected space to live in.

Acknowledgement

I want to thank Margreet Visser, clinical psychologist in the KJTC (Child and Juvenal Trauma Centre) with whom I developed the project *No Kids in the Middle*. I also want to thank Judith Brown and Kristof Mikes-Liu who edited our article, *No Kids in the Middle: Dialogical and Creative Work with Parents and Children in the Context of High Conflict Divorces* for the Australian and New Zealand Journal of Family Therapy. Some small parts of this chapter are taken from this article. (Van Lawick & Visser 2015).

References

Alon, Nahi & Omer, Haim (2006). *The Psychology of Demonization: Promoting acceptance and reducing conflict.* London: Lawrence Erlbaum Associates, Publishers.

Andersen, Tom (1990). *The Reflecting Team: Dialogues and Dialogues about Dialogues.* Broadstairs: Borgmann.

Bakhtin, Mikhail M. (1981). *The Dialogical Imagination.* Austin: University of Texas Press.

Bateson, Gregory (1972). *Steps to an Ecology of Mind: Collected Essays in Anthropology, Psychiatry, Evolution, and Epistemology.* Chicago: University Of Chicago Press.

Bateson, Gregory (1979). *Mind and Nature: A Necessary Unity.* New York: Bantam Books.

Boscolo, Luigi; Cecchin, Gianfranco; Hoffman, Lynn & Penn, Peggy (1987). *Milan Systemic Family Therapy: Conversations in Theory and Practice.* New York: Basic Books.

Cecchin, Gianfranco (1987). Hypothesizing, circularity, and neutrality revisited: An invitation to curiosity. *Family Process*, 26(4), 405–413.
Cottyn, Lieve (2009). Conflicten tussen ouders na scheiding. *Systeemtheoretisch Bulletin*, 27, 131–161.
Keeney, Bradford (1983). *Aesthetics of Change*. New York: The Guilford Press.
Keeney, Hillary & Keeney, Bradford (2012). What Is Systemic About Systemic Therapy? Therapy Models Muddle Embodied Systemic Practice. *Journal of Systemic Therapies*, 31(1), 22–37.
Maturana, Humberto, & Varela, Francisco (1988). *The Tree of Knowledge*. Boston: Sharnbhala New Science Library.
McCarthy, Imelda (1995). Serving those in Poverty: A Benevolent Colonisation? In Justine van Lawick & Marjet Sanders (Eds.) *Gender and Beyond*. Heemstede: LS Books.
McCarthy, Imelda (2010). The Fifth Province: Imagining a Space of Dialogical Co-Creations! *Context*, December 2010.
Omer, Haim (2010). *The New Authority: Family, school and community*. Cambridge: Cambridge University Press.
Rober, Peter & Seltzer, Michael (2010). Avoiding Colonizer Positions in the Therapy Room: Some Ideas About the Challenges of Dealing with the Dialectic of Misery and Resources in Families. *Family Process*, 49(1), 123–137.
Satir, Virginia (1972). *Peoplemaking*. New York: Science and Behavior Books.
Shotter, John (2005). Goethe and the refiguring of intellectual inquiry: from 'aboutness' thinking to 'withness' thinking in everyday life. *Janus Head*, 8(1), 132–158.
Spruijt, Ed & Kormos, Helga (2014). *Handboek scheiden en de kinderen*. Houten: Bohn, Stafleu & van Loghum. (2nd Ed.)
Stern, Daniel (2004). *The Present Moment in Psychotherapy and Everyday Life*. New York: W.W. Norton.
Van der Valk, Inge & Spruijt, Ed (2013). *Het ouderschapsplan en de effecten voor de kinderen*. Jeugd & Gezin, Departement Pedagogische Wetenschappen: Universiteit Utrecht.
Van Lawick, Justine & Visser, Margreet (2014). *Kinderen uit de Knel, een interventie voor gezinnen verwikkeld in een vechtscheiding*. Amsterdam: SWP.
Van Lawick, Justine & Visser, Margreet (2015). No kids in the middle: Dialogical and Creative Work with Parents and Children in the Context of High Conflict Divorces. *Australian and New Zealand Journal of Family Therapy*. 36, 33–50.
Watzlawick, Paul; John Weakland & Robert Fisch (1974). *Change: Principles of Problem Formation and Problem Resolution*. New York: Norton and Company.
White, Michael (2007). *Maps of Narrative Practice*. New York: W. W. Norton.
Wilson, James (2007). *The Performance of Practice*. London: Karnac.

16 Creating Islands of Safety for Victims of Violence
A critical systems approach

Catherine Richardson/Kinewesquao

There are times when I catch myself believing that there is such a thing as something: which is separate from something else.
Gregory Bateson / Nora Bateson 2010

What is a system?

What is a system that functions holistically? Is it being more than each part or individual but relying on the growth potential of each integral part for adaptation and flourishing in the world? Indigenous peoples may find examples of this holism in an eco-system, in a tribe or in a ceremony. Scientists have attuned to this holism in physics and quantum theory for almost one hundred years. Scientist Michael Jackson (2003) writes about creative holism as a "critical systems approach to complex problem situations in relation to management addressing issues within an organisation and with employees" (Jackson, p.62). I would also add that there is something about a system that transcends the "sum of its parts". While this has been stated widely, I would also say that there is something of the *creative spirit* or *life force* at work in a holistic system; something of the magnificent that can be transformed or created from what was previously considered. While many family therapists sprung from either a scientific background or a more Marxist or secular oriented approach to social work, I believe there was something more at work that extends into the realm of the creative, the mysterious, the transcendent even, although that would be experienced uniquely by each person. Indigenous practice has never distanced itself from spirituality and *mamatowisowin*, the life force and the interconnectedness of all things or the Great Mystery which will be explored later in the chapter. Nora Bateson's film about her father's life and thought evokes a recognition of Gregory Bateson's attunement to these non-secular attributes... a life force that connects us all as beings in nature (Nora Bateson 2010). It was perhaps for this reason that it was impossible to categorise Gregory Bateson into any one particular discipline. However, it is clear that his contribution to systemic thought reverberated widely in the world of social work and family therapy.

Holistic approaches in relational social work and family therapy in a context of colonisation?

Research in the field of social work and family therapy with Indigenous families in Canada has shown that relational, holistic approaches and practice that considers the whole being of the person and not just the immediate issue, lead more readily to successful outcomes (Carriere & Richardson 2013; Ermine 2000; Freedberg 2015; Littlebear 2000; Rice 2005; Thomas & Green 2007). A holistic approach would generally be client-centred or family-centred, involve mutuality, empathy, decentring of the worker, uplifting of the client's perspective, life experience and ways they have tried to resist mistreatment and preserve their dignity. Dignity is a central human concern, but particularly so in working with Indigenous people who have suffered great humiliation due to colonialism in Canada. In other words, all levels of context from the larger social context to the more immediate contexts of the moment are included.

Segregation is still an issue in Canada. The "Indian Act" (1876) remains in place and there are still barriers to moving beyond it in terms of administering funds to First Nations communities. A much higher proportion of Indigenous people are controlled by every measure of state intervention. They suffer disproportionate prison sentences, child removals, institutionalisation and involuntary psychiatric treatment than the general population (Statistics Canada 2011; Carriere & Richardson 2013; Richardson & Wade 2008). Their experience of injustice, violence, corruption and ignorance at the hands of the Canadian state institutions is apparently greater than any other minority. Their level of education, health and income is lower than the general population. They suffer every indication of poverty and isolation. In response to generations of mistreatment, Indigenous people are gradually becoming less separated from their own cultures and languages as they recover from the previously purposeful effort of the Canadian government to integrate them by systematically annihilating their cultures. It is important to consider this particular history of colonial interaction in order to provide helpful and appropriate social services for Indigenous families (Carriere & Richardson 2013; Richardson & Wade 2008).

Holistic or systemic child protection work also involves considering the multiple contexts of the family, including socio-political conditions, the particular circumstances of the interaction, and the situational logic through which a victim of violence resists those micro-acts of aggression. It is possible and important to understand the interaction within the family system while recognising the power/power imbalances that are at work within the system. The notion of "gender power" or gender imbalance does not exist in natural ecosystems as it does in human society. The "separate but equal" conditions of many species involved in sexual reproduction have not resulted in human constructed culture, ideologies, values, and priorities that come from abstract thinking and social imperatives. In an attempt to sort out the relationship between mind and nature and the land of *creatura*, where not only material/energetic processes are found but also information processes that he found informed Bateson's ideas of human interaction with systems. Bateson spoke of the "double description" as his method for investigating the interaction between life forms (Hui et al 2008). In relation to this interaction, Bateson also posed the question:

> *What pattern connects the crab to the lobster and the orchid to the primrose and all the four of them to me? And me to you? And all the six of us to the amoeba in one direction and to the backward schizophrenic in another?*
>
> (Bateson 1979, p.8)

His interest in relationality resonates with the Indigenous epistemology described later in this chapter, indicating there is something at work along the lines of inherent and integral connections between us all. This kind of attention to relationality has much to contribute to health and social care and the ways we hold each other up as part of life on the planet.

Systemic analysis can assist practitioners working with families and in communities to understand interaction in context without blaming victims of violence, asking appropriate questions about the deliberateness of violence in the human realm, about the conditions that engender violence and embolden perpetrators. As systemic or relational practitioners, we can find answers in the social ecology that explain the foundations of violence (e.g. colonialism, patriarchy, social inequality, unfair laws, abuses of power with impunity) rather than seeking explanations for victimhood within the victim. It is important to contest theories about false consciousness and internalised oppression as they are hyper-generalised and abstract sociological theories created by individuals with relative power who do not consider the immediate context of people's lives. Often, these theories are imposed by people of relative power onto those with a lower socio-economic standing which can be both unhelpful and elitist. For example, Allan Wade writes that Karl Marx constructed the theory of false consciousness to explain why the proletariat were not rising up to overthrow their oppressors when they failed to live up to his prediction. (Wade, public communication, Mind the Gap, 2015). Marx blamed the poor for over-identifying with the bourgeoisie and upper classes; that they sought to emulate their lifestyle rather than overthrow it. Erving Goffman (1963) has offered some insight into this conversation by reminding us that people both identify with what they love and appreciate while resisting that which they oppose.

Similarly, we can contest popular descriptions such as "co-dependency", or psychodynamic binaries (e.g. he is aggressive because she is passive; I am racist because you have dark skin) in that they fail to acknowledge and understand the resistance and responses of the victim as well as the deliberateness of the violence. Thus, they reproduce a false assumption that victims are passive. A way to avoid engaging in practices that obscure differences in gender, power and access to resources is to elicit both accounts of violence/mistreatment and resistance to aggression (Gilligan, Rogers & Tolman 2013; McCarthy 2010a, Richardson 2009; Richardson & Wade 2012, 2008; Wade 1997). In so doing, it becomes clear that the victim is not passive, did not just "take it", and that they possess particular, situational knowledges related to safety and protection. These knowledges can be explored through therapeutic conversation and embedded into the safety planning process. When we elicit and elucidate the acts of resistance against violence, these safety knowledges show, for example, how a mother has been trying to protect her child and keep herself safe simultaneously. Due to the unequal power relations between perpetrator and victim, she is unlikely to be able to stop the violence so she must make the best decisions possible within that context. When resistance is understood "in situ", the situational logic becomes clear and intelligent. Such a conversation can also serve to strengthen the victim's sense of themselves, their knowledge and acumen, thus putting them in a better position to manage the system and restructure their lives on a more secure foundation. Our role is to help put events (which have often been decontextualised by others) back into context.

Systemic structuring in the Canadian 'Islands of Safety' process

"Islands of Safety" is a child protection intervention developed on the West Coast of Canada by Allan Wade and me in order to assist and facilitate safety planning with First Nations, Metis and Inuit families in the context of spousal assault. This method offers culturally-based, family therapy informed, response-based approaches to addressing violence and creating more harmonious relationships within families (Richardson & Wade 2008; Richardson & Wade 2013). The Islands of Safety process can also accomplish the following therapeutic tasks: 1) restoring the mother-child bond which is often attacked and damaged by male intimate partner violence, 2) restoring preferred and more culturally-designated family roles and interaction in a way that could be called "decolonising" (e.g. both taking into account past and current colonisation of Indigenous families while attempting to exist outside and beyond it to some degree, while also acknowledging the structural violence within the system). The development of the Islands of Safety model included a process of community consultation with relevant "stakeholders". This included receiving feedback from Indigenous mothers involved in the child welfare system, fathers who have used violence, child protection social workers, Aboriginal/Indigenous child welfare agencies, shelter workers and Indigenous cultural advisors. The model is embedded in a cultural model of traditional Metis/Cree family life (Anderson 1990) and "rounds" of questions informed by preferred ways of living/being. These questions also serve to articulate the ways family members have been resisting violence and its indignity. Research has shown that highlighting resistance knowledges leads to better outcomes for recovery and well-being (Brown 1991; Gillian, Rogers & Tolman 2013; Richardson 2013; Richardson and Wade 2008: Wade 1995, 1997). A typical series of response-based questions would be "When he hit you, how did you respond in that moment... What did you do?" In order to establish the interviewee as a competent person with pre-existing abilities, we would regress chronologically and ask "When did you first notice that he was becoming dangerous?" We would then list and summarise her acts of resistance in context and asking a connecting or "transference of knowledge" question such as "How did you know to do this?"

Application of a critical systems approach

A framework known as a "critical systems approach" was developed by social scientists (Bateson 1979, 1972; Capra 1996; Jackson 2003) to bring to bear more analysis of imbalances, such as social inequality, to systemic thinking. Jackson believed that holistic systems could be used creatively for problem-solving:

> *Creativity, in a systemic sense, has become possible because of more recent developments in systems methodology.... The "hard systems" methodologies developed were, and still are, efficient at tackling a particular range of problem situations.... System dynamics, organisational cybernetics, complexity theory, soft systems thinking, emancipatory systems thinking and postmodern systems methods were developed.*
> (Jackson 2003, p.62, 12.6)

One example of systems change that can help the entire eco-system is to stop the adding of toxicity into the system. This could mean addressing pollution but metaphorically, it could refer to addressing violence or mistreatment so that the other (e.g. human) parts of the system may live unimpeded by harm or violence. In the helping professions, social disruption relates to the colonialism, (structural) violence, displacement and the denial of life-sustaining activities. As such, applying a critical systems approach to an activity such as safety planning could be viable. It is important to acknowledge that natural systems do not necessarily refer to human beings who act with intent and deliberation.

Jackson offers a critique of cybernetics (2008), offering discernment between natural and human systems. He says that the defining feature of social organisations is the fact that their component parts are human beings who attribute meaning to their situations and act according to their own purposes. He believes that effort needs to be placed into managing processes of negotiation between different viewpoints and value positions. He writes, "Although cybernetics pays lip service to notions of empowerment and democracy, it actually says little about how individuals can be motivated to perform and how participation and democracy can be arranged." (Jackson 2008, p.108). There isn't an explicit analysis of what happens if there isn't an explicit analysis of what should be done if one individual within the system decides to abuse power and mistreat others. This is a limitation which lies within the systems metaphor. In the family therapy world, there was a famous debate between Jay Haley and Gregory Bateson about this very issue. I will briefly present this debate further along in the paper.

In the Islands of Safety work, we found the systems analysis and metaphor helpful in our work with Indigenous families. Most women continued to include their view of the male abusers as part of the family needing help and healing rather than a part of the system they wanted extricated. In fact, the child protection worker often took issue with the mother's efforts to include and assist the perpetrator. We were guided by the question, "How could it be safe enough for the child to be in the presence of their father?" Our team prepared and strategised around how to address limitations of the child protection system. For example, we knew from experience that 1) mothers are often encouraged to end their relationships with their partners (which leads to various larger social concerns) in order to keep custody of their children; 2) mothers are often "forbidden" from meeting the violent partner. Through a response-based lens, we understood and acknowledge the mother's safety knowledge. The mothers often found it helpful to talk to her partner and ascertain his state of mind. Child protection professionals saw this as risk rather than risk reduction, even though the child was not present. Finally, it was problematic that 3) the actions of the mother (and father) are often considered outside of any particular context and explained through the use of de-cultured, abstract theories (e.g. she has boundary issues or problems of discernment). Perhaps the most detrimental issue is that of mother-blaming.

Mother-blaming is one form of victim-blaming that is found in the human services. In particular, policies known as "failure to protect" tend to be used to designate the mother as neglectful and responsible for the family crisis (Strega et al 2012). The child protection logic has been that if the father is using violence against the mother it is, in some way, the mother's fault for choosing to be with him. As such, the child tends to be removed from the mother, not the father. Mothers are often subjected to psychological testing with the assumption that she must be psychologically "damaged", either by the violence or even before the violence, and therefore unfit to parent. In applying a systems approach, we would see the problem as located in between people, in the social world and not inside any one individual. Of course, the abuse of power by one member of the system can and must be addressed, but we would avoid individualising a systemic or social problem. We would question society's granting of impunity for male violence in certain contexts and the social systems which fail to adequately address the issue.

The logic of victim-blaming is found less with crimes such as stranger assault, or violence in social settings, such as bar-fights, bank-robberies or muggings; this logic is reserved for cases when the woman has been in an intimate relationship with the perpetrator (Strega et al 2012; Richardson and Wade 2012). One example from our practice is the issue of the victim choosing to meet with the perpetrator. We have observed that women often increase their safety when they meet with their violent partner at a time and place of their choosing, even if there is a "no contact" order in place. Trying to control a woman's actions around safety can undermine her process. Her situational analysis informs her decision to preserve the relationship, on her terms, with the perpetrator can be useful for information gathering. This decision should not be the business of child protection workers when the child is kept safe in the process, because safety is the goal, not "mother control".

It became important for achieving a positive outcome to continuously re-focus from criticism, judgments and stereotyping to the safety of mother and child. Many of these judgements are underlined by state power and undermine the mother's ability to provide safety (e.g. "Why doesn't she just leave him?", "This is the third time that she has called the police!"). When we focus on what the mother is already knowing and doing, guided by her situational logic and in relation to her understanding of the violence, we access more insight into her safety awareness and orientation. In general, in our experience the absence of a systemic or family therapy orientation to child protection work, along with an application of decontextualised and individualistic psychological theories and labels, undermines safety planning and simply builds a case against the mother (or the non-offending parent in cases of a violent mother). These issues comprise a foundation for how child protection systems do not deal fairly or appropriately with First Nations, Metis and Inuit families in Canada.

Cybernetics

Gregory Bateson was a "grandfather" of cybernetics and systems theory (Bateson 1979, 1972; Boscolo et al 1987). Keeney (1983) identifies other key cybernetic researchers as Heinz von Foerster, Humberto Maturana and Francisco Varela. Bateson was interested in how all life forms were connected and how people and environment were mutually influential. He was in awe of the natural world and was masterful at posing thought-provoking questions which highlighted these sacred relational qualities.

Later, his ideas were taken by family therapists, such as Tom Andersen (1987) and the Milan Team (1987) and applied to the study and practice of family therapy and what was called "cybernetic circularity" (Boscolo et al 1987, p.9). The Milan team explained:

> *by circularity, we mean the capacity of the therapist to conduct his investigation on the basis of feedback from the family on the*

> basis of the information he elicits about relationships and therefore about difference and change.
> (Selvini-Palazolli, Boscolo, Cecchin & Prata 1980, p.11)

Therapists noticed that it was more difficult to invite or provoke change if the family was insulated and too isolated from social influences and outside experiences. For example, when parents integrated some of the learning children were experiencing at school, feedback from teachers, psycho-educational information about social issues and family life, they were more likely to begin to incorporate changes in interaction. A kind of openness was helpful for resolving problems and improving relationships. This knowledge was applied to the concept of "an open system".

Allan Wade and I were both moved and inspired by the contribution of family therapy, including the work of the Milan Team, to addressing problems within families. Nora Bateson's film (2010) about her father's life and work depicts both a practical and an aesthetic interface with Gregory's understanding of the relationship between all things. The ideas shared in this film resonate with Indigenous cosmology in a way that began to explain some of the numinous and what could be considered sacred aspects of inter-species relationships. However, Bateson's articulation of these concepts only takes a few steps down a path into what could be called a spiritual cosmology as depicted by the various belief systems of Indigenous peoples, such as one that guides me, *mamatowisowin*...the Cree word referring to the interconnectedness of all of life, everything and everyone. This experience is knowledge (Ermine 2000, p.106).

Indigenous theory

Mamatowisowin is described by Indigenous cosmologist Willie Ermine as "the capacity of tapping into the "life force" as a means of procreation." It is a "capacity to tap the creative force of the inner space (inside one's being as opposed to in the external world) by the use of all the faculties that constitute our being – it is to exercise inwardness" (p.106). Ermine talks about how the elders, the Old Ones:

> *Experienced a totality, a wholeness, in inwardness, and effectively created A physical manifestation of the life force by creating community. In doing so, they empowered the people to become the "culture" of accumulated knowledge. The community became paramount by virtue of its role as repository and incubator of total*

> tribal knowledge in the form of custom and culture. Each part of the community became an integral part of the Whole flowing movement and was modeled on the inward wholeness and harmony.
>
> (Ermine 2000, p.106)

There is something about this knowledge and holism that is sought in the Islands of Safety process, in the interaction with Indigenous families. There is also something of "two worlds colliding" in child protection processes that necessitate facilitators to be advocates for families, to contest oppressive and colonising processes whenever they interfere with the process. For example, Islands of Safety is based on the practice of upholding and highlighting human dignity and the presence of safety. Dignity is restored by acknowledging past humiliations through colonialism or in social service settings. When a space is created for this type of introductory conversation, the level of trust and risk-taking tends to increase. It is important that the family experiences enough safety to be invited into "risky conversations," a term borrowed from the Fifth Province work in cases where abuse had occurred (McCarthy 2003; Richardson & Reynolds 2015) and that the workers/facilitators are genuinely concerned with how the family is treated in health and social care settings. The facilitators then use the information about "what didn't go well" in other health and social care situations to inform guidelines for the interaction this time around.

In subsequent rounds of questioning, related to the family's safety knowledges and the social responses they have been receiving, professionals and family members around the table are reflect and identify the presence of dignity in the family's interaction or in the mother's attempt to resist her partner's violence. We begin the first round by asking "How is everyone doing now?", "How do things look when your family is getting on well?" and "Is this your first interaction with child protection workers?" The intent of these questions is to establish the competency and dignity of each person, to highlight their preferred ways of being together. We ask about previous interaction with professionals so we can ascertain how that went and if they felt their dignity was upheld or violated. Acknowledging past humiliations in similar processes is one way to demonstrate our commitment to doing a better job this time. We might ask the question, "If we were to really mess up here today and do a bad job, what would that look like?" Often the humour creates a lighter atmosphere in which the family can list their preferences and their fears.

The second round of questioning aims to elicit events – who did what to whom and how did the victims respond to and resist abuse. After documenting a list of resistance strategies and the acts of violence to which they were responding, we ask them "Who else knows about what happened?" This leads into discussing the social responses to the family. We understand that victims of violence and families in which violence has occurred can easily become stigmatised. Once we find out how they are being treated by others (family, friends and professionals), then we elicit and document their responses to the social responses of others. As such, their pre-existing safety knowledge and strategies become apparent. Perhaps most relevant, women can see themselves as active, responding agents and not "someone who just took it!" Perhaps the greatest suffering of victims, after the betrayal and heartbreak, is the feeling that they didn't do enough to stop it —that is was in some way their fault. We contest this notion implicitly through the questions we ask and through the assumptions embedded within these questions.

In efforts to uphold the dignity of each person, we believe that perpetrators are capable of desisting violence (as many do, often without counselling). We also believe that treating people with dignity is more likely to be helpful than applying shame or righteousness. It is important that the facilitation team share this orientation. In one Islands of Safety meeting, one of the social workers representing the government said she would "pass", meaning she refused to comment on the dignity of the family. The facilitators had not "prepared" this worker for the meeting, nor known that she would attend, we would not have permitted her to join the meeting unless she was committed to abiding by the process and taking a "one down" position to assume human equality with the family. Generally, it is not difficult to name "dignified interaction" one has witnessed on the part of the family and reflect this back to them. This kind of acknowledgement creates a safer and more uplifted space, similar to that of "The Fifth Province," where conversation is acknowledged as sacred and where people can share anything with a commitment of all parties to listening and respect (Byrne & McCarthy 2007; McCarthy 2010b). The Fifth Province is a metaphor for a Celtic province in ancient Ireland, a site where Chieftains would meet to discuss matters of state. The Hill of the Kings existed in the centre of Ireland where the four political provinces met thereby constituting a fifth province. It was imagined to be a Druidic site where the Kings and chieftains of various clans came to sort out difficulties, not by fighting. They would lay down their arms and come and talk, and receive counsel from the Druids. It was a place where oppositions came and collided. It was a place of work,

Creating Islands of Safety for Victims of Violence

of negotiation, to identify what the issues were... their relationship to other issues. In this way, conversation is a means of weaving together action, interaction and the context in which it is embedded. The ritualistic focus on creating a "sacred space" resonates both through Fifth Province and Islands of Safety work. There is no desire to minimise, categorise or individualise, privatise, de-contextualise or de-genderise asymmetrical interactions involving violence and responses to it, including resistance. Acknowledging that these are issues of life and death, the greatest attention is paid to "the small acts of living" (Goffman 1963) and how they contribute to staying alive in dangerous situations (Wade 1997). Some of the crucial safety practices have been recently documented in an article (Richardson and Reynolds 2015) entitled "Structuring safety in conversations with survivors of torture and residential school." As well, safety is attended to by focusing on human dignity in all aspects of the gathering, although safety is meant to be a "bottom line" rather than a defining goal of human interaction. Through highlighting resistance, knowledge and preferences, Islands of Safety participants may re-envision their highest aspirations for a preferred life.

These aforementioned processes articulate informal guidelines for the process. Islands of Safety is not a "talking circle" where people can say just anything; nor is it a restorative justice process. It is a meeting where the safety of those most harmed is held up over all else in the process of safety planning. The voices and desires of victims are given precedence in guiding the process. The perpetrators have committed to participating safely, without intimidating others and are willing to hear how the violent behaviour has elicited particular responses and resistance of others who are trying to create safety and dignity. For the perpetrator to be included, we used particular criteria to ensure that participation would be meaningful and that there would never be any "backlash" for victims (Richardson and Wade 2008). Unlike some processes of mediation or circles, we do not assume there is an equality of resources, privilege or safety. Rather, we acknowledge the risks, differences in power and what is necessary to create immediate safety in the process.

Collapsing gender and difference – Bateson and obfuscations of power

Islands of Safety is about assisting people to create safety and overcome violence. A key part of understanding, assessing and addressing violence involves a study of power. Power is about the ability to exert one's will in an unimpeded manner (*puissance*) and to make things happen in one's world (*pouvoir*) (Deleuze cited in Marks, p.60). Foucault (1991) saw power as being at work everywhere, as diffused, embodied in discourse and knowledge. He believed that we are all affected by power and that it is not necessarily a bad thing, sometimes it is just leverage. In terms of exercising power, the role of the Islands of Safety facilitator involves holding knowledge of the system and making sure its policies are realised to the benefit of "safety". For example, this means contesting systemic discrimination against abused mothers. It also means relying on accurate accounts and avoiding misrepresentation. It means upholding the dignity of the person in every interaction and contesting the unjust power of the state where there is unfairness in application of policies.

In some contexts, pouvoir involves impunity. Wherever there is power, and particularly oppression and violence at work, there is resistance. The 1960s/1970s West, saw a rise in feminist praxis and a movement towards attention to gender and equality within the context of a largely patriarchal North American society. Sexism was being challenged both in western societies at large and in the patriarchal family (Mander & Rush 1974; Byrne & McCarthy 1999; McCarthy 2001). Wife assault was being identified as a critical social issue and women's resistance to violence in the home would eventually emerge as an important part of analysis and contextual understanding. Inspired by the work of feminists, Indigenous people and writers from the anti-colonial movement, Allan Wade writes:

> *Whenever persons are badly treated, they resist. That is, alongside each history of violence and oppression, there runs a parallel history of prudent, creative and determined resistance.*
>
> (1997, p.23)

These points were introduced into therapeutic conversations by feminist therapists, inviting the field to consider the existence of violence, inequality and imbalances of power in both society and in the therapy room (Mander & Rush 1974; Byrne & McCarthy 1999; McCarthy 2001). An important debate between therapist Jay Haley and Gregory Bateson in debate around the issue of power. Bateson presented his view that power was a myth (1972) but acknowledged that those parties who believed in power were often corrupted by it or sought to abuse it. Rather than believing in the existence of unilateral power, he believed that the parts of the system influence each other (p.486). Haley believed that humans regularly sought to influence one another and often organise themselves into hierarchies, seeking advantage over others (Carr 1991, p.16). Haley would address this strategically in the therapy session in ways which he believed would improve the functioning of the family. Carr (1991) suggests that both Haley and Bateson worked with only one simplistic definition of power where there are actually several different kinds (p.20). In our work with Islands of Safety, we paid attention to the earlier feminist critiques and were perhaps most moved by Carr's idea that "Mutuality of influence does not imply equality of power".

> *A central problem with Bateson's position is the assumption that mutual influence implies "a mutual amount of influence". There is no doubt that in any social influence situation both parties are influenced by each other. However, often one party is influenced more than the other. For example, wives are more often seriously physically injured by their husbands than visa versa (Neidig & Friedman, 1984). Children are more often abused by their parents than vice versa.*
>
> (Goldstein et al, 1985)

As such, we would contest practices of victim-blaming as well as mutualisations of unilateral violence, such as co-dependency, complementarity (Richardson and Wade 2012). Today, I would add children and children's authors to the list of those who have inspired response-based practice. Indeed, we have had to look beyond the fields of psychology and psychiatry for the inspiration of survivors, former political prisoners and women targeted by men's violence. Wade's article "Small Acts of Living" (1997) documents how the theme of "healthy" resistance is absent from the psychotherapy literature, apart from a few important exceptions (e.g. Burstow 1992; Epston, Murray & White 1992; Gillian, Rogers & Tolman 1991; Kelly 1987; McCarthy & Byrne 2001). What does it mean for our field when the majority of theorists ignore the fact of resistance to violence and that victims are already engaged in dignity preservation and safety planning throughout their experience, not just at the coaching of professionals. The article "Taking Resistance Seriously" (Richardson & Wade 2008) provides examples of psychological theories of abuse survivors which could be described at least as women-unfriendly and victim-blaming. Today, theories such as the Johnson Typology (2008) construct women who resist violence as aggressors thus further confounding self-preservation with violent aggression and potentially criminalising self-defence. These types of ideas also negative the reality that resistance is much more than merely fighting back physicality but involves a multitude of spiritual, emotional and intellectual processes (Richardson & Wade 2008). These blurring of lines is avoided by adhering to a definition of violence as being unilateral, deliberate, and social (e.g. it takes place in the social world, not in the mind of the victim). "For years psychologists have been trying to address men's violence by tampering in the minds of women" (Wade personal communication, Mind the Gap 2015). It hasn't worked.

Twenty years later, response-based practice was developed partially to address this crucial absence relating to how victims of violence are construed and treated in society, "stigmatized" as James C. Scott (1990) and Erving Goffman (1963) would state. Coates and Wade (2004) knew that until this stigmatisation of violence victims was addressed, there would neither be peace in family life for many women and children, NOR gender equality.

Concluding by embracing the sacred in Islands of Safety

The Islands of Safety process was developed in consultation with Indigenous women, men, elders, cultural teachers as well as child protection social workers. It has been informed by many therapists, practitioners and individuals/families who embrace the sacred in their daily lives. Inspired by processes of ceremony, medicine wheels, the sweat lodge, the Fifth Province, as well as studies of interpersonal dignity. One of the things we learned from Indigenous women is that they want their men to heal too. They acknowledge a brutal history of colonial/state violence and that both men and women were targets of this harm; as such, both men and women deserve support for living lives free of violence. There are still areas of Canada that are rampant with multiple forms of violence due to ongoing state neglect. At the same time, Indigenous people everywhere are active through protest, through ceremony, through identity-strengthening for the victims of state child welfare and child internment. Their work includes prayers, sharing teachings, travel to ceremonies and blessings for Earth. It is my view that dignity is the path to restoration and social harmony. Dignity involves autonomy, sovereignty, mutual aid and a full-on effort to address structural violence and racism. The official count of murdered and disappeared Indigenous women in Canada today is 1186, a figure dating back 30 years (CBC 2014). Many Canadians are waiting for an end to the impunity experienced by many perpetrators and a whole-hearted commitment to address such forms of racist, sexist and class-based violence.

It is possible to work with families who suffer violence, serve as allies, support victims and hold perpetrators accountable whilst treating them with dignity. We can work as advocates and activists, within our role as therapists, to help create societies that are more just for marginalised and First Peoples. If fifty years of therapeutic knowledge and evolving family practice cannot be used to help create safety for families, then what is the point of the work, after all. For me, it is about creating these islands of safety and care... not about exploring what is wrong with people.

Acknowledgement

Thanks for Robin Routledge for his interest and feedback on the chapter. It is much appreciated. You are intricately part of my eco-system and community of the heart!

References

Anderson, Kim (2000). *A Recognition of Being: Reconstructing Native Womanhood.* Toronto: Sumach Press.

Andersen, Tom (1987). Dialogue and Meta-Dialogue. *Family Process*, 26, 415–428.

Bateson, Gregory (1979). *Mind and Nature.* New York: Dutton.

Bateson, Gregory (1972). *Steps to an Ecology of Mind: Collected Essays in Anthropology, Psychiatry, Evolution, and Epistemology.* San Francisco: Chandler.

Bateson, Nora (2010). *An Ecology of Mind.* Film. Reading, PA: Bullfrog Films.

Boscolo, Luigi; Cecchin, Gianfranco; Hoffman, L. & Penn, Peggy (1987). *Milan Systemic Family Therapy.* New York: Basic Books.

Brown, Lyn (1991). Telling a Girl's Life: Self-Authorization as a Form of Resistance. In Gilligan, Carol, Rogers, A.G. and Tolman, D. (Eds). (2013). *Women, Girls and Psychotherapy: Reframing Resistance.* Binghampton, NY: Harrington Park Press.

Burstow, Bonnie (1992). *Radical Feminist Therapy: Working in the Context of Violence.* London: Sage.

Byrne, Nollaig & McCarthy, Imelda (1999). Feminism, Power and Discourse in Systemic Family Therapy: Fragments from the Fifth Province. In I. Parker [Ed.], *Deconstructing Psychotherapy.* London: Sage.

Byrne, Nollaig & McCarthy, Imelda (2007). The Dialectical Structure of Hope and Despair: A Fifth Province Approach. In Carmel Flaskas, Imelda McCarthy & Jim Sheehan (2007). *Hope and Despair. in Narrative and Family Therapy: Reflections on Adversity, Forgiveness and Reconciliation.* New York: Hove-Brunner Routledge.

Carr, Allan (1991). Power and Influence in Systemic Consultation. *Human Systems: Journal of Systemic Consultation and Management*, 2, 15–20.

Carriere, Jeannine & Richardson, Cathy (2013). Relationship is everything: Holistic approaches to Aboriginal child and youth mental health. *First Peoples Child and Family Review*, 7(2), 8–26.

CBC News. (2014) Posted 1st May 2014: http://www.cbc.ca/news/politics/report-of-1-000-murdered-or-missing-aboriginal-women-spurs-calls-for-inquiry-1.2628372

Coates, Linda & Wade, Allan (2004). Telling It Like It Isn't: Obscuring perpetrator responsibility for violent crime. *Discourse & Society*, 15(5), 499–526.

Epston, David; White, Michael, & Murray, Kevin (1992). A Proposal for a Re-Authoring Therapy: Rose's revisioning of her life and a commentary. In Sheila McNamee and Kenneth. J. Gergen (Eds.), *Therapy as Social Construction* (96–115). London: Sage.

Foucault, Michel (1991). *Discipline and Punish: The Birth of a Prison*. London: Penguin.

Ermine, Willie (2000). Aboriginal Epistemology. In M. Battistes & J. Barman (Eds.) *First Nations Education in Canada: The Circle Unfolds*. Vancouver, B.C: UBC Press.

Faith, Erika (2007). Seeking "Mamatowisowin" to create an engaging social policy class for Aboriginal students. *First Peoples Child & Family Review*, 3(4).

Flood Robert & Jackson Michael (1991). *Creative Problem Solving: Total Systems Intervention*. Wiley: Chichester.

Foucault, Michel (1977). *Power/Knowledge*. New York: Pantheon Books.

Freedberg, Sharon (2015). *Relational Theory for Clinical Practice*. New York: Routledge.

Gilligan, Carol: Rogers, Annie & Tolman, Deborah. (2013). *Women, Girls and Psychotherapy: Reframing Resistance*. New York: Routledge.

Goffman, Erving (1963). *Stigma: Notes on a Spoiled Identity*. New York: Doubleday.

Hui, Julie: Cashman, Ty & Deacon, Terrance (2008). Bateson's Method: Double Description. What Is It? How Does It Work? What Do We Learn? In Jesper Hoffman [Ed.], (2008). *A Legacy for Living Systems: Gregory Bateson as Precursor to Biosemiotics*. New York: Springer Books.

Jackson, Michael (2003). *Systems Thinking: Creative Holism for Managers*. Chichester: Wiley.

Johnson, Michael (2008). *A Typology of Domestic Violence: Intimate Terrorism, Violent Resistance and Situational Couple Violence*. Boston, MA: Northeastern University Press.

Keeney, Bradford (1983). *Aesthetics of Change*. New York: The Guildford Family Therapy Series.

Kelly, Liz (1988). *Surviving Sexual Violence*. Oxford: Blackwell Press.

Little Bear, Leroy (2000). Jagged Worldviews Collide. In M. Battiste (Ed.), *Reclaiming Indigenous Voice and Vision*. Vancouver, BC: UBC Press.

Marks, John (1998). *Gilles Deleuze: Vitality and Multiplicity*. London: Pluto Press.

McCarthy, Imelda & Byrne, Nollaig (2001). Resisting Daughters: Father-Daughter Child Sexual Abuse Disclosure. In A. Clearly, M. Nic Ghiolla Phadraig & S. Oui, [Eds], *Understanding Children, Vol. 2: Changing Experiences and Family Forms*. Dublin: Oak Tree Press.

McCarthy, Imelda. (2001). Fifth Province Re-Versings: The social construction of women lone parents' inequality and poverty. *Journal of Family Therapy*, 23(3), 253–277.

McCarthy, Imelda (2010a). A Traumatic Intrusion with Transgressive Possibilities: Power as a relational and discursive phenomenon. *Context*, Oct. 2010.

McCarthy, Imelda (2010b). The Fifth Province: Imagining a space of Ddalogical co-creations. *Context*, Dec. 2010.

Rice, Brian (2005). *Seeing the World with Aboriginal Eyes: A Four Dimensional Perspective on Human and Non-Human Values, Cultures and Relationships on Turtle Island*. Winnipeg, Manitoba, Canada: Aboriginal Issues Press.

Simpson, Leann (2000). Anishinaabe Ways of Knowing. In J. Oakes, R. Riew, S. Koolage, L. Simpson, & N. Schuster (Eds.), *Aboriginal Health, Identity and Resources*. Winnipeg, Manitoba, Canada: Native Studies Press.

Richardson, Cathy & Reynolds, Vikki (2015). Structuring safety in conversations with survivors of torture and residential school. *Canadian Journal of Native Studies*. xxxiv, 2, 147–164

Richardson, Cathy (2012). Witnessing life transitions with Ritual and Ceremony in Family Therapy: Three examples from a Métis therapist. *Journal of Systemic Therapies*. 31(3), 68–78.

Richardson, Cathy & Wade, Allan (2012). Creating Islands of Safety: Contesting "Failure to Protect and Mother-Blaming in Child Protection Cases of Paternal Violence Against Children and Mothers. In S. Strega, J. Krane, S. LaPierre & C. Richardson (Eds.), *Failure to Protect: Moving Beyond Gendered Responses to Violence*. Winnipeg, MB: Fernwood.

Richardson, Cathy (2009). Islands of Safety and the Social Geography of Human Dignity: A child and mother safety planning initiative for cases of paternal violence in child welfare. *Federation of Community Social Services of BC, Research to Practice Network*, 1–12.

Richardson, Cathy & Wade, Allan (2008). Taking Resistance Seriously. In [Eds]. Susan Strega & Jeannine Carriere. *Walking This Path Together: Anti-Oppressive and Anti-Racist Social Work*. Winnipeg: Fernwood Publications.

Scott, James (1990). *Domination and the Arts of Resistance.* New Haven, USA: Yale University Press.

Statistics Canada. *Aboriginal Peoples in Canada: First Nations, Métis and Inuit National Household Survey.* (2011). Ottawa: Government of Canada.

Systems Research and Behavioral Science Syst. Res. 23, 647–657 (2006) Published online in Michael C. Jackson (Ed.) *Wiley InterScience Creative Holism: A Critical Systems Approach to Complex Problem Situations.* Hull, UK: The Business School, University of Hull.

Smith, Linda Tuhiwai (1999). *Decolonizing Methodologies: Research and Indigenous peoples.* New York: Zed Books.

Strega, Susan; Krane, Julia; LaPierre, Simon & Richardson, Cathy (Eds.) (2012). *Failure to Protect: Moving Beyond Gendered Responses to Violence.* Winnipeg, MB: Fernwood.

Thomas, Robina & Green, Jacquie (2007). A Way of Life: Indigenous perspectives on anti-oppressive living. *First Peoples Child and Family Review*, 3(1), 91–104.

von Bertalanffy Ludwig (1968). *General Systems Theory.* Penguin: Harmondsworth.

Wade, Allan (1997). Small Acts of Living. *Contemporary Family Therapy*, 19(1), 23–39.

Wade, A. (1995). Resistance Knowledges: Therapy with Aboriginal persons who have been subjected to violence. In P. H. Stephenson, S. J. Elliott, L. T. Foster & J. Harris (Eds.) *A Persistent Spirit: Towards Understanding Aboriginal Health in British Columbia.* (167–206). Vancouver: University of British Columbia.

Wiener Norbert (1948). *Cybernetics.* Wiley: New York.

Walker, Polly (2004). Decolonizing Conflict Resolution. *American Indian Quarterly*, 28(3 & 4), 527–549.

Walsh-Tapiata, Wheturangi (2008). The Past, the Present, and the Future: The New Zealand Indigenous experience of social work. In M. Gray: J. Coates & M. Yellow Bird (Eds.), *Indigenous Social Work Around the World: Towards Culturally Relevant Education and Practice.* Burlington, VT: Ashgate Publishing.

Systemic Practice in a Complex System
Child sexual abuse and the Catholic Church

17

Marie Keenan

Introduction

Having worked with victims of sexual crime and with sex offenders for more than twenty years my interest in the subject matter of this chapter specifically arose from my clinical experience as a systemic psychotherapist who, along with two colleagues, established a community-based treatment programme in Ireland in 1996 for child sex offenders. There we also saw victims of Catholic clergy. From its inception the treatment facility attracted a number of Roman Catholic priests and religious brothers for treatment of sexually abusive behaviour, and the therapeutic model that we developed was a systemic one that also included narrative approaches. At the same time, the model respected the "evidence-based" literature that deemed cognitive behavioural approaches to treatment of men who had sexually offended as meeting the gold standard, and we incorporated this approach too. What, in fact, developed was an amalgam of treatment methodologies that were coherently organised within a systemic conceptual frame, and in order to do so, we used the "as if" perspective to cognitive work – "as though" cognitive "distortions" existed. However, this chapter focuses on systemic interventions with Catholic clergy who had sexually abused minors. In this chapter I will use the term "victim" when referring to people who have experienced sexual abuse as children, for reasons of brevity and to signify the fact that sexual abuse is also a crime. I will use the term "offender" when referring to individuals who have perpetrated sexual offences, for reasons of brevity and to signify the fact that offender is the term used in the criminal justice system for such individuals. Later, I discuss the limitations of such identity descriptions.

Despite occasional mutterings in the public press and the rare suggestion in empirical literature, there is no evidence to suggest that Catholic clergy enter clerical and religious life with the purpose of gaining access to children to abuse them. In fact, the most comprehensive research ever carried out on sexual abuse by Catholic clergy, conducted by researchers in the United States (John Jay College, 2011), reports that whatever else formed the men's motivation for joining, there is no evidence to suggest that gaining access to children in order to abuse them was part of it. My own experience confirmed this. The more I met with the clerical men who had abused, the more intrigued I became. Put simply, I was not in the presence of "monsters", nor was I in the presence of individuals who had an "illness". I began to think there must be more to this problem – situational, organisational and institutional – that must also be considered.

Apart from offering treatment to clerical men who had offended and to victims of sexual crime, I realised from the early days of my involvement with the clerical offenders that there was another dimension to the abuse problem – the handling of abuse complaints by the church hierarchy. This has become apparent in almost every country in the world in which child sexual abuse by Catholic clergy has come to light. Whilst seen by some as two separate and distinct problems, it was clear to me from the outset, that the two problems were interlinked. I formed the view from research and clinical work with both cohorts and with their broader systems, including non-offending clergy, canon lawyers and theologians, that some of the factors that contributed to a climate in which the clerical men could sexually offend also contributed to the conditions that made it possible for the church hierarchy to act as they did in the handling of abuse complaints. In essence, they were both part of the same institutional culture and I began to be curious about a number of matters: What kind of an organisation could accommodate a story of abuse like this? What would the rest of the organisation have to be like for its members to behave like this? What would the workings of this institution have to be for individual bishops to act as they did? What would the workings of the institution have to be for local church organisations – as far apart as Cork and Canada, Boston and Berlin – to act with such uniformity as they did? With the response to the problem by the national church organisations indicating universal similarities, I found that all roads led to Rome and to the heart of the Roman Catholic Church in the Vatican, and my therapeutic work and curiosity took me to these places, in various ways and in various forms.

While within the clerical culture of the Catholic Church not all priests were abusive, it was also important to determine the particular dynamic circumstances that gave way to sexual offending on the part of some clerical men. This could not be done without remembering the larger cultural landscape within which this abuse took place. The same held for the "erring" bishops. That was part of my project which I have fully elaborated in earlier works on the topic (see Claffey, Egan and Keenan, 2013; Keenan, 2009, 2012, 2013).

Background and context

My mother was a central character in my life. Formally uneducated but with an insight into the human condition that none could teach, and I, the first of her five children, was to be a beneficiary of a depth of wisdom that flowed effortlessly as she and my father coached their five children from childhood to adulthood in an Ireland that was undergoing great social change. A significant aspect of this change included the position of the Catholic Church in Ireland which, until the 1980s, was a mono-cultural, and predominantly Catholic country. Here, the lessons that I now see as resonating with social constructionist thought began: Rules are man-made and meant to be questioned; never judge a book by its cover; never underestimate the power of the human spirit; trust your instinct, but always remember that your view is not the only one; do not fear those in authority, such as doctors and clergy, and never take as "gospel" what they tell you; doing what you think is right often involves risks (of rebuttal or rejection); tread gently for life is difficult. Within the parameters of this humble working-class enclave, I learned "to avoid isolation" and "refuse indifference" (Weingarten, 2007: 15) and that by doing so, lives and worlds can change. In these early years, I also learned the importance of having allies in life, and finding people who were interested in standing with me in solidarity in my professional endeavours.

My primary training as a social scientist, later as a social worker, and later still as a systemic and forensic psychotherapist, equipped me with the intellectual skills to undertake my professional life and to evolve and expand my intellectual horizons over what is now a period of more than 40 years. The myriad of clients whose lives intertwined with mine gave shape to that learning, teaching me the small but important lessons in what it means to be a compassionate and courageous worker. In translating compassion and courage into activities that fight against isolation and indifference and work on behalf of inclusion and relevance, I learned to welcome folks, to be hospitable, to avoid labels, to be humble but not self- effacing, to lead and be led, to listen carefully to what people said, to honour silence, to be sceptical of certainty, to be curious and to take risks (Foucault 2001, pp. 1–24). The more I learned about clients' lives (both victims and offenders) the more the distinctions between "us" and "them" became increasingly unsustainable. "They" were "us" and "we" were "them" – connected by more than divided us. This became increasingly clear when both worker and client managed to "show up" (Fisher 2008) and particularly when the dialogue moved to the sphere of hopes, dreams, values, and intentions for life. For Fisher "showing up" means that the person, with their skills, knowledge, intentions, pain, and vulnerabilities, show up and allow themselves to be seen and heard in dialogue with others.

As I reflect back on my introduction to social constructionism proper, four important forces came together to sway my life and work in that direction: my work as a probation and welfare officer in a Dublin prison, my training as a systemic therapist in the first family therapy programme in Ireland my introduction to the narrative work of Michael White and meeting Art Fisher, a narrative therapist who runs a programme in Nova Scotia for responding to love, hurt, and violence in families. (For further information the reader is directed to http://www.alternativesinstitute.com).

While the work in the prison offered humbling evidence of embodied resilience and marginalised despair in the men whose lives had taken them into confinement, my systemic training offered a questioning site of much new learning. Run by Imelda McCarthy, Nollaig Byrne, and Philip Kearney of the Fifth Province Associates, the systemic family therapy training programme also provided support and challenge as my exposure to the philosophy of social constructionism took hold. Imelda and Nollaig, who were to become lifelong friends and mentors, were also unknowingly to become the guardians of my new social constructionist and systemic home, as I learned to witness and meet with imprisoned men and those who loved them. The work of Michael White (2000, 2004) led me to consider the multiple meanings of "imprisonment" and the "life sentences" imposed by Western psychiatric practices. Having worked in adolescent and adult psychiatry, I developed scepticism towards the promises offered by psychiatric practices, for example as pathways to liberation from emotional pain, which contrasted with the stigmatised identities and side-effects of medication that often came instead. I learned that diagnostic classification systems are instruments of power that mask the power relations involved in their very construction (Foucault, 1991, 2004). I concluded that diagnostic classification systems served interests other than of those of the so-called diagnosed. The work of Fisher (2008, 2009) showed me the lengths to which we must go to create new narratives and to thicken the plot of alternative identity descriptions with clients and the role of love and emotion in the therapeutic process, especially with victims and offenders for whom violence has been part of their lives.

Systemic Practice in a Complex System

All of these experiences compelled a professional coming-of-age and a wake-up call from which there was no return. Going forward, all taken-for-granted ideas and truths, particularly in the human sciences, became "truth in parenthesis" and just one version. No longer could truth claims in the social sciences be accepted as outside of the context of their creation (Foucault, 1991, 2004), which included the sphere of influence of vested interests, ideology, and power relations. Going forth, all taken-for-granted truths in the "soft" sciences would have to be deconstructed and challenged, in the name of ethical practice, and any suggestion that certainty or truth could be arrived at through "scientific" methods, "objective" instruments and "objective" researchers was no longer acceptable. Grand theory would have to be "held lightly" (McCarthy, 2002). In its place came my interest in the omnipresence of power, ideology, and emotion and the influence of this trio on the creation of knowledge and on how human beings live. I also became interested in the power of language and in the stories that get told and that people tell about themselves and their lives. It was also during this time that I committed myself anew to working *with* the people who sought my help rather than *on* them. I decided that the only way forward was to offer *with-ness* work (Shotter, 2005), with people whose life met with mine, rather than *aboutness work* or *on-ness* work that engaged clients, whether victims or offenders as object-subjects. I also committed myself to joining with the individuals who consulted me in the search for meaning. My belief and subsequent experience was that in the creation of such conversational and human meetings that lives and worlds can change.

Finding a place to stand

All systemic practice is a form of reflexive inquiry and it was clear to me in undertaking my work with victims of clergy and with clerical men who had sexually abused children, both as a Catholic citizen of the Republic of Ireland and a mother of two children that I was an insider and an outsider to the process and that the journey would necessarily be a reflexive one in which all assumptions and prejudice must be held "in parenthesis".

Confronting sexual abuse of minors goes to the very heart of what most adults appear to abhor, and in working with victims and particularly with men who had abused I had a number of concerns. Whose truth matters and whose account can claim to be final? Whose story is to be privileged and whose is to be marginalised? Can a space be created in which all voices are held and honoured, and in which no one is disqualified? What position or observation point should a therapist take when it comes to criminal acts that have been committed? What about "us" and "them" distinctions? Should perpetrators tell their story or should they be listened to only through the lens of lawful and clinical assessment and through legal judgment and punishment?

While I was always clear about the powerlessness of the child victim in situations of sexual abuse and in their attempts to get "justice" as adults within the criminal courts and in relation to the Catholic Church, I also wondered about other dimensions of victimhood and perpetrator-hood and who defines and reifies these crucial distinctions. While registering differences in scale, in different situations and different contexts, I wondered whether we have all been victims in some contexts while taking on the perpetrator role in others. Furthermore, are there contexts in which we have all been bystanders, particularly in situations that involved sexual violence? In contemplating the personal violence involved in sexual abuse of minors, I wondered about social violence and how it too goes unaddressed. I also wondered if our reactions to the violence and the continued trauma could be transformed into compassionate witnessing for all, with the potential for addressing and finding healing from the pain (Weingarten, 2003, p.7).

It is always challenging to try to locate oneself in the place of another person. To do so with victims of sexual abuse has often been a challenging lesson in humility as I was continually taught to listen carefully to the entirely subjective nature of their experience, irrespective of the type or level of the offence. To locate myself in the place of the other when the other is someone who has sexually abused a child also brought forth existential, uncomfortable moments that took me to the core of human dignity and sexuality. To locate myself in the place of the bishops who were seen as covering up the defilement of children has also posed significant challenges.

It is not easy to acknowledge or accept one's own potential for inflicting pain on another person, most especially a child, or to contemplate for a moment that I could be like "him". We all like to think that we would do the right thing. The psychological threat of identification with the "otherness" of people who abuse children, or with bishops who are said to have covered up their abuses, which is always challenging, is even more difficult when one is in the midst of a problem of truly global proportions, and involving seemingly privileged men who have broken the most sacred of sacred trusts. Discourses of guilt, shame, blame, sorrow, rage, and disqualification are omnipresent in such a constellation, and I encountered all in my professional journey with this work.

Systemic Practice in a Complex System

Many people are directly and personally affected by child sexual abuse, primarily the immediate victims, but we also know that the effects extend way beyond the immediate and identifiable victims—to their families, the perpetrators' families, their colleagues and friends, the perpetrators themselves, church leaders, and those who work with them. However, the social-psychological processes necessary to live through such extreme emotions and the life trajectories and stories that underpin them are not usually part of the public conversation. Almost no public debate focuses on the psychological process involved in living through such public/personal trauma for the victims, public humiliation and vilification for the perpetrators, and the pain of their families and those who love them. Little public debate focuses on how difficult it must be for aged and sometimes unwell bishops to be the focus of intense public anger on a daily basis. The debate is usually limited to typical themes such as deviance, pathology, and betrayal by perpetrators, trauma and damage to victims and their families, and "cover-up" and betrayal by the church leaders. Understandable as this might be at one level, it also leaves a psychosocial void.

The shock that we experience as a result of the revelations of sexual violence against minors has no useful place to go either. No appropriate language is easily available that allows for compassionate witness; all healing language seems to be eclipsed by the language of blame. This is the general context in which I set out work in this area and to find a place to stand in which I could do so. I wanted to embrace all stories and silence no one. However, if sides had to be taken I knew where I stood. I had found that place many years ago in working with other victims and perpetrators of trauma and violence, as I walked and talked and sat in witness. I take a stand on the side of all human beings who are trying to find a way through life in the best and only way possible, while taking a radical stand against cruelty, violence, injustice, and institutional and personal hypocrisy in all its many manifestations.

Resisting totalising descriptions of the victim

Beyond serving the important function of providing a language for legal proceedings and of giving emphasis to the criminal aspects of the behaviour of sexual abuse and violence that has hitherto gone in the main unrecognised, the language of "victim" and "offender" is actually a limiting one, acting as a constraint and barrier in any endeavour to understand the complex issues involved, and to find a way forward. When can one stop being cast as a victim, or is this always the description that accompanies one through life? When does one stop being cast as an offender: one year, ten years, forty years after the offence? When is the attribution of these descriptions something personal and when is it a public process?

Although a full examination of the experiences of the survivors of sexual abuse by Catholic clergy is beyond the scope of this chapter, the Ryan Report (2009) revealed that emotional, physical and sexual abuse was endemic within child care institutions run by the religious orders on behalf of the Irish state. It was reported that children were regularly subjected to severe, violent and arbitrary corporal punishments that were designed to maximise pain and humiliation. This created a pervasive climate of fear as children never knew when or why the next beating would occur. Their emotional trauma was exacerbated by constant ridicule and other practices designed to elicit feelings of shame and degradation. Children were often separated from families and some were even informed (falsely) that their parents were dead. In addition, malnutrition, inadequate clothing, oppressive regimes, austere accommodation, poor hygiene, and limited education and training opportunities contributed to a culture of physical neglect. Sexual abuse was also common in male institutions. Studies have found that survivors of child sexual abuse may experience long-term psychological, economic and social consequences. Carr et al. (2010) studied the psychological well-being of 247 survivors of institutional abuse and found that over 80% were suffering from psychological disorders, including anxiety, mood and substance abuse, and had weak social attachments. In addition, Barrett, Kamiya and O'Sullivan (2014) found that male victims of child sexual abuse are three times more likely than the general population to be unemployed as a result of illness or disability.

In modern society sex acts with children are illegal because of the likelihood of harm to children. However, there is evidence to show that children are not universally harmed by sexual abuse (Clancy, 2010), although some very clearly are, as suggested above. For some individuals it is a relatively unimportant event in their lives, or even a challenge from which they have gained strength. Clancy argues that survivors of childhood sexual abuse are victimised not only by their abusers (whose acts often leave them confused and sometimes frightened), but also and inadvertently by well-intentioned health professionals, whose interpretations of abusive experiences are often more traumatic than the actual events and effects themselves. Here Clancy is drawing attention to the social discourse in which the problem is embedded. Drawing on case studies, statistics, and technical data, Clancy opposes the view that abusive acts destabilise the neurobiology of the victim, as in other traumas. Positing that the trauma model damages victims of sexual abuse with inaccurate predictions and ineffective treatments, she suggests that what hurts most victims is not the experience itself but the meaning of the experience and how victims make sense of what happened, in line with the available societal and therapeutic discourses, and how these understandings make them feel about themselves and others. My work with victims of sexual abuse was respectful of the fact that some experience deep trauma as a result of the experience while some people who experienced sexual abuse are not affected adversely by the experience. Such individuals however often require solidarity and support in making the offender accountable, in redressing power imbalances in relationships and in attending to child protection concerns. They also need acceptance of their claim that they are not psychologically or in any other way "damaged".

For those individuals who were adversely affected by the sexual abuse my commitment was to "hold lightly" any pathologising labels that they acquired through their lives and instead to see the trauma as a shock to their system, an intrusion into their normal functioning and something from which they could reclaim their lives. However, I was respectful of (but not held captive to) classifications and labels – such as post-traumatic stress disorder – in circumstances in which a victim felt that such were helpful to them. In most cases with victims I joined with the outrage at what had occurred, joined in solidarity with them in their efforts to regain power in their lives, heal what needed to be healed, seek accountability and social justice through the courts and restorative justice mechanisms and ensure that other children would be protected.

However, at the core of my work was the idea that the identity of children who suffered child sexual abuse must not be totalised as victim. It has been my experience that modern popular culture now appears to accept that there are unjust limitations imposed on individuals who have experienced abuse when their identities are totalised as victims. In response to calls from victims themselves, society accepts some of the other descriptions them, such as "survivor" or "thriver". However, even these labels do not always do justice to the complexities and richness of the lives and the skills and knowledge that many individuals who have experienced sexual abuse in childhood give testimony. In the public domain we all too often focus on the negative effects of trauma. This is, of course, important and must be highlighted time and time again. However, we usually do so without ever considering the importance of the individual's "response" to trauma and what this shows about the wisdom and bravery of abuse survivors. We know from the trauma literature that wherever there is a story of oppression, there is a parallel story of resistance, and it is in these small, maybe even ordinary or neglected stories of resistance that we see the bravery and "agency" of even the smallest child, who took on the offender in the most skilful of ways (McCarthy and Byrne, 2001; Wade, 1997; White, 2000, 2004). In neglecting to focus on human responses to trauma and the enormous steps that individuals, including children, take to prevent abuse and to resist its after-effects, we are disqualifying or rendering invisible huge reserves in the human spirit.

I have long been persuaded by the work of Michael White, an Australian psychotherapist, who tells us that the ways in which people respond to trauma are based on what they give value to, or what they hold precious (White, 2004, p.48). What is often really striking in trauma work is how individuals continue to privilege certain values in life and to preserve what is precious to them such as love or justice, despite everything they have been through. So what is required is actually a double listening: listening for the effects of trauma and being open to the responses to trauma too (p.48). By having an open ear for both, we are listening not just for disempowerment, but for personal agency, in the magnificent and incredible ways all victims of trauma try to resist, prevent, or modify its effects. Sometimes the language of "victim"neglects or omits to capture such vital skills, wisdom, and bravery.

Resisting totalising descriptions of the offender

Whatever the problems are with the broad acceptance of the limited view that identifies and totalises victims of abuse as "victims", popular culture is less prepared to even think about its own black spots when it comes to defining "perpetrators." By totalising the identity of men who have perpetrated sexual abuse as solely "perpetrators" we are rendering invisible aspects of the men's lives that either stand in contrast to the abuse or that bear testimony to an otherwise blameless life of good works. The public discourse on sexual offenders presents the offenders as "embodied evil," and research is often unfairly cited to confirm a view that sex offenders are fundamentally different from the rest of mankind (Keenan 2009). Despite the best of intentions of therapists and do-gooders, so the argument goes, no help in the world can change these men. The common belief and perception of clerical perpetrators is that they are fundamentally flawed and fundamentally bad; they just managed to

Systemic Practice in a Complex System

hide that fact for a long time. Public belief rests on the premise that "once a child sexual offender; always a child sexual offender." The idea of "flawed nature" dominates reports and public debate. In the paradigm of criminal essentialism (Maruna, 2001, p.5), the sexual offender is bad and cannot ever be good. In the somewhat popular paradigm of paedophilia, the sexual offender is simply regarded as sick and cannot ever recover from his condition. Reductionist models of explanation and intervention are en vogue. In the rush to condemn, some things get noticed but even more gets missed. The stage is set for extremes of hate. In the world of good versus evil, the good are allowed the occasional mistake, but "the essentially evil" deserve no consideration whatsoever. In the current climate, Catholic clergy who have perpetrated sexual abuse against minors are largely seen and treated as a cast of unreformable men. They have almost become "untouchables", total outcasts. Members of the church hierarchy who are accused of "cover-up" are also seen as beyond redemption.

For me the unhelpful dichotomies and dangers that arise from identifying and totalising the identity of any individual had to be addressed in the therapeutic rooms and in my input into public discourse. Against the prevailing popular perception, I maintained that victims of abuse do not constitute a homogenous group, and neither do the abuse perpetrators. Rather than enforcing what Tocqueville has called "the tyranny of the majority", I argued that we would do better by remembering that what really matters is the subjective experience. If the latter assumption holds true, this means also that there must be room for all in their different manifestations and experiences. By casting "victims" and "perpetrators" as homogenised groups, each with identifiable symptoms and absolute and unchangeable identities, further social injustices were likely to occur, this time couched in the language of social justice or therapeutic work.

The therapeutic aim of my work with offenders was to put all children beyond risk (Lang 2003) and to help the men in therapy to live non-abusive lives. I also wanted to offer a systemic ear to individuals who consulted with me so that the experiences of all could be held and honoured in the interest of healing, collective restoration, and transformation. The therapy involved individual, group, and family therapy modalities, as well as accountability meetings, workshops on specific topics, and self-help groups for families. For the men who had perpetrated sexual abuse, weekly group therapy sessions of five hours, supplemented by weekly or fortnightly individual counselling sessions, formed the core of the treatment programme. Accountability meetings involved the offender, significant people in his social and professional network, and key treatment staff, and took place at regular intervals. In the case of the Catholic clergy who attended for therapy, these meetings involved the cleric's bishop or his immediate superior and other church personnel. Members of the cleric's family of origin were also offered help and support. The family support group for the families of all of the men attending the treatment centre met on a monthly basis and consisted of family members, mainly women, who had played an important role in clients' lives.

The focus of many therapy programmes for sexual offenders is on gaining detailed accounts of the offending act, with the implied contingent risk of further offending (Eldridge & Wyre 1998: 86; Loftus & Cameron 1993: 300; Wyre 1996). Professional and legal discourses caution against "believing" the offenders' accounts (Eldridge & Wyre 1998: 82; Wyre 1996) because of the assumed denial, minimisations, and rationalisations that are thought to be hidden in their stories. Working with such a conceptual framework inevitably silences and marginalises first-person accounts. As a result the voices of men who had abused were absent from public debate. The perpetrators' silence in response to exposure was interpreted in public discourses as evidence of further deviance and pathology. Such an interpretation troubled me. By engaging in therapeutic work and research with clerical perpetrators my aim was to create the space for more personal and context-specific narratives to emerge. All of the therapeutic work had to be contextually sensitive to the men's lives and in engaging in this work I had to become familiar with Catholic theology, doctrine, traditions, spirituality, ecclesiology and canon law. Without such a working knowledge I was in danger of engaging in colonising practices that would not take account with sensitivity of the context of the men's lives and histories. This work involved constant reflection on the importance of Power, Gender, Religion, Age, Class, Culture, Economics, Sexuality, Sexual Orientation, Spirituality, Conscience and Masculinities in the work in which I was engaged with the clerical men.

Conclusions

This chapter represents an overview of my work with clerical men who had sexually abused minors, with victims of clergy and with the church hierarchy who responded to their complaints. My work in relation to sexual abuse in the Catholic Church was premised on a systemic perspective that linked detailed knowledge of the church administration and the institution of the Catholic Church to the personal narratives of some offenders and to Catholic bishops as each reflected back on the other. When my own micro-therapeutic and research work are interpreted in the larger context, it becomes obvious that there are noticeable links between what happens on the grand scale of things and on the local level, and that the individual, the organisation, and the institutional dimensions are actually influencing each other and bound together in particular dynamic relations. Such observations might reveal that the classic micro/macro distinction is a rather artificial construction and rather that both must be kept in view at all times. As Clifford Geertz has pointed out, it makes sense to see social interpretation as "a continuous dialectical tracking between the most local of detail and the most global of global structure in such a way as to bring both into view simultaneously … Hopping back and forth between the whole conceived through the parts that actualise it, and the parts conceived through the whole which motivates them, we seek to turn them, by a sort of intellectual perpetual motion, into explications of one another" (Geertz 1979, p.239). I believe that the strength of my work as a systemic practitioner and researcher is in the very process of systemic thinking and thinking in terms of systems – holding the wider context in a systemic mind no matter how macro or micro the system that happened to be as the particular focus of my brief.

References

Barrett, Alan; Kamiya, Yumiko & O'Sullivan, Vincent (2014). Child Sexual Abuse and Later Life Economic Consequences. *Journal of Behavioural and Experimental Economics*, 53, 10–16.

Carr, Alan et al. (2010). Adult Adjustment of Survivors of Institutional Child Abuse in Ireland. *Child Abuse and Neglect*, 34, 477–489.

Claffey, Pat; Egan, Joe & Keenan, Marie (Eds.) (2013). *Broken Faith: Why Hope Matters*. Oxford: Peter Lang.

Clancy, Susan (2010). *The Trauma Myth: The Truth about Sexual Abuse of Children and its Aftermath*. New York: Basic Books.

Geertz, Clifford (1979). From the Native's Point of View: On the nature of anthropological understanding. In Paul Rabinow and William Sullivan (Eds.), *Interpretive Social Science: A Reader*. Berkley: University of California Press.

Eldridge, Hillary & Wyre, Ray (1998). The Lucy Faithfull Foundation Residential Program For Sexual Offenders. In William Marshall and Yolanda Fernandez. (Eds.), *Sourcebook of Treatment Programs for Sexual Offenders*. London: Plenum Press.

Fisher, Art (2009). *Leading-edge Developments in Narrative Practice Responding to Violence*. Workshop given at the European Conference of Narrative Therapy and Community Work, Brighton, UK, July 2009.

Fisher, Art (2008). *Power and Practices of Documentation in Working with Clients, Especially Those Involved in Family Violence*. Three day Intensive Workshop held in Maynooth, Ireland, November 24–26 2008.

Foucault, Michel (2004 [1972]). *The Archaeology of Knowledge*. Translated by A. M. Sheridan Smith. (6th edition.). London: Routledge Classics.

Foucault, Michel (2001). *Fearless Speech*. Edited by Joseph Pearson. Los Angeles, CA: Semiotext(e).

Foucault, Michel (1991). *Discipline and Punish: The Birth of the Prison*. Translator: Alan Sheridan. London: Penguin.

John Jay College of Criminal Justice (2011). *The Causes and Context of Sexual Abuse of Minors by Catholic Priests and Deacons in the United States, 1950–2002*. Washington DC: United States Conference of Catholic Bishops. Accessed March 10th 2015. Available at: http://www.usccb.org/mr/causes-and-context.html)

Keenan, Marie (2013). Senior Diocesan Officials and the Murphy Report. *Studies: An Irish Quarterly Review*. Winter 2013, 434-446.

Keenan, Marie (2012). *Child Sexual Abuse and the Catholic Church: Gender, Power and Organizational Culture*. New York: Oxford University Press.

Keenan, Marie (2009). 'Them and Us'. The Clergy Child Sexual Offender as 'Other'. In Tony Flannery (Ed.), *Responding to the Ryan Report*. Dublin: The Columba Press.

Lang, Peter (2003). *Putting Children Beyond Risk and Perpetrators Beyond Suspicion*. Workshop held in Department of Social Policy and Social Work, University College Dublin. April 23rd 2003.

Loftus, John & Camargo, Robert (1993). Treating the Clergy. *Annals of Sex Research*, 6, 287–303.

Maruna, Shadd (2001). *Making Good: How Ex-Convicts Reform and Rebuild their Lives*. Washington DC: American Psychological Association.

McCarthy, Imelda (2002). The Spirit of the Fifth Province: An ancient metaphor for a new millennium. *Feedback: The Magazine of the Family Therapy Association of Ireland*, 9(2), 10–13.

McCarthy, Imelda & Byrne, Nollaig O'Reilly (2001). Resisting Daughters: Father–Daughter Child Sexual Abuse Disclosure. In Ann Cleary, Maire Nic Ghiolla Phadraig, & Suzanne Quin. (Eds.) *Understanding Children: Changing Experiences and Family Forms*, Vol 2. Dublin: Oak Tree Press.

Ryan, Sean (2009). *Commission on Child Abuse Report*. Dublin: Government Publications.

Shotter, John (2005). Goethe and the Refiguring of Intellectual Inquiry: From "about-ness" thinking to "with-ness" thinking in everyday life. *Janus Head*, 8(1), 132–158.

Wade, Allan (1997). Small Acts of Living: Everyday resistance to violence and other forms of oppression. *Journal of Contemporary Family Therapy*, 19(1), 23–39.

Weingarten, Kathy (2007). Hope in a Time of Global Despair. In Carmel Flaskas, Imelda McCarthy & Jim Sheehan (Eds.), *Hope and Despair in Narrative and Family Therapy: Adversity, Forgiveness and Reconciliation*. London: Routledge

Weingarten, Kathy (2003). *Common Shock. Witnessing Violence Every Day: How We Are Harmed, How We Can Heal*. New York: Dutton.

White, Michael (2000). Re-engaging with History: The Absent but Implicit. In Michael White, *Reflections on Narrative Practices: Interviews and Essays*. Adelaide, South Australia: Dulwich Centre Publications.

White, Michael (2004). Working With People Who are Suffering the Consequences of Multiple Trauma: A narrative perspective. *International Journal of Narrative Therapy and Community Work*, 1, 45–76.

Wyre, Ray (1996). Personal Communication on a visit to The Lucy Faithfull Treatment Programme, Birmingham, England.

18 Hope and Risk
Systemic practices for supervision and assessment in child protection

Ernst Salamon & Imelda McCarthy

...if we look with love, then the colours of heaven are revealed to us ...

Stephens 1982

We get wise by asking question.

Stephens 1923

Something has become clear to the two of us in our work over thirty years with child protection social workers in many countries in Europe. And it is this: while these social workers perform admirably in extremely difficult social and professional contexts, one of the major stumbling blocks for them stems from the dual, seemingly contradictory assignments of support and protection (control). In our work we describe this as the *help vs. control dichotomy*. We also want to draw attention to the possibility of a democratic systemic practice in complex systems where professionals clarify for themselves as well as for their clients and supervisees, the basis and reasons for actions taken and not taken (Featherstone et al 2014). In this chapter, we offer thinking and practices from two systemic approaches developed in Sweden and Ireland respectively – the Commission Model (Salamon et al 1991; Salamon 1994a, 1994b) and the Fifth Province Approach (Byrne 1995; McCarthy 2010; O'Brien 2014). The approaches will be interwoven throughout the chapter.

How we see what we see!

In our writing of this chapter we want to offer an analysis of complex help-giving situations so that we can foster more systemic and reflexive seeings, positionings and interventions in ourselves and for others who would find this way of working useful. Working as a social work academic (Imelda, IMcC) and as supervisors (IMcC and Ernst, ES), we have witnessed that child protection workers have been publicly criticised BOTH for being over-judicious AND for incompetence in dealing with situations of disclosed and suspected abuse (Wintour 2015). For many workers in this area it is a lose-lose dilemma and can lead to large-scale resignations in child protective services (ISPCC 2015). Prejudicial over-reaction that a

Hope and Risk

suspected abuse is indisputable without adequate corroborative evidence AND an apparent non-acknowledgment of the seriousness of disclosed abuse are the most frequent complaints (see also Payne 1999, p.255). At a time of huge media comment and demands for accountability everywhere, we are among the many colleagues who feel that there is a need to recognise the social reality of a vigilant press and the needs for more open, clearer assessment criteria as part of the professional context.

We suggest therefore, that approaches are needed which, (1) help us to deal with the dual functions of support and control/protection; (2) clarify *who* asks for help with what; and (3) make explicit who our commissioners are. We attempt to accomplish that clarification in this chapter.

Support and control: towards non-contradictory practices in child protection

We have seen that when we do not clarify who defines the situation as problematic or what counts as help then it can hide an execution of power, justify controversial interventions, and enable the violation of individuals or groups. We have also seen this recursively captured in the macro relationship between social institutions and citizens and also in the micro relationship between an individual social worker and his/her clients. Within the Fifth Province Approach we have referred to this recursion as a way that a control of abuse can often re-present as an abuse of control by statutory services (Byrne & McCarthy 1988). This was poignantly captured in the words of a young adult who described her childhood disclosure of abuse to a State agency as "my own personal holocaust".

Many child protection service workers have told us of their difficulties in integrating and uniting the double functions of social control and support in their work due to heavy caseloads and the pressure of risk and safety issues. So, we have come to the conclusion that these difficulties emerge largely from the ambiguity that is built into systems of help-giving. We say this as the split becomes harmful and often abusive in cases where the child protection worker, on the discovery of neglect and abuse, must let the control and authority function take precedence over the support function. In these scenarios the professional frequently has to carry out actions against the client's will and become the focus of their anger. Having to work constantly in situations of ambiguity and frequent client anger does not lay conditions for good practice or worker – client satisfaction! So, how can we be "helpful"?

Who does what for whom?

In order to be helpful in such ambiguous situations we feel that we need to clarify *who* is doing what for *whom* as we have found in our work that the incongruity between support and control diminishes when we take into account whom the professional is serving in any one instance. Furthermore, when we think about it, the words, "social services" are indeed an accurate description of the task of the child protection worker. These words encompass most of the functions of the profession, but only if it is stated clearly whom the professional serves at any point in his/her duties. In our view, it is most important to acknowledge that primarily a child protection worker is a public servant who carries out the services, which society's institutions (including their profession), laws and elected representatives define. We, as child protection workers, therefore can be said to serve society both when we act in a role of social control on behalf of the State/Society and when we offer supportive services to the public.

As such, the primary mandate and what we are calling the commission of a child protection worker comes from the state via an employing body and not from its service users. Put another way, the Social Service Agency is the Primary Commission Giver (PCG) while the service user may become a Secondary Commission Giver (SCG) should they agree to the service being given. Otherwise, should they not agree they may not have a choice and can become Target Persons (TP) in relation to "imposed" or mandated actions. We refer to these latter actions as "Taking Measures" and differentiated them from the actions of "Help-Giving".

Defining the actions of 'help' and 'taking measures'

As a result of this analysis of the systemic context of "help giving" in social services we have therefore always found it important to define clearly the terms, "help giving" and "taking measures". Unpacking these terms and discourses as it were helps to reveal where relationships of unequal "power" and control have the potential to operate. The term or concept of "help", in our approach, refers to those collaborative actions taken only with the prior agreement of the client. In other words for an intervention, premised on co-operation and co-creation, to be classified as "help" there needs to be prior agreement for the actions to be taken in the future both by the social worker and the service user/client. However well-intentioned the protective mandates or actions taken by professionals may be they are referred to by us as "taking measures" (Salamon et al 1991; Salamon 1994b).

We believe this distinction between "help" and "taking measures" to be important for the following reasons. Very often, as professionals, we can assume that actions are helpful which have not been agreed and are frustrated and upset when clients do not seem to understand or appreciate our efforts. In order to work with this conundrum we propose that when we understand that only commission-givers may tell us whether our actions have been helpful or not then we have a way of clarifying the situation for ourselves and the people who use services. The Primary Commission Giver who is requesting or employing our services might deem certain actions to be protective or helpful for children whilst at the same time these very actions may not be viewed as helpful by the parents of the children. So, what might be helpful to the Primary Commission Giver (PCG) in trying to prevent child abuse may not be experienced as helpful by a parent suspected of abusing or neglecting their children. In this instance where the parent does not agree with the action taken they become Target Persons (TPs) for the intervention. In this instance what is seen as "help" by the PCG is experienced by the non-agreeing TP as the professional taking measures against them.

This is also a situation that we referred to earlier and that is that we could see where attempts to control abuse may in a recursive flip flop end up as being abuses of control? In distinguishing clearly between these twin tasks, support and control, help and taking measures we feel that we can become more transparent in relation to our own systemic positionings and involvements. This is why we would stress that as the issues in child protection refer to children, adults and professionals in particular family and social contexts, it is always important, in our experience, to subjectively and socially situate each assessment and evaluation. In this way each analysis for us always involves a second order systemic positioning. We, as supervisors, therapists and social workers are inevitably part of the frame of analysis. A commission is therefore clarified according to the situation and place in which one is living and working and is never based on objective criteria. The British Prime Minister, David Cameron's threats to imprison social workers, show us clearly who is the primary commission giver in the context of Britain (Wintour 2015). Forgetting this can trap us into either ignoring hierarchical implications of this work and so risk further abusing those coming for both supervision and social services or imagining that we can only work to the mandates of those who use our services. Both these stances obscure the complex contexts of social service mandates and policies even when we may not like them! To illustrate these systemic dilemmas let us introduce an example from Ernst's work in Sweden.

Case presentation

The context is a Swedish social services agency, divided into two groups, one caring for adults while the other cares for children and youth. Together they had external supervision with Ernst every third week.

In the supervision group, two of the social workers, Monica and Eva, whose names we have altered together with those of family members, presented the following case:

> Monica worked in the children's section and was commissioned by social services to carry out to an assessment following the request by a mother we are calling Gun, to resume custody of her ten year old daughter who we are calling Rachel. The other social worker, Eva, served with the unit for adults and was involved in the task of helping Gun to resolve the difficulties of drug abuse, housing, and unemployment in her life with the aim of having her daughter live with her again.
>
> Eight years previously, when Rachel was two she had been placed in foster care against Gun's wishes. The reason for the removal from her mother was that, at the time, Gun was judged by social services to lack the ability to adequately take care of her daughter. This was mainly due to drug abuse and its accompanying lifestyle, such as irregular attendance by Rachel at the day care centre, inadequate hygiene, financial debts and threats of eviction. At the time of this first assessment Gun denied any drug abuse on her part and did not go along with any measures instituted by the social services. A further complicating factor was that, at the time of the investigation, there was a serious suspicion that Rachel had also been sexually abused. The social workers were unclear whether this abuse was perpetrated by Gun or by one of her temporary boyfriends. The suspicion itself was based on observations by staff of the little girl's behaviour at the day care centre.
>
> However, at the time it was judged that the suspicion of sexual abuse was difficult to prove due to Rachel's young age and Gun's lack of co-operation. The key social workers had decided not to investigate the suspicion further as there were sufficient other reasons to remove Rachel from the care of her mother. A short time later, when Gun was confronted with the suspicion by her social worker, she had protested her innocence and also expressed doubts about whether there had been any abuse at all. Eight years on, it

was now reported that Gun had made great changes in her life and that she would like to have her daughter live with her again. Over the previous year she had admitted her drug-abuse, received and completed treatment for it. She had also started training towards employment, was taking good care of her finances and had regular contact with her daughter and with her social worker, Eva.

Dilemmas: Contradictory needs and rights

During the supervision session, the dilemmas that Monica and Eva, presented related to many seemingly contradictory needs and wishes which were brought forward in Gun's, request to have Rachel, back to live with her.

These different commissions, issues and possible dilemmas are highlighted below under the following headings:

- Rachel's right to safety and stability vs. Gun's right to have the situation reassessed: Introducing a hierarchy of commissions
- Family reunion from the child's and the parent's point of view
- Child Protection: Hope for safety versus fear of risk

Key questions

When faced with complex system's issues, which are often contradictory and potentially dangerous to a child's welfare, we have experienced that we need to be clear about the mandates we are working to. Therefore, these, two key questions have emerged:

1. Has Gun changed enough to offer safety and a good enough life to Rachel?
2. If Rachel returns to Gun will this be a good or bad situation for Rachel?

To clarify the presented dilemma further, Ernst asked Monica and Eva what the present status of their assessment was. It emerged that both felt torn between the different needs and rights of those involved and experienced themselves facing a crucial choice between two radically different alternatives:

They must *either* i) immediately initiate the beginning of a long and cautious process of having Rachel move back home with Gun or ii) work for a permanent foster care placement by applying for a custody order for Rachel whereby the foster parents would be awarded full custody. We are deliberately using the terms, "good" and "bad" as these are the words that the social workers themselves used during supervision. Of course different contexts will generate different words to capture the situations of protection and risk being worked with.

Why either/or – emotional factors?
Because the dilemmas were presented so starkly and the perceived alternatives had far reaching consequences Ernst proceeded to ask both Monica and Eva about their feelings in regard to different aspects of the case. It emerged that the most common emotional difficulties were worry and fear in relation to two issues:

1. The delicate task of removing Rachel from her foster home where she had been rooted. They also feared that irreversible injury might occur if she were to be uprooted for a second time, together with the fear and risk if her return to Gun did not work out.
2. The outstanding suspicions about the sexual abuse of Rachel when she was in the care of her mother eight years previously and the resultant worry for Rachel's security if she did return to her mother.

Through the ongoing discussion about the social workers' emotional reactions, it became clear that many in the group felt antipathy towards the mother. This was because they were concerned that she might either have sexually abused her daughter or that she did not protect her against abuse. Furthermore, they had the impression that she did not show any signs of remorse or worry when confronted with the suspicions of the day care centre staff eight years previously.

From this brief vignette one can see how the social workers' antipathy towards Gun was producing a context of fear in relation to Rachel's safety. However, in talking further it became clear in the group that this was also occurring for them in the absence of a sound assessment of what was happening at this point in time. Introducing the element of time, then and now, allowed the team to begin to shift their perspective. Given that Gun had made a request for help to have her daughter home the team began to realise that if they were to be helpful in this situation that they needed to address how these previously unrecognised past prejudices, fears and ideas might recursively constitute their current fears and risks. In this way drawing the distinction in time (then and now) and between the concepts of "help" and "taking measures" together with the recognition that Gun had shifted her position from being a Target Person to being a Secondary Commission Giver also recursively

Hope and Risk

enabled the team and the supervision context to shift in a more democratic and collaborative direction.

Deconstructing fixed ideas through the assessment process

Following on from the previous example and in order to begin such a collaborative and democratic process we propose that supportive actions in the arena of child protection work could be construed as, deconstructing fixed ideas through introducing scales of difference and thereby co-constructing possibilities for new solutions and ideas to emerge for service users and social workers.

In simple terms child protection endeavours would begin to address themselves towards the movement from an either/or position to both/and positions as in the example above. This means moving from a mutually excluding dichotomous position to positions which consider apparent oppositions as positions of difference on continua and scales. This deconstruction of dichotomies (either/or scenarios) introduces possibilities (more and/or less) for greater manoeuvrability for professionals and greater opportunities for co-operative democratic participation with help-seekers and in supervision.

For example, the questions "Should Rachel return to her mother?" and, "Should Rachel stay in foster care?" pushes the professionals into either/or (dichotomous) thinking. However, when we ask for both the possibilities and the risks of each alternative we have found that it helps deconstruct "all or nothing" reasoning and opens up possibilities for "more or less" options. Questions can then be brought forth, such as, "On a scale of 1 to 10 where 1 refers to very bad situations and where 10 refers to optimal situations, what are the possibilities and risks of Rachel returning to her mother?" and "How much contact shall Rachel have with the foster home in the future?" In the posing of such questions we have the possibility to move from dichotomised Good/Bad situations, Risk/Safety situations and Change/No Change situations towards placing the dilemmas on continua or scales towards their deconstruction.

The deconstruction of 'a bad mother'

Before he could proceed, Ernst had to follow up some of the feelings that Monica and Eva had expressed in relation to Gun. So, he asked the supervision group members to dwell for a moment on their hypothesis that the mother had taken part in the abuse or had not cared about it. He asked questions such as, "How was it that a mother might do such a thing?"

These questions prompted the group to speculate on the background of the mother, and in the generation of these reflections the antipathy against Gun noticeably diminished. The professionals stated that they realised they had become stuck in their dilemma (in either/or thinking) because they saw Gun as "a bad mother". When they realised this they could begin to view her more empathically and to look at the changes Gun had actually made in her life. Gun's capabilities as a parent in the present time could now be evaluated with less prejudice.

When Gun was deconstructed as a "bad mother" it was possible to introduce questions, which would address other possibilities on a continuum from one extreme solution to the other:

- How could the transfer of Rachel back to Gun's care be done with as little harm as possible?
- What preventative actions needed to be taken in such a scenario?
- What changes would have to take place to guarantee Rachel's safety and security with Gun?

After a thorough discussion a plan is co-constructed where the Eva and Monica would gradually increase the time that Rachel and Gun spent together and where they would monitor the developing relationship. They realised also that the foster parents would carry an important role and task. As such it was deemed important by Eva and Monica to help them consider a range of options (from fostering to support of Rachel living with Gun) in relation to their ongoing emotional involvement and positive attachment with Rachel. The child protection workers, in considering commissioning issues, realised also that they must clarify for the foster parents that part of their primary commission included the aim of striving for the reunion of the family of origin where possible. However, they would also offer to provide any support that the foster parents needed in order to carry out the decisions of the social services.

The next step in the supervision process was a discussion where the necessary and desirable, changes could be spelled out. This occurred alongside the consideration of different protective mechanisms that would provide sufficient safety and security for Rachel both in the situations of increased interaction and access between Gun and Rachel and in any prospective move to the full-time care of Rachel by Gun.

An important factor was also an investigation of Gun's awareness of the risks and consequences of child sexual abuse. In addressing these questions, in relation to security, Monica and Eva began to include others within the child's network as resources to her and to them. A list was drawn up of Rachel and Gun's resource people in order to find persons whom Rachel had confidence and trust in and who would observe and support Rachel and Gun's relationship while also supporting the foster parents. These included the child's grandmother who could maintain links to the family and to the child's mother, a therapist with whom the child had a good relationship and her foster parents with whom she could continue to visit for weekends, etc. Within a fifth province approach these activities has been referred to as identifying "resource systems" and creating a "safety net" to ensure ongoing protection against serious risk scenarios developing (Byrne & McCarthy 1995).

Little by little a picture emerged during the supervision session where a continuum of different alternative routes and possibilities emerged for situations of safety and minimal risk with the best interests of Rachel at centre stage. Through this emergence the dichotomised, either/or alternatives, which were present at the outset of the discussion, no longer dominated the minds and actions of the key social workers and their team.

We have found that what is often designated as, "forbidden" in relation to child protection depends largely on whether the worker has a feeling of "hope" that the situation can change within a specific time frame and in a particular direction. Certain behaviours may be permitted in the short term while some change is taking place but not in the longer term. The fact that time frames often play a part in what might happen also indicates for us that hope plays a big part in what will happen in relation to a child and his or her parents. If we analyse what contributes to feelings of hope then we may find that it depends on the parent(s) co-operating in protective actions with the social worker and showing a willingness to change their behaviour and/or situation. Conversely we might say that if the parent does not co-operate within a designated time frame they are deemed not to be willing to change along the parameters desired by social workers and child protection systems. The inclusion of hope into the scenario links to the definition of "Problem" in the Commission Approach (Salamon et al 1991). Here, a "problem" is defined as being a person's hope/desire for change that they do not know how to achieve.

This also relates closely to the concept of "dilemma" used in the Fifth Province approach (McCarthy & Byrne 1995). In the absence of "hope" on the part of parents and professionals the professional is frequently required to take measures. Questions which address the issue of hope would include the following: "What does the parent have to do to satisfy the social worker that change is happening/possible?" and "What would have to happen so that you (the professional) can maintain the hope necessary to continue with an assessment based on co-operation and voluntary help giving?"

At one end of the continuum, in very bad, forbidden situations, it is often required that child protection workers are mandated to intervene and *take measures.* Of course, it is also expected that *help* is offered prior to measures being taken. However, in the absence of a voluntarily agreement to co-operate with social services, measures usually have to be taken to protect children. Here again as we will have seen in our case example above, the professional group would be invited to work with their prejudices and emotions in order that they can be deconstructed so that they can more clearly assess the information at different points in the process.

There are two Conditions for Workers to act without parental consent (take measures):

> A. The situation in which the child lives is legally forbidden (as in the earlier situation of Rachel where she was removed to long-term foster care).

or

> B. The situation will continue to be non-permissible without intervention. However, it may change with intervention thereby avoiding the necessity of removing the child or just having to remove a child in the short-term.

One of the traps that a child protection worker might find themselves in is that if one concentrates on solutions only (e.g. child protection as a solution for the problem of child abuse) then one is often confused about or does not look at what precise problematic behaviours or contexts need to change. In other words, and in our experience, we need to be asking, what are the particular goals that either the professional or the parent needs to or wants to change in order to solve the problem of child abuse/neglect. In addition, we would also propose that there would be an exploration of the most feared situation, what security measure are already in place and if they are sufficient in this particular scenario. If the answers to these questions point to inadequate safety then there needs to be an exploration of what measures might need to be introduced. We have found that the major dilemmas for professionals working in the arena of child protection frequently centre around whether, enough sustainable change is happening or not; change is possible or not; change is happening as quickly as it needs to or not; and change is more and/or less in the desired direction or not according to the primary commission. Alongside the clarifying of precise problems in context and goal setting we have seen that there needs to be an ongoing focus on clarifying Commissions in the different circumstances, So, for example a systemic supervisor might ask, "What is your task in the specific/general situation?", "What does the law say?", "What does the Senior Social Worker/Director of the Service say?" These situating and commissioning questions have been simplified in the following four questions which are always context related:

- What do you want to do?
- What can you do?
- What are you allowed to do?
- What must you do?

Conclusion: bringing hope to child protection

Given the huge mandate on child protection workers to change a situation and to protect a child indicates and implies that "hope" really must play a big part in any evaluation. In this, it may be useful to consider what it is that "hope" depends on co-operation by parents for change within a situation that is deemed, according to the parameters of a child protection commission, a bad situation warranting intervention by the State. It has been our experience that such situations are often among the most difficult for workers charged with child protection to maintain "hope".

The violation of a child is one such problem for which we could say that child protection is a hopeful solution. However, as we have said, very often in our conversations with child protection workers and students, protection – while often thought of as a goal – is also seen as a problem. In our view the prevention of child abuse might be an initial goal in promoting safety. However, we would propose that overall child protection be seen more as a "solution" for the problem of risk and danger. For example, child protection work in this light is no longer premised primarily on questions of whether or not to remove a child from his or her parents in situations of abuse and neglect. Rather it is premised on a process, which encompasses a range of possible actions that might be taken by both the child protection worker and the parents. In other words. we would ask, "HOW might the solution of child protection work in this situation?" Such thinking, we have found, facilitates opportunities for the generation of more collaborative conditions in the generation of safety along certain specified and hopefully agreed parameters on a scale or continuum. In our experience it also facilitates the combining of *support and control; help and taking measures* in state mandated commissions. Above all, it clarifies a complex social system and field for observation, releases us from contradictory (either/or) binds and opens up possibilities for compassion, co-operation and hope in very distressed families who are frequently living lives of great adversity.

References

Braye, Suzy & Preston-Shoot, Michael (1995). *Empowering Practice in Social Care.* Buckingham: Open University Press.

Burnham, John (2011). Developments in social GRRAAACCEEESS: Visible and invisible, voiced and unvoiced. In Britt Krause (Ed.) *Mutual Perspectives: Culture & reflexivity in systemic psychotherapy.* London: Karnac Books.

Byrne, Nollaig O'Reilly & McCarthy, Imelda C. (1988). Moving Statutes: Re-Questing Ambivalence through Ambiguous Discourse. In *Radical Constructivism, Autopoiesis and Psychotherapy,* a special issue of the *Irish Journal of Psychology,* 9, 91–100.

Byrne, Nollaig O'Reilly (1995). Diamond Absolutes. *Human Systems: Journal of Systemic Consultation and Management,* 6(3/4), 255–277.

Byrne, Nollaig O'Reilly & McCarthy, Imelda. C. (1995). Abuse, Risk and Protection: A Fifth Province Approach to an adolescent sexual offense. In Charlotte Burck & Bebe Speed (Eds.), *Gender, Power and Relationships.* London: Routledge.

Featherstone, Brid; White, Susan & Morris, Kate (2014). *Re-Imagining Child Protection: Towards Humane Social Work with Families.* Bristol: Policy Press.

Irish Society for the Protection of Children (ISPCC) (2015). *The ISPCC expresses concerns over the number of child protection workers resigning their posts and the impact this has on vulnerable children.*

O'Brien, Valerie (2014). Navigating Child Welfare and Protection in Ireland with the Help of the Fifth Province. Special Issue. *Feedback,* 91–117.

Payne, Malcolm (1999). The Moral Basis of Social Work, *European Journal of Social Work*, 2(3), 247–258.

Salamon, Ernst; Andersson, Mia & Grevelius, Klas (1991). *The AGS Commission Model*. Stockholm: AGS Institutet.

Salamon, Ernst (1994a). The Commission Model: An attempt to avoid Therapeutic Abuse. *Context*, 19, 31–34.

Salamon, Ernst (1994b). Who is a Customer for Social Services: Some Risks for Abusive Practices in the Transition to Purchaser-Provider Systems in Swedish Social Services. *Human Systems: Journal of Systemic Consultation and Management*, 5: 305–318.

O'Hagan, Kieran & Dillenburger, Ken (1995). *The Abuse of Women Within Child Care Work*. Buckingham: Open University Press.

McCarthy, Imelda C. & Byrne, Nollaig O'Reilly (1988). Mis-Taken Love: Conversations on the Problem of Incest in an Irish Context. *Family Process*, 27: 181–199.

McCarthy, Imelda C. (1997). Power, abuse discourses and women in poverty. *Human Systems: Journal of Systemic Consultation and Management*, 8, 239–249.

McCarthy, Imelda C. (2010). *Fifth Province Diamonds: Contrasts in Co-ordinated Play*. Available at: http://www.imeldamccarthy.com/Publications_and_Downloads.html

Stephens, James (1982). *The Demi-Gods*. Dublin: Butler Simms.

Wintour, Patrick (2015). "Jail those who turn a blind eye to child abuse, says Cameron." *The Guardian*. 3rd March 2015.

19 'Double Jeopardy' and 'Professional Jeopardy'
Stories of shared identity

Gill Goodwillie

A single mother with a son diagnosed with attention deficit hyperactivity disorder (ADHD) had wanted him to go on an educational trip with his school. She had struggled to get the non-refundable deposit to secure his place but with support from her mother, she had duly paid and the school confirmed her son's place for the trip. At some point in the three months leading up to the school trip, her son was involved in a number of misdemeanours within his school. The school wrote to his mother to cancel his place on the trip and refused to return her deposit.

In this episode, the young boy and his family were punished twice – firstly, by not providing a disabled child with an educational trip and secondly, in depriving a poor family of precious money. Thus the idea of a "double jeopardy" was kindled as I reflected on the above. The child with a diagnosis of ADHD faces considerable challenges in relation to their learning and this can have a serious negative impact on academic achievement. They also face the double jeopardy that they may have restricted opportunities to develop their social skills.

Introduction and working context

The practice described in this chapter is drawn from my experience working in the National Health Service (NHS) in a Child and Adolescent Mental Health Service (CAMHS) in England. The service serves an inner city population that is diverse and recognised nationally as deprived and impoverished. The title *Double Jeopardy* is intended to attract your attention to the experience that I have increasingly come across with families being somehow punished doubly for the difficulties that they face. I am introducing the concept of "professional jeopardy" to describe the struggle to continue to provide an ethical systemic psychotherapy service to young people and their families within the UK's National Health Service (NHS).

The term "double jeopardy" describes a legal principle of some 800 years within the British Justice system that stopped a defendant from being tried again on the same charges following acquittal or conviction. Sir William Macpherson (1999) recommended that it was abolished after his inquiry into the murder of Stephen Lawrence and this was enacted when The Criminal Justice Act 2003 came into force in 2005.

It is easy to applaud the thinking behind this recommendation – a virtuous response to the situation faced by the Lawrence family and others that sought justice. However, there are sometimes unintended consequences to well-intended actions. What other forms of "double jeopardy" might there be if we apply this idea to social relationships and social justice?

I was prompted to write about the issue of social justice … or indeed injustice … facing many families and the story of the cancelled school trip chimed with many accounts shared by parents when I was conducting research into parental experiences of having a child diagnosed with Attention Deficit Hyperactivity Disorder (ADHD) (Goodwillie 2013, 2014).

Parents talked about the social isolation often experienced by their child and one of the key themes that emerged in the research was the belief that their child had restricted opportunities to develop their social skills and form peer relationships: "He wasn't a child that was invited around after school"… "He has no idea how to interact with them… he tries so hard"… "Everybody thought she was the naughty kid… it's like if she is being naughty then I am going to get tarred with the same thing and they drift away".

Parents talked about the choice of peer groups becoming restricted within the school setting because their child would be placed in a learning group with other children who were presenting with behavioural problems. Parents felt that this meant their child was exposed on a daily basis to non-compliant and challenging behaviour in the classroom and therefore had limited opportunity to experience positive role modelling by their peers. Parents expressed the view that this strategy promotes a subculture within a school of children who misbehave and this unwittingly reinforces poor behaviour.

For the parent of a child diagnosed with ADHD, who wishes to help their child to acquire social skills, a school trip can hold significance in terms of its potential to make an important contribution to the child's social development. A school trip can be a financial stretch for a parent on a limited income whilst a wealthy family will not have to consider the affordability in the same way. How did the mother feel about losing the deposit that had been so hard to find? How did this affect the relationship with her son? How did the school response affect the relationship not only the parent had with the school but also the relationship the child had with their teachers and the peers with whom he would have shared the experience? What impact does this kind of action have on these relationships? I began to think of the combination of lone parenthood, low income, and ADHD diagnosis as a kind of double jeopardy that might also be thought of as a "multi-jeopardy" when the contextual lens is widened to include the multiple and recursive connections between the macro level of society and services and the micro level of families.

This chapter illustrates two examples of jeopardy that I have encountered in my clinical practice and is followed by a personal reflection of professional jeopardy drawn from my experience of working in the NHS. At the end I will also describe how I met both families again when I arranged for them to read the draft of this chapter and they gave consent for their stories to be told.

1. Loving both sons: A lone parent attempting to house her eldest son due to be released from prison following a sexual offence, her younger son's reaction to this and work conducted in CAMHS.
2. Living with ASD: Trans-generational work with a family affected by Autistic Spectrum Disorder across four generations.
3. Systemic practice in the NHS: My own experience of "professional jeopardy" whilst attempting to provide an ethical and high quality systemic service within the NHS.

Loving both sons – double jeopardy

This example addresses the multiple jeopardies of a mother and her sons within a complex and contradictory system. This work was taking place in consultation with other agencies monitoring child and social protection of the family and public.

Some six months after his older brother's sentencing to a custodial term for a sexual assault on a young relative. This thirteen year old (let us call him Andrew) was referred to CAMHS because of "anger problems". I learned from Andrew's mother (let us call her Amy) that she had discovered the assault and had immediately reported it to the police and Andrew's brother (let us call him Aaron), was arrested at the family home and following his trial; imprisoned.

Aaron had been in a young offender's institution for eighteen months when I first met Andrew. Amy felt that Andrew's anger related to the shame and humiliation regarding his brother's crime and she requested therapeutic work to help him address this. Aaron was due to be released on license in twelve months. Amy was concerned that the brothers could have a future relationship on his return.

The work focussed initially on the relationship between Amy and Andrew and their upset about what had happened with Aaron. Andrew had not visited his brother-he felt too angry with him and Amy visited the young offender institution on her own.

The work involved individual sessions with Andrew to explore the anger he felt was overwhelming him. Practical strategies and an exploration of his feelings toward his brother created space for him to talk. His shame in relation to his brother's offence and his sense of himself as contaminated and also guilty by association were recurring themes.

The work progressed well. Amy and Andrew recognised they could not forgive Aaron for the act he had committed but Andrew appeared more accepting of his mother's wish for Aaron to come home.

The terms for Aaron's release on license came through with the shocking news that he could not return home to the same address. If Amy was to have her son home, the family would have to move from their two bedroom council house where they had lived for many years to another with three bedrooms. This had serious potential repercussions for Andrew as a move might mean him living outside his school catchment area.

A school move meant leaving a settled educational environment with friendship groups at a time when this stability could make the difference to things working out within the family home. The risk of jeopardising his education and the risk of resentment that could arise if this were to occur could sabotage any psychological gains that had been made to date.

My role as a systemic psychotherapist involved liaison and negotiation with different agencies, criminal, education, social services and housing to explore alternative possibilities to the unacceptable position for Amy, of making some kind of choice between her sons. An important idea within systemic thinking is to adopt the notion of both/and instead of, either/or in order to free the therapist to think in a manner that is about holding apparently oppositional positions and occupying a space where this can be thought about.

Andrew now accepted that his brother should come home but the question of geographical area in the terms of Aaron's license meant that there was a limited choice of possible addresses in council stock that could enable the family to keep their tenant status and for Andrew to remain in his current school. The potential disruption to Andrew's education should he be forced to change schools was a clear concern as well as the risk that the relationship with his brother might be further jeopardised if this occurred.

A war of attrition between Amy, the Prison Authorities and the local Housing Department then developed. Initially supportive of her stance to move to alternative council accommodation, as long as it remained within the catchment area of Andrew's school, the authorities support began to erode as no alternative housing appeared to be on offer. Amy was encouraged to think about giving up the security of her tenancy and move in to the private housing sector.

My experience of working with families in the short life, private sector influenced my stance in relation to this and in addition to therapeutic work with Amy and Andrew; I sent numerous letters, faxes and emails to those departments directly involved. Amy's anguish was palpable as the countdown to Aaron's projected release date began. The Housing Department began to adopt a distinctly threatening tone as the months went past as did the prison authorities... unless Amy could find a suitable place, Aaron would go to a bail hostel.

The family prepared to move from their home with little notification and their possessions were put in boxes... their life put on hold. Amy's own mental health became increasingly fragile as she struggled with the pressure being exerted. I supported her as the weeks went by, then finally five days before Aaron's release date; she was given a key to a house that met the requirements that would enable her to provide a home for both sons. Needless to say the house had not been well maintained – Amy appeared to be given a property that was a previous crack house and in her view was not fit for human occupation. Amy scrubbed all the rooms from ceiling to floor, removing unused needles in the house and garden, prior to moving in. And, exhausted from the move, she found she needed to

'Double Jeopardy' and 'Professional Jeopardy'

drive 100 miles to collect her son on his release date as no transport had been provided for Aaron to get from the prison to his new home.

Multi-jeopardy
This is clearly not even a case of double jeopardy but multi-jeopardy for the family and individual members.

- Amy loves and cares for both of her sons.
- Amy's courage and tenacity has remained an untold story of a mother's commitment to doing the right thing – initially reporting her son to the police when she realised what he had done and then standing by both her sons in spite of professional pressure to do otherwise.
- If Aaron had been placed in a bail hostel, he would be vulnerable to abusive experiences and it would be unlikely he would get sufficient support to pursue further positive opportunities.
- Andrew, as brother of a sex offender, was unwittingly caught up in the stigma and fall out of his older brother's behaviour.
- The risk that Andrew's education could have been disrupted and his future life chances seriously affected.

Post-release work was then conducted for a further eight months in sessions with the brothers together, their mother individually, and as a family group, to help reconcile the past and find a way of going on together as a family. Aaron obtained an apprenticeship and began to work.

Since the date of the original referral of Andrew to our service, the referral criteria for Tier 3 CAMHS have changed and become much more restrictive. If no mental health issue is identified at referral, the referral is not accepted. Anger is not seen as a mental health diagnosis and Andrew would now probably have to be referred to Tier 2 (however Schools now hold the budget for Tier 2 mental health services in our area so this would be dependent on the School recognising the need) If a referral was to be made currently, there is a high likelihood that Andrew's anger would be perceived as his individual problem and he would probably be referred to an anger management programme delivered by less experienced practitioners. The complexity of his family context is unlikely to have been thought about or explored.

It is important to note that increasing numbers of young people are presenting in CAMHS with issues relating to frequent house moves incurred for families within the private rental sector. In tandem with loss of peer relationships, the impact on their education has the capacity to adversely affect their life chances while the stress of frequent house moves recursively increases family stressors. Here is another stark example of how systemic multiple jeopardies impact families. The privatisation of previous public housing stock contributes to the increasing marginalisation and stress of families in poverty.

Living with ASD – double jeopardy

This family came to the attention of the systemic psychotherapy team because a young man we shall call Bobby (now seventeen years of age), had been finally diagnosed with Autistic Spectrum Disorder (ASD) and there were relational conflicts with his siblings that we were asked to help the family address.

CAMHS had been involved for some years in a protracted diagnostic process – (Did he or did he not meet the diagnostic criteria for ASD?) Eventually medication was prescribed to manage Bobby's angry outbursts. Bobby regularly attended medication review appointments accompanied by his mother Brenda, and he was seen for individual sessions to help him manage his behaviour using a CBT approach. No one had met other members of his family.

At our first meeting with Bobby's family, his two sisters and both parents present, we observed the style of communication and listened to their descriptions of family life. We noted how long it had taken for the service to meet these important people in Bobby's life. Both daughters described poor experiences within school and had left without any qualifications. Both sisters shared a love of animals and the family described a small menagerie in their garden where rabbits, chickens and other creatures were loved and cared for. Brian their father was described as a loner shunning activities that involved socialising with others but content to go out fishing in his free time regardless of the weather. Sometimes Bobby would go with his father on these trips and he seemed to particularly value their times together. We learned that Brian could not read or write but had maintained a job as a night watchman for the past 20 years. He could not tell the time and could not drive so the family solution had been for Bobby's mother to take her husband to work in time for his shift and he would walk home in the morning. He would be relieved of his post in the morning by colleagues arriving for work. We were struck that through Brenda's support; Brian had been able to stay in stable employment which meant that he had been able to be the sole provider for his family.

We learned that both of Bobby's older sisters had now left school and were looking for employment although they had little hope of getting regular work. We realised that each member of the family, other than Brenda, seemed to show characteristics of autism. Brenda appeared to hold the whole family together co-ordinating and managing the complexities of the various needs of the individuals in the family. Bobby's relationship with his sisters was confrontational and he resented the introduction of their respective boyfriends to the home. Bobby struggled with the changes in the family dynamics and appeared to view his sisters' boyfriends as rivals within the home. He would retreat to his own room following angry outbursts in which he expressed resentment over minor infringements of his personal space.

Work was initiated to explore more harmonious ways of living together. Some months into working with Bobby further events occurred that had a seriously disruptive impact on the family's capacity to survive. These events powerfully affected the family sense of identity and brought with them issues of pride and shame.

Bobby had been sitting on a wall outside a local park when a couple of youths had thrown him a mobile phone and told him he could have it. Unknown to Bobby the phone had been stolen and a few minutes later the police arrived and promptly arrested him for possession of the stolen phone. He was taken to the local police station and put in a cell. The fear and panic for Bobby whilst in the cell was overwhelming. Being held for a crime he had not committed yet unable to understand or explain his actions to the officers who experienced his increasing agitation as potential violence.

At the time, our CAMHS had a funded partnership project with the Local Youth Justice Service that meant a CAMHS worker could liaise with the police and intervene in situations like this to prevent unnecessary detention. Bobby was released on bail to appear in court in a couple of weeks. Liaison with criminal justice involved putting the case that because of his diagnosis, Bobby did not have capacity to commit a crime (The Mental Capacity Act 2005) and the case was eventually dropped. It took months of work to help Bobby recover from the trauma of this experience.

The second event had an equally profound impact on the family. Brian was made redundant as the company he worked for had become bankrupt in the economic downturn. Brian was devastated; sinking into a depressive mood but refusing to attend his GP. He was irritable and bad tempered.

Around the same time one daughter became pregnant and moved out of the family home with her boyfriend. We met her newly born baby when she was five days old. In this session we observed that the baby was positioned on respective family laps facing outwards with little opportunity for close eye contact. We commented on this in the reflecting team and wondered whether the family could practice holding the baby differently? Some sessions later we met the baby again at around nine months. Baby Bella seemed to be developing well physically and it was clear that the family had taken on board the need to hold her in a manner that encouraged eye gaze. We noted however, that she seemed gaze avoidant and requested that we make a referral to our Infant Mental Health team (subsequently de-commissioned through cuts).

Multi-jeopardy

- Brenda's central role within the family to mediate with the external world on behalf of family members who experience such contact as hostile and threatening.

- Bobby's vulnerability in relation to his peers and susceptibility to negative influences.

- Brian had held a job for many years that did not challenge his preference to be solitary and avoidant of social interaction.

- The loss of Brian's role as provider for his family and the impact on his self-esteem led to increased friction within the home.

- Brian was faced with the prospect of applying for job seekers allowance. In my experience these forms are complex and difficult to fill out-how does a man with literacy issues ever cope with them?

- Baby Bella's future developmental path within a family environment in which genetic influences may also pre-dispose her to developing autistic traits.

Systemic practice in the NHS – professional jeopardy

The clinical work I have described in this chapter has arisen in my work as a systemic psychotherapist within CAMHS. So, now I will reflect on how the idea of double jeopardy connects with my experience of providing psychotherapy in an ethical manner for clients who come for therapy within a budget conscious NHS.

I started work as a paediatric social worker in a psychiatric outpatient unit in the early eighties in London. Trained in psychodynamic ways of thinking, I began to work with families engaged in an intensive therapeutic programme, with children under the age of five, referred to child psychiatry.

Co-working with colleagues who had skills in working with families, my initial encounters with this work left me uncomfortable and uncertain about some of the practices that seemed manipulative and the use of "paradoxical injunctions" left me cold. I later learned these methods were informed by structural and strategic models of working... it took many years for me to get rid of my prejudices about structural family therapy that arose from this experience.

However a colleague with some basic systemic training changed this and when we co-worked together. I started to witness changes in the families we met. I observed an approach that was non-directive, but challenging and the technique of circular questioning (Tomm 1987, Penn 1985) fascinated me. I subsequently trained as a systemic psychotherapist at Kensington Consultation Centre in London.

So why does it matter so much to me that thirty years later systemic psychotherapists are not more widely represented within the workforce for psychological therapies in the NHS? Working effectively with families across the lifespan need not just be an ideal. When I started out in my career most psychotherapy was delivered privately or from the voluntary sector –it was simply not on offer within mental health services.

Over the past thirty years I have seen the growth of counselling and psychotherapy delivered by practitioners in the NHS and it is acknowledged that the original conception of a health service "free at the point of delivery" by Bevan (1948) was a holistic vision that included mental health services.

Founder and Director of the Centre for Economic Performance (1990) at the London School of Economics, Professor Richard Layard, acted as a policy advisor to the British Labour Government from 1994 to 2010. Layard's role in mental health issues was informed by his interest in health economics and the cost to the State of a benefits system, if people are long term unemployed. Posing the question of how better mental health could improve social and economic life at both individual and societal level; he was involved in the publication of The Depression Report in 2006. Following this The Improving Access to Psychological Therapies (IAPT) programme was developed to address the imbalance in accessing mental health services in the NHS in England and Wales in comparison with physical health. Calls for parity with physical health services have continued and the Royal College of Psychiatrists published a paper in 2013 that critiques the strong relationship between mental health and physical health and how this influence is mutual.

The results of the second National Audit of Psychological Therapy Services for depression and anxiety (2013) used ten audit standards measuring access, acceptability, appropriateness and outcomes in IAPT services. This showed a gloomy picture with only waiting list times apparently improving nationally. This was probably related to findings illustrating that the first million people accessing IAPT showed half a million users did not return for a second appointment. So, questions were raised regarding engagement, attrition rates and the inability to measure outcomes based on the returned data. One aim of IAPT had been to reduce GP prescribing of anti-depressants however in the previous three years there had been a reverse trend with an increase in GP prescribing-practices of 10% year on year.

Some people argue that the introduction of IAPT with an emphasis on cognitive behavioural therapy (CBT) has led to the loss of skilled practitioners from other psychotherapeutic modalities. It seems to me to be another example of unintended consequences to well-intended actions and a professional jeopardy for fully trained psychotherapists in other modalities such as systemic and psychoanalytic approaches.

A further area of concern was that 30% of psychological therapists within high intensity IAPT services were delivering a therapy without any formal training. The risk to the public of psychological therapists delivering therapies in the NHS that they are not trained to deliver is an example of the double jeopardy for the NHS in misleading the public when psychological therapies are delivered by inadequately trained clinicians. This also represents a contradiction to the principles of clinical governance. Dissatisfaction may then be expressed in the form of complaints and client drop out. This in turn begs the question, what recourse people have if they are dissatisfied with the psychological treatment they have received? Is it strategically easier for NHS Trusts to restrict the range of psychological treatments on offer?

The NHS is now made up of different geographically based health trusts that may not necessarily serve the local community for whom services are delivered in spite of the mantra of local Clinical Commissioning

Groups (CCGs) commissioning health services that are based on local need. In this situation, tenders are bid and contracts are won through the commissioning process. Described as the "Mental Health's Market Experiment" in a report by Griffiths, Foster et al (2013) they showed that the tendering process is seriously flawed as successful tendering may not be indicative of quality.

The current political context and the introduction of an austerity programme for all public sector services in the UK has resulted in draconian cuts on services for young people since 2010. Young people do not have a powerful voice within British politics and like other marginalised groups within society, services for young people become easy targets for politicians. The impact of these cuts are all too apparent to anyone working within Child and Adolescent Mental Health (CAMHS) as increasing rates of depression, anxiety and self-harm are reflected in the rates of referral to a diminishing group of professionals within these services. For example, in my CAMHS there were 32.5 Whole Time Equivalent (WTE) practitioners in 2011. In 2012-2013 this had reduced to 19.1. By 2015 this had further reduced to 13.4 WTE.

The role of clinical commissioning groups (CCG) further complicates the manner in which NHS Trusts respond to demand. The Trust I work in for instance, has six different clinical commissioning groups wanting different things/holding different priorities. As a single organisation this makes it difficult to harmonise services as senior managers find themselves attempting to accommodate these differences.

The imperative to manage budgets and the costing of particular psychotherapeutic interventions has seen the adoption of care pathways and payment by results. Thus a particular presentation is put on a particular pathway. Family Psychotherapy is only offered for those conditions that are supported by the evidence determined by the National Institute for Clinical Excellence (NICE).

During the past thirty years the increasing medicalisation of childhood and the use of diagnoses to determine criteria eligibility for access to services, a system of care pathways have been developed. These pathways can split off elements of care that may be cherry-picked and delivered by organisations that have profit at the heart of their business model. The logical consequence of this process is that the most challenging and complex presentations will remain within the NHS at a time when the NHS is haemorrhaging experienced and skilled staff. The impact on the remaining front line practitioners is a corrosive blend that undermines confidence and creates a context within which "unsafe uncertainty" (Mason 1993) may impact in such a way that it is hard for clinicians to work at their best and promote hope within the therapeutic endeavour.

I also acknowledge that the fear of being the focus of a client complaint certainly influences my clinical practice and creative risk-taking within the therapeutic process may be deferred until I am confident that the therapeutic relationship is robust enough to manage challenge. I have also noted that increasingly families who are employed struggle to get time off from their employer to attend an appointment with their child/young person during working hours. This has equally applied to families with parents employed as nurses within the same Trust as myself.

The introduction of private contracts within mental health services represents a particular challenge for psychotherapists interested in working relationally; together with Information Technology (IT) systems within the NHS that discriminate against the practitioner working with family groups. Clinician workload is judged by the number of weekly clinical contacts. In my Trust, if you run a group with seven people from different families the group will count as seven contacts for the clinician running the group each time the group meets. When I meet with a young person and their significant relational system (family members or others such as carers or close friends), I may have seven people participating in the session but the contact is counted as one. Thus the measure of throughput with the counting of contacts in such a manner that only the named *individual* is understood as having the contact means that the extent of the work is never counted (Lather 1991). In spite of good evidence for the effectiveness and efficacy of systemic interventions that shows a decrease in the rate of attendance at medical services for other family members (Crane 2008, 2011, 2012), systemic psychotherapy then does not demonstrate the value for money that is deemed to be so important in the context of tight budgets.

Of the two clinical examples I have presented in this paper, Andrew would no longer be seen within the CAMHS that I work in. The criteria for our service have been rewritten to exclude any young person who is not seen as meeting the criteria of an enduring mental health condition. The referral for Andrew having problems with his anger would now be directed to a practitioner working within the community who, unless they are systemically trained, is more likely to see the anger as a problem intrinsic to him and none of the wider systemic work would be undertaken. Bobby, with a diagnosis of ASD, would have received a service but with a colleague not trained to "Think Family" (2008).

Over the course of my career I have witnessed the introduction of systemic ideas and practices into mental health services within the NHS. In spite of increasing supporting evidence that systemic psychotherapy is effective as stated in National Institute of Clinical Evidence (NICE) guidelines in relation to particular presentations, the recruitment of this workforce into the NHS has not reflected this trend. Those who have been recruited have tended to be employed within Child and Adolescent Mental Health and there have been reductions in these posts over the past years. Few Adult Mental Health Services employ sufficient numbers of systemic psychotherapists to have a significant impact.

Loyalty to the Trust and its business model appears to be the highest context marker for employees. In my role as Head of Family Therapy I have produced yearly annual reports with referral and outcome data initially using early SCORE questionnaires to the current SCORE 15. Last year I was informed that this was not required as there was a risk this information could be leaked to competitors. How can a National Health Service historically founded on collaboration and partnership operate, if the notion of competition is introduced in this manner?

Systemic Psychotherapists have had historical problems delivering therapy with some private providers that maintain a focus on the individual. Private insurance for instance may exclude family members participating in sessions. The Professional Affairs Committee (PAC) within the Association of Family Therapy and Systemic Practice (AFT) had been challenging this for some years and only recently managed to achieve a limited breakthrough with one private health insurance company.

Professional jeopardy

There are several facets illustrated here culminating in a picture of professional jeopardy.

- As highlighted earlier, a reduction in staffing levels increases the workload for those remaining within services and there is a toxic combination of complex clinical presentations with stressed and over-worked practitioners. What is the cost to a clinician of the pressures of working in an organisation that is not mindful of the psychological impact of the work on staff?

- Because of the scarcity of clinical resources, it seems to me that multi-disciplinary competition is encouraged as each discipline attempts to get posts in their specialty at the expense of a more considered skills mix. Furthermore, because of the manner of data collection, systemic psychotherapy is then disadvantaged by IT systems that are not set up to reflect the work that is conducted and thus the depth and extent of the work remains invisible.

- Systemic Psychotherapy represents a small minority professional group, without Department of Health funding for paid trainees in the differing areas of service provision in the way that clinical psychology and child psychotherapy are supported at a governmental level. What are the politics that only recognise individual ways of working therapeutically? It is a sad indictment of the politics at play when Think Family was such a mantra in the years of the Labour Government (1997-2010).

- As a systemic psychotherapist I value multiple perspectives and a team approach enables our practice to connect with the multiple views of those within the therapy room. From a cost perspective, with just one contact being logged against two other colleagues at the same time as myself on the IT system, it looks as if it is an expensive therapy although the outcomes in the family therapy clinics could counter this idea. Unfortunately these outcomes appear to be less significant than the cost burden to a manager tasked with keeping the finances within budget.

- At a personal level I worry increasingly about the risk of burn out or a complaint being made about my practice that would be investigated by a non-clinical manager, with insufficient experience to appreciate the clinical dilemmas being presented. I have reflected earlier in the chapter about the impact on my clinical practice and creative risk-taking. Systemic psychotherapy is not in my opinion always able to be a soothing, listening therapy but an active intervening into the system that involves challenge and conflict at times.

- An annual report of clinical activity by the family therapy clinics was an effective method of providing feedback to me and the team of our clinical outcomes and also often identified changes we could make in response to this information. For example, we were able to highlight in a twelve month period that 40% of the families referred to Family Therapy had parental mental health as a factor impacting on the children's mental health and psychological well-being. How come there are no Systemic Psychotherapy posts in the Adult Service in the Trust?

- Auditing the impact of a telephone call the day before an appointment we were able to demonstrate that a telephone call reduced the "Did

Not Attend" rates significantly. We were given secretarial support to make the phone call but this has now ceased as the secretaries were "too busy". The ethics of being too busy as clinicians, yet knowing that this was good practice meant that we took on the role ourselves. The associated costs for a clinician making the telephone call are much higher than the organisational support that used to be provided to support this action.

- The ethical dilemmas came to a head for me when a senior manager, attempting to justify the organisational stance on the above issues, advised that I should no longer aim to deliver a gold standard service and to recognise we should be "aiming for bronze". I believe this idea breaches the United Kingdom Council of Psychotherapy (UKCP) code of ethics that informs my clinical practice and contradicts key principles of the therapeutic endeavour. How do the ethics of psychotherapy provision fit within this kind of ethos?

Meeting the families again

I have referred to the use of outcomes as a way of demonstrating effective therapy but these are usually recorded at the ending of therapy and without a research mandate it is unusual for clinicians in the NHS to hear the longer term outcomes for their client families unless there is a later re-referral.

Writing this chapter created an opportunity for me to make contact with Andrew's and Bobby's families and find out for myself whether the account I had given of our work together coincided with their experience and whether working together had been useful on a longer term basis.

Amy invited me to her home, she welcomed me with a hug and after making me a coffee told me how things had been for Andrew, Aaron and her since we had last met two years ago. Andrew was doing well in school; Aaron had finished his training as a motor mechanic and now had a job. Amy had started work as a part-time care assistant and was really enjoying her work and feeling fulfilled by doing a psychologically rewarding job. The home looked beautifully cared for and the little garden was an oasis of calm for her. Amy was quite clear how helpful the work had been and felt that the support provided had kept her going when she was vulnerable and enabled the family to get on a positive future track. Amy agreed with the draft and talked at various stages of the memories evoked when reading about the different issues she had faced.

Brenda arranged to meet me at my office and brought Bobby's eldest sister with her to also read what had been written. They described their dismay at the loss of a family therapy provision as Bobby had now transitioned to Adult Mental Health. Bobby sees a psychiatrist for brief medication reviews but there is no service for families to meet together. Bobby is struggling to know what to do with his life and he has no girlfriend at the moment. Brenda talked about him being stopped and searched by community police officers on six occasions in the preceding eight months. She worries about his future. Brenda described how helpful it had been to come to a space where conversations could be held that were managed and containing-family members could say the things they might not otherwise say to each other. Both Brenda and her daughter reminisced about some of the sessions we had had together and felt happy that their story be told.

My thanks go to both families for the privilege I have had of entering their lives for a brief period and for their generosity in letting me share this experience with you.

References

Bailey, Sue; Smith, Greg & Thorpe, Lucy (2013). *Whole-Person Care: From Rhetoric to Reality*. Occasional paper. OP88. The Royal College of Psychiatrists.

Bell, Simon; Clark, David; Knapp, Martin & Layard, Richard (2006). *The Depression Report: A New Deal for Depression and Anxiety Disorders*. London: London School of Economics.

Cabinet Office, Social Exclusion Task Force. (2008). *Think Family: Improving the life chances of families at risk*.

Crane, D. Russell (2008). The Cost Effectiveness of Family Therapy: A summary and progress report. *Journal of Family Therapy*, 30: 399–410.

Crane, D. Russell & Payne, Scott (2011). Individual Versus Family Therapy in Managed Care: Comparing the costs of treatment by the mental health professions. *Journal of Marital and Family Therapy*, 37, 273–289.

Crane, D. Russell & Christenson, Jacob. D. (2012). A Summary Report of the Cost Effectiveness of the Profession and Practice of Marriage and Family Therapy. *Contemporary Family Therapy*. 34, 204–216.

Goodwillie, Gill (2013). The Impact of Attention Deficit Hyperactivity Disorder on Family Relationships: Parental Perspectives. *The Journal of Psychological Therapies in Primary Care,* 2(2), 157–173

Goodwillie, Gill (2014). Protective Vigilance: A parental strategy in caring for a child diagnosed with ADHD. *Journal of Family Therapy*, 36 (3), 255–267.

Griffiths, Steve; Foster, Joan; Steen, Scott & Pietroni, Patrick. (2013). *Mental Health's Market Experiment: Commissioning Psychological Therapies through any Qualified Provider Centre for Psychological Therapies in Primary Care*. University of Chester.

Lather, Patti (1991). *Getting Smart: Feminist Research and Pedagogy with/in the Post-Modern*. Oxford: Routledge.

Mason, Barry (1993). Towards Positions of Safe Uncertainty. Human Systems. *Journal of Systemic Consultation and Management*, 4, 189–200.

MacPherson, William (1999). *The Stephen Lawrence Inquiry*.

Penn, Peggy (1985). Feed Forward: future questions, future maps. *Family Process*, 24(3), 299–310.

Stratton, Peter; Bland, Julia; Janes, Emma & Lask, Judith (2010). Developing a practicable outcome measure for systemic family therapy: The SCORE. *Journal of Family Therapy*, 32(3), 232–258.

Tomm, Karl (1987). Interventive Interviewing: Part III. Intending to ask lineal, circular, strategic or reflexive questions? *Family Process*, 27, 1–15.

20 Paths to Transformative Conversations

Francesca Balestra & Laura Fruggeri

Introduction

What makes a conversation a therapeutic conversation, a conversation that can be considered transformative of stories, meanings, and perspectives? What is the path through which a conversation generates new meanings? These are the questions that we will address in this chapter.

We want to start by inviting you as readers to take a look at the following excerpts taken from our practice, and see if there is anything that strikes you in terms of differences between them.

Excerpt 1 – The Oranges: Patrizia (wife), Alberto (husband)
Topic: A couple's dynamic in arguing

Therapist: You both go haywire.

Alberto: It is beyond our control, and we start to see ourselves as two enemies.

Therapist: You become hostile to each other.

Alberto: Yes! We become hostile.

Therapist: Do you become violent?

Alberto: I break some stuff.

Therapist: Are you violent toward each other?

Alberto: We are not.

Patrizia: No. (Smiles)

Alberto: Absolutely not.

Therapist: What is the dynamic of these crises?

Alberto: She feels that she is going to be abandoned or challenged, which is something that I absolutely don't want to do. Two evenings ago I said, "If we want to stay together, which is fine to me, we have to solve a problem". And she said, "You cannot call our relationship into question".

Patrizia: Actually he said, "If we want to stay together." To me, there's no "if". We want to stay together. Do we have to say "If we want to stay together"?

Paths to Transformative Conversations

Therapist: Patrizia says that she feels that you haul out an episode to question the entire relationship, and that you exaggerate by raising doubts. This dynamic makes Patrizia feel insecure. She clams up. The dynamic that you Alberto told us is that you feel that Patrizia positions herself in a corner, and when she doesn't get out from there, so you pull her.

Alberto: I raise the volume.

Therapist: You make her step out of this dynamic. Do you agree?

Alberto: Yes. Through the years I realised that sometimes, even if everything is going well between us, a drama is needed. Usually the tension grows until a tornado blows off, and then pouf! we work it out.

Therapist: It seems like for him it is important to feel that you somehow need him, so when he finds out that it is not so, he is shocked, frustrated because in his view being helpful is part of being in a relationship.

Patrizia: Yes.

Alberto: She is a bottomless pit. What I give her in terms of confirmations and presence is never enough.

Patrizia: I have to admit I am complicated. Maybe I am a little bit, ehm, I am extremely demanding, first and foremost to myself.

Therapist: Yes, but the point is not that you are wrong and he is right, the thing is how the two aspects connect.

Patrizia: I honestly think that now he is attributing to me expectations that, actually, I don't have.

Therapist: But he seems sorry for this.

Patrizia: (Joking, but slightly seriously) I also told my son Filippo "We have to be careful in asking Alberto to buy things, because he immediately brings them to us".

Therapist: Could the dynamic be this: Alberto feels triggered by practical requests, like a request to buy something. But you are not asking it literally, you are somehow saying "Show me that you care about me".

Excerpt 2 – The Reds: Franca (wife), Samuele (husband)
Topic: Divorce

Therapist:	Is it your separation consensual?
Franca:	Yes.
Samuele:	Yes.
Therapist:	So you have come to this decision in a shared way?
Franca:	Calm way? (Overlapping therapist) Not so much.
Therapist:	Shared. Well, these things are not calm, but they can be shared. I mean, at the moment do you both agree about the separation?
Samuele:	Yes.
Franca:	(nods)
Therapist:	And did you analyse the causes of the separation?
Franca:	Well essentially... According to me...
Therapist:	Later Samuele will tell his interpretation.
Franca:	I discovered that he had a story with a woman. He says that she was only a friend, but the tone of the text message that I saw was not friend-like. I have never monitored anything because I trusted him 100%. I checked the phone twice and I caught him.
Therapist:	How come you decided to check your husband's phone if you never monitored him?
Franca:	Because he was changed, he was always at the phone.
Therapist:	And your interpretation?
Samuele:	Well... I met this person with whom I talked and shared my problems, because I could not do it with my wife.
Therapist:	So, the separation is... something that you feel like... a solution that is good for each of you.
Franca:	Definitely. Together, we can no longer go on.
Samuele:	No longer.

Excerpt 3 – The Silvers: Lisa (wife), Michele (husband).
Topic: Partners' needs

Therapist:	What hurt you?
Lisa:	Well, the "I absolutely cannot" that he said because he had to go to his friend's birthday.
Therapist:	Mmh, mmh

Lisa:	And so I instinctively didn't feel considered or at least not considered as I would like to be, the reasons of our relational problems were connected to this aspect. We are in a very particular phase. Seeing if, if we can re-establish our relationship or not.
Therapist:	You didn't feel considered by him?
Lisa:	I felt little considered because he found hard to say no to his friend. I don't care about the appointment with your friend. If I am the priority, you have to tell him.
Therapist:	So the problem for you is that you want to be a priority for Michele, you want to come first always. This is important for you.
Lisa:	I mean, when we had a good relationship, I never restrained him because I myself wish to have my own spaces.
Therapist:	And you Michele, what has disappointed you in your relationship?
Michele:	Well, it is... that sense of guilt that we already talked about, a sense of inadequacy that I felt towards her.
Therapist:	This relates to what Lisa has expressed towards you. Instead if you were to express something to Lisa, regardless of her complaints so to speak.
Michele:	Yes, as I always said, I would like to buy a home. I would like to keep many possibilities open, which range from changing home, to even... change lifestyle.
Therapist:	Listen Lisa, I would like to ask you...
Lisa:	(nods)
Therapist:	You say, "I would like to have a relationship in which he is not protective anymore". But doesn't this fit with Michele saying "We can go out every day, but not on my friend's birthday". Isn't this his way of not being protective? In this case he didn't protect you, but you don't seem to be happy either.
Lisa:	What I had spontaneously understood was "he did not consider me" not "he did not protect me". Now with my individual therapist I'm considering this aspect, this need to feel loved because I have been an unseen daughter.

Therapist: Yes, yes.

Lisa: And right now I feel this need in a impetuous way, and it is difficult for me to control it.

What differences did you notice between these excerpts?

For us these excerpts represent different ways to engage in a transformative conversation. In the first excerpt, the conversation stimulates the emergence of a new perspective on the presented problem. This type of interaction differs from that of extract two, where the conversation promotes the deepening and the specification of the "divorce" topic, thus letting the different family members' viewpoints emerge. Even if the conversation opens space for all family members to express their opinion, new ways of looking at things do not seem to emerge yet. Finally, the third extract shows an even different type of conversation, where old descriptions of feelings and needs coexist with new ones.

We often think of therapeutic conversations as transformative or non-transformative. The above examples remind us that there are also conversations that are transformative in different ways: the first generates meanings, the second explores different perspectives, and the third opens space for different ways of dealing with the issue at stake. In everyday clinical practice, all these kinds of conversation can occur even during the same session.

Is it important for a therapist to be able to observe, distinguish and describe these different ways of participating in a transformative conversation? Does this methodological attitude count as systemic practice? We argue that the answer is that it does matter. As described by Sluzki (1992), the change processes in psychotherapy are favoured by a redefinition of both the content of the narration and the way the content is narrated. This implies that there are ways of talking about issues that may or may not produce change. Thus it is important for the therapist to be aware of which kind of conversation she is involved. But how can we, as therapists, carry on the analysis of a conversation while it unfolds? Are there criteria or hints for identifying different kinds of therapeutic conversations as they flow? Are there guidelines helping therapists to move from a non-transformative to a transformative conversation?

Drawing from research on therapeutic process, in this chapter, we will propose some ideas useful to answer to these questions.

Therapeutic competences and process research

According to the systemic approach, a psychotherapeutic session can be conceived as a space where therapist and family members engage in a process of negotiation of new meanings. Such a process can be analysed from two different perspectives: individual and relational. From the individual point of view, the analysis focuses on how each individual (therapist included) makes sense of what is happening, the personal claim that people have in mind coming to the encounter, the reaction they have to each other's stances, the emotions expressed by participants, the questions raised by therapist, and so on. But research, even the outcome research, has pointed out another level embedded in the therapy: the relational one (Sprenkle, 2003). From that perspective a therapeutic process emerges as a mutual and shared activity (Rober 2005), that the language, the constructs, the notions used to describe the individual processes do not capture. Relationship is not a background of the therapeutic intervention, it is not the container, it is the very web through which therapy takes shape. In this sense we do not understand how therapies work until we find ways to understand how the therapeutic relationship works (Burck 2005; Pinsof 1989). Interestingly enough, the systemic approach that is based on relationships, is still struggling to identify conceptual resources to reflect and analyse in details the therapeutic relationship in the systemic practice. Systemic practitioners and researchers have provided coherent and effective methodologies for the analysis of clients' relationships but seem to lack instruments for the analysis of the therapeutic relationship. The research field known as Process Research aims to fill the gap. The object of process research studies is the on-going process through which the therapeutic intervention unfolds. The major concern is methodological, that is the elaboration of conceptual tools that are appropriate to analyse the mutual and complex nature of the therapeutic process (Heatherington et al. 2005; Oka & Whiting 2013). The pursuit of such a goal is very important, since process research would provide the tools for the development of an overlooked skill of systemic therapists: the relational competence, that is the ability to analyse the therapeutic process as it unfolds (Fruggeri, 2012). We claim that it is important to make a distinction between technical competence and relational competence. The first one is the ability to apply a model; the second is the ability to monitor the interpersonal process as it emerges from the therapist-clients interchange. The two competences do not overlap. Making the right questions and exploring themes which may seem useful to understand the story of one family, may indeed become unhelpful when it merges with clients' previous experiences, feelings, beliefs, and so on. The therapist might "do the right thing" according to the model, yet the conversation that takes place does not seem to introduce novelty, to enhance connectedness, create sharing and trust (Roy-Chowdhury 2006; Fruggeri 2012; Patrika & Tseliou 2015). The technical competence orients therapists to reflect on the rules of the model, the relational competence invites therapists to observe and reflect on the happening of the therapeutic intervention. The technical competence guides the thinking and the actions of therapists, the relational competence orients therapists to observe the interactive effects of their actions.

The search for the methodologies that fit the goal of analysing and shedding light on the development of the therapeutic relationship has called on those fields that study peoples' talk.

In marital and family systemic therapy, the studies conducted within the process research field over the years can be distinguished in three main areas, depending on the adopted methodologies and the research aims.

The *first area* includes the research conducted through the framework of Conversation Analysis (CA). In particular, CA studies detach the grammar of a conversation through its regularities and procedures. By pointing out the linguistic actions performed by therapists and clients, this research has described the conversational structure of the psychotherapeutic dialogue (Peräkyläet al. 2008).

The *second area* consists of studies that adopt Discourse Analysis (DA) methods. DA examines how people use language in interactions to build certain accounts of events, thus enhancing some positions, and undermining others (Potter & Wetherell 1987). Research conducted within this methodology described the discursive construction of a wide range of phenomena (Tseliou 2013), such as: psychotherapeutic techniques, therapeutic relationship, institutional psychotherapeutic practices, gender, blame, power and culture.

Finally, the *third area* can be identified in those studies that developed innovative methodologies for the study of psychotherapeutic dialogue. In general terms, the third research area is more heterogeneous than the previous ones, and it includes a combination of methods aimed at exploring different aspects of the therapeutic process, e.g. relational control sequences (Family Relational Communication Control Coding System, Friedlander & Heatherington 1989), narrative understanding of family therapeutic process (Laitila et al. 2001), therapeutic alliance (System for Observing Family Therapy Alliances, Friedlander et al. 2006), responsive processes (Dialogical Methods for Investigations of Happening of Change, Seikkula et al. 2012). Like a prism, process research has elaborated procedures that allow separating the conversational flow into its different components, and helps us to see structures, peculiarities and redundancies of interactions. In this, they all contribute to provide tools for identifying interactive/communicative forms that are connected with the generation of new systems of meanings.

A guide to observe patterns of interaction

Within the stream of process research, we performed a study aimed at identifying specific dimensions of change that can account for different forms of therapeutic conversation, and can offer clinicians some empirically supported information to improve their practice. Central in our study has been the notion of positioning, which underlines that in every conversation participants interact by taking different perspectives that are linked to the subjects' multifaceted identity, and orient them to perceive others, hear, feel and act in a specific way (Hermans 2006; Van Langenhove & Harré 1994).

The positions of participants are bonded by the context of the on-going discourse; on the other side a change in positioning can modify what people are doing together, that is the context within which they interact (Harré et al. 2009). During the course of every dialogue the positioning for themselves and for the others can be accepted or refused: they can be challenged and can change through the course of interaction (Markova et al. 2007; Seikkula et al. 2012). This process, which is embedded in everyday interpersonal exchanges, is emphasised in the psychotherapeutic dialogue, where clients express themselves both in the interaction with the therapist and in the autobiographical narratives they are telling. This means, according to Wortham (2001), that in analysing a therapeutic conversation it is necessary to look at the positioning adopted both in the on-going interaction, and in the narrated events.

Positioning can change in its content, according to the thematic issues addressed in a specific dialogue. But positioning can change also according to other dimensions that point out the dynamic features of this construct (Grossen & Salazar Orvig 2011; Harré et al. 2009; Hermans 1996; Marková et al. 2007; Vion 1998).

In our study we found that changes in positioning occur in different ways (Balestra 2014): The narration can be made through an individual and a collective positioning which can be expressed in a more or less emotional intensity and be connected to specific time slots. A positioning can be introduced by family members as they tell their story, or by the therapist, and can be proposed also for persons which are not present (evoked others). Moreover, the positions adopted by each participant for her/himself (or for others) can be consistent throughout the narration, or oscillate between opposing aspects. At the same time the interlocutors can contribute to the dialogue in a synchronous way, by adopting similar types of positioning, or in an asynchronous way, by taking positions that express different and even diverging aspects. Finally, the taken positioning can adhere to the storyline or refer to unrelated issues.

Alongside with these changes, during the development of the conversation therapists may position themselves in different ways. As a "co-narrator", the therapist joins clients in narrating new stories, whereas as an "explorer", s/he seeks details of the family's story. Being "curious", s/he is interested and open to clients' point of view and explanations, while as an "expert", s/he uses her/his professional knowledge to interact with clients. A therapist could take the position of a "listener" or an "observer", but can also be a "coordinator" when s/he decides who talks. As long as s/he listens and comprehends clients' emotional states therapist adopts an "empathic" positioning, while challenging the story of the family, s/he takes a "provocative" one.

As dialogue unfolds, all the above mentioned elements of positioning can take different trajectories: (i) *morphogenic*, when there is an irreversible change in positioning (e.g., the shift from emotional to non-emotional positioning or vice versa); (ii) *morphostatic*, when changes in positioning constantly oscillate between different forms (e.g., the shift from absence to presence of positioning for evoked others goes back to the initial absence); (iii) *static*, when there is no change in positioning (e.g., there is only a flat emotional tone). These trajectories of the positioning moves allow describing different forms of transformative conversations.

Let's go back to the initial excerpts and capture the differences between them through the lens of the above-described changes in positioning. We remind the reader that the excerpts refer to a generative, an explorative and an oscillating form of conversation, respectively. It might be of interest to the reader to know that each of the above excerpts is an example of a typology that we identified in our study by analysing 11563

Paths to Transformative Conversations

utterances. All the conversations included in each typology present the features here described.

If we consider the extent of family members' and the therapist's positioning, all the three forms of conversation have similar features. The clients go to and from individual and collective positions, e.g., as "worried couple" and "wife sure of the relationship" (excerpt 1), or as "couple in crisis" and as "partner who does not feel considered" (excerpt 3). The therapist oscillates between different positions with a morphostatic trajectory throughout the development of the topic. In the first excerpt, s/he adopts the position of "co-narrator" and "explorer", then moves across different positions (e.g. "coordinator" and "expert"), to return in the end to the position of "co-narrator"; in the second excerpt s/he shifts from "explorer" and "expert" (adopted mostly at the beginning and at the end of the conversation), to "coordinator" and "provocative" in the middle of the conversation; in the third excerpt, s/he presents a varied range of positionings that oscillate all the time between "curious", "explorer", "listener", "coordinator", "co-narrator" and "provocative".

Being sessions of couple/family therapies, the alternation of the I/WE positions on behalf of clients is not a discriminatory feature of the dialogue. But even more interestingly, the multiplicity and oscillation of the therapist positioning does not discriminate the type of conversation either, thus pointing out how it is not by analysing only the therapists' actions that we understand the development of the therapeutic process.

Let's observe the other features of positioning that, instead, allow differentiating the three forms of conversation.

In the generative conversation, positioning always relates to the topic at stake (e.g. the dynamic of the couple's arguments in excerpt 1), while in both the explorative and the oscillating conversations, positioning sometimes fits the topic, sometimes it does not. In the second excerpt, e.g, positioning is congruent with the topic of divorce at the beginning and at the end of the conversation, while in the middle part of the dialogue positioning is related to the betrayal. Similarly, in the third excerpt positioning does not always fit with the topic "partners' needs", as we can see when Lisa positions herself as an unseen daughter (excerpt 3).

The emotional dimension of positioning specifies the generative conversation, in which the emotional tone becomes more intense as the conversation goes on. In fact, through the development of generative conversations we can notice a shift from the expression of neutral positioning (e.g. "wife sure of the relationship", excerpt 1) to the expression of emotionally connoted positioning (e.g. "complicated wife", excerpt 2); while in the explorative and oscillating conversations we can observe a continuous fluctuations of the emotional intensity of family members' positioning. The latter movement is particularly evident in the second excerpt, where clients repeatedly oscillate between the positions of "wife/husband who has difficulties", and "spouses in the process of consensual separation".

Generative conversations are also characterised by a shift from past to present and future issues. In the first excerpt, in fact, clients and therapist start talking about the past conflicting moments, then move to present, by talking about how the couple feels. On the contrary, in the explorative and oscillating conversations, the dialogue develops by oscillating through present and past (e.g. the here and now of the divorce, and the past betrayal, 2nd excerpt; the inadequacy of Michele and Lisa's individual therapy in the 3rd).

Coherence and synchronicity of family members positioning, instead, differentiate oscillating conversations from generative and explorative ones. In oscillating conversations, in fact, each family member expresses a set of contradictory positions, and contributes to the dialogue in an asynchronous way, by taking positions that express diverging aspects. In the third excerpt: Lisa adopts inconsistent positions, like "partner who wants to be a priority" and "permissive partner"; and the couple underlines different aspects: Lisa points out her feelings, while Michele focuses more on the couple needs and opportunities. In generative and explorative conversations, positioning of family members change but they are always consistent and synchronous. These particular features of positioning point out how the oscillating kind of conversation is far away from a shared story.

Finally, authorship of positioning and positioning for evoked characters are the elements that clearly distinguish each type of conversation. In generative conversations family members move from proposing positions to accepting positions proposed by therapist, like e.g. husband as "partner who cares" (excerpt 1). Differently, in explorative conversations, positioning is always introduced by family members who express their point of view in answering to the therapist's questions. In oscillating conversations, instead, both the therapist and the clients, in turn, introduce new elements. As we can see in excerpt 3, the therapist positions Michele as "partner expressing needs", and in the next turn Michele accepts this interactive position by expressing the desire to change home; at the same time, e.g., Lisa positions herself as a "partner who wants to be a priority" and therapist adopts this position for Lisa in the next turn. Finally, positioning for evoked others is introduced during the course of generative conversations, it is consistently present in explorative conversations and it is sometimes present, sometimes not in oscillating conversations.

Conclusion

It is quite easy in clinical practice to identify a change when it is connected with a redefinition of a narrative or with a change in behaviours. However, this is not the only way in which change can occur through the course of a session. We can have conversations that are transformative in a more subtle way. For example, exploration does not necessarily bring dramatic changes in behaviours, but it can facilitate the emergence of different viewpoints and opinions never expressed before or never heard by family members. We can have conversations that produce new descriptions that are later withdrawn, thus giving the idea that novelty is possible but not now. In our chapter, we attempted to offer some guidelines that can be used to identify whether the unfolding conversation is of a generative, an explorative or an oscillating kind.

Constantly adhering to the addressed topic, generative conversations are characterised by the fact that: i) emotional tone gets more intense as the conversation goes on; ii) positioning moves from past towards present and/or future; iii) there is a progressive emergence of new positioning proposed by the therapist and accepted by the family members.

On the other hand, the explorative and the oscillating conversations show similar features: in both cases almost all dimensions of positioning oscillate without fostering any novelty. However, the exploration pattern is recognisable by the fact that the therapist never introduces new positioning; s/he rather deepens the other dimensions of the proposed positioning without changing the content of the story. The oscillation pattern is instead recognisable by the fact that all the elements of positioning do not change, but they introduce a movement in the content of the story. This conversation is characterised by ambivalence and asynchrony, which means that each participant maintains positions expressing opposite aspects, and contributes to the development of the topic in opposite ways.

Why are these results relevant for practitioners?

They help practitioners to become aware of the kind of dialogical construction they participate in. According to the systemic-constructionist approach, a session is not just an application of technical therapeutic devices. It is rather a "joint action" whose consequences are not unilaterally determined but co-constructed through the interaction itself (Shotter 1993). This is why it is important for therapists to develop a relational competence that is the ability to read the interaction as it unfolds through the dialogue among participants. But the relational competence needs instruments to rely on. The operationalisation of the different kinds of transformative conversation in terms of positioning is an attempt that we made to offer instruments that can support and feed the competence of therapists to read processes.

This kind of research provides guidelines to the self-reflexivity of the therapist, who can then ask her/himself questions such as: what is my position in the conversation? How do clients respond to this? Are they generating new positioning? Are they oscillating between this and that? What is the quality of their emotions? What the time dimension?

The generation of new meanings and stories is a goal to which all therapists aim. But sometimes generative conversations are too premature with respect to the timing of the family; accepting to go along with the oscillation of clients' positioning allows novelty to emerge in a bearable way. Thus, being aware of the above-mentioned characteristics of different transformative conversations, a therapist might choose to participate and stay in an oscillating or in an explorative conversation according to different therapeutic needs. On the other side, if the therapist is able to distinguish the features of the positioning characterising conversations that have or have not the potentials for generating new meanings, she doesn't need to change the content of the positions adopted by clients, she can rather work on the features of the proposed positioning, like projecting them in another time dimension or elaborating on the emotional tune, or addressing the inconsistency or a-synchronicity of the adopted positions, thus giving a different direction to the on-going process.

References

Balestra, Francesca (2014). *Mappare il cambiamento. Analisi dei processi interattivi in terapia familiare* (Unpublished doctoral thesis). University of Parma, Parma, Italy.

Burck, Charlotte (2005). Comparing Qualitative Research Methodologies for Systemic Research. *Journal of Family Therapy*, 27, 237–262.

Friedlander, Myrna L. & Heatherington, Laurie (1989). Analysing relational control in family therapy interviews. *Journal of Counselling Psychology*, 36(2), 139.

Friedlander, Myrna L.; Escudero, Valentin & Heatherington, Laurie (2006). *Therapeutic Alliances in Couple and Family Therapy: An Empirically Informed Guide to Practice*. Washington DC: American Psychological Association.

Fruggeri, Laura (2012). Different Levels of Psychotherapeutic Competence. *Journal of Family Therapy*, 34(1), 91–105.

Grossen, Michelè & Salazar Orvig, Anne (2011). Third Parties' Voices in a Therapeutic Interview. *Text & Talk*, 31(1), 53–76.

Harré, Rom; Moghaddam, Fathali M.; Pilkerton Cairnie, Tracey; Rothbart, Daniel & Sabat, Steven R. (2009). Recent Advances in Positioning Theory. *Theory & Psychology*, 19(1), 5–31.

Heatherington, Laurie; Friedlander, Myrna L. & Greenberg, Leslie (2005). Change Process Research in Couple and Family Therapy: Methodological challenges and opportunities. *Journal of Family Psychology*, 19(1), 18–27.

Hermans, Hubert (1996). Voicing the Self: From information processing to dialogic interchange. *Psychological Bulletin*, 119, 31–50.

Hermans, Hubert J. M. (2006). The Self as a Theatre of Voices: Disorganization and reorganization of a position repertoire. *Journal of Constructivist Psychology*, 19(2), 147–169.

Laitila, Aarno; Aaltonen, Jukka; Wahlström, Jarl & Angus, Lynne (2001). Narrative Process Coding System in Marital and Family Therapy. *Contemporary Family Therapy*, 23(3), 309–322.

Marková, Ivana; Linell, Per; Grossen, Michèle & Salazar Orvig, Anne (2007), *Dialogue in Focus Groups: Exploring Socially Shared Knowledge*. London: Equinox.

Oka, Megan & Whiting, Jason (2013). Bridging the Clinician/Researcher Gap with Systemic Research. *Journal of Marital and Family Therapy*, 39(1), 17-27.

Patrika, Pinelopi & Tseliou, Eleftheria (2015). Blame, Responsibility and Systemic Neutrality: A discourse analysis methodology to the study of family therapy problem talk. *Journal of Family Therapy*. doi: 10.1111/1467-6427.12076

Peräkylä, Anssi; Antaki, Charles; Vehviläinen, Sanna & Leudar, Ivan (Eds.) (2008). *Conversation Analysis and Psychotherapy*. Cambridge: Cambridge University Press.

Pinsof, William M. (1989). A Conceptual Framework and Methodological Criteria for Family Therapy Process Research. *Journal of Consulting and Clinical Psychology*, 57(1), 53–59.

Potter, Jonathan & Wetherell, Margaret (1987). *Discourse and Social Psychology*. London: Sage.

Rober, Peter (2005). Family Therapy as a Dialogue of Living Persons. *Journal of Marital and Family Therapy*, 31, 385–397.

Roy-Chowdhury, Sim (2006). How is the Therapeutic Relationship Talked into Being? *Journal of Family Therapy*, 28, 153–174.

Seikkula, Jakko; Laitila, Aarno & Rober, Peter (2012). Making Sense of Multi-Actor Dialogues in Family Therapy and Network Meetings. *Journal of Marital and Family Therapy*, 38(4), 667–687.

Shotter, John (1993). *Conversational Realities*. London: Sage.

Sluzki, Carlos E. (1992). Transformations: A blueprint for narrative changes in therapy. *Family Process*, 31(3), 217–230.

Sprenkle, Douglas H. (2003). Effectiveness Research in Marriage and Family Therapy: Introduction. *Journal of Marital and Family Therapy*, 29(1), 85–96.

Tseliou, Eleftheria (2013). A Critical Methodological Review of Discourse and Conversation Analysis Studies of Family Therapy. *Family Process*, 52(4), 653–672.

van Langenhove, Luk & Harré, Rom (1994). Cultural Stereotypes and Positioning Theory. *Journal for the Theory of Social Behaviour*, 24(4), 359–372.

Vion, Robert (1998). De l'instabilité des positionnements énonciatifs dans le discours. In Jef Verschueren (Ed.), *Pragmatics in 1998: Selected Papers from the 6th International Conference*, Vol. 2. Antwerp: International Pragmatics Association.

Wortham, Stanton (2001). *Narratives in Action*. New York: Teachers College Press.

Systemic Conversations with Military Families
Research as intervention

21

Ann-Margreth E. Olsson

Suddenly everything had changed. He found himself lying in a little shed close to his wounded colleague. With bullets whistling around them, the shed was giving little cover. He was not afraid of dying but very worried about his family. He had promised them to return home safe and sound.

Peter did return. However, at heart he was never the same Peter as before. His family noticed the change. Peter always avoided talking about what he had been through. Not until he decided to participate in this new veteran research study. Now, through the research, he invited his closest family members into conversations exploring his and their experiences of the deployments and their consequences.

In this chapter, I invite the reader into my meeting with Peter and in his family. You are invited into my practice of action research using systemic, dialogical and narrative ideas in an ongoing study with Swedish military families, or as they prefer to be called, families with a family member employed as a soldier. The research project is directed, by means of a dialogical participation action research (DPAR) method (Olsson, 2014a, 2014b), towards the discovery of the right tools that can serve military individuals and their families, and which act as a buffer against the challenges they face. DPAR may also guide professionals in social services, education and health care and volunteers who work to reduce the distress experienced by soldiers, veterans and their families while also promoting individual and family resilience. I invite the reader into my narrative exploring a striking example from the families participating.

A striking example of the ongoing research study in systemic practice

Twenty years ago, Anna's son, Peter, had decided to go away to the Middle East, deployed as a soldier in a UN Peace Support Operation to which Sweden contributed troops. Peter was 21-years-old and left without any special information or support to his family from the Swedish Armed Forces (SAF). His mother would have preferred him to stay in Sweden.

However, she did not wish to interfere with her son's plans, especially as her husband (Peter's father) and the rest of the family (an older daughter and her husband) seemed to be in favour of the idea. They saw it as an opportunity to go in search of adventure, to do something different and contribute to a better world. However, neither they, nor the young soldier could imagine what he was going to meet and carry with him in the future.

Two decades later, as a systemic researcher, I interviewed the family about their experiences concerning Peter's deployments. I also interviewed Peter, now a 41-year-old veteran, and we talked about and reflected on his memories and his situation today. The focus of this research study was on the support of soldiers, veterans (soldiers been deployed abroad) and military families might need from the Swedish welfare system and/or SAF, and how they manage to give each other support, as well as others in a similar situation.

In this family, the individual dialogues in the mother's sewing-room, later in the evening, turned into a network meeting with the whole family in the living room. The dialogical interplay and collaboration in the family was already in progress, before my visit, and intensified in the dialogue in the kitchen, waiting for their turn to be interviewed. This process had actually started when the veteran decided to join the research and invite his family to join in too. As they revealed in the interviews, this was the first time they felt that the soldier had invited them to take part, or at least get something more than fragments from his experiences of three military deployments in the Middle East and the Balkans; to learn what these experiences had done to him, how they had changed his attitudes towards his loved ones, towards himself and his way of life. His sister, Karin, captured this change in the following quotations:

> "Of course I had considered that him going into war would affect him, and become a difficult experience for him. However, I had never ever imagined the extent of the impact – how much it affected and changed him."

> "I remember him as another person before he went away. He became a completely other person afterwards. His personality changed. However, as he has commented on this change: 'Perhaps I would have become like this anyway?' We will never know. But he is quite another person ..."

Systemic Conversations with Military Families

According to the plans at the time, Peter was going to be away for six months in the first deployment. In the spring, his grandfather died and then Peter returned for a few days to Sweden for the funeral, however he was also going to be home again in another few months. Shortly after the funeral his mother, Anna, was at work when she suddenly heard something on the radio news. His sister Karin, who was at home cleaning, also heard something on the radio news. Her husband, at work, called his wife immediately when he also heard the news about Swedish soldiers involved in combat, soldiers probably killed or wounded, and, which made things even worse, shut in somewhere out of reach. This took place in the area they expected Peter to be.

At this time, the Swedish Armed Forces did not have any procedure as regards preparing the soldiers' families or giving immediate information about Swedish soldiers involved in incidents abroad. The sister started to call SAF, asking for information. However, at this stage nobody seemed to know anything – or perhaps they did not want to divulge unverified information.

At the same time, Peter had concerns about his family and their reactions. Here is an extract of the interview with Peter and me (AMO):

AMO:	Do you want to talk about it?
Peter:	No – yes, I don't know what you already know. It was [...] Swedish soldiers being kidnapped [...] firing broke out and a soldier died, several wounded.
AMO:	It sounds as if you're reading a newspaper, but you were there, in this.
Peter:	I remember what the newspapers wrote. I still have the press cuttings. It is very difficult to talk about this in my own words. I have read those articles so many times.
AMO:	Mm.
Peter:	What I remember which wasn't in the newspapers was: "Is this how it will end?"
AMO:	OK, a feeling?

Peter:	I think we were all convinced that we were going to die there: "Is this how it will end?" When we were in training for the deployment we listened to a recorded incident where the participating soldier [his name], in the midst of grenade attacks and explosions, he was wounded and said: "Is this how it will end?" Now, a year later, that's in my brain. I remember thinking this. I was not afraid of dying, but I was very worried about my family and what they were going to think. In fact I had told them: "This is not dangerous – nothing will happen – everything will be fine".
	[...]
AMO:	What you now remember, when you are narrating, you remember from within the occurrence. remembering as if you had a sense of guilt in relation to your family "I had told them this wasn't going to happen" – you had concerns, cared about your family in the middle of everything ...
Peter:	Yes, it was like that somehow. In one way I didn't have any concerns about what they were going to say or think about what I had told them, but I was very worried about them: This would affect them deeply – how would they be able to deal with this? I was going to die, I was sure about that.
AMO:	A very unselfish thought in this.
Peter:	Yes, but that's one way to react – I don't know if I would react in same way today – you never know until afterwards.
AMO:	No.
Peter:	I think, when you realise you are going to die, you become egoless – unselfish we say. If you reconcile yourself to "this is the end, this is it" then you can become completely unselfish and only have considerations for others ...

In the dialogue the soldier also uncovered why he wanted his family to participate in this research study:

Peter:	This is part of my way of processing what I have been through I think. Important to talk about and I am bad at getting this off my chest and talk.

Systemic Conversations with Military Families

AMO:	You could have fooled me.
	[both laughing]
	[...]
Peter:	Those who have understood me are my UN friends. I talk with them now and then, a few of them, we still keep in touch ... after 20 years.

He also reflected on how he had changed:

Peter:	I have changed. However, this might have been the case anyway. I'm a little bit more introvert, reflecting and pondering a lot, having difficulties opening up and letting people in [...] It might be about things I've experienced, seen and lived through, having an impact on me somehow, even though I can't understand how or how it has affected me. However, I have been kidnapped, been fired at, I have been digging up, excavating mass graves. There is so much that could have scarred me for life ...

The impact of the ongoing dialogues

Peter had invited me to his parents' house and asked them, his sister and her now former husband to participate. He wanted them all to go there together. I met them and was eager to listen to their narratives about their experiences of having a son and brother deployed, injured and returning for more deployments.

I had asked Peter to invite important people and had suggested that we start with individual interviews followed by a joint network meeting at the end. What I had not expected was that they all arrived simultaneously and sat in the kitchen waiting together in a joint dialogue, while I interviewed them one by one in the mother's sewing room upstairs. During the evening, I began to realise that something unique was emerging in the kitchen downstairs. The sister gave some clues in the interview:

Sister:	[...] Perhaps this could help him find a new direction. Earlier he didn't want to talk to anybody about this ...
AMO:	Something very special – you sitting in the kitchen all together.

Sister: Yes, we do talk now. That's what we said, this could be a part of his progress, finding a new direction in how to go on, perhaps for us as well. I think it is. After his deployments we didn't talk but we are now. I don't think anybody can imagine how it was down there (in the context of war). He's telling us that: "You can never ever understand how it was down there if you haven't been there".

The sister's ex-husband also pointed to the conversation in the kitchen:

Ex-husband: We've been talking about all sorts of things from electric light bulbs to ... he is telling us new things more and more. Not gigantic disclosures but perhaps this will become a spur for him to starts to opening up more. As a matter of fact it felt a bit different – it did.

After four hours and five individual interviews we assembled in the living room. Everybody seemed pleased with the impact of the dialogues, both in the sewing room and in the kitchen. Everything in the sewing room was recorded but not the conversations that took place in the kitchen. In the living room, Peter's father made a video recording of our conversation for the research. Even though it was quite late in the evening, I invited them into an open dialogue. I asked them to reflect upon their own understanding of the emerging dialogues and interplay, including how this might have been heard and experienced from the Peter's perspective. After they had listened to each other's answers, and reflected upon what was heard, we rounded off listening to Peter reflecting on the evening from his point of view. I expressed my thanks and gratitude to them all, especially to Peter who invited me into his life, giving me the opportunity to listen to his and his family's narratives and getting to know them all.

Context

Sweden has had peace for two hundred years and upholds a policy of neutrality based on tradition. However, Sweden has a long tradition of taking part in major peacekeeping operations and other peace missions around the world (Michel, 2005). Since 1948, Sweden has an unbroken tradition of participating in military peace operations worldwide, for example, in Cyprus, the Middle East, Bosnia, Kosovo, Liberia and

Afghanistan (Swedish Armed Forces, 2015). The so-called Suez Battalion in 1956 was the first armed squad that Sweden placed at the UN's disposal. Otherwise, it has been operations with unarmed observers. In total, over 100,000 Swedish soldiers have served in international force and international peace support operations (Swedish Armed Forces, 2011). In the years that Sweden has sent out men and women in different contingents to war zones round the world, the soldiers have not been asked about their families, not registered if they have children and only recently started to ask about their marital status. While a country like USA knows the number of children involved in military families (cf. Kelty, Kleykamp, & Segal, 2010; Robertson, 2008), Sweden cannot produce any historic data about the soldiers' marital status or their children. In the Swedish context, neither the families nor the soldiers live on campus. They are part of the same community and the same universal welfare system, with rights and obligations, as everybody else. Professionals in social services and health care are supposed to recognise, identify and supply support if and when the need arises for a veteran and a military family when they cannot provide for themselves with own resources (cf. the Swedish Social Service Act). How these professionals manage to do this could be interesting to shed some light on in further research studies.

The Swedish Armed Forces started to invite their families into network meetings with other military families only recently, informing them about the work and the contingent their soldiers have joined. When the soldiers arrive home they all participate in de-briefing group meetings and are given the opportunity to talk and make a soft landing (Molin & Salomonsson, 2013). Then they go home, home to their families, alone and not thoroughly prepared for the homecoming, as they say. Some return to their parents and siblings, some to their spouses and children, others to an empty flat or house, hopefully with friends and relatives nearby. Nevertheless, it is a huge change and needs – both for home-comers and recipients (loved ones at home) – adjustment. Veterans living with or close to their parents can appreciate the instrumental and emotional support (Worthen, Moos, & Ahern, 2012). Parents can probably stand an egocentric reaction from grown-up children returning home from deployments. As one mother told me, with three sons in the military, all veterans:

> *"You have to put up with them sitting in an armchair for three days not saying anything and then suddenly they are back to their old selves again."*

This patience and forbearance is not easy for a waiting spouse or partner to produce or for a longing child to accept. They need their homecoming family member, just as he or she needs them. For this communication to run smoothly, after all, needs a miracle. Anyhow, that is what is expected, both of those involved and others. No offer of family support is given or heard, not at this stage nor later. Individual soldiers could ask for support and therapy, but if the soldier wants and is planning for a military career he/she will avoid offers from within the military system. This is because it would not look good if the soldier revealed weaknesses or injuries other than physical ones. In the view of SAF, the forces are primarily the soldier's employer and have responsibilities towards the soldier, the employee. Formally, they haven't employed the whole family. Recently increasing awareness of the importance of approaching the individual soldier as member of a family system is seen in the military context. The support of, and emerging interest in, this research study is evidence of this. Introducing a family system framework focuses on the interrelatedness of individuals and relationships within families together with a social ecological framework (Bronfenbrenner, 1979), this view broadens the lens to include also the larger systems which families are embedded and how the families' interactions with those systems shape the deployment experiences of the soldiers (Everson & Figley, 2010; Paley, Lester, & Mogil, 2013).

The research study and the dialogical interviewing

The research was begun with a dialogical conference (cf. Shotter & Gustavsen, 1999) in 2011 involving 40 participants from diverse sources including representatives of SAF, both local and from the Headquarters, the veterans' organisations, voluntary family support networks, politicians, researchers and teachers in higher education, and the general public. A group of researchers/teachers at Kristianstad University (HKR) coordinated the conference and subsequently formed a centre for research on and support to military families. I headed the centre and was instrumental between the university and SAF forming a joint venture to fund research on social support to military families between 2013 and 2015. Research on civil social work for soldiers, veterans and their families is rare in an international context and up to that point, non-existent, in Sweden. The focus of the research was to contribute to improvements for concerned families and their network as well as individual members.

Systemic Conversations with Military Families

In collaboration with participating family members, I have arranged open dialogue meetings (cf. Seikkula, Arnkil, & Esa, 2003), in which the researcher-practitioner is moving and switching between listening, narrating, using listening questions – questions arising in response to the interplay (Olsson, 2010) – and reflecting (cf. Anderson & Jensen, 2006). In this, I introduced systemic techniques, such as exploring different positions (for example ethical and moral) and different perspectives, involving the participants in each other's point of view (Lang & McAdam, 1994; Shotter, 1984) and, in particular, seeking to explore this from involved children's points of view (not included in this chapter). These movements, and the impact they might have made, are an important part of the actions in the conducted action research together with the participants (cf. Whyte, Greenwood, & Lazes, 1991). Using dialogical ideas, and invited to participate in the emerging research as well as in the results, co-created the processes of the Dialogical Participatory Action Research (DPAR) used in the study (Olsson, 2014a, 2014b). My own intervention was to be at their disposal totally here and now, ready to listen and inquire, to put myself in the other people's shoes, listening from his or her point of view and perspective (cf. Anderson, 1999), getting a hang of the meaning in use in the context (cf. Bakhtin, 1986) – the participants' understanding of what was told and heard. In this, I tried to be open with my responses, maintaining my curiosity, following and exploring the emerging narratives and narrating (Lang, Little, & Cronen, 1990). I was using different forms of questioning as circular (cf. Penn, 1982; Tomm, 1988), externalisation (White, 2007), and opening questions. When other participants were listening, I asked for their reflections in and on what they had heard and the meaning in use similar as in use of reflecting teams (cf. Andersen, 1987), and I asked for their views or to continue the narrating. The intervention could be seen and recognised in family systemic therapy which in other studies have appeared warranted for these individuals and families (cf. Ford et al., 1998; Hollingsworth, 2011)). All in all, I have met representatives from 51 families and have over 160 dialogues recorded, which I am now watching in this final analysing phase. Watching, listening and transcribing the dialogues bring me back to the meetings with the participants and invites me to continue the dialogue with them.

Reflections from within the research study

Returning home, Peter, like many of his colleagues, found it difficult to talk about the deployment, what it had done to them and others, what they had done and what they had become. He preferred to talk and reflect on the experiences with other veterans participating in the same platoon or from other contingents. They reasoned that they have the same, or at least similar experiences, that they speak the same military language, "so you do not need to explain everything over and over again, as you do with civilians". They are involved in the military system, so they already "know" and they can easily put themselves in another soldier's shoes. They do not have to explain or adapt whatever they express in a new context. They respect and understand why they need to tell their story over and over again, re-narrate and keep their old story. It is co-creating their narrative identity, the dominating story about themselves, and strengthening their belonging in the military system (cf. Lang & McAdam, 1994; Ricoeur, 2000). They do not have to take a final step out of the system, at least not outside of the veteran's community. Other veterans they can trust to understand and rely on, to give them respect, to be patient listeners who do not question or challenge their story while also being able to bear whatever they disclose. Movements outside the military system are viewed as more unpredictable and unreliable, leading to alienation. The veterans say that they simply cannot relate to ordinary people – those who have not lived through the exceptionally stressful experience of combat and have no idea what the veterans have been through (Calhoun, 2011). All these soldiers have a story to tell. However, soon after arriving home, they seem to become disappointed in how friends and family members listen to their stories. It seems as if the veterans have developed a strong sensitivity towards the responses of others and otherness in their surrounding – a sensitivity well warranted and needed for survival in war zones, but co-creating another meaning and causing other unexpected consequences at home.

This sensitive interplay can be seen as dialogical. Inspired by John Shotter's dialogical ideas (cf. for example Shotter, 2009), I liken it to the mutual spontaneous living bodily expressed responsiveness in dialogical interplay and collaboration. My hypothesis is that this capacity and capability is a survival competence for the soldiers in the field. Adapted and used in other contexts, such as at home, at other workplaces or in the family, it could be an excellent skill and qualification for dialogical collaboration. The emergence of dialogical interplay hinges on the actors' capacities to be mutually spontaneously responding to each other and otherness in the context. This extreme sensitivity, which soldiers need in the combat, could, however become tricky to deal with in relation to people at home and in relation to what can be heard in the environment of everyday life in the homeland. Soldiers/veterans talk about how their bodies remember how to react when the body,

Systemic Conversations with Military Families

for example, hears bangs sounding like detonations. A soldier told me how he was walking with his mother in their hometown in the south of Sweden and suddenly, after a bang in the area, hurled himself over his mother ready to draw her to safety. His reactions were embodied and the body made its own interpretations of the situation even before the veteran had a chance to become aware of what he was doing. This was an example of explicit response/sign of the soldier's ability to survive and readiness to protect others in extreme situations. The veteran's family network could ask the veteran to tell them more about these challenges – changing from the deployment system to the family system and how to readjust him/herself both as a soldier and a family member, moving between the systems. However, also these inquiries might feel difficult to make, especially when the soldier/veteran does not seem to be open to any dialogue about the deployment – not inviting the family into his or her perspective as a soldier and a veteran – as in the family above. As one of the family members said:

> *"We had plans. We were going to talk when he returned home. But we never did. It came to nothing. I don't know why ..."*

It might be that the family feel that the veteran soldier is not ready to share his experiences, or it could be about, the soldier is protecting his family members in not telling them details about trauma or violence witnessed or experienced.

Summary and conclusions

The participants in the study were invited to participate in dialogical network meetings with their families to explore their experiences of deployment as well as managing on the home front before, during and after deployments. In the dialogical interviews, I met individual family members, whole families or parts of families and soldiers' networks. Some of them, like the family I introduce in this chapter, have had a family member deployed many years ago and deployed several times. Others had both old experiences and new. For others, this was their first time. I followed the families just before the contingent was going to leave Sweden, during the deployment and after. I can see and hear, notice, that the dialogical approach and emerging collaboration in open dialogue co-create differences for the participants, including myself, and also introducing a "difference that makes a difference" (Bateson, 2000), as for the family of the soldier presented in this chapter. After twenty years, this family managed to improve their dialogical interplay and collaboration in the context of the dialogical interviews. And perhaps this is what this study is all about: as systemic and dialogical practitioners, how we can support families and trust the emerging processes.

References

Andersen, Tom (1987). The Reflecting Team: Dialogue and meta-dialogue in clinical work. *Family Process*, 26, 415–428.

Anderson, Harlene (1999). *Samtal, språk och möjligheter. Psykoterapi och konsultation ur postmodern synvinkel* [*Conversation, Language, and Possiblities: A postmodern approach to therapy*] (C. Brodin & K. Hopstadius, Trans.). Stockholm: Mareld.

Anderson, Harlene & Per Jensen (Eds.). (2006). *Innovations in the Reflecting Process. The Inspirations of Tom Andersen*. London: Karnac.

Bakhtin, Mikhail Mikhailovich (1986). *Speech Genres and Other Late Essays* (V. W. McGee, Trans.). Austin, Texas: University of Texas Press.

Bateson, Gregory (2000). *Steps to an Ecology of Mind: Collected Essays in Anthropology, Psychiatry, Evolution, and Epistemology*. Chicago and London: the University of Chicago Press.

Bronfenbrenner, Urie (1979). *The Ecology of Human Development: Experiments by nature and design*. London: Harvard University Press.

Calhoun, Laurie (2011). The Silencing of Soldiers. *The Independent Review*, 16(2), 247–270.

Everson, R. Blaine & Figley, Charles R. (Eds.). (2010). *Families Under Fire: Systemic Therapy with Military Families*. New York London: Routledge.

Ford, Julian D.; Chandler, Patricia; Thacker, Barbara; Greaves, David; Shaw, David; Sennhauser, Shirley & Schwartz, Lawrence (1998). Family Systems Therapy After Operation Desert Storm with European-theater Veterans. *Journal of Marital and Family Therapy*, 24(2), 143–250.

Hollingsworth, W. Glenn (2011). Community Family Therapy with Families Experiencing Deployment. *Contemporary Family Therapy*, 33, 215–228. DOI: 10.1007/s10591-011-9144-8

Kelty, Ryan; Kleykamp, Meredith & Segal, David R. (2010). The Military and the Transition to Adulthood. *The Future of Children*, 20(1), 181–207.

Lang, Peter; Little, Martin, & Cronen, Vernon E. (1990). The Systemic Professional: Domains of action and the question of neutrality. *Human Systems Journal of Consultation and Management*, 1, 39–56.

Lang, Peter & McAdam, Elspeth (1994). Stories, Giving Account and Systemic Descriptions: Perspectives and positions in conversations. Feeding and fanning the winds of creative imagination. *Human Systems Journal of Consultation and Management*, 6(2).

Michel, Per-Olof (2005). *The Swedish Soldier and General Mental Health Following Service in Peacekeeping Pperations*. PhD Digital Comprehensive Summaries of Uppsala Disertations from the Faculty of Medicine 17, Uppsala, Uppsala. Acta Universitatis Upslaiensis database.

Molin, Lena & Salomonsson, Gustaf (2013). *Berättelsen om bao2. Källmaterial och metoder för att studera veteraners fysiska och psykiska hälsa, utifrån ett fallstudie på bao2*, [*The Bao2 Story: Sources and methods concerning military veterans long-term health*] (Vol. FOI-R-3704-SE, 70). Stockholm: Försvarsanalys/Defence Analysis.

Olsson, Ann-Margreth E. (2010). *Listening to the Voice of Children: Systemic dialogue coaching: Inviting participation and partnership in social work*. Professional Doctorate in Systemic Practice PhD, University of Bedfordshire, Luton. http://hdl.handle.net/10547/243770

Olsson, Ann-Margreth E. (2014a). Dialogical Participatory Action Research in Social Work Using Delta-reflecting Teams. In Franz Rauch, Angela Schuster, Thoms Stern, Maria Pribila & Andrew Townsend (Eds.), *Promoting Change Through Action Research* (163–172). Rotterdam: Sense Publishers.

Olsson, Ann-Margreth E. (2014b). The Impact of Dialogical Participatory Action Research (DPAR): Riding in the peloton of dialogical collaboration. In Gail Simon & Ales Chard (Eds.), *Systemic Inquiry: Innovations in reflexive practice research* (230–243). Farnhill: Everything is Connected Press.

Paley, Blair; Lester, Patricia, & Mogil, Catherine (2013). Family systems and ecological perspectives on the impact of deployment on military families. *Clinical Child Family Psychology Review*, 16, 245–265. doi: 10.1007/s10567-013-0138-y

Penn, Peggy (1982). Circular Questioning. *Family Process*, 21, 263–280.

Ricoeur, Paul (2000). *The Just* (D. Pellauer, Trans.). Chicago: The Univerity of Chicago Press.

Robertson, Rachel (2008). Understanding the Cycle of Military Deployment: How it affects young children and familes. *Exchange: The Early Childhood Leader's Magazine Since 1978*, 180, 24–26.

Seikkula, Jaakko; Arnkil, Tom Erik & Eriksson, Esa (2003). Postmodern Society and Social Networks : Open and anticipation dialogues in network meetings. *Family Process*, 42(2) 185–203.

Shotter, John (1984). *Social Accountability and Selfhood*. Oxford: Blackwell.

Shotter, John (2009). Listening in a Way that Recognizes/Realizes the World of "the Other." *International Journal of Listening*, 23(1), 21–43. DOI: 10.1080/10904010802591904

Shotter, John & Gustavsen, Bjørn (1999). *The Role of "Dialogue Conferences" in the Development of "Learning Regions": Doing "from within" our lives together what we cannot do apart*. Stockholm: Stockholm School of Economics.

Swedish Armed Forces (2015). *Historiska internationella insatser*, [*Historical International Deployments*]. Retrieved March 25th, 2015, from http://www.forsvarsmakten.se/sv/information-och-fakta/var-historia/internationella-insatser/

Swedish Armed Forces (2011). *Internationella insatser*, [*International Missions*]. Retrieved 19 July, 2011, from http://www.forsvarsmakten.se/sv/Internationella-insatser/#

Tomm, Karl (1988). Interventive Interviewing: Part III. Intending to ask linear, circular, strategic or reflexive questions? *Family Process*, 27(1), 1–15.

White, Michael (2007). *Maps of Narrative Practice*. New York: W.W. Norton & Company.

Whyte, William. F., Greenwood, Davyedd J., & Lazes, Peter (1991). Participatory Action Research: Through practice to science in social research. In W. F. Whyte (Ed.), *Participatory Action Research*. London: SAGE Publications.

Worthen, Miranda; Moos, Rudolf, & Ahern, Jennifer (2012). Iraq and Afghanistan Veterans' Experiences Living with Their Parents After Separation from the Military. *Contemporary Family Therapy*, 34, 364–375.

Heresies from Practice: a Case of Obsessive–Compulsive Disorder 22

Padraic Gibson & Don Boardman

Returning requires leaving. Stopping needs going, releasing follows holding. Since each arises from other, then speak to find silence, change to know unchanging, empty to become full.

From moment to moment, mind tricks mind and thoughts follow thinking in circles. The way out is in. The way in is out. Through is between.

Take hold of both halves and swing the doors of mind wide open or closed shut. Full mind is the same as empty mind.

R. Grigg, *The Tao of Relationships*

Obsessive–Compulsive Disorder treatment

In this chapter we will present a pragmatic therapeutic practice for the treatment of human distress. In it, we will use the case of an Obsessive–Compulsive Disorder (OCD) treatment process which has been developed from a radical constructivist epistemology and has been researched by the first author for over a decade and by both authors in a three year outcome study. The chapter starts with a theoretical exposition of OCD during which we expand on how the logical processes employed by OCD sufferers in managing their problem, is generally inaccessible to those outside the problem and how we can introduce other forms of logic (Gibson et al, 2014; Nardone & Portelli; 2013; Bateson 1979).

The chapter continues by demonstrating how these ideas were grounded in therapy with a man in his 30s who had laboured with the yoke of OCD during the previous five years. This problem by extension had a profound domino effect on both his family and work systems. In spite of this man's best efforts to get help from a number of other mental health services, his problem continued to grow.

Finally, we describe ideas we have drawn from non-ordinary logic (Gibson et al, 2013; Nardone et al, 2013; Nardone & Watzlawick 2005), which facilitates our understanding and capacity to work with the logic of those suffering with OCD. OCD logic (Gibson et al, 2014) once employed can become impervious to rational and linear attempts to uproot it. We will describe how rational, linear attempts to help OCD sufferers are usually unsuccessful and how the importance of tracking the structure of OCD and its persistence is required in order to reverse its direction; thus creating change.

An understanding of Obsessive–Compulsive Disorder

Obsessive–Compulsive Disorder (OCD) is a problem characterised by recurrent or persistent thoughts, impulses or images that are experienced as intrusive or distressing (obsessions) and repetitive behaviors or mental acts (compulsions) often performed in response to an obsession (Keeley & Storch 2008). Epidemiological studies report a lifetime prevalence of 1-4% in the general population (Abramowitz, et al, 2009; Foa, 2010; Karno et al, 1988), equal for men and women, although the disorder is more commonly found in boys than girls (Abramowitz et al, 2009; Geffken et al, 2004). Co-morbid psychological disorders associated with OCD include major depression (Doron et al, 2008), additional phobias, panic attacks, generalised anxiety disorder (Keeley et al, 2008) as well as severe occupational, social and family dysfunction (Abramowitz et al, 2009; Nardone & Portelli 2013; Storch et al, 2008). However, because of the subtle nature of the disorder and because of the seemingly common sense logic that underlies these rituals, many patients go undiagnosed with OCD. (For example: health anxiety, general anxiety). Most of the therapeutic research on OCD has been conducted on the efficaciousness of Cognitive Behavioural Therapies (CBT). These Cognitive and Behavioural Therapies are based primarily on a rational and linear logic, which is also the primary logic underlying most psychotherapies including those in the "systemic" field.

The metaphorical image that best represents the underlying logic of OCD is gleaned from a story told by Gordon Alport and quoted by Paul Watzlawick (1993), "A man claps his hands every ten seconds...and when asked about the reason for this strange behaviour, he explains: 'I do it in order to scare away the elephants'. When told there are no elephants present, the man responds: 'Precisely!'" Obsessive–compulsive ideas emerge as repetitive fixations which are often unreasonable but from which the client cannot free him/herself. The typical perceptual and behavioural system of obsessive–compulsive disorders is based, from our experience on fear or on pleasure which in turn drives the patient to repeatedly react by carrying out specific compulsive thinking, formulas or ritualised actions in an attempt to either reduce his fear or to achieve a pleasurable sensation (Gibson et al, 2013; Nardone & Portelli 2013; Portelli 2004).

Clients with OCD usually only seek therapy when they begin to lose the power to control their rituals and these rituals begin to impede on the most important aspects of their life, despite their best attempts at controlling them. Samuel Johnson states that (1709–1784): "The chains of habit are too weak to be felt until they are too strong to be broken". With our action research project for developing effective systemic treatments for anxiety, depression and eating disorders (Gibson et al, 2014; Nardone & Salvini 2007; Nardone & Watzlawick 2005, 1990.), we can now see that in the case of OCD it carries its own specific practical commitments and unique phenomenology.

There are no simple cases of OCD for a therapist because the first port of call for these clients is usually the medical route which often can, in the initial phases, facilitate a reduction of some of the symptoms of the problem. However, clients often struggle to get beyond some initial "first order" gains. Many clients in our experience, also drop out of CBT treatment and have described a lack of optimism from professionals regarding the outcomes for OCD. Sadly, many of these clients do not seek further help and continue to suffer in silence.

Emotions and their importance – fear-based problems

Our experience has repeatedly shown that clients afflicted with OCD generally seek help from the "specialist" – someone they feel not only understands the problem but more importantly, can facilitate them to resolve it. We have observed that sufferers of OCD are generally seeking a therapist who is confident in their methods and someone who they believe has the tools to help them. We have repeatedly noted with OCD clients that they have sought control over a fear and found it, only to now find that they are controlled by this very control. In order to resolve these complicated problems it is important that therapeutic efficaciousness is built on the use of non-ordinary logic (Boardman 2015, 2014; Gibson, et al, 2014; Nardone & Portelli 2005).

Strategic communication is key

In order to re-orient the symptom towards its self-annulment we have observed through our clinical practice that it seems necessary to first convey to clients that what they think and do makes sense. Then in our experience we can offer clients the illusion of holding a more efficacious way to manage the situation. In other words, as therapists we follow the logic that underlies the patient's ideas and actions (Gibson et al, 2014, 2013; Gibson & Ray 2014; Portelli 2005) in order to change their perception and to avoid any inherent resistance arising from the problem's persistence. These are, after all, clients that have sought control and believe that they have found it but soon discover that they are now controlled by the very control they have sought, leaving them feeling stuck in a self-made prison locked from the inside. In regard to holding this particular therapeutic stance, we have found it useful to have, and to demonstrate confidence in the therapeutic option we are providing.

Rigorous but not rigid interventions

The therapeutic model that we are advocating is built on a foundation of strategic and constructivist theory (Gibson et al, 2014; Nardone & Watzlawick 2005) which has shown effective outcome results in treating many forms of psychological suffering when compared to CBT (Gibson et al, 2014; Nardone & Portelli 2005). One significant difference that exists between this approach and that of CBT, the gold standard treatment for OCD, is that the later derives from learning theory whereas the former approach builds upon theories of change, (Watzlawick et al, 1973) communication theory and cybernetics. While a CBT therapist guides the patient through a process of awareness and voluntary effort to learn how to fight and handle the problem, the strategic constructivist therapist adopts ad hoc therapeutic interventions that create a corrective emotional experience that is accompanied by a felt sense of change (Gibson et al, 2014; Nardone & Salvini 2007).

In our opinion effective interventions transform how the person feels, perceives and reacts towards "reality", thus allowing the individual to later acquire awareness of the problem and the ability to prevent it recurring. However, this approach also results in a more efficient, intervention leading to faster healing and reducing relapses in the long term (Gibson et al, 2014). This therapeutic stance echoes von Forster's imperative, "if you desire to see learn to act" (Watzlawick 2015). This idea challenges one of the deeply held beliefs of many therapists, namely that insight precedes change. Rather, we hold that insight follows change.

Matching intervention to problem structure — an isomorphic process

Depending on the structure of the ritual an essential and unique aspect of the working model, which we will now present, is that we have devised several counter-rituals specifically prescribed to fit the different typologies of compulsive symptomatology (Gibson et al, 2013; Portelli 2005; Nardone & Portelli 2013, 2005). These counter rituals, when adopted by the patient, paradoxically break the ritualised behaviours usually quite rapidly, as reported in a case of treatment for self-harm (Boardman 2014). We will now present a case study which illustrates how we worked with one man suffering from OCD.

Chains of habit

Liam is a 30 year old married father of two young girls. He was referred by a community psychiatric service having attended there for over six months, in relation to a growing problem of anxiety in his life. The psychiatric service offered this client Cognitive Behavioural Therapy and medication, which according to Liam had quite limited results. Liam presented for systemic therapy with a listless, emotionally flat almost ghostly pallor. His answers were short and un-expansive and his response to most questions was confused, stilted and generally required further clarification. He did however describe in great detail how, in addition to feeling anxious much of the time, he also had a specific compulsion to continuously check before going to bed that his home was secure and his family were safe against the threat of intruders.

This was something he found extremely difficult to talk to others about, even his wife. Liam described being quite consumed by cognitive "white noise"; a type of mental fog. The effects arising from the problem left him adrift in social interactions and exacerbated a sense of alienation. This description, as we will acknowledge later, is consistent with an operative diagnosis of OCD based on obsessional doubt. This problem formation usually results in highly structured and rigid pathology/experience/interaction.

Case presentation

In this case study we will represent the process in which Liam struggled free from the confines of OCD. We will discuss the stranglehold that Liam felt this problem exerted in his life in wider systemic terms. Liam's OCD had a ripple effect and adversely affected his relationships with family members, in addition to contributing towards a faltering performance within an employment context due to his constant obsessing. Liam had reluctantly begun to write himself out of the script as a "good husband, committed father and an effective worker". It was clear through Liam's presentation that he was deeply concerned at how his OCD had driven a wedge between himself and others.

It could easily be underestimated how isolated and marginalised even a white, middle class man feels when everywhere he has sought help he has not found it. Liam spoke in a matter of fact way about how he had internalised the message that perhaps there is no appropriate help available and that this problem is a personal failing on his part. Everywhere Liam has looked, he observes others appearing to be managing their problems and getting on with their lives.

As practitioners attempting to work therapeutically with this client, we are faced with a very complex case involving someone feeling disenfranchised who, in addition, has low expectations and wonders whether these expectations can be raised through therapy. It appeared to us that Liam's almost apologetic voice, which barely registered above a whisper, bore testimony to this internalised dialogue. We also noted the secondary effects of this problem on those involved with such an individual who have done all they can to support him, yet are left feeling little has helped or made a difference.

By the time Liam had finished therapy, he had reflected on and described his changed self-perception, social interactions and self narrative to that of a competent man able to resolve complex problems. He also spoke of having become the kind of husband and father he did not think he was capable of being, in addition to feeling that he had regained a sense of control which extended to his work context.

We are born into relationships and it is through these relations that we manage our activities in ways that construct patterns of action; "forms of life" (Wittgenstein 1953). We will recount in this chapter how, through returning to a pragmatic approach (Watzlawick et al, 1973, 1967) in our therapeutic practice, we facilitated change, in this instance with one man who described feeling severely constrained by a problem that was consuming him for most of his waking life. By the time Liam finished in therapy, he reported having exited his self-made prison and was enjoying life as a free man. In addition Liam described feeling that now he was controlling the problem rather than the reverse.

Heresies from Practice

We would suggest that von Foerster's ethical imperative that is to act so as to increase choice (Glanville 2003), provides the driving impetus for our work. To this end we sometimes venture outside apparently rational lines. Lines that Bateson himself began to transgress when he and his colleagues introduced Russell and Whitehead's (1925) work on paradoxes and later seen in the form of the double bind theory in the seminal text Pragmatics of Human Communication (Watzlawick et al, 1967).

The presenting problem

In the early phase of therapy we sought a specific description of the functioning of the problem that Liam would like us to focus on as his objective for therapy. Where our work may differ from others in the field is that we seek to explicitly introduce change at every single stage in the process. Our dialogue (and this is especially true for OCD clients) seeks to influence the way the client makes sense of a problem through the use of metaphor, questions offering the illusion of alternative and evocative paraphrasing to promote or inhibit specific patterns of interaction. We see the dialogue as being both interventive and discriminative: the questions and the answers we receive help the therapist to discriminate between types of problems (or classes of problem) and to intervene on the client's perception (Gibson et al, 2014; Nardone & Salvini 2007). We will speak in detail about the epistemological, ethical and practice underpinnings of such an approach later in the chapter.

During the session Liam described how a ritual had developed which he had enacted in response to his perceived fear that his family would be harmed. The ritual that Liam described went as follows. Every night he would engage in a series of checks to ensure that all the windows and doors of his house were properly secured. From humble beginnings this ritual was now occupying between 60-90 minutes of his time every night of the week, excluding time spent obsessing about the ritual. For Liam, the more he obsessed with checking, the more unavailable he became to his family. This unavailability further ratcheted up his anxiety. Liam described how he felt caught in a double-bind (Bateson et al, 1956) where on the one hand he wanted to stop but did not feel strong enough to, and on the other hand if he did stop he would be exposed to his biggest fear – that his family would be harmed.

Perception, interaction and outcome

If we hold, like Von Foerster, that the world is an outcome of our perception/s (1979) and when we say perception, we are talking here about the emotional, behavioural, cognitive and interactional elements that construct our realities; then we can suggest that what Liam was experiencing was the reality he had created himself. This created reality, like that of many of our OCD clients, is self-perpetuating and based on irrational logic (Gibson et al, 2014; Nardone 2007). We can also see that the problem here is maintained by an obsessional doubt and that in every movement to appease or resolve the doubt, it is reinforced.

Therapeutic intervention

When we arrived at a working description of the functioning of the problem we then carefully considered how to devise a useful therapeutic intervention. Liam described how this obsessive ritual to check his home to ensure that it was safe from intruders, had started on a much smaller scale but required more and more energy and effort until he felt like he had completed the ritual satisfactorily. Initially this ritual took 15-20 minutes to complete before Liam's anxiety would subside but it kept growing until it occupied 60-90 minutes before the anxiety subsided.

With Liam we used the "counter ritual" based on the paradox of prescribing the symptom (Watzlawick et al, 1973, 1967) with the following intervention: "if you choose to enact this ritual of checking once, you must do it 3 times, not one time more and not one time less, exactly 3 times or not at all". This injunction contains the illusion of an alternative and renders a ritual which was once spontaneous and involuntary, now prescribed and voluntary.

In the following session Liam reported undertaking this ritual in the exact manner specified. He began to find this immensely tedious and spontaneously he began to check only once per night. He reported that even checking once with his fastidious nature could last 20 minutes and even this exerted unreasonable pressure on him, he said that this should take him 10 minutes or less. In conclusion, at the end of the fourth session Liam said that he had chosen to only check once for 10 minutes or less. He said in his understated manner that this had made a big difference to his connectedness to his family and that this change had lent itself to a generally more positive "emotional temperature" at home. In addition, he said that his checking was no longer a problem and was back within what he described as a normal range of concern.

Upon his return after one month, Liam said that his anxiety was no longer a problem. He concluded by saying that the issue had now been resolved and that he believed that this would continue. A six month follow up appointment confirmed that the therapeutic gains were sustained. Liam reported that both his own and his family life were expanding exponentially and that a new found confidence had replaced the old anxiety.

We have described how we used therapeutic interventions that facilitated this client to discover that one way to suffocate the fire is to add more wood. We tracked the client's "logic" and how the problem was functioning and followed the direction it led. The challenge for us then was to determine how to develop a counter ritual which would turn a spontaneous involuntary problematic behaviour into a voluntarily one and thus in so doing, steal away its potency thereby creating the conditions for it to collapse under its own weight.

Changing in order to change

From the start of therapy, we explained to Liam that we are interested in maintaining a 360 degree perspective on the effects of OCD in all areas of his life, in order to notice how his relationship with OCD was changing. What emerged during the subsequent sessions, arising from his feedback, was an increasing sense of feeling more in control of his thoughts, feelings and behaviour, ironically as a result of now losing control in a safe way. These changes he described were not just specifically related to his OCD but extended to his perception of an improvement in the quality of his relationships. Liam described in detail his increased physical and emotional availability to his children. He said it resulted in him being able to play with them more. This attunement to his children's needs was something that he felt was very important for his family not just in terms of aiding connections to his children but also for taking some of the pressure off his wife. Arising from these changes Liam expressed feeling closer to his wife and feeling relieved that he was not adding to her woes with his burdens.

Much of the feedback that Liam gave about the differences he was noticing at home, were not focused on specific ideas that had been discussed directly through our therapeutic enquiry. With this model we expect that client changes will often happen "spontaneously" and enquire accordingly. We often use the analogy with clients of describing the changes that happen during therapy as; "wild mushrooms popping up all over a field".

As our work progressed we sought an understanding of the systemic effects arising from our therapeutic input. This feedback was elicited by the client being asked questions like, "What difference, outside of that we have discussed, has this work made in your relationships with your loved ones?" In Liam's case, it brought him great pleasure to describe how he was becoming the husband and father that he thought he would never be.

A radical-constructivist-systemic model for working with OCD

Similia, similubus, curantor: prescribing the problem

We experience changes in our everyday life (that is spontaneous change) when our perceptions, relationships or emotions are called into crisis thus leading to some form of growth or maturity (Watzlawick et al, 1973). We generally accept such change as valid or appropriate and our training programmes aim at helping psychotherapists to wait for such spontaneous, non-instructive change (Hoffman 1993). However, we have seen with this case that we can purposefully facilitate clients to make the changes that they would like but either "feel" they can't, or "feel" they have tried everything to change but to no avail.

Change is something of real importance in the treatment of OCD. In our experience, patients tend to drop out very quickly if they do not experience change. This type of complex problem is not based primarily on the relationship with self and others but with the relationship with self and self; it is a closed system (Maturana & Varela 1987). What is usually perpetuating this problematic system is the logic that the client is bringing to solving the problem. This self-sustaining, self-referential feedback loop maintains the problem. The solution is achieved by the recognition of the systemic nature of the problem and by a systemically informed therapeutic response.

What this means is that the client's apparent "solution" is his problem and his problem is at the same time the only solution. We have observed that trying to rationally explain this adds little in terms of therapeutic effect; on the contrary, it appears to reinforce the client's view that not only are they stuck with a big problem but even the professionals cannot help them to find a solution!

We have also found that focusing on dialogue surrounding the wider aspects of the client's life not related to solving their OCD to be of limited benefit. When we have found ourselves widening the focus of enquiry, it is our contention that we often increase the client's sense of hopelessness (and our own!) resulting in the client then asking at the end of the session; "That's all well and good but what do I do about my OCD?"

We hold the view that it is important to introduce a tangible change to the system via an intervention/s that creates a corrective emotional experience (Alexander & French 1946; Satir 1967). This is something that facilitates a shift in how the client perceives their problem, which then has a ripple effect in creating change on how a client feels, acts and thinks.

In the case of a client suffering from OCD, we have found that it is counterproductive to use reason with someone to stop his or her pathological rituals. These clients have described to us over and over in detail how they feel they can't stop. When we employ a rational, logical frame in working with them, they are then left doubting whether we understand just how difficult it is for them feeling controlled by the problem, in addition to being left with the doubt of whether you are able to help them resolve it! However, a prescription based on the same logic underlying the problem will turn the force of the symptom against the disorder itself, breaking its perverse balance.

Counter ritual
With OCD treatment the following prescription of the counter ritual is one we regularly use: "each time you enact one of your rituals, you must repeat it three times, precisely, three times, no more, no less. You can avoid doing it at all, but if you do it once, do it three times no more and no less than three times" (Boardman 2014; Gibson et al, 2014; Nardone & Salvini 2007;). The injunction to ritually repeat the ritual paradoxically leads the person to construct a different reality from the one characterised by uncontrollable compulsions. We can then request that they can consider the possibility of not performing the ritual since they are not spontaneous anymore but prescribed voluntarily (Gibson et al, 2013; Nardone & Watzlawick 2005).

The logical structure of this apparently simple prescription helps to avoid the usual resistance that comes with this problem typology. If the individual chooses to perform the ritual once, he has to do it three times. Therefore, it is the therapist suggesting how many times he is to repeat it, thus taking control of the symptom and giving to the patient the injunctive permission to avoid doing the ritual. Usually we find that following the prescription literally at first, clients usually suspend the ritual after a few days unable to explain why. The way the prescription is communicated is fundamental and ought to be delivered through the use of a redundantly repeated, hypnotic linguistic assonance and of a posthypnotic message expressed in a more marked tone of voice (Erickson & Rossi 1974).

Specific interventions on the cybernetic loop of interaction that nourishes the problem
As we explain below, we hold that the clinician is responsible to devise specifically tailored interventions for the client, instead of trying to

shoehorn a client into a particular theoretical paradigm. Depending on the structure of the OCD ritual, we now have a number of counter rituals based on the structure of the problem's persistence.

Structure of intervention

1. When the ritual holds a sequence, and thus is numerical, the intervention proceeds in giving the patient a specific numerical pre-set counter-ritual, which fits the particular pathological ideas and actions leading to a catastrophic change. This is the case of the person that needs to check something for a number of times ensuring it has been done correctly.

2. Progressive violations of the sequence of the ritual are encouraged, from small to total violation, in order to break the established rigid control.

3. The technique of postponing the ritual to a specific and prescribed time. This is aimed at making boring, then annoying and unpleasant what, previously acted on impulse, appeared pleasurable to the subject. This strategy has been proven particularly useful with vomiting syndrome, a compulsion based on pleasure. Once again, the attempted solution of vomiting for weight control after having binged gradually becomes the problem, and the reason it persists, lies in the pleasure provided. Since any repressing intervention would only exacerbate the desire to binge and vomit, by altering the spontaneity of the cycle, the interval technique takes away the enjoyment of the liberating act of vomiting, usually accompanied by the feeling of an almost orgasmic urgency, which progressively become more difficult and unpleasant. Thus, a ritual based on pleasure is transformed into an act of self-torture.

4. Ritualising the pathological compulsion in specific space and time set aside during the day, first numerously then progressively reducing this ritualised-ritual to zero, allows the person to take control of it, gradually demolishing the pathology.

5. Introducing "a small disorder that maintains order", the objective is to break the rigid control until the unstoppable need for the compulsion becomes completely de-structured. A client who fears contamination, for example, will often continuously wash, clean, and sterilise self, house and other belongings in order to prevent infection or contamination. However, once this state of cleanliness or sterilisation is reached the client then fears they may not be able to hold on to it. In this instance, a "strategic dialogue" is useful firstly to reframe the client's rigid construction of the problem before slowly preparing the client to understand the idea that "a small disorder

Heresies from Practice

maintains order"; that when everything is spotless, there is only one way things can go. When we introduce a small disorder, we actually maintain order. A little bit of dirt then becomes the way to actually protect the person from total cleanliness. When a client is striving for control through something being satisfactorily cleaned, it is the belief that they are safer this way that is responsible for the person's increasing fear (Gibson et al, 2013; Nardone & Portelli 2013).

Conclusion

We have described a model which facilities a systemic/cybernetic, constructivist practice with clients presenting with OCD. This pragmatic approach strives to adapt the theory we draw from, as we hold that "knowledge is only as good as how you use it" and that knowledge is not made for the classroom.

We have outlined the rigorous theoretical basis for our approach which facilitates a lightness of touch in our practice. Any meta-theories, presuppositions, along with any grand ideologies are parked outside the door to allow for the emergence of a more nuanced higher order embodied cybernetic approach (Keeney & Keeney 2012). This model calls for being truly present "in the here and now" with no one interpretation dictating or blocking the organic process of circularly responding to interactions happening in real time. We feel that it is not enough for the systemic practitioner to "not know" (Anderson 2008) as even "not knowing" can be an imposition on effective practice, where the interpretation is valued above all else. Rather "acting in order to know how to act" places the therapist and the client inside a cybernetic process which embodies circularity in practice. This cybernetics of cybernetics requires the therapist to continually change in order to facilitate the client changing (Keeney & Keeney 2012, p.26-33).

Due to the brief nature of this chapter there is a lot more we could say about our work which is absent. We have seen how attempted solution/s often becomes the problem. We have highlighted how these ideas were used clinically with a complex case involving a man who had previously received extensive CBT and Psychiatric support.

In applying strategic and constructivist theories to our clinical work we have found a pragmatic, playful and relationally sensitive way to resolving obsessive–compulsive disorders. Through the use of ad-hoc therapeutic interventions, in-session injunctions and the use of performative language, this therapy bypasses the individual's usual rational mechanisms. In our experience this usually quite quickly leads to the self-destruction of the vicious cycle maintaining the problem and leads to its rapid resolution.

References

Abramowitz, Jonathan S. Taylor, Steven & McKay, Dean. (2009). Obsessive–Compulsive Disorder. *The Lancet* 374, no. 9688, 491–499.

Abramowitz, Jonathan S. (1996). Variants of Exposure and response Prevention in the Treatment of Obsessive–Compulsive Disorder: A meta-analysis. *Behavior Therapy* 27, 583–600.

Alexander, Franz & French, Thomas M. (1946). The Corrective Emotional Experience. In *Psychoanalytic Therapy: Principles and Application*. New York: Ronald Press.

Anderson, Harlene. (2008). *Conversation, Language, and Possibilities: A postmodern approach to therapy*. Basic Books.

Bateson, Gregory; Jackson, Don D.; Haley, Jay & John Weakland, J. (1956). Toward a Theory of Schizophrenia. *Behavioral Science* 1(4), 251–264.

Bateson, Gregory. (1979). *Mind and Nature: A Necessary Unity*. New York: Dutton.

Boardman, Don. (2015). A Leopard Changing its Spots, an Old Dog Learning New Tricks: Advanced Brief Strategic therapy with a septuagenarian. *Context: The Magazine for Family Therapy and Systemic Practice in the UK*.

Boardman, Don. (2014). Engaging with Resistance and Ambivalence: Facilitating a therapeutic shift in clients from window shoppers to customers for change. *Feedback: Journal of the Family Therapy Association of Ireland*.

Boardman, Don. (2013). A Single Case Study of a Clinical Intervention in a School Context: A Systemic Constructivist approach using Strategic Logic. *Feedback: Journal of the Family Therapy Association of Ireland*.

Doron, Guy; Moulding, Richard; Kyrios, Michael & Nedeljkovic, Maja. (2008). Sensitivity of Self-beliefs in Obsessive Compulsive Disorder. *Depression and Anxiety* 25, No. 10: 874–884.

Erickson, Milton H. & Rossi, Ernest L. (1974). Varieties of Hypnotic Amnesia. *American Journal of Clinical Hypnosis* 16, No. 4: 225–239.

Foa, Edna B. (2010). Cognitive Behavioral Therapy of Obsessive–Compulsive Disorder. [Historical Article]. *Dialogues ClinNeurosci*, 12(2), 199–207.

Geffken, Gary R.; Storch, Eric A.; Gelfand, Kenneth M.; Adkins, Jennifer W. & Goodman, Wayne K. (2004). Cognitive-behavioral Therapy for Obsessive–Compulsive Disorder: Review of treatment techniques. *J PsychosocNursMent Health Serv*, 42(12), 44–51.

Geller, Daniel A.; Biederman, Joseph; Stewart, S. Evelyn; Mullin, Benjamin; Farrell, Colleen; Dineen Wagner, Karen; Emslie, Graham & Carpenter, David. (2003). Impact of Co-morbidity on Treatment Response to Paroxetine in Pediatric Obsessive–Compulsive Disorder: Is the use of exclusion criteria empirically supported in randomized clinical trials? [Clinical Trial Multicenter Study Randomized Controlled Trial]. *J Child AdolescPsychopharmacol*, 13 Suppl 1, S19–29.

Gibson, Padraic; Manzoni, Gian Mauro & Pietrabissa, Gaida. (2014) A 4-year Observational Study on the Efficacy of BST Treatment for OCD in an Irish Clinic. *Journal of Therapies in Medicine*.

Gibson, Padraic; Papantouomo, M. & Portelli, Claudette. (2014) *Winning Without Fighting: A Handbook of Effective Solutions to Social, Emotional and Behavioural Problems in Schools*. Kindle.

Gibson, Padraic, & Ray, Wendel. (2014): *Family Therapy Pioneers: No:1: Don D Jackson. Analysis of Transcript of Jackson's Therapy as a lesson to us all*. (Unpublished).

Gibson, Padraic & Ray, Wendel. (2014): *Family Therapy Pioneers: No:2: John Weakland. The Subtle Art of Doing Nothing:* (Unpublished).

Gibson, Padriac; Castelnuovo, Gianluca; Pietrabissa, Giada & Manzoni, Gian Mauro. (2013). *A Pilot Study on the Effectiveness of Brief Strategic Therapy in the Treatment of Postnatal Depression*.

Glanville, Ranulph. (2003). Heinz von Foerster. *Systems Research and Behavioral Science*, 20(1), 85–89.

Grigg, Ray. (1989). *The Tao of Relationships: A balancing of man and woman*. Green Dragon Books.

Hoffman, Lynn. (1993). *Exchanging Voices: A collaborative approach to family therapy*. Karnac Books.

Jónsson, Hjalti; Hougaard, Esben & Bennedsen, Birgit E. (2011). "Dysfunctional beliefs in group and individual cognitive behavioral therapy for obsessive compulsive disorder." *Journal of Anxiety Disorders* 25, no. 4 (2011): 483–489.

Karno, Marvin, Golding, Jacqueline M.; Sorenson, Susan B. & Burnam, M. Audrey. (1988). The Epidemiology of Obsessive–compulsive Disorder in Five US Communities." *Archives of General Psychiatry* 45, no. 12 (1988): 1094–1099.

Keeley, Mary L. & Storch, Eric A. (2008). The Nature, Assessment, and Treatment of Pediatric Obsessive–compulsive Disorder. *Behavioral Psychology* 16(3), 535–551.

Keeley, Mary L.; Storch, Eric A.; Merlo, Lisa J. & Geffken, Gary R. (2008). "Clinical Predictors of Response to Cognitive-behavioral Therapy for Obsessive–compulsive Disorder. *Clinical Psychology Review* 28, no. 1 (2008): 118–130.

Keeney, Hillary & Bradford Keeney. (2012). What is Systemic about Systemic Therapy? Therapy Models Muddle Embodied Systemic Practice. *Journal of Systemic Therapies* 31, no. 1 (2012): 22–37.

Kim, Suck Won; Dysken, Maurice W. & Kuskowski, Michael. (1990). The Yale-Brown Obsessive–Compulsive Scale: A reliability and validity study. *Psychiatry Research* 34, no. 1 (1990): 99–106.

Lewin, Adam B.; De Nadai, Alessandro; Park S. Jennifer; Goodman, Wayne K.; Murphy,Tanya K. & Storch, Eric A. (2011). Refining Clinical Judgment of Treatment Outcome in Obsessive–Compulsive Disorder. *Psychiatry Research*, 185, no. 3 (2011): 394–401.

Mahoney, Michael J. (1991). *Human Change Process: The Scientific Foundations of Psychotherapy*. New York: Basic Book.

Maturana, Humberto R. & Varela, Francisco J. (1987). *The Tree of Knowledge: The biological roots of human understanding*. New Science Library/Shambhala Publications.

Meyer, Victor. (1966). Modification of Expectations in Cases with Obsessional Rituals. *Behav Res Ther*, 4(4), 273–280.

Nardone, Giorgio & Portelli, Claudette. (2013). Ossessioni, compulsioni, manie. *Newsletter* 27, no. 28 (2013): 29-30.

Nardone, Giorgio & Balbi, Elisa. (2008). Solcare il mare all'insaputa del cielo. *Ponte alle Grazie*, 2008.

Nardone, Giorgio & Salvini, Alessandro. (2007). *The Strategic Dialogue: Rendering the diagnostic interview a real therapeutic intervention*. Karnac Books.

Nardone, Giorgio & Portelli, Claudette. (2005). *Knowing Through Changing: The Evolution of Brief Strategic Therapy*. Crown House Publishing.

Nardone, Giorgio & Watzlawick, Paul. (2005). *Brief Strategic Therapy: Philosophy, Technique and Research*. Lanham, Maryland: Jason Aronson.

Nardone, Giorgio Verbitz, Tiziana & Milanese, Roberta. (1999). *Prison of Food: Research and treatment of eating disorders*. Karnac Books.

Nardone, Giorgio & Watzlawick, Paul. (1990). *The Art of Change: Strategic Therapy and Hypnotherapy Without Trance*. San Francisco, USA: Jossey-Bass.

Portelli, Claudette. (2005). Brief Strategic Interventions for Obsessive Compulsive Disorders: Acquiring the maximum with the minimum in the first session. *Brief Strategic and Systemic Therapy European Review* 2.

Portelli, Claudette. (2004). Advanced Brief Strategic Therapy for Obsessive–Compulsive Disorders. *Brief Strategic and Systemic Therapy European Review* 1.

Rosa-Alcázar, Ana I.; Sánchez-Meca, Julio; Gómez-Conesa, Antonia; & Marín-Martínez, Fulgencio. (2008). Psychological treatment of obsessive–compulsive disorder: A meta-analysis. *Clinical Psychology Review* 28, no. 8 (2008): 1310–1325.

Russell, Bertrand & North Whitehead, Alfred. (1925). *Principia mathematica*. 1, no. (2) : 3.

Satir, Virginia. (1967). *Conjoint Family Therapy: A guide to theory and technique*. Palo Alto. CA: Science and Behavior Books.

Storch, Eric A.; Larson, Michael J.; Muroff, Jordana; Caporino, Nicole; Geller, Daniel; Reid, Jeannette M.; Morgan, Jessica; Jordan, Patrice & Tanya K. Murphy. (2010). Predictors of Functional Impairment in Pediatric Obsessive–Compulsive Disorder. *Journal of Anxiety Disorders* 24, no. 2 (2010): 275–283.

Storch, Eric A.; Abramowitz, Jonathan & Goodman, Wayne K. (2008). Where Does Obsessive–Compulsive Disorder Belong in DSM-V? *Depress Anxiety*, 25(4), 336–347.

Storch, Eric A.; Geffken,Gary R.; Merlo, Lisa J.; Jacob, Marni L.; Murphy, Tanya K.; Goodman, Wayne K. ; Larson, Michael J.; Fernandez, Melanie & Grabill, Kristen. (2007). Family Accommodation in Pediatric Obsessive–Compulsive Disorder. *Journal of Clinical Child and Adolescent Psychology* 36, no. 2 (2007): 207–216.

Tek, C.; Uluğ, B.; Gürsoy Rezaki, B.;Tanriverdi, N.; Mercan, S.; Demir, B. & Vargel, S. (1995). "Yale-Brown Obsessive Compulsive Scale and US National Institute of Mental Health Global Obsessive Compulsive Scale in Turkish: Reliability and validity." *Acta Psychiatrica Scandinavica* 91, no. 6 (1995): 410–413.

Van Oppen, Patricia; De Haan, Else; Van Balkom, Anton J.L.M.; Spinhoven, Philip; Hoogduin, Kees & Van Dyck, Richard. (1995). Cognitive Therapy and Exposure In Vivo in the Treatment of Obsessive–Compulsive Disorder." *Behaviour Research and Therapy*, 33, no. 4 (1995): 379–390.

Von Foerster, Heinz. (1979). Cybernetics of Cybernetics. , 1, 83–85. In Klaus Krippendorff (Ed.) *Communication and Control in Society*, Gordon and Breach, New York: Routledge, 5–8.

Wang, Yuan-Pang, & Gorenstein, Clarice. (2013). Psychometric Properties of the Beck Depression Inventory-II: A comprehensive review. *Revista Brasileira de Psiquiatria* 35, no. 4 (2013): 416–431.

Watzlawick, Paul. (2015). If You Desire to See, Learn How to Act. In *Evolution Of Psychotherapy..........: The 1st Conference*, p.91. New York: Routledge.

Watzlawick, Paul. (1993). *The Situation is Hopeless, But Not Serious: The Pursuit of Unhappiness*. WW Norton & Company.

Watzlawick, Paul; Weakland, John H. & Fisch, Richard. (1973). *Change: Principles of Problem Formation and Problem Resolution*. W.W. Norton & Company.

Watzlawick, Paul, Beavin Bavelas, Janet; Jackson, Don D. & O'Hanlon, Bill. (1967). *Pragmatics of Human Communication: A Study of Interactional Patterns, Pathologies and Paradoxes*. W.W. Norton & Company.

Wittgenstein, Ludwig. (1953) *Philosophical Investigations*. Trans. G. Anscombe. New York: Macmillan.

Woody, Sheila R., Steketee, Gail and Chambless, Dianne L. (1995). Reliability and Validity of the Yale-Brown Obsessive–Compulsive Scale. *Behaviour Research and Therapy* 33, no. 5 (1995): 597–605.

23 Family Semantic Polarities as a Guide for the Therapeutic Process

Valeria Ugazio

Coming back to a forgotten project

Naven (Bateson 1936/1958) has always fascinated me. It contains two extraordinary intuitions. The best-known one advanced the central hypothesis of the Positioning Theory, half a century before Harré & van Langenhove's (1999) developed it. Bateson's extraordinary intuition is that the "character" is at least partially the result of a position in the conversation, constructed by symmetrical and complementary schismogenetic interactions. In his study of the Iatmul tribe, Bateson was struck by the rigid opposition dividing the lives and the characters of men and women. Men carried out spectacular, and often violent activities around the ceremonial house, a magnificent building compared to the simplicity of the huts around which the life of the women was organised. Responsible for gathering and cooking food and raising children, women performed their activities privately and quietly. Men were proud, theatrical and superficial; they spent the majority of their energy asserting themselves. They showed a prestige that in fact they did not have: there wasn't any fixed hierarchy in the tribe, the men were too individualistic to make it possible. Arrogance, boastfulness and buffoonery were accepted as respectable male behaviour, whereas women were spontaneous, cooperative, lively and good-humoured.

Through the concepts of complementary and symmetrical interactions, Bateson tried to prove that men's arrogance, pride, theatricality were constructed by the women's spirit of observation, their curiosity, their willingness to be enchanted and their looks of admiration. There is no theatre without an audience. Likewise, the simplicity, humility, non-dramatic cheerfulness of the Iatmul women were a response to the imperious needs for self-assertion of their men. Through the concept of schismogenesis, Bateson highlighted and explained the polarisation of the Iatmul's respective characters. He also focused on the risks created by the polarisation of characters for the cohesion and stability of the tribe and on the tools – as the enigmatic *naven* ceremonies – they collectively developed to control and counteract the polarisation processes.

The second amazing intuition of *Naven* is that meanings, and consequently emotions, are at the core of character. In his monograph,

Family Semantic Polarities

Bateson focused on the semantic contents to which the complementary and symmetrical interactions were applied. Although included in the rather obscure concept of ethos – defined as "a culturally standardised system of organisation of the instincts and emotions of the individuals" (Bateson 1958, p.18) – the semantic content were identified with antagonist polarities such as admiration/exhibitionism, dominance/ submission. Also in *Morale and National Character* (Bateson 1942) and in his essay on Bali (Bateson 1949), the core of the ethos is identified with polar semantic structures tightly linked to emotions.

In later years, Bateson (1972) and the Palo Alto school focused increasingly on the interactive processes in the here and now and on the pragmatic aspects of communication, ignoring the semantic as well as the relationship between interactive processes and individual identity. In order to understand the role of meaning and of interactive processes in the construction of identity in conversation, attention must be focused on all the temporal dimensions, including the past, but these dimensions were disregarded specially by Bateson's direct descendants brought together in the Mental Research Institute in Palo Alto.

The concept of family semantic polarity and the clinical conceptualisations that I developed from this concept can be seen as a further development of Bateson's aforementioned intuitions. Certainly these intuitions were for me the main source of inspiration along with a focus on meaning deriving from my belonging to the Milan approach. From *Paradox and Counterparadox* (Selvini-Palazzoli, Boscolo, Cecchin & Prata 1975/1978) onwards, the Milan approach was characterised by an interest in meanings and in redefining meanings. Looking back, counterparadoxes were triadic reframings, which gave sense to the prescription of symptoms.

After having summarised the concepts of semantic polarity and family semantics, I will attempt to demonstrate the usefulness of the concepts of semantic polarity and family semantics for the therapeutic change, through two clinical cases.

The semantics of freedom, goodness, power and belonging as a matrix for identities and a resource for therapy

According to the model of semantic polarities, conversation in the family as in any other group with history is organised through polarities of opposing meaning, such as intelligent/dim-witted, generous/selfish, sensitive/hard-hearted. The model applies a constructionist approach to the old idea that meaning is constructed through opposing polarities (Kelly 1955; Osgood, Suci & Tannenbaum 1957). As a result, "polarities are not considered as something in the mind of each individual, but a discursive phenomenon" (Ugazio 2013, p.21), able to contribute to the intersubjectivity, so crucial given the social nature of human beings. In this perspective:

> *"The semantic contrasts present in all languages constitute a 'universal' characteristic whose function is to render individuals interdependent at a semantic level as well as a pragmatic level.* It is precisely because the structure of meaning is polar that individuals cannot position themselves or be positioned as 'generous' or 'intelligent' unless there is at least one other individual in their relational context who occupies the opposite position of "selfish" or "stupid." In this way, however, their position, and that part of their identity which is fuelled by that position, come to depend on those who position themselves in complementary positions".
> (Ugazio 2013, p.36, original italics)

Let me delve into this point. A family is a family inasmuch as those belonging to it construct the conversation within specific semantic polarities, which form a shared plot that generates consequent narratives and storylines.

If you belong to a family where, for example, the central polarities are sadness/cheerfulness and good-luck/misfortune, the dominant episodes created by conversations will be about people – friends, relatives or members of the same family – struck down by illness or by economic crisis or, on the contrary, kissed by luck, thanks to their ability to take life lightly or simply because they are in the right place at the right time. Sadness will spoil marriages and careers, whereas cheerfulness can console who is in trouble or can resolve a tangled situation. No matter how different the members of your family are, they will share these polarities and the consequent narratives.

> "The similarity between members of the family is limited – in each family group – to this sharing of a plot of semantic polarities which is derived from the conversational history of the family".
> (Ugazio 2013, p.22)

Family Semantic Polarities

All members have to take a position within the dominant polarities in their family and in the other groups they belong to. Obviously, the importance that the conversation assigns to each semantic polarity continually changes and is negotiated in the family as well in the other groups. Likewise, the possibility of creating new meanings is always open.

Positioning themselves with others within the plot of semantic polarities dominant in their own groups, conversational partners anchor their own identity to those of the other members of their groups. The organisation of meaning according to opposing polarities makes individuals interdependent. They can position themselves as "honest", " welcoming", "loyal", but in order to occupy these positions others will have to be "dishonest", "chilly" and "untrustworthy". That is why, when someone in therapy tells me: "I am a good person", I immediately ask: "Who is the bad one in your family?"

I receive many requests to provide therapy for children with learning disabilities. Usually the parents are colleagues of mine met while teaching at University or their friends. In these families the polarity "intelligent/dim-witted" is relevant, as often happens among academics.

> *"The members of these families will position themselves with people who are intelligent or very intelligent but will also be surrounded by people of limited intelligence or who are actually dim-witted. They will marry people who are intelligent, bright, stupid or clueless. They will strive to become intellectually brilliant or will help those who are unfortunately less bright to become so. They will fight and compete to ensure that their intellectual abilities are recognized and they will end marriages and friendships or, alternatively, develop new relationships when intellectual problems arise."*
>
> (Ugazio 2013, p.24)

Some members of these families, as my university colleagues, are intellectually brilliant, while others will prove to be intellectually lacking, like their children with learning disabilities. It is not at all difficult to imagine what happens in an academic family when a child comes home with poor or negative results. Alarmed, the parents rush to see the teacher who will confirm the child's difficulties. Naturally they ask themselves the reasons of the failings of their child, arguing, and sometimes blaming the less intellectual individuals who look after the child (grandparents, babysitters, and so on). Finally, they change their arrangements and often their life style. Before, they had no problem leaving the child with the grandparents or babysitters, while they participated in congresses or concentrated on their research. Now, they dedicate time and energy to the child, who takes on a central position – a situation that could actually worsen the problem.

Of course, the polarity intelligent/dim-witted might be irrelevant among other families, troubled by other problems. But what interests me for the moment is to highlight that all family members need their conversational partners to occupy a different position so as to maintain their own identity. Only by doing this, each member contributes to continuing the discursive practices which generate the meanings on which their identity is based and maintained. Because more than one polarity is relevant in each family, "the organization of meaning into opposing polarities, besides making identities interdependent, guarantees the multiplicity of the self" (Ugazio 2013, p.25).

From what I have summarised above, it is clear that the model of semantic polarities envisages the family as a co-position of individuals united by their differences. In many families we find people who are polar opposites such as *The Brothers Karamazov* in Dostoevsky's masterpiece (1880) or in other literary families such the *Buddenbrooks* by Mann (1901) or *Dombey and Son* by Dickens (1846-1848). Living in the same family, for example, makes siblings more different than similar, as many studies have proved (Towers, Spotts, Reiss 2003).

In an attempt to look at the system in its entirety, family therapists have developed concepts that transcend the individual, such as "rules", "homeostasis", "myth", "family paradigm", "structures", "boundaries" and "enmeshment" (Anderson & Bagarozzi 1989; Ferreira 1963; Minuchin, Rosman & Baker 1978; Reiss, 1981; Watzlawick, Beavin &Jackson 1967). Although useful, these concepts cannot differentiate the contribution of each person in the construction of a shared family dynamic. Families can differ profoundly even when they belong to the same culture. "Those things that one whole family fights, rejoices or despairs over are entirely irrelevant for another" (Ugazio 2013, p.21).

One central thesis of the model of semantic polarities is that people with eating, phobic, obsessive–compulsive disorders and depression are involved in the here and now and have grown up in families where certain specific semantic polarities predominate. I have defined these as "family semantics" firstly because they are primarily learned in the

Family Semantic Polarities

original family and are continually renegotiated in the families and in the groups the individual subsequently belongs to. Secondly, because they are coherent configurations of meaning fuelled by the same emotions. These are the semantics of freedom (phobic disorders), goodness (obsessive–compulsive disorders), belonging (mood disorders), power (eating disorders). I will shortly examine them.

Freedom versus dependence and exploration versus attachment are the main semantic polarities that organise the conversations in the families where the semantic of freedom dominates the conversation. They are fuelled by the emotive opposition fear/courage. Consequently:

> *"[...] members of these families will feel, or be defined as fearful or cautious or, alternatively, courageous, even reckless. They will find people who are prepared to protect them or will meet up with people who are unable to survive by themselves, who need their support. They will marry people who are fragile and dependent, but also individuals who are free and sometimes unwilling to make commitments. They will suffer for their dependence. They will try in every way to gain their independence and freedom, which they will defend more than everything else. Admiration, contempt, conflict, alliances, love and hatred will be played out around issues of freedom/dependence."*
>
> (Ugazio 2013, p.84)

The more these polarities dominate the conversation, the more probable is the polarisation of the identities within the family:

> *"In the same family we will therefore have the globetrotters as well as people who have never moved away from the district where they were born. And there will be those – like agoraphobic patients – who are so dependent and in need of protection that they will require someone to accompany them in dealing with the most ordinary situations in daily life, and those who, on the other hand, will be so independent as to seem self sufficient."*
>
> (Ugazio 2013, p.84)

Rooted in the guilt/innocence emotive polarity, "bad/good "and "alive/dead" are at the core of the semantic of goodness. Approaching families where this semantic dominates the conversation, is like opening a page in Dostoevsky. A dramatic pathos characterises this semantic because life stands on the side of badness. The conversation in these families is frequently focused on:

> *"...episodes which bring into play the deliberate intention to do harm, selfishness, greed, guilty pleasure, but also goodness, purity, innocence, asceticism, as well as sacrifice and abstinence. As a result, members of these families will feel, and be seen as, good, pure, responsible or alternatively bad, selfish, immoral. They will meet people who will save them, improve them, or, on the contrary, who will initiate them into vice, lead them to behaviour that will make them feel guilty. They will marry people who are innocent, pure, capable of self-denial or, on the other hand, cruel egoists who will take advantage of them. Their children will be good, pure, chaste or alternatively will express their feelings without restraint, be aggressive in affirming themselves and their sexuality. Some of them will suffer for the selfishness and malice of others, or for the intrinsic badness of their own impulses. Others will be proud of their own purity and moral superiority. And some will feel gratified by the satisfaction of their own impulses."*
>
> (Ugazio 2013, p.129)

When the semantic of power prevails in the family conversation, the main polarities are "winner/loser" and "strong-willed/yielding", fuelled by the emotive polarity shame/boasting. Members of these families feel shame when they are in a losing position, whereas they boast when their superiority is recognised by their conversational partners.

Winner/loser polarity has a specificity: "...its content is purely relational. People can only regard themselves as winners or losers in comparison to others" (Ugazio 2013, p.182). As a consequence, the conversation in these families is focused on comparisons and is devastated by conflict over the definition of the relationship. All are involved in a game of one-upmanship.

What matters when the semantic of belonging prevails in conversation is to be "in the group, included or to be out of the group, excluded" and "honourable/unworthy". Some members of the family are welcomed, honoured, worthy of being remembered, whereas others, like those prone to depression, feel excluded, marginalised, defrauded and forgotten. They crave belonging to a family, a community, and an all-absorbing marital relationship. They yearn to be at the centre of their partner's emotional world, but end up feeling rejected, alone, misunderstood and abandoned, oscillating between anger and despair.

Family Semantic Polarities

This thesis, linked to a branch of research on meaning and psychopathology initiated by Guidano (Guidano & Liotti 1983; Guidano 1987, 1991; Arciero & Bondolfi 2009), has recently received many empirical confirmations (Castiglioni, Faccio, Veronese & Bell 2013; Castiglioni, Veronese, Pepe & Villegas 2014; Ugazio, Negri, & Fellin 2015; Ugazio & Fellin 2016; Veronese , Procaccia, Romaioli, Barola, Castiglioni 2013).

Nevertheless, it is important to highlight that the four semantics shortly described here often dominate the conversation in families where nobody suffers from a psychopathology. The positions mutually assumed within the critical semantic by the family members play a more important role in the transition from "normality" to psychopathology than the semantic itself. The identification of the client's dominant semantic – regardless of the psychopathology – helps the therapist formulate a therapeutic path.

> *"Certain therapy stories that are possible in one semantic—in the sense of being productive, easy to implement, boding well for change – are forbidden in another, in the sense that they are difficult to develop, incapable of making best use of personal resources, destined to encourage dropping out or dysfunctional circuits."*
> (Ugazio 2013, p.275)

Two reasons explain this. Values, the definitions of themselves and others, attachment bonds and the relationships with those outside the family are different in each semantic. The motivation driving the persons toward change are consequently different. Above all, each semantic tends to construct peculiar constraints that therapists have to take into account, and resources that are a wealth for the life of the individual, as well as for the psychotherapy. A second reason is that we have as many different ways of building the therapeutic relationship as the number of semantics. Therapists, taking part in the family conversation inevitably end up co-positioning themselves within the client's semantic.

> *"The crucial variable that shapes the therapeutic relationship is not so much the psychopathology but the dominant semantic in the patient's conversational context."*
> (Ugazio 2013, p.275)

The semantics of freedom, of goodness, of power and of belonging construct the therapeutic relationship in different ways. The expectations, the therapeutic alliance and its possible fractures or dysfunctions, are different in each semantic. For example, when the semantic of goodness prevails – as with the obsessive–compulsive patients and their families but also with clients with other kinds of problems – the "judging/rendering someone an accomplice" polarity often implicitly characterises the therapeutic relationship. The therapist may, therefore, unknowingly find themselves in the position of a benign judge during the family sessions, able to disentangle the moral dilemmas troubling some family members, freeing them from guilt, re-establishing justice in the group, condemning or correcting the behaviour of some members if necessary. But the therapist may also find themselves, especially if they try to hold a neutral position avoiding judgements, as an accomplice, for better or worse, of those who have behaved immorally or are considered corrupt by other members of the family (Ugazio & Castelli 2015).

When the semantic of power takes over, therapists may find themselves in the uncomfortable position of rivals of their clients. Challenged by the asymmetry of the patients-therapist relationship, which these clients interpret through the metaphor of power, they feel humiliated and regard the setting and its rules as a plot to put them in a one–down position. The semantic of power also offers therapists the more promising position of ally. To win over an ally, clients may be willing to accept entering in a close relationship with the therapist. Unfortunately, this is an alliance that is a bit different from the kind the therapist wants, since it is an alliance against someone else (Ugazio 2013, p.273).

I cannot set out the specific therapeutic approaches for each semantic. I will only discuss two clinical cases and the first intervention with each of them, appropriate (at least according to me) for the dominant semantic which was different in each case.

An unexpected betrayal within two different semantics

The critical event that induces both couples discussed here to request a consultation is the same: an unexpected betrayal. Both would like to move on, especially as the third party, who entered their lives, does not seem to be a credible alternative to the betrayed partner for different reasons. But they fail to do so. A separation seems to be a likely, although undesirable, outcome. Both couples are at a stage in their lives where children are becoming independent, have been successfully married for a long time and their mutual expectations have been substantially met. The life they had planned has become a reality. They wanted to start a family and they really did. Both wanted a fulfilling career and they got it. Despite these structural similarities, the narratives of their histories, of their betrayals and the dilemmas that are now endangering the very existence of the couple are completely different, as different as the semantic that characterises the conversation.

"Protected/against the odds", "unpredictable/reliable", "risk/ safety", "exploring/staying put" are the main polarities with which Stella and Matteo reconstruct their problems during the session. Fear, caution and disorientation are the main emotions that emerge in the session. From time to time however, Stella makes courageous standpoints. These are polarities and emotions that are characteristics of the semantic of freedom.

The conversation with the other couple is dominated instead by the semantic of power. In the world of Vittoria and Leo there is someone who is overbearing, challenging, strong-willed, and someone who is submissive, yielding, who fights and who surrenders or is forced to do so. Their conversation creates a moral order dominated by success/failure. Professional, economic and family success is an undisputed value to them and of course the fear of failure is always looming. The strongest emotions during their sessions are pride and shame. Proud of their economic success, they both want to impress their therapists, seek their alliance, and have them take their side. Sometimes one tries to humiliate or challenge or diminish the other, but at other times they value each other.

Let's see how the two couples describe the betrayal, the situation from which it stemmed and the dilemmas it unleashed.

A 'Don Juan' inserts himself into a quiet marriage
"I never tried to find someone to replace Matteo," says Stella, "I had everything, we have always been fine together. (...) I found myself in this affair almost without noticing. He (the lover) confided his emotional problems to me... and in the end... yes in the end I found myself inside this affair." Stella really has a hard time identifying significant problems in her marriage. Matteo suggests, "Perhaps our life was a bit monotonous, I'm a bit sedentary, she's more adventurous..." Stella does not deny that she would like to travel more and see more friends, but this is not the reason for the betrayal. "If you really want to look for a reason, it's probably because I got married too young, I had little experience besides him because my parents were too protective." In the individual session that we initially reserve for each partner within the couple consultation, especially in those cases where there is a third party or we suspect there is, Stella confides: "He made me dream, I was feeling so well in this new dimension that I wasn't worried; it was like being in a

magic bubble. And it all happened so fast..." Then she added: "Perhaps I was attracted to his own adventurous, reckless life..."

When her husband realises she is having an affair, just three months after it began, thanks to insistent phone calls from her lover, he feels doubly betrayed: the lover is one of his three closest friends from childhood whom he had helped economically, on at least a couple of occasions. The man has always been his polar opposite. Matteo is responsible and quiet, whereas the other is restless and unreliable. He changed lots of jobs; sometimes it went well but most often he ended up in trouble. Inconsistent and intolerant towards any hierarchy and routine, he threw himself into risky situations, many of which ended badly. His love life was even more messy: "He's a Don Juan – even now that he's over fifty!" says Matteo. "Friendship for me was sacred. I knew I was a fool, but I didn't think he would do such a thing to me."

Matteo does not understand how his wife could have fallen into his trap, as Stella knew what kind of man he was: "Anyone but him!" The idea that a man like this could involve Stella sentimentally was so far away from Matteo's mind, that he had recently let him borrow a small apartment adjacent to them, initially bought for their children. Having left his wife and two sons, having been thrown out of the house by his last companion who was tired of his betrayals, in need of money, the man was struggling to find a place to stay.

Matteo now gives a negative description of his friend. But I do not find it hard to understand that until the critical event, he was full of admiration for his adventurous friend, albeit ambivalently. He regretfully remembers, for example: "When he used to tell me of his amorous adventures, I had fun, I listened to him. Recently he even told me that he was making a move on a forty-year-old woman.... I guess he was referring to you (to his wife). Now I could slap myself...". The discovery of the affair leaves Matteo appalled and disoriented. He feels he has lost his anchor: "She was my strength, she gave me security.... now I think anything can happen at any moment." He did not expect anything like this, especially since everything between him and Stella was fine, including their sex life.

The discovery of betrayal unleashes disruptive emotions also in Stella. "It's strange but I didn't think it would all come out. It was a shock for me too. I felt hunted. The first feeling was fear, then suffocation, I felt trapped." And Stella breaks away from the trap immediately; she confesses to her husband that she is feeling something that cannot be

Family Semantic Polarities

ignored. "I knew she had feelings for him even before she told me." Matteo invites her to follow her feelings and not be influenced by his grief – he was visibly overwhelmed – but wants the lover to assume his responsibilities. "This might sound strange to you," Matteo addresses the therapist, "but the strongest feeling was to protect her. I didn't feel angry with her; I was worried about her, so I put aside my pride....". Matteo asks for a meeting with Stella and her lover. After having reprimanded his friend for his disgraceful behaviour, Matteo made it clear that he would not come between him and Stella, but the man would have to be clear, he had to say that there were strong feelings involved, stronger feelings than those that bound Matteo and Stella, and above all he had to take responsibility for what he did. "I threatened him: careful how you behave! Stella is very different from the women you are used to. I'll leave you two alone, but you must respect her."

The lover is in trouble; he doesn't deny the affair, the emotional involvement, but he takes a step backwards. The same evening he calls Stella and tells her that they cannot be together: "It would be terrible for Matteo, it would destroy him. It would be an act of cowardice if I didn't give a chance to your marriage." Stella is deeply disappointed, it's like a cold shower, especially because, knowing the economic difficulties the man was facing at the time, she didn't propose moving in together. She would have temporarily stayed at her parents' house. She understands she is being rejected and refuses the man's proposal of seeing each other anyway. "At that point it didn't make any sense." Stella and the lover never saw each other again but between Stella and Matteo a sort of "wall" was raised and they are not able to tear it down. Matteo is no longer able to trust Stella. He does not say it but you can sense that he fears that the other man might come back at any moment and seduce Stella again, because she is still not totally free of him. Matteo managed not to loose Stella, but his self-esteem has been damaged.

He would like to control and protect her, but he knows he might make things worse by limiting her freedom. Also Stella feels she is at a dead end: more than three months have passed now since the fairy tale was shattered. She thinks her husband is right "but when I see him sad and suffering I don't know what to do: I feel helpless and I get nervous. I'm limiting my independence so not to make him suffer, but I can't carry on like this..." Even her self-esteem is jeopardised: continuing her independent life means hurting Matteo, but to give up her autonomy, to accept being controlled, to her it means losing all value, a price she can not pay, especially after the disappointment inflicted by her lover.

A betrayal that overturns the positions of power within the couple
It was Leo that induced his wife to discover his betrayal, after nearly a year of seeing another woman. All this time he continuously sent and received text messages from his lover, right before her wife's eyes. Vittoria didn't think it would ever happen. Aware of her beauty, extroverted, she had always thought that if one of them were to betray, it would have been her, especially as the betrayal was in stark contrast to the mentality of her husband. Leo had always criticised friends who betrayed partners and tried hard to behave in an exemplary manner in front of their children, friends, acquaintances and employees. In the individual session, Leo tells the therapist that it was very difficult for him to betray Vittoria, despite being the subject of attention from other women. Physically attractive, with a prestigious social position, well mannered, he probably had many opportunities to betray his wife. Vittoria was initially surprised by the betrayal, but she did not make a scene, mostly because the lover is a former girlfriend of her husband, a couple of years older than her and less attractive. Initially she considers his betrayal as a kind of competitive game that she herself had solicited. A couple of years earlier she had suggested to her husband that he cheat on her to put a bit of spice in their love life.

A few days after she discovered the affair, she therefore asked a friend to take her to a movie: it had never happened before. The underlying message was: "Be careful! I can humiliate you right away." Leo makes things worse by going out at night: he never went out at night, except for business meetings in which his wife sometimes participated. The competitive game and the fun end when Leo tells Vittoria he doesn't love her anymore. Vittoria falls apart, cancels her work schedule and goes for a week to her mother's house to be comforted. She is crushed – no one had ever seen her like this. His lover, as her husband also tells me in the individual session, is not his ideal woman. She is certainly less attractive, less sincere and loyal than his wife. She is also awkward in public, so inadequate for his social life. Yet, for a few months he had thought it was better to spend the rest of his years with a socially inferior woman, less intelligent than him, but accommodating and mild, than keep fighting with his wife.

The narratives that are built around the situation that generates a betrayal are different only in appearance. Both agree that the leader in the family was Vittoria, "She has the temperament of a leader (...) even if I have succeeded more in my career. It was me that gave Vittoria and the kids a pampered life. But it was Vittoria who inspired me and motivated me..." Leo recognises that his wife has supported his career but he is full

Family Semantic Polarities

of resentment towards her. In the last six, seven years, just when her husband obtained the success they both hoped for, Vittoria had inexplicably become assertive, overbearing, and sometimes even provocative. Unsatisfied with a sex life she believed to be monotonous, she had asked her husband to buy sex toys. "I had to drive around the city," said Leo, "and look for a sex shop far from home and from my office where I hoped no one knew me.... I was ashamed ... it was humiliating to buy these sex toys and use them ... having to resort to this to have sex with her...." What hurt him most was that Vittoria did not value what he did for her and for the family. Especially in front of the children, their friends and relatives she never missed an opportunity to put him back in his place. She seemed jealous of her husband's successes. Vittoria denies ever being dissatisfied and overly critical, but in the individual session she reveals a great and inexplicable dissatisfaction that accompanied the recent years of her marriage: "I cannot explain why. I still love my husband; he is physically my type. But I couldn't stand him. He got on my nerves."

Now that the worst is over, he has understood that his lover will never be his companion, and Vittoria has changed a lot, but they still cannot forget what has happened. He had left his lover but when Vittoria started violently attacking and provoking him again, he went back to the other woman. Since then, they repeated the pattern several times. Whenever he ended the relationship with the other woman, she would attack him. "It seems as if she does it on purpose," Leo emphasises. Although the relationship with his lover now seems worn out, Leo seems worried about leaving her lover for fear of losing the winning position that he acquired with the affair. However, to continue the relationship with his lover would mean probably losing Vittoria and much of what they have built together. For Vittoria, letting him return without retaliation would mean putting herself in a losing position that does not suit her personality. Ending her marriage involves losing the man she loves and the prestige she enjoys thanks to him. Unable to break the deadlock, the two of them are wondering if they really want to get back together and avoid a separation.

How can we use the semantic that have helped create the problem, to overcome the dilemmas that have trapped these couples? How can we transform their semantic from constraint to resource in the therapeutic process? The first step – which I will explain here – is to change positions within the semantics that dominate their conversation.

An imprudent couple

In their reading of the events Stella and Matteo are on opposite sides: she has betrayed the trust of her husband weaving a story with one of his closest friends, an unrepentant "Don Juan", something she knew very well thanks to the stories her husband shared with her. She is therefore reckless and unreliable. It was her desire for adventure and her superficiality that led her in a trap. "I hurt you," recognises Stella, "but my feelings…" Stella never ends this sentence she repeats several times in the first session, but the meaning is clear: she was in love with the lover. The deception of his wife and friend deprived Matteo of his securities, disorienting him. Also, his self-esteem was destroyed. Matteo does not say it, but there is a suggestion that the protection manifested towards his wife reveals that he depends on Stella. The lover in fact, said to Stella: "How can we do this to Matteo. Don't you see? We've destroyed him!" Also Stella's self-esteem was damaged: she let him make fun of her, and she is considered unreliable and someone to be kept under control – she who always considered herself autonomous and independent. From this point of view, Stella can only emphasise her feelings for her lover. They allow her some self-esteem, but at the same time, they undermine Matteo's self-esteem, creating such a situation of deep uncertainty and anxiety that a separation is preferable, although hard to accept. The reframing I propose puts both of them in the same position in relation to the lover.

Therapist:	It's not strange that you felt the need to protect your wife (when you discovered her betrayal), because you are in the same position with this person. You brought him into your house, because you trusted him (her lover).
Matteo:	That's true, but he has betrayed me.
Therapist:	Your wife trusted herself and began to listen to him.
Stella:	Because it was years that he (the lover) had been coming to our house and nothing ever happened between us…
Matteo:	He didn't start coming to our house just two months ago…
Therapist:	Sure, I understand, he was a friend of the family.
Matteo:	It's 20 years that he (the lover) has been coming …20 years!
Therapist:	God knows how many times he set his sights on your wife … but she never gave him a chance ….knowing the type he is.
Matteo:	She knew everything…

Family Semantic Polarities

Therapist:	[addressing the wife] Did you believe your husband or did you think he was exaggerating about his friend's bad behaviour?
Stella:	No, no, I never thought he exaggerated. Sometimes he even omitted some details to avoid criticising him. He was one of his friends.
Therapist:	Then you are exactly in the same position, because you, Stella, also knew everything about him (her lover) and you trusted yourself, you listened to him talking about his sentimental problems, so you encouraged him. Weren't you afraid that he could come between you two?
Stella:	No, I never thought he would have done something like that, he was so close to my husband... and my husband did so much for him. It was inconceivable. And then I... I...
Therapist:	You wouldn't have done it.
Stella:	Sure, I never even dreamed about it.
Therapist:	You are both exactly in the same position. You both trusted him.
Matteo:	We are two silly geese. [looking at his wife and touching her knee with his hand]
Stella:	So, we are two silly geese. [looking at her husband]
Therapist:	Silly geese? You simply trusted him. Perhaps you were a little careless...
Matteo:	No, I never thought he would have done such a thing to me...
Therapist:	It's in his DNA... didn't you tell me that he is a professional seducer?
Matteo:	Sure! He told me all his affairs... about the betrayed husbands... it was ending badly with one of them... he has always liked risk... he was not interested if there was no risk.
Therapist:	It was like keeping a thief in your house. You think he won't steal, because he is a friend of yours, but sooner or later... What's more, you didn't realise that for him it would have been an irresistible temptation to come between you two.

This reframing immediately makes them to come closer. The husband, who until then had kept his head down like a beaten dog, not looking at his wife, turns to Stella looking at her affectionately, putting his hand on her knee, gently telling her "we are two silly geese". It's a reinterpretation that is in tune with the semantic of the couple, therefore it is very plausible. In this perspective, the critical episode is the expression of the vulnerability of the human condition. Stella was seduced as anyone could be, given that her husband's friend is a "professional" seducer. The betrayal is yet another confirmation of the many dangers in the world, a conviction rooted in everyone living in contexts where the semantic of freedom dominates. Also those who position themselves in the appreciated pole of this semantic, and are therefore free and independent, are well aware of the dangers and fragility inherent in the human condition. Despite being in tune with the semantics of Stella and Matteo, the new reading of the events completely overturns the positions and definitions of themselves, something that makes it difficult for them to forgive the betrayal. They were deceived, but together they can recover the emotional and economic security that the lover has threatened but not destroyed because they were able to defend themselves. Matteo forced her lover to admit that it was only an affair for him; Stella woke up from the fairy tale when she understood that he did not really love her.

A daughter who tries to raise her mother's self-esteem
Also the first redefinition that therapists introduce with Vittoria and Leo remains within their semantic (power), overturning their positions. They both describe their behaviour that prevents them from resolving the critical episode, as real acting out. As soon as Vittoria diminishes him or criticises him, he feels an impulse to return to his lover. He doesn't want to, but he does. As soon as she feels she got rid of the other woman, she can't help provoking him: "I plan to stay quiet, not to attack him, not to make fun – something that drives him crazy.... (...) But I can't help it, I can't. I can't accept him coming back as if nothing happened between us ... "

The reframing we offer is all within the semantic of power but it unexpectedly widens the field of observation. Other actors are included which modify the meaning of the power struggle between Leo and Vittoria and their positions. These actors are Vittoria's parents and their marital history. It's a reinterpretation that relies on an unexplained aspect in the story of Vittoria and Leo: why did Vittoria start to become spiteful towards her husband, attacking and diminishing him, just when the man takes on an important position they both worked hard for? The hy-

Family Semantic Polarities

pothesis suggested by her husband, that Vittoria was envious, is scarcely credible. In the same period, Vittoria achieved a permanent position at the University and numerous awards. Disagreements seem to emerge just as the success of the couple is publicly sanctioned.

Therapist:	Have you ever thought about how the marital situation of Vittoria's parents has had an influence on you?
Vittoria:	In what sense?
Therapist:	You are deeply attached to your mother, aren't you?
Vittoria:	Certainly, yes. We have a very close bond.
Leo:	My wife has always had a great relationship with her mother and also esteems her greatly.
Vittoria:	You too [turning to Leo] have great esteem of her, haven't you?
Leo:	Certainly. I have often talked to her over the last two years, even if it wasn't easy because she takes her daughter's side. She's a great woman. She has Vittoria's temperament but is more balanced.
Therapist:	And she had a very difficult life, didn't she? She was a sort of martyr from what I understood from your stories, wasn't she?
Vittoria:	Yes, my father was despotic and she put up with him, not because she was weak but to keep the family together.
Leo:	He was in the Army, and with a dictator's character. Even after the stroke, he didn't change towards his wife or anyone else.
Vittoria:	Yes, he didn't show any appreciation for my mother, who looked after him.
Leo:	He preferred to die rather than bow down. He refused treatment in the end...
Therapist:	Was it very difficult for your mother not to have any sign of gratitude, any appreciation even when she took care of him?
Vittoria:	Certainly, but she took care of him anyway.
Therapist:	And this stroke happened seven years ago, didn't it?
Vittoria:	Yes and he died two years later. A living hell for my mother.

Therapist:	Then... while you were having all these successes in your life, when you bought your large apartment in the of centre of Milan and the house by the sea, your mum [addressing Vittoria] ended her married life badly.
Vittoria:	Very badly.
Leo:	Very badly and she didn't deserve anything like that.
Therapist:	So you, Vittoria, were involved in a family drama for most of your life.
Vittoria:	Yes, but I have always lived my own life. My mother has never asked me for help. On the contrary, she helped me with the children. Of course she knew that both my husband and I were on her side.
Leo:	I intervened... at least in one occasion.
Vittoria:	That's true.
	[...]
Therapist:	So as long as your father was alive, you both, powerful, competent, with many influential connections were useful for your mother... you could contain her husband.
Vittoria:	Perhaps, but not that much.
Therapist:	Your mother was disregarded by her husband until the very end... Once he was dead, she must have looked back at her life... and felt it a failure... Am I wrong?
Vittoria:	No... I saw her very embittered more than once...
Therapist:	Exactly the moment when you had everything – a loving husband, economic success, finally a permanent position at your university. The children well...
Vittoria:	But my Mum has never been envious... After my father's death she became more reserved, she was less willing to come to us because she was sad and didn't want to burden us and the children.
Therapist:	But perhaps it was you who felt you had to take a step backwards. You could not stand having everything, while your mother had nothing.
Vittoria:	I'm very tied to my mum. It's true that seeing her depressed hurts me, but...

Family Semantic Polarities

Leo:	I don't know... I had never thought about that... but it is true that after her father's death, Vittoria changed. I have always said that, and I never understood why, given that she wasn't attached to him...
Therapist:	And sure enough she chose a man like you who is quite unlike her father. You are opposites.
Leo:	That's true!
Therapist:	You [addressing Vittoria] told me of a period of unjustified discontent that began with your father's illness and death – if I remember correctly. I wonder if you were unable to handle so much success in front of your mother who ended her married life so badly. And her married life was a fundamental part of her... she was a housewife.
Vittoria:	The children were more important for her.
Therapist:	Undoubtedly. On the other hand, as soon as Leo's betrayal drove you crazy, you ran to your mother. Who else did you talk to about your husband's betrayal?
Vittoria:	No one. Nobody. I have a lot of friends and I'm very close to them but I don't speak about my problems with him (her husband) to them. My children know.
Therapist:	By going to your mother and asking her to comfort you, staying there for a week, it's a bit like saying: "All men are the same! It was not only dad who behaved as he behaved... Even Leo, who seemed so different..."
Leo:	The fact that she went to her mother for a week really surprised me. I was alarmed too. It was not like her... It wasn't in tune with her character.
Vittoria:	... I don't know, maybe... I have to think about it.

It's certainly an unexpected point of view and it is comprehensible that Vittoria wants to reflect on this point. The hypothesis introduced changes not only the significance of the symmetrical interactions that exacerbated the last years of their married life, but also the positions of the spouses. And above all, it eliminates the motivation behind the behaviours that make reconciliation impossible. The perspective introduced makes Vittoria's provocations an unaware self-injurious type of behaviour. These provocations do not arise from envy towards the success of her husband, as suggested by Leo. Instead, they are a sort of "gift" for Vittoria's mother, who not coincidentally, is the only one receiving Vittoria's confidences of betrayed wife. It's a way for Vittoria to restore some of her mother's self-esteem, which was lost due to a husband who always disregarded her. The idea suggested by Leo that his wife did not accept his successes because she was secretly competitive, should be reviewed, as well as the idea that to return to her, Leo must assume a submissive position. The real problems are very different! Although unexpected, the reinterpretation is consistent with the semantic of the couple, and therefore is plausible. Whoever is in a conversation where the semantic of power prevails, often feels alone when they become successful, and the first to move away from them are the very people who are in a losing position, even if that success brings them benefits.

The semantics of freedom and power within broader cultural systems

The semantics and the connected dilemmas we have just dealt with are linked to specific premises. Matteo and Stella are prisoners of "the idea of freedom as an absolute and solitary independence from the relationships" at the core of the semantic of freedom (Ugazio 2013, p.122). This is why Matteo before, and Stella afterwards, have for years been under the spell of a man who, within other semantics, could be considered a loser (semantic of power), despicable (semantic of belonging), immoral (semantic of goodness).

Also Stella's willingness – frankly surprising – to leave her husband and children for someone with whom she was having an affair for just three months, a man without a house, with a messy life, is an expression of this premise. Of course we do not know what she would have done if the lover hadn't taken a step back. But her intention was certainly indicative of the same pervasive premise, along with the therapeutic request. Even if secretly desiring to overcome the betrayal, the couple highlighted the possibility to separate during the beginning of the consultation. It seemed that they both had looked for therapists who could help them to find enough courage to end their relationship, fearing that the bond, which each felt toward the other, was the result of a mutual dependency, and therefore at least partly negative.

It was "the idea of equality as a breaking down of differences" (Ugazio 2013) at the base of the semantic of power, that made it difficult for Vittoria and Leo to get out of the impasse. As among all couples and families where the semantic of power prevails, they were in extreme difficulty in confronting differences. Every difference is interpreted in terms of superiority/inferiority and therefore regarded as harsh and disturbing in the semantic of power. And what worried Vittoria and Leo was to be put in an inferior position towards each other. Ending his affair, Leo feared losing the "power" he acquired thanks to the betrayal. Allowing the husband to come back with his head held high, Vittoria feared losing the upper-hand. They could not find any position assuring equality between them. In the individual session, Vittoria confided to the therapist: "Even if I betray him, now, even if I fall in love with another, now, it would seem spiteful, something done on purpose....." Also playing tit for tat, Vittoria could not restore equality in their couple, given that Matteo betrayed first.

Both the ideas of equality as a breaking down of differences and of freedom as independence of the relationships are far from systemic thinking. They are expressions of Western individualism (Ugazio 2013), linked to a vision of the individual cuthese it off from the group, independent from relationships, without differences and shortcomings that lead them to achieve completion with others.

In order to be able to help the couples to overcome the dilemmas in which the betrayal has placed them, the therapist has to take a reflexive stance on these ideas. Nevertheless, particularly at the beginning of the therapeutic process, the therapist can look for the resources able to develop the couple's resilience within the couple's own dominant semantic. Both the proposed interventions were in tune with the clients' semantics. The first, with Matteo and Stella, slightly changes the moral order of the semantic of freedom, increasing the value of security, protection, both of which are devalued meanings in their semantic. The second, accepts the competitive premise of the semantic of power, that the success of one is the failure of the other, but places the competitive dynamic outside the couple, focusing on another relationship, Vittoria and her mother. But when, in the subsequent session, Vittoria and Leo developed a narrative that they had to find the courage "to win alone" – i.e. taking the distance from Vittoria's mother and other relatives and friends who were supposedly envious of their success – the therapists bypassed this pathogenic premise – to deepen this kind of courage see Ugazio & Salamino (2016). They focussed on the conversation around this question: how could the couple involve Vittoria's mother and others into their success, making them feel part of it together. The "quasi-physical metaphor", of power as a "quantitative phenomenon"(Bateson 1979, p.248), implying that, you loose it if someone close to you gains it, was challenged.

The moral order of each semantic is not monolithic, it contains resources capable of turning over its own pathogenic premises. The model of semantic polarities helps the therapist to identify and respect the clients' semantic and its values, but also helps avoid the dysfunctional premises inside it. Sharing the clients' semantic makes it easier to develop the therapeutic relationship, without which therapy is impossible. Later on, when the therapeutic alliance is constructed, the therapist will try to reduce the dominance of one semantic favouring the entry of new meanings in the family conversation.

References

Anderson, Stephen. A. & Bagarozzi, Dennis A. (Eds.) (1989). *Family Myths: Psychotherapy Implications*. New York and London: Haworth.

Arciero, Gianpiero & Bondolfi, Guido (2009). *Selfhood, Identity and Personality Styles*. Oxford: Wiley-Blackwell.

Bateson, Gregory (1936/1958). *Naven*. Stanford: Board of Trustees of the Leland Stanford Junior University.

Bateson, Gregory (1942). Morale and National Character. In G. Watson (Ed.), *Civilian Morale*. Boston: Houghton Mifflin.

Bateson, Gregory (1949). Bali: The Value System of a Steady State. In M. Fortes (Ed.), *Social Structure: Studies Presented to A. R. Radcliffe-Brown*. Oxford: Clarendon Press.

Bateson, Gregory (1972). *Steps to an Ecology of Mind: Collected Essays in Anthropology, Psychiatry, Evolution, and Epistemology*. San Francisco: Chandler Press.

Bateson, Gregory (1979). *Mind and Nature*. New York: Dutton.

Castiglioni, Marco; Faccio, Elena; Veronese, Guido & Bell, Richard C. (2013). The Semantics of Power Among People with Eating Disorders. *Journal of Constructivist Psychology*, 26(1), 62–76.

Castiglioni, Marco; Veronese, Guido; Pepe, Alessandro & Villegas, Manuel (2014). The Semantics of Freedom in Agoraphobic Patients: An empirical study. *Journal of Constructivist Psychology*, 27(2), 120–136.

Dickens, Charles (1846-48). *Dombey and Son*. London: Penguin Classics.

Dostoevsky, Fyodor (1880). *The Brothers Karamazov*. London: Penguin.

Harré, Rom & van Langenhove, Luk (Eds.) (1999). *Positioning Theory: Moral Context of Intentional Action*. Oxford: Blackwell.

Kelly, George A. (1955). *The Psychology of Personal Constructs*. New York: Norton.

Ferreira, Antonio J. (1963). *Family Myth and Homeostasis*. Archives of General Psychiatry, 9, 457-463.

Guidano, Vittorio F. (1987). *Complexity of the Self*. New York: Guilford.

Guidano, Vittorio F (1991). *The Self in Process*. New York: Guilford.

Guidano Vittorio F., & Liotti, Giovanni (1983). *Cognitive Processes and Emotional Disorders*. New York: Guilford.

Mann, Thomas (1901/1924). *Buddenbrooks: The Decline of a Family*. London: Vintage Books.

Minuchin, Salvador; Rosman, Bernice L. & Baker, Lester (1978). *Psychosomatic Families: Anorexia Nervosa in Context*. Cambridge, MA: Harvard University Press.

Osgood, Charles E.; Suci, George J. & Tannenbaum, Percy H. (1957). *The Measurement of Meaning*. Urbana: University of Illinois Press.

Reiss, David (1981). *The Family's Construction of Reality*. Cambridge, MA: Harvard University Press.

Selvini Palazzoli, Mara; Boscolo, Luigi; Cecchin, Gianfranco & Prata, Giuliana (1975/1978). *Paradox and Counterparadox*. New York: Aronson

Towers, Hilary; Spotts, Erica & Reiss, David (2003). Unraveling the Complexity of Genetic and Environmental Influences of Family Relationships. In F. Walsh (Ed.). *Normal Family Process*. New York: Guilford.

Ugazio, Valeria (1998). *Storie permesse, storie proibite* [Stories allowed, stories forbidden]. Torino: Bollati Boringhieri.

Ugazio, Valeria (2013). *Semantic Polarities and Psychopathologies in the Family: Permitted and forbidden stories* (R. Dixon, Trans.). New York,: Routledge.

Ugazio, Valeria & Castelli, Daniele (2015). The Semantics Grid of the Dyadic Therapeutic Relationship (SG-DTR. *TPM. Testing, Psychometrics and Methodology in Applied Psychology*, 22(1),135-159.

Ugazio, Valeria & Fellin, Lisa (2016) Family Semantic Polarities and Positionings: A semantic analysis. In Peter Rober & Maria Borcsa (Eds.). *Research Perspective in Couple Therapy*. Springer: London.

Ugazio, Valeria; Negri, Attà & Fellin, Lisa (2015). Freedom, Goodness, Power and Belonging: The semantics of phobic, obsessive–compulsive, eating, and mood disorders. *Journal of Constructivist Psychology*, 28(4), 293–315.

Ugazio, Valeria; Negri, Attà; Fellin, Lisa & Di Pasquale, Roberta (2009). The Family Semantics Grid (FSG): The narrated polarities. *TPM. Testing, Psychometrics and Methodology in Applied Psychology*, 16 (4), 165-192.

Ugazio Valeria & Salamino, Ferdinando (In press). The Shades of Courage. *TPM. Testing, Psychometrics and Methodology in Applied Psychology*, 17(3).

Veronese, Guido; Procaccia, Rossella; Romaioli, Diego; Barola, Gianpiero & Castiglioni, Marco (2013). Psychopathological Organizations and Attachment Styles in Patients with Fear of Flying. *The Open Psychology*, 6, 20–27.

Watzlawick, Paul; Beavin Bavelas, Janet & Jackson, Don D. (1967). *Pragmatics of Human Communication*. New York: Norton.

24 Beyond Biology and the Linguistic Turn
Event, singularity, sense and the work of imagination

Marcelo Pakman

> *Being prepared for an event consists in being in a state of mind where one is aware that the order of the world or the prevailing powers don't have absolute control of the possibilities.*
>
> Badiou with Tardy 2013, p.13

Robert tells me he fears that his productivity will not be up to the standards of the business he works for. The job promotion he expected may not happen, and he even fears losing his job. Robert describes the situation in a sober and somewhat guarded way but similar situations brought by members of different types of organisations come to my mind. These include people tormented by physical symptoms of stress, compounded with the use of street drugs as a way out of those tensions; those with relational problems with their spouses and/or conflicts with their children; people dealing with a lack of communication with friends frequently immersed in similar crises, among others. Robert says: "It would be unfair to be seen and exposed as incompetent." He appears concerned, but I have an unclear sense of the way this is affecting him. When I ask him to elaborate more specifically, he remains vague. He has volunteered to present a situation to work on during a workshop I am conducting concerning conflicting situations in everyday life. I respect his vagueness trying to remain within the boundaries of this setting. When I ask Robert: "Who knows about your concerns?" he says: "I talk with my wife... We joke about it with friends... some people working with me... but we do not discuss it much really". I ask about the jokes and he says: "Oh, those jokes, you know, about bosses... and allusions to getting the one way ticket out... But I have not believed I needed a therapist for this. It is a job problem basically... Not personal." While I listen to him, I think that, although these situations seemed to be more frequent among men, I have heard women involved in business organisations in different capacities talking about similar struggles and fears while focusing on the "invisible ceiling" restricting them to compensation lower than for men in comparable positions. But women seemed able to discuss these situations more easily with friends (mostly women) in ways other than through jokes about peers and bosses that the men more typically make. This includes the difficulty in addressing what their male colleagues refer to as "human factors". Robert stresses that his fear is not unfounded. He has been part of performance evaluation meetings in front of peers that were typically the platform for a public exposure of the employees' inability to deal with the so called "challenges" of their jobs. He says, talking about his co-workers: "I wouldn't like to be in their shoes... I don't know... it's humiliating". I feel closer to him when he says this, and I remember being touched at other times by people's voices shaking in anticipation of similar meetings.

Change and the political

I invite you to read Robert's situation that follows as part of my own previous developments on systemic therapy as a critical social practice (1998, 2005). While sharing Gregory Bateson's misgivings about the anti-ecological role of conscious purpose leading human interventions (1968a; 1968b), I further elaborate on the importance of action oriented towards eventful change and towards the opening of what Badiou (2013) calls in the epigraph "states of mind" beyond conscious purpose. This opening, mediated by the introduction of concepts from different traditions of argumentation, enriches the systemic work, which was also informed by philosophical concepts, the narrative perspectives of Michel White and David Epston (1989, 1990, 1992) and the feminist perspective of Marianne Walters, Betty Carter, Peggy Papp and Olga Silverstein (1988). These different perspectives also introduced a more overtly political lens to systemic therapy. This work also brings to attention what Hubert Dreyfus and Charles Taylor (2015) call the process of *disenchantment* of the world (2015) that accompanied the emergence and dominance of the Cartesian dualist paradigm between body as an extended substance (*Res extensa*) and mind as a thinking substance (*Res cogitans*) that was a constant preoccupation of Gregory Bateson.

Image

The meaning of the term *image* is usually linked to the classical philosophical polarity between essence and existence. If essence stands for the ultimate reality of transcendent being, usually attributed to Plato (1991) and his Idea, existence would stand for the everyday impure copies of that ideal form. In this instance, if image is an *appearance* opposed to the ultimate reality of the Ideas it copies, everyday images are appearances of those appearances, and thus degraded forms of reality. This view of the image as appearance endured in the mimetic conceptions of images as copies of what we would get directly without mediation, through the sensual perceptions of empirical reality. It is also present in the productive view of images as fictions because, even when they are not defined as copies, they are still considered unreal compared to what is actually present to our senses. Thus, this concept of the image as appearance, either as a copy of reality or as a fictive production without a mimetic goal but a creative one, has been naturalised as a common sense meaning.

Immanuel Kant was the first (1998) to abandon this classical polarity between essence and existence to oppose instead phenomenal life, the only territory of the knowable, to the unknowable *noumenon* of things in themselves, and thus, as Gilles Deleuze remarked (2006), founding phenomenology, in a broad sense of the term, as a critique of transcendental essences. This shift implied a momentous change in the conception of images, becoming *apparitions* of the world instead of being mere *appearances*. With Jean-Luc Nancy (1997, 2008, 2012), Kant's conception of the image, that was linked to a transcendental subject, becomes an ontology of worlds or realities discontinuously coming into existence, making themselves present without assuming any transcendent place of origin or ultimate being, either divine or metaphysical, ideal or material, subjective or objective, conscious or unconscious. However, as Nancy says (2005), this is not "the ordinary presence of the real" that would provide data directly to our sense perception, as in an empirical scientific approach. Images, in all their modes, are pulses of reality putting themselves forward, distinguishing themselves from a background created in the very act of presentation, and affirming the material exteriority of a world while always having, in principle, as they appear, a vivid textural quality (Pakman 2014, p.120). Thus, an image would be the *apparition, the coming to presence or the birth to presence of the real of a world*. Images are then *poetic* givens because the term *poiesis* (Chateau 2014; Goyet 2014) also means coming to presence or appearing as existent.

Sense

A consequence of the adoption of the conception of the *image as apparition* by Nancy is that *images*, in their simultaneously sensual and material quality, belong to a dimension of *sense* (Nancy 1997, 2000, 2003, 2013), breaking with the Cartesian dichotomy opposing the processes of abstraction that underlie both scientific and linguistic turn projects. If we conceive images as apparitions of worlds or realities, we legitimate that they offer themselves as vivid presences, and we participate in them in ways that are not limited to words or language. This is neither a return to

Beyond Biology and the Linguistic Turn

a naive realism, nor an affirmation of the primacy of language as a signifying process, such that *sense is not a synonym of meaning, but its root*.

This concept of *sense* aligns with others searches for a dimension of language that could not be reduced to meaning, even though a linguistics discipline centred mostly on signifying processes and the signifier/signified distinction became dominant, stressing these two aspects (Deleuze 2005). In the systemic field, the search for a dimension of communication distinct from meaning is central to Gregory Bateson's ecology of mind, where it appears as the logic of sacrament as opposed to that of the symbol (1979) or as an idiosyncratic view of metaphor embodied in nature beyond language (1972).

The sense of the world is what we inhabit well before we learn to speak and we become taken by language into what Lacan would refer to as a symbolic order (2007), in what Giorgio Agamben (1993, 1995) called the inaugural moment of disjunction between the living subject and the speaking subject. Systemic biologist Francisco Varela (2010) also shows how, with the acquisition of language, a discontinuity occurs that amounts to a lack of the primordial body within these more evolved sociolinguistic forms of meaning making, allowing us to speak about discrete objects in an abstract and detached way.

For Nancy (2001), this dimension of language precipitated around the term *sense* and became part of an ontology that reached the extra linguistic world. The mind cannot be the origin of images as Nancy understands them, because they belong to the dimension of sense that precedes and exceeds the constitution of the speaking subject; there is no world to which we add a meaning from outside but *a world that is sense*. Sense is then a dimension that precedes and exceeds the dimension of representation or meaning and becomes constitutive of our being in the world. *Sense* thus becomes the centre of the continuity between life and language that Gregory Bateson and Francisco Varela (1991, et al. 2011) had already stressed within the systemic field. It precedes it because it is the dimension of what I have called, following in their steps, *the ecology of the lap* in which we all live before we acquire language as signifying processes to talk about this or that. However, it exceeds the meaning of speech because, no matter how hidden that language before speech may appear, once speech acquires primacy, the complex processes of the sensory-motor *ecology of the lap* are still present within the world of representations without being reducible to them (Pakman 2014). The dance of intuited directions in a given interaction, the sense of fear or comfort, the many subtle although blurry channels of communication between or within people, even the communication between people and domestic animals, the insinuated understandings in a culture whose language we do not know at all, the ethos of a people, the everyday poetic expertise of an artisan, among other phenomena, all bear witness to a language that is not based on signifying processes and that is prior to speech while it persists as a testimony of the ecology of the lap.

Imagination

Going back to our clinical situation, we encounter first an image of an institution in which Robert feels fearful and fragile. Sensitive to this image, I let other images inhabit the situation as memories of other people, institutions, and fears. I am touched by the simultaneous vagueness of the presentation. Still other images appear as thoughts — men, women, friendships, "human factors", psychotherapies — all come forward in a rapid succession of fragmentary presentations of a complex situation, always pertinent to the *sense* of this situation, not of its meanings, multiple and unclear, unknown or even unknowable. I feel then touched by Robert's fear anticipating a meeting to evaluate his performance. Also, images touch each other in a "contagious" way (Nancy 2005) such as when I present images to you as readers and you put them together with your own images of the world, be they memories, perceptions, thoughts, and/or emotions. *Imagination* can be conceived as the work one creates with these images, a composition putting them next to the each other, one with the other, one through the other, instead of being, as in academic psychology, a mental function of the individual mind along the lines of perception, memory, thought, emotion, attention, whatever definitions of it were given (Pakman 2014). Instead of being this productive function of images understood as fictive, *imagination is an experiment of making images compose-able with each other*. Perceptions, rational thoughts, fictionalisations, memories, emotions would be only modes of these images or apparitions, and the boundaries among them could vary according to how these images are composed in the work of imagination that puts them together. But this attempt at "composing" images, to use a term of long philosophical tradition (Deleuze 2006, 2008), without the composition destroying any of them but rather holding them together, is not for the sake of a unity. It is a continuous navigation within a life whose sense we sustain, despite the fragmentary quality of its coming to presence, without a thorough comprehension of the meanings at play.

Robert's initial presentation of his predicament was vague and could easily escape our attention and pass by as a superficial allusion. However, I persisted in order to secure a place for these images of fluctuating intensity, responding sympathetically to Robert's account of his fear of performance meetings, which he qualified himself, although in passing, as humiliating. I asked: "Do you know, Robert, why the organisation sets up a ritual that risks publicly humiliating people?" He appears surprised and says, "Well...no... I know these people.. don't get me wrong...I appreciate them.. They know their stuff..." and then he tries to rapidly change the subject saying, "Every job has its difficult moments... I don't know. Any advice?" I continued trying to put together both images displayed before me that we now both inhabited — not only Robert's fear about his performance evaluation and of potential humiliation his supervisors could inflict, but also his reluctance to share his fears, his vagueness while doing it, and then his retreat and his quasi excuse of the organisation. So I said, "I am thinking that as much as you extend your understanding and your appreciation of your organisation, you feel you are in a difficult position and you fear what can happen and also you are going through some of the bad things your colleagues went through." But suddenly and surprisingly, a "new person" appeared in Robert, who increased even further his support for the organisation, stating, "It is a mandate of good business: you shall not have emotional considerations based on friendship interfering with the principles of efficiency. And our enterprise is one of the leading ones in our field." The anguished person with difficulties in relation to his organisation was gone, and now I felt I was with one of his employers. His use of the plural signalled my exclusion from an organisation he was actively supporting. I thought he also wanted to emulate his bosses with the thought that, if successful, he could be the one doing those performance evaluations to others in public meetings. But after a pause he said, "You have to be confidential when you discipline people..." At first I wondered if he was returning to a critical position of the organisation, but he added, "It is tough out there. People can take advantage of knowing that someone is in trouble." So I said: "So, do you mean there are public meetings that could make you feel humiliated if you don't fare well but there are also confidential meetings, still difficult if they are disciplining you, but at least protective of people from colleagues taking advantage of them?" He confirmed, "That is exactly right." He didn't take my cue about humiliation still being present and problematic, nor my stressing that both situations were difficult and that the organisation was only protecting itself against people taking advantage in terms of business but not protecting people from humiliation. I thought that, in that Hobbesian world, the fear of colleagues taking advantage combined with the fear of public humiliation, as well as the "protection" the organisation employed was ensuring that collegiality would not be a source of resistance to the rules of the game, so typical of the macropolitics of "free" market organisations. I asked, "Does all this functioning affect friendships?" He said: "It helps actually. They are very ethical in this regard. They would not protect people based on personal reasons, sympathies or friendships. We are all equal over there."

Presence and intensities of existence

The sequence shows how images, although being all in principle apparitions of realities, do not always have the same value as materials for imagination to work with because, as Alain Badiou conceptualises it (2009, 2013), realities do not have a digital quality as if they either exist or they do not, but have instead different *intensities of existence* that can go between a maximum and a minimum. In Robert's situation the rules of the organisation maintain certain realities at a low level of existence: his fears of potential humiliation, of losing his job, of not having a place to talk about this, the impact this may have on his friendships, his family and emotional life in general, his assumption of a different ethics that may conflict with some of the practices of the organisation (as shown by his vagueness to talk about these issues), his oscillating identification and distancing from those he works for, etc. For Badiou (2005) what is present in a situation could count more or less as a representation. Besides, going from being to existence, thus starting to count for a given situation, requires a *presentation*. Although what is represented makes for the official *state of the situation* (Badiou 2007), *realities are made also of what is present but not represented in language or inscriptions.* Thus Badiou breaks with the concept that existence necessarily requires signifying language. Reading Badiou with Nancy, we could say that the realities of everyday life come to presence in a way similar to Nancy's images as apparitions to existence (Pakman 2014). There is what is present without existing at a significant level or counting as an element of the situation, be it idea, emotion, perception, fiction. And as a part of this intermediate dimension of poetic sense, there is what is present in speech as an expression, which is not ineffable, although it doesn't have a clear and distinct meaning. Between what is signified and what is ineffable there is the *dimension of presentation, sense, images and imagination*. Coming to existence is a process of localisation of being in a situation in which some realities acquire different intensities according to the rules of the situation in which they appear (Badiou 2009).

Beyond Biology and the Linguistic Turn

Macropolitics and micropolitics

The ideology Robert is presenting with his volte-face from his initial concerns is part of the standard macropolitical *status quo* of a capitalist enterprise. But macropolitics at the social level is not conveyed automatically to the level of lived experience without micropolitical processes where the social and the mental become intertwined. The social is embodied in lived experience, and the mental shows its social constitution. Without a micropolitical level, therapeutic processes could become programmatic interventions with a prior agenda, and the distinction between coercion and consent could become blurred. I call *micropolitics of a given situation the creation, maintenance and regulation, both explicit and implicit, of objectifying mechanisms of subjectivation/subjection of the human experience* (Pakman 2011). *Micropolitics* is articulated by four elements explored by Michel Foucault (2000):

1. *Power relations* that operate as *dividing practices*, separating, for instance, normals from abnormals (2003) or dividing people internally between aspects, like body and soul, or consciousness and the unconscious. This is a distributed, local, positive and horizontal *power*, unlike the sovereign or state, the repressive and vertical power at work in macropolitics (Foucault 1980, 2000).

2. *Knowledge* includes both what is *said* and what is *seen* at a given social moment within historical formations (Foucault 1985, 1994; Deleuze 2013). Power/knowledge is articulated in *apparatuses* that, in Agamben's reading of Foucault are: "Anything that has in some way the capacity to capture, orient, determine, intercept, model, control, or secure the gestures, behaviours, opinions, or discourses of living beings" (2009, p.14).

3. *Subjectivities* are both the *identities* and the *subjective positions of enunciation* that we assume as micropolitical subjects, acting as agents who create, support and maintain the apparatuses while, at the same time are shaped by them. Thus they become objects of knowledge and points of origin and application of power relations (Foucault 1985, 2008; Pakman 2011).

4. The *social imaginary* made of images that instead of being marginalised to a low level of existence, as in Robert's case, acquire a high level of intensity, but only as a sensual everyday illustration of certain dominant meanings. This happens when Robert displays the preferred emotions, ideas, ways of talking, attitudes, clothing, gestures, etc. that come with being part of, for instance, his successful organisation. Images, which are either marginalised or incorporat-

ed into the social imaginary find it difficult to enter into the work of imagination. Thus, the social imaginary becomes central to the configuration of micropolitics as life scripts guiding our whole life in what Jacques Rancière considers a *partition of the sensible*: what to say and not to say, what to perceive and not to perceive, etc. (2000).

Hegemony

Unlike the concepts of *image* and of *imagination*, both of which have been largely unexplored in the systemic context or taken in their everyday meaning without further elaboration or the concept of *sense* whose territory has only been signalled under other names, the concept of *power* as related to politics has occupied centre stage in the systemic field. This is seen in the work of, for instance, Michel White and David Epston (1989, 1990, 1992), Imelda McCarthy (2010) from a narrative, dialogical and feminist perspective, John Shotter from a dialogical perspective (1993), and feminist authors like Marianne Walters, Betty Carter, Peggy Papp and Olga Silverstein (1988), among others.

Our conception of power adds an important element, not only distinguishing macro from micropolitics, but also stressing the way that micropolitical forces do not dominate, coerce or control us as is especially apparent in dictatorial systems. Instead, micropolitics works by *consent* in what Antonio Gramsci elaborated as processes of *hegemony* (1991, 1996, 2007). Although the boundaries and the balance between coercion and consent are always mobile and at the macro-political level the more resistance a system encounters the more its tendency is to slide towards coercion, the hegemonic everyday element is secured by a subject able to govern him/herself in freedom as stressed by Foucault (2011). We witness *hegemony* at work when all of a sudden Robert switches to speak as one of his feared employers and praises their ethical stance while going against his own emotional expression and collegiality. Hegemonic freedom in not simply a mechanism of co-option, and it is always open to being reversed and put at the service of what can actually oppose the rules of the system. As Foucault insisted, wherever there are mechanisms of power relations there are *points of resistance* (2000), a concept that Alan Wade (2007) with Linda Coates (2005) and Nick Todd (2004) have used in the systemic field from a narrative perspective without the incorporation of the micropolitical distinction or this hegemonic element.

Poetic events

With the work of imagination starting from these points of resistance within the micro-politically shaped situations, certain images can be either amplified to increase its intensity of existence or rescued from the social imaginary. In this way they can be put to the service of what can become a *poetic singular event*, deviating in a transformative way from the life scripts adopted thus far and going beyond assumed identities and subjective positions, including our own usual positions concomitant with our assumed models of therapy.

In Robert's case his initial anguish, his sharing of his fears of losing his job, his sense of humiliation about the public performance meetings, his varied attachment to the use of the plural to talk about the organisation he works for, can operate as *points of resistance*. Unpredictably, even to myself, I present him with this image, "I remembered, while I was listening to you, the Moscow trials during the Stalinist era. Have you heard about them?" When he says he knows about Stalin but not about the trials, I tell him, "For a few years in the 1930's several trials happened in Moscow against people accused of conspiring against the soviet state, although they have been companions during the Revolution and close friends in some cases. Most people, against their own interest, confessed and were punished with death or imprisonment. Although they were partly coerced by threats to their families and torture, many scholars who studied these processes agree that many self-accusations were genuine and that these accused people really believed they deserved to be punished for deviating from the behaviour of good citizens. They felt they were guilty in spirit if not in fact." Robert leans forward and takes a breath indicating he wants to say something. I wait while he makes a long pause and then says, "They had been friends, that's killing me." "How so?" I ask him and he tells me that, "It doesn't have to happen within communism only, right? Because this is capitalism all right... And yet, you just touched something that is tearing me apart." So I tell him, "It is not me, it is our old visitors from Moscow who are bringing us news." He smiles and says, "I am sacrificing a lot, even friendships." "What do you mean?" I ask him. And he says with teary eyes: "I stopped talking even to people that were friends more than just colleagues and all because it was not good to share business and ... It is mistrust. People can be promoted or fall behind and ... Friendship is difficult then... Even if they are not my only friends, they could understand better what we deal with over there..." When I give room to the fleeting appearance of the Moscow trials, an exercise of *poetic sensibility* to potential events prompted by the points of resistance to the dominant micropolitics of the situation, we are not just making an analogy or using a metaphor. In spite of the shortcomings of this uninvited presence in terms of its meanings, we are taking an image from the social imaginary where they illustrate the wrongs of a regime and we put it to use in imagination to become a vivid enhancer of what was otherwise marginal to the hegemonic micropolitics Robert was sustaining. Thus, a poetic event takes shape that carries both of us beyond our subjectivities, and a new agency appears around this unique singular presence in the micro community we configure at that moment, and I invite you to participate in right now. Driven by this poetic event Robert has a dilemma both pragmatic and ethical more than a solution or a dissociated conflict within a dominant micropolitical conflict. A careful exploration of this enhanced presence of otherwise devalued friendships can now be experimented within imagination, putting it together with all the complex aspects of the situation at hand. This is not an abstract condemnation of capitalistic logic but a vivid engagement with a limited human situation. I say, "Now you have a dilemma Robert: can you have this type of job that you value and need, within this or another organisation, without sacrificing something you feel central to your life as well?" He says, "It is a tough one. I cannot afford losing the job, nor [sic] I probably want to but there are other people feeling this way... I have to think and talk about this but at least I don't really have to be more of a papist than the Pope!" Between the impotence felt from hard realities and the elusive pseudo transformation of abstract words of good intention, it is possible for a different conception of imagination to carry forward singular presences against the commonplace and the clichés plaguing both human problems and human solutions, therapeutic or otherwise. Thus it can foster poetic events that do not have to be earth shattering to be transformative of lived experience within the local communities of social interventions. If, as Badiou has Socrates say in his version of *Plato's Republic*, "the proper virtue of the human species is justice!"(2012 p.12), the critical poetic perspective I have outlined embodies an ethics of truth that, far from enforcing it dogmatically or bringing back a correspondence between signs and realities, opens us up to unique events in the flesh of life and beyond the known. Critical social practice then meets a poetics of change.

References

Agamben, Giorgio (1993 [1978-2001]). *Infancy and History: The Destruction of Experience*. Translated by Liz Heron. London and New York: Verso.

Agamben, Giorgio (1995 [1985]). *The Idea of Prose.* Translated by Michel Sullivan and Sam Whitsitt. Albany: Suny Express.
Agamben, Giorgio (2009 [2006]). *What is an Apparatus? and Other Essays.* Translated by David Kishik and Stefan Pedatella. Stanford: Stanford University Press.
Badiou, Alain (2005 [1992-98]). *Infinite Thought.* Translated by Oliver Feltham and Justin Clemens. London-New York: Continuum.
Badiou, Alain (2007 [1988]). *Being and Event.* Translated by Oliver Feltham. London-New York: Continuum.
Badiou, Alain (2009 [2006]). *Logic of Worlds. Being and Event II.* Translated by Alberto Toscano. London: Bloomsbury Academic.
Badiou, Alain (2012). *Plato's Republic. A Dialogue in 16 Chapters.* Translated by Susan Spitzer. Introduction by Kenneth Reinhardt. New York: Columbia University Press.
Badiou, Alain (2013). *The Subject of Change: Lessons from the European Graduate School.* Edited by Duane Rousselle. New York-Dresden: Atropos Press.
Badiou, Alain & Tardy, Fabien (2013). *Philosophy and the Event.* Cambridge-Malden, MA: Polity Press.
Bateson, Gregory (1968a). Conscious Purpose and Nature. In *Steps to an Ecology of Mind: Collected Essays in Anthropology, Psychiatry, Evolution, and Epistemology.* 1972. California: Jason Aronson.
Bateson, Gregory (1968b). Effects of Conscious Purpose and Human Adaptation. In *Steps to an Ecology of Mind: Collected Essays in Anthropology, Psychiatry, Evolution, and Epistemology.* 1972. California: Jason Aronson.
Bateson, Gregory (1972). *Steps to an Ecology of Mind: Collected Essays in Anthropology, Psychiatry, Evolution, and Epistemology.* 1972. California: Jason Aronson.
Bateson, Gregory (1979). *Mind and Nature.* New York: Dutton.
Baudrillard, Jean (2010). The Agony of Power. New York: Semiotext(e).
Chateau, Dominique, "Art", in Barbara Cassin (Ed.) (2014) [2004]). *Dictionary of Untranslatables: A Philosophical Lexicon.* Translated by S. Rendall et al. Princeton and Oxford: Princeton University Press, p.42–47.
Coates, Linda and Wade, Allan (2005). Language and Violence: Analysis of Four Discursive Operations. *Journal of Family Violence*, 22(7), 511–522.
Deleuze, Gilles (2005 [1973]). *Derrames entre el capitalismo y la esquizofrenia.* Parte II. Buenos Aires: Cactus.
Deleuze, Gilles (2006 [1980-86-87]). *Exasperación de la filosofía.* El Leibniz de Deleuze. Buenos Aires: Cactus.
Deleuze, Gilles (2007 [1981]). *Pintura. El concepto de diagrama.* Buenos Aires: Cactus.
Deleuze, Gilles (2008 [1980-1981]). *En medio de Spinoza.* Buenos Aires: Cactus.

Deleuze, Gilles (2013 [1985]). *El saber. Curso sobre Foucault*. Tomo I. Buenos Aires: Cactus.
Deleuze, Gilles (2014 [1986]). *El poder. Curso sobre Foucault*. Tomo II. Buenos Aires: Cactus.
Descartes, René (2000 [1637]). *Discourse on Method and Related Writings*. New York: Penguin.
Dreyfus, Hubert & Charles Taylor (2015). *Retrieving Realism*. Cambridge-London: Harvard University Press,
Foucault, Michel (1985 [1969]). *The Archaeology of Knowledge and the Discourse on Language*. New York: Vintage Books.
Foucault, Michel (1994 [1966]). *The Order of Things: An Archaeology of the Human Sciences*. New York: Vintage Books.
Foucault, Michel (2000). Power. *Essential Works of Foucault 1954-1984*. Edited by James Faubion. Volume II. New York: The New Press.
Foucault, Michel (2008 [1973]). *This is Not a Pipe*. Edited and translated by James Harkness. Oakland: University of California Press.
Foucault, Michel (2011). *The Government of Self and Others*. Lectures at the Collége de France 1982-1983. Edited by Frédérick Gros. English edition by Arnold I. Davidson. Translated by Graham Burchell. New York: Palgrave MacMillan.
Foucault, Michel (2013). *Lectures on the Will to Know*. Lectures at the Collège de France 1970-1971 with Oedipal Knowledge. Edited by Daniel Defert, English edition by Arnold E. Davidson, translated by Graham Burchell. New York: Palgrave Macmillan.
Goyet, Francis, "Art of the Ancients, Art of the Modern: The rules of art", in Barbara Cassin (Ed.) (2014) [2004]. *Dictionary of Untranslatables: A Philosophical Lexicon*. Translated by S. Rendall et al. Princeton Oxford: Princeton University Press.
Gramsci, Antonio (1991, 1996, 2007 [1929-1933]). *Prison Notebooks*. 3 volumes. Edited and translated by Joseph A Buttigieg. New York: Columbia University Press.
Kant, Immanuel (1998 [1791]). *Critique of a Pure Reason*. Edited and translated by Paul Guyer and Allen W. Wood. Cambridge: Cambridge University Press.
Kearney, Richard (1995). *States of Mind: Dialogues with Contemporary Thinkers*. New York: New York University Press.
Lacan, Jacques (2007). *Écrits: The First Complete Edition in English*. Translated by Bruce Finks. New York: Norton.
McCarthy, Imelda (2010). A traumatic intrusion with transgressive possibilities. Power as a relational and discursive phenomenon. *Context*, October 2010, 21–24.
Moore, Thomas (1997). *The Re-enchantement of Everyday Life*. New York: Harper Collins.
Nancy, Jean-Luc (1997 [1993]), *The Sense of the World*. Translated by Jeffrey S. Librett. Minneapolis: Minnesota University Press.

Nancy, Jean-Luc (2000 [1996]), *Being Singular Plural*. Translated by Anne E. O'Byrne and Robert D. Richardson. Stanford: Stanford University Press.
Nancy, Jean-Luc (2003 [1990]), *A Finite Thinking*. Edited by Simon Sparks. Stanford: Stanford University Press.
Nancy, Jean-Luc (2005), *The Ground of the Image*. New York: Fordham University Press.
Nancy, Jean-Luc (2008 [2005]), *Dis-Enclosure, The Deconstruction of Christianity*. Translated by Bettina Bergo, Gabriel Malenfant and Michael B. Smith. New York: Fordham University Press.
Nancy, Jean-Luc (2012 [2010]). *Adoration: The Deconstruction of Christianity II*. Translated by John McKean. New York: Fordham University Press.
Nietzsche, Frederic (2001 [1882]). *The Gay Science: With a Prelude in German Rhymes and an Appendix of Songs*. Edited by Bernard Williams. Cambridge: Cambridge University Press.
Nietzsche, Frederic (2006 [1883-1891]). *Thus Spoke Zarathustra*. Edited by Adrian del Caro and Robert Pippin. Cambridge: Cambridge University Press.
Pakman, Marcelo (1998). "Education and Therapy in Cultural Borderlands: A Call for Critical Social Practices in Human Services." *Journal of Systemic Therapies*, 17(1), 18–30.
Pakman, Marcelo (2005). Toward Critical Social Practices: Hermeneutics, Poetics and Micropolitics in Community Mental Health. In Anita Lightburn and Phebe Sessions (Eds.) *Handbook of Community-Based Clinical Practice, Oxford University Press*, Chapter 7, pages 84–98.
Pakman, Marcelo (2011). *Palabras que permanecen, palabras por venir: Micropolítica y poética en psicoterapia*. Barcelona: Gedisa.
Pakman, Marcelo (2014). *Texturas de la imaginación: Más allá de la ciencia empírica y del giro lingüístico*. Barcelona: Gedisa.
Plato (1991 [c.380BC]), *The Republic of Plato*. Second edition. Translated, with notes, and interpretive essay and a new introduction by Alan Bloom. New York: Basic Books.
Rancière, Jacques (2000). *Le partage du sensible: esthétique et politique*. Paris: La Fabrique.
Shotter, John (1993). *The Cultural Politics of Everyday Life*. Toronto: University of Toronto Press.
Todd, Nick and Wade, A. (2004). Coming to terms with violence and resistance: From a language of effects to a language of responses. In T. Strong and D. Pare (Eds.) *Furthering Talk: Advances in the Discursive Therapies* (145–161). New York: Kluwer Academic/Plenum.
Varela, Francisco (2010). *El fenómeno de la vida*. Santiago de Chile: J.C.Sáez Editor.

Wade, A. (2007). Despair, Resistance, Hope. In C. Flaskas, I. McCarthy & J. Sheehan (Eds.), *Hope and Despair in Narrative and Family Therapy: Adversity, Forgiveness and Reconciliation.* Hove: Brunner-Routledge.

Walters, Marianne; Carter, Betty; Papp, Peggy and Silverstein, Olga (1988). *The Invisible Web: Gender Patterns in Family Relationships.* New York: Guilford Press.

White, Michael & Epston, David (1989) *Literate Means to Therapeutic Ends.* Adelaide: Dulwich Centre Publications.

White, Michael & Epston, David (1990). *Narrative Means to Therapeutic Ends.* New York: Norton.

White, Michael & Epston, David (1992). *Experience, Contradiction, Narrative and Imagination: Selected papers 1989-1991.* Adelaide: Dulwich Centre Publications.

Systemic Psychosexual Therapy
A guided tour

25

Desa Markovic

Within two weeks of my arrival in London from Belgrade, the first clinical session on the systemic therapy course was with a young couple whose opening words were: "We are in love and totally committed, and really looking forward to our imminent wedding. However... our sexual relationship is not working. And this is why we came to see you." Having explored their relationship, their cultural and familial contexts I consulted the team and supervisor behind the one-way screen. They thought it was unlucky that my very first session should present a sexual problem but reassured me that I was doing well by exploring the clients' wider contexts and engaging them in mapping out rich and interesting material. In the post session the team congratulated me on creating client rapport. This felt like a significant step in my learning about a new approach as well as about conducting sessions in English, and in a new and different culture. I was looking forward to continuing the work however the couple never returned, and I searched for a coherent explanation for that over time. It took me years to begin to question the story told that if clients bring sexual topics to therapy, that is exceptional and unlucky. My avoidance of talking about sex was obvious whilst that was the primary topic for the clients. Although we had an interesting conversation about their families, culture, and religion, it detracted from the very reason for therapy. None of my systemic therapy training or literature addressed sex. Many of my colleagues have commented over time, they "didn't feel qualified"; or would "shy away" from the subject raising more questions and puzzlement for me: how come we were trained to work with relationships, yet we didn't feel qualified to work with sex? This took me on a journey to qualify as a psychosexual therapist and sparked my interest in combining psychosexual therapy with the systemic approach.

Introduction

The first couple session described above, even though it took place back in 1991, still resonates with me, as often clients declare that they have been unable to talk about sex with previous therapists. Whilst I believe that practitioners have many creative ideas, most of the psychotherapy trainings in the UK do not include very much about sexual issues. The systemic approach is rich with resources for working with sex and sexual relationships however these are rarely applied. I researched ways in which systemic therapists work with the topic of sex, the resources they saw as helping them and the constraints they saw as hindering that work (Markovic, 2007). All interviewees agreed the topic was important but that they addressed it only in a limited way; they believed conversations about sex were potentially risky, inappropriate, and self-exposing. However, they reflected that having addressed it, the results had been therapeutically beneficial. Subsequently I expanded this research to experienced psychotherapists from UK and Europe, practicing from Humanistic, Psychodynamic, Existential, CBT and Integrative perspectives. The absence of the topic of sex and sexual relationships in therapeutic practice was recognised with some concern at several psychotherapy conferences in which I took part. I also reviewed the syllabi and reading lists of a number of psychotherapy training programmes. This confirmed that the subject is noticeably lacking from psychotherapy courses, literature and clinical practice (Markovic, 2011).

I feel it is important to treat sex as a form of communication and an integral part of the human condition and relationships. Social and cultural contradictory messages about sex, oscillating between sensationalist approaches on the one hand and silence and suppression on the other, aggravate the anxiety underlying sexual problems. The task of therapy is to be irreverent (Cecchin et al, 1992) to such treatment of sex, which exacerbates the stigmatising and self-deprecating picture that clients often present. This chapter is a step in that direction and describes how I integrate sexology and systemic therapy, using a medical framework in conjunction with systemic social constructionist ideas.

Integration of systemic and sexology approaches

I define systemic social constructionism as an approach which views reality as constructed through communication and language, objectivity as impossible (Burr, 2003) and the aim of therapy as creating a context for change through collaborative therapeutic relationships (Anderson, 2000); and sexology as a sexual science guided by scientific knowledge within the field of sexual medicine (Wylie et al, 2004).

These approaches hold radically different and often contrasting epistemologies. Using a fundamental systemic principle of "both/and", I integrate these in my practice as a psychosexual and systemic therapist and

Systemic Psychosexual Therapy

supervisor. Within this context each approach can be enriched through the inclusiveness of the other: balancing quantitative with qualitative research; holding multidimensional perspectives; appreciating both neutrality and normative judgments; embracing linear, circular and reflexive positions; appreciating the concepts of socially constructed realities as well as of truth and facts; making use of both instructive and exploratory interventions; acknowledging shared expertise of both clients and therapists; valuing both medical diagnoses and systemic deconstruction.

Balancing quantitative with qualitative research

Whilst large scale quantitative studies are typically applied in sexology and qualitative research is more pertinent to psychotherapy, both types of enquiry are combined in this integrated framework. In my experience, clients often seek information about the pervasiveness of the difficulties they are experiencing and are curious to hear about outcome predictions of their treatment. I deeply believe in the clients' right to have clear responses to their queries, which is also coherent with the Declaration of Sexual Rights (WAS, 2014) and I ensure to answer them to the best of my knowledge. In sharing this knowledge I often rely on quantitative evidence from sexology that I convey within a collaborative social constructionist framework.

For example, my clinical experience confirms statistical data from sexology that a vast majority of women worry about not reaching orgasm through vaginal intercourse. The percentage of worry regularly outweighs the actual extent of the physical problem. I believe that normalising interventions so fundamental to the systemic approach (Hare-Mustin, 1994) are crucial in response to such concerns and are most effective when supported by specific findings such as, in this example, that the majority of women reach orgasm via clitoral stimulation and that sexology science considers this as just one of the ways in which women may experience sexual pleasure and climax. Thus, using statistical facts arrived at through sexology research, affirms the diversity of female orgasmic experience.

Sexology provides a rich evidence base for psychosexual therapy; sharing statistical data with clients can be an important and effective therapeutic intervention in providing a window into others' experiences. Often clients feel isolated with their problem which reinforces the problem itself. One client presenting lack of sexual desire verbalised thus: "I feel like a freak and think all the time what is wrong with me, psychologically, emotionally, physically...? Am I so abnormal I am not meant to have sex?" Quantitative sexology studies exploring factors influencing sexual desire (e.g. Weeks & Gambescia, 2002) informed me in normalising her experience within the context of multiple pressures such as: work stresses, family illness, relationship conflict. Normalising interventions that emphasised these as typical factors that influence sexual interest enabled her contextual understanding of her sexual concerns thus reframing her self-pathologising focus.

The knowledge base developed within sexology is shared through the social constructionist framework in that it is not presented as the ultimate truth but it is contextualised within particular research and offered as a relative guide. Any discrepancies from the statistical norm can be considered as clients' idiosyncrasies rather than abnormality. For example, statistics may suggest that typically it is women who need foreplay as a prelude to intercourse however it is important not to pathologise the opposite situation. I have encountered male clients with strong inclinations for foreplay and gentle, loving, "soft" sexual interaction and females who favoured short, sharp and strictly genitally focused sex. Given how complex and delicate the subject of sex is, it is paramount for therapists to allow for a wide spectrum of sexual preferences and consider statistical normality (Tiefer, 2004) a relative and approximate indicator.

The multidimensional perspective: remembering the body
Working with sexual issues requires appreciation of the multidimensional nature of sexuality (Iasenza, 2004; Markovic, 2013). Whilst emotional, cognitive, behavioural, relational and cultural dimensions of human lives and relationships are addressed in psychotherapy approaches to various degrees, the bodily dimension is typically underestimated and sometimes forgotten. As far back as 1989, a family therapy article (Attwood & Weinstein, 1989) describes the case of a client presenting vaginal pain on intercourse for which no organic cause could be found. Only after three years of psychotherapy and no improvement, did it transpire that she was taking off-the-counter medication which had the side effect of drying soft tissue thus causing her genital pain. In systemic psychosexual therapy the physical dimension is equally important and regularly included. I recall a female client who came to the clinic accompanied by her partner, a woman who was extremely worried about the client's lack of sexual desire. They were both adamant that everything else in their relationship was going well. The clinic's multidisciplinary team approach involved a routine blood test, which showed severe anaemia. This proved to be the direct cause of the lack of sexual interest as the appropriate physical treatment resulted in immediate improvement. With clients present-

ing low sexual desire I now recommend that they undertake blood tests being aware that conditions such as anaemia, or high cholesterol or high sugar levels can be a sole cause of low desire. Prescription of appropriate medication, change in nutrition, or supplements may resolve the situation rendering psychotherapy unnecessary.

On the other hand, I have also seen several clients where improved couple communication, enhanced self-image and general satisfaction coincided with improved hormonal levels thus indicating a likely correlation between these areas. One such client with extremely low testosterone levels was put on a priority list for testosterone replacement therapy in the NHS. After several months during which the couple made good use of psychosexual therapy she reached the top of the waiting list when new hormonal tests showed a completely normal result.

In my consulting room I have a wealth of ever-expanding resources including educational DVD's, leaflets, books and articles, lists of websites, pictures and drawings. With clients who feel their genital organs to be abnormal for example, I often show photographs of the range of male and female genitalia to normalise the diversity of their appearance. The importance of the clitoris is often illustrated using visual tools, when women feel abnormal if vaginal penetration itself does not create pleasure. I then explain that female sexual functioning can be complex, and that women's erogenous zones vary greatly. Furthermore, a particular kind of stimulation may be needed. Sometimes men are puzzled by the complexity of female sexual response. I remember a man's comment in one couple session that, "sometimes it's half a millimetre here or there", to which his wife replied: "I gave you a guided tour!" Indeed, a guided tour may be the answer!

Appreciating both neutrality and normative judgements
I see the richness of systemic neutrality in encompassing many different perspectives, multiple possibilities, and "not falling in love with your hypothesis" (Cornwell 1989), and "entertaining the myriad of applicable stories describing one interaction" (Cecchin 1987).

However, one can become a prisoner of this openness (Radovanovic, now Markovic 1994) in that it is possible to get trapped between too many options, and feel confused and lost in a vast space of countless possibilities. In their writings on irreverence, Cecchin, Lane, and Ray (Cecchin et al 1992) suggest that, in such situations of confusion a narrow, uni-directional, even instructional approach can be liberating for clients. Strictly adhering to neutrality often prevents therapists from discussing subjects until brought up by clients, leaving space for clients to choose which issues to talk about. Often, in my experience, the opposite approach facilitates clients' choice more effectively. The topic of sex is often difficult for clients so when I raise it in both a direct and invitational way, it seems to assure them, normalising such conversations and taking the stigma out of sex.

Various different ways to introduce sex could include, suggesting a link with a presenting issue:

> *"How have conflict and anger impacted on your emotional and sexual intimacy?"*

Or, announcing the topic:

> *"I understand you are here to talk about your relationship and that may include communication, your sexual relationship..."*

The subject could be offered as an option with an open question:

> *"What would be most useful to focus on: your sexual relationship, conversational patterns, cultural differences, or something else...?"*

It could also be put forward directly whilst leaving the choice to clients:

> *"I'm wondering whether it may be relevant to talk about sex."*

Within this context, systemic neutrality also relates to appreciation of the variety of sexual practices and preferences. A couple in their 50s said, shyly: "We haven't had sex for the last ten years..." It emerged their sexual preferences were unusual (Iasenza, 2010); they had no interest in penetration but they regularly engaged in playful humiliation games, bondage and restraint. In spite of describing this experience as: fun, play, adventure, sensuality, imagination and intimacy, they felt they were involved in something shamefully abnormal. I embraced neutrality as a non-judgmental approach to sexual diversity. At the same time I was not neutral in directly affirming this was within a wide scope of normality:

> *"You have the right to your sexual choices."*

Systemic Psychosexual Therapy

> *"You are communicating your desires openly and clearly."*

> *"It is important you understand each other's signals."*

Where relevant, I may include the following types of affirmations:

> *"Anger is a typical barrier to sex."*

> *"Blame closes down desire for intimacy."*

> *"Penetration is a choice"* and, as Zilbergeld wisely puts it, *"Orgasm is an option"* (Zilbergeld, 1992).

With regards to systemic neutrality to treatment outcome I both respect the clients' ultimate choice including the option of staying the same, and am keen to support and encourage them in a freer expression of their sexuality, their sexual rights and decision making processes. This enthusiasm may be seen as not strictly systemically neutral however I believe it plays an important part in achieving positive outcomes.

Embracing linear, circular and reflexive positions

The Milan team's concept of circularity (Selvini-Palazzoli et al, 1980) brought forth an epistemological revolution in psychotherapy, postulating that it is difficult and even detrimental to determine what causes certain behaviours. For example, one person may withdraw because of the partner's anger or, perhaps, the partner is angry because the other withdraws. Searching for a cause of a problem was conceptualised as evoking blame and reinforcing unwanted repetitive patterns (Pearce, 2007).

Circularity is a major part of Basson's (2000) revision of the Masters and Johnson's pioneering model of human sexual response (Masters & Johnson 1966). Their four stage model evolving from excitement, plateau, and orgasm to resolution, was a leading paradigm for many decades. However, it was criticised as linear, normative and pathologising by sexologists including Basson whose model has had a transformative impact on sexology. At the heart of her revision are fundamental systemic concepts: context, circularity, variety, connectedness, relatedness, multidimensionality, reflexivity, and sensitivity to gender differences.

Alongside these concepts, within the framework I propose, I see it as essential to also appreciate a linear perspective. Paradoxically, I propose expansion of the boundaries of the systemic approach by inclusion of narrow, uni-dimensional linear perspectives. For example, rigid masturbation patterns can be a direct cause of restricted couple sexual interactions, thus impacting unilaterally in a linear way on their sexual relationship. A female client had a well-rehearsed ritual over many years: setting up the room in a certain way, starting to touch herself at the beginning of the same CD, using the same movements, type of touch and fantasy to always bring herself to orgasm during the last track. She had constructed a strong arousing stimulus by way of mental, physical and erotic association. This ritual created a problem in the sexual relationship with her partner whom she met subsequently, in that it affected her ability to experience arousal through a different pattern of stimulation in an interpersonal context.

The lineal causal links are well known in sexology for example in cases where men who have been culturally brought up to believe that masturbation is sinful, practice it in a rush for fear of being discovered; this practice can lead to premature ejaculation in later sexual relationships.

Behavioural exercises developed within sexology are suggested to alter habitual masturbation patterns allowing for different ways of experiencing sexual arousal and orgasm. In this way, the lineal cause of the problem is being directly treated. In addition, it can be helpful to deconstruct deeply embedded feelings of sexual shame and guilt often accompanying this condition, by employing systemic exploratory questioning such as: "What are you worried may happen if you become aroused by your partner?" or, introducing a hypothesis through normalisation: "Many cultures and societies condemn masturbation and it seems during your upbringing it was regarded as a shameful thing to do. How do you think it has impacted on your ideas about sex, touch, and erotic pleasure that may be affecting your current relationship?"

The social construction of truth
Social constructionist philosophy applied to systemic therapy appreciates diversity of constructions of reality. In addition, systemic psychosexual therapy opens space for the inclusion of notions of truth, facts and scientific evidence. The sexology concept of sexual myths implies that sexual facts, truths, and misinterpretations exist (Zilbergeld 1992; Weeks & Gambescia 2000). Widely held sexual myths such as, that "proper sex" necessitates genital intercourse, or that vaginal as opposed to clitoral orgasm is the mature response, have oppressed many clients who then come to therapy to cure their so-called inadequacies.

A lively and well educated woman in her 30s came to my practice crushed by her boyfriend's comment that her "clitoris was too small". I explained, using drawings to reinforce the message of truth and certainty, that the clitoris typically appears as very small on the outside whilst being connected to a vast number of nerve endings. She came back letting me know that the book I recommended The Clitoral Truth (Chalker, 2000) had usefully expanded her insights. There was no need for continuing therapy, as she felt sufficiently supported and empowered by these educational interventions which enlightened her understanding of current scientific facts.

I recall a mature, attractive woman whispering to me: "My husband and I never had proper sex". By this she meant they never had simultaneous orgasm, and so she faked orgasms not wanting to disappoint him. In dispelling this misconception, I explained that not only can this be difficult to achieve but it is not necessarily a measure of a well-functioning sexual relationship, according to contemporary thinking in the field of sexology. I normalised her situation by sharing my knowledge that the myth of simultaneous orgasm has caused many people to feel sexually abnormal and ashamed. I also empathised with her anxiety tuning into her perspective in the context of socially and culturally restricted conversations about sex which leave people to draw their own conclusions, lacking in confidence to approach the subject and fearful of being judged. Psychosexual therapy is often the first place where sex is openly discussed and reflected upon, notwithstanding clients' gender, sexual orientation, age, culture, religion, education, class or intellectual ability. A highly educated, middle aged, professional, family man hesitated in his first session: "I never talked about sex with anyone, including my wife"! I responded: "I know, people don't talk about it as if there is something wrong with it!"

A case of a male client aged 88 whom I saw with an experienced sexologist at the beginning of my psychosexual training made me aware of my own sexual prejudices. I was surprised that a man of his age would seek help for an erectile problem and was astonished when my colleague conducted a full assessment followed by a course of suggested treatment. From that I learned the fact that erectile ability is not necessarily lost at any age. Indeed he was also active in pursuing his bisexual interests as a single man full of life force, vibrant energy and exuberance. This experience prompted in me the concept of "professional sexual myths" highlighting different scientific and therapeutic discoveries that have been proven over time to be inaccurate and misleading. Schnarch (2000) talks about "first and second generation approach to sexual desire" describing how sexology evolved from seeing desire as a natural, biological drive to appreciating the psychological, relational and cultural aspects, thereby removing the pathological emphasis. These changes are deeply systemic and I propose a third generation, shifting towards socially constructed realities, the Self of the professional and their self-reflexive questioning, as Tomm elegantly puts it: "Listen to your listening, think about your thinking, question your questioning..." (Tomm 1992).

Instructive and exploratory interventions
Whilst believing that instructive interaction (Maturana 1988) has a practical and ethical edge, I also believe that instructions within a collaborative relationship can contribute to therapeutic effectiveness. For example, a widely used sexual therapy technique "sensate focus" (Masters & Johnson 1966; Weiner & Avery-Clark 2014) consists of a series of instructions to clients over a period of time. Instruction and collaboration are combined in that basic parameters are set by the therapist whilst there is scope for clients to use their own imagination and exercise choice within set boundaries.

When working with discrepancy of sexual desire, I often address typical multiple influences including: stress, tiredness, life worries, bereavement, illness, redundancy and so on. Despite conversations mapping out this multifactorial picture, a male gay couple still kept asking the same question, "why did this happen to them?" I drew a diagram summarising the factors referring to our previous sessions. The visual map seemed to amaze them, even though nothing new was presented in terms of content however the new presentation seemed to move them. The clarity and straightforwardness of the map apparently impacted on them more strongly and significantly than previous conversations. Since then I have been frequently using such maps, to support verbal exchanges, combining elements of instructional guidance with opportunity for reflection. It feels important to temporise the maps by adding a date on the drawing so they become a snapshot rather than a fixed picture of the couple.

Interventive interviewing, (Tomm 1987) through open, exploratory and reflexive questions, a distinctive feature of the systemic approach, has the potential to bring forth self-healing. For example:

> *"If instead of withdrawing or leaving when she got upset you simply sat with her or put your arm around her shoulder, what would she do?"* (Embedded Suggestion)

> *"In most couples after childbirth there is a huge change in their sexual behaviour. Do you think you are coping with this transition better or worse than other couples?"* (Normative Comparison)
>
> *"When she talks about her difficult sexual experiences from the past, do you think she wants to create an excuse for not having sex with you or she wants to feel reassured and understood by you?"* (Distinction Clarifying)

On the other hand, closed linear questions are necessary in obtaining clarification, gathering information or establishing some facts. For example:

> *"Is it OK if I ask you about your sex life?"*
>
> *"How often do you have sex?"*
>
> *"How long after penetration do you ejaculate?"*

As part of engaging clients' active participation, I encourage their questions, sometimes by asking a simple linear question: "Do you have any questions?" and equally importantly, making sure they are answered. Typical anxieties that I have encountered in systemic psychosexual therapy concern the underlying questions about being "normal". I have come to appreciate the importance of both providing straightforward answers and exploring the meaning of normality and the meaning of such concerns.

Shared expertise of both clients and therapists

In sexology, expertise is in the hands of the medical professional who conducts their assessment, diagnosis and treatment according to the vast body of evidence based scientific knowledge (Bancroft 2009). Systemically, the client is the expert (Anderson 2000) and the therapist facilitates clients' self-reflection and their choice of action. In systemic psychosexual therapy I propose, both the clients and the therapist are the experts (Markovic 2010) as may be illustrated by this transcript from a formulation session:

> Therapist: ...we talked about your understanding about the sexual problems you are experiencing, starting with you feeling that it takes you too long to orgasm...

Client:	[nodding]
Therapist:	From my perspective and working experience, this wouldn't be necessarily a problem in itself... Individual times vary; people take longer, shorter... it is not classified as a dysfunction. Problems often arise between people, so, if your partner wasn't thinking "this is too long", maybe you wouldn't... From that point of view it is a relational thing... and how couples negotiate their intimacy. I think that is something that you felt through experiences with your partners, that they were frustrated and felt it was too long.
Client:	My ex-boyfriend used to make me orgasm because he used to persevere then he'd complain about how long it took and criticise me after...
Therapist:	You see that kind of criticism fuels the idea that there is something wrong with you... and then with the next partner you feel that you are not adequate...
Client:	I don't want to keep him that long... My boyfriend now doesn't understand why I never come with sex, as all women do; he mentions it a lot...
Therapist:	So you don't go into the sexual encounter with enthusiasm, looking forward, you're not relaxed which doesn't help your arousal. It actually stops it. Anxiety, worry... these are usual things that affect sexual feelings.
Client:	I do worry that this has ruined my relationships.
Therapist:	However on self-stimulation you are able to reach orgasm.
Client:	I do it better myself.
Therapist	That is very important information for our understanding of what you're experiencing, that you are able to reach orgasm. We know that you have that capacity, and you know how your body works. If the partner was doing what you were doing yourself to keep you aroused... if the criticism, anxiety, were all out of the way... which I suppose when you're on your own, you don't feel...
Client:	...obliged...
Therapist:	...anxious, obliged... there is no worry about the partner, how they are experiencing it, are they frustrated... So you are more relaxed into it, that's what helps you.
Client:	[nodding]

Therapist:	It's slightly more complicated sometimes with women... working out where's the sensitive area... It's very unusual for women to have sexual pleasure and orgasm through penetration only. So I think what needs to happen is clitoral stimulation. We talked about it didn't we...
Client:	Yeah.
Therapist:	And something that particularly gives you pleasure is oral sex isn't it. Something you are particularly sensitive to, particularly able to enjoy, your sensuality is in it...
Client:	Yeah... I can orgasm orally... when we play about but not always with sex.
Therapist:	So, oral sex is not sex?
Client:	[laughing] Don't know why...
Therapist:	It isn't unusual to think that.
Client:	I'd like to think it is...
Therapist:	What would need to happen so you start thinking it is?
Client:	Maybe I can talk to my boyfriend... or better I should talk to my best friend, she may be easier... I never talked with anyone...
Therapist:	That sounds a good idea. Can I make another suggestion?
Client:	[nodding]
Therapist:	I'd like to suggest a few things to you, as a first step at the beginning in a kind of a programme here. Then you see what you can do and come back and tell me. If things didn't quite work out, we can talk about it. Is that OK?

My experience suggests that clients feel best supported when the therapist confidently carries their expertise whilst allowing plentiful space for the clients' voice. I aspire to present my point of view and make sexology knowledge accessible to clients, make suggestions without imposition, lay out treatment options, and offer advice whilst listening to the clients' perspectives with utmost care.

Diagnosis and deconstruction

Systemic approach has critiqued psychiatric diagnoses as degrading and pathologising, in objectifying and reducing the person to a set of symptoms thus jeopardising personal agency (White 2007). Such an oppressive tradition is seen as enforced by the social and political systems based on hierarchy, power and domination (Foucault 1976). An emphasis on diagnosis may close down curiosity thus blocking therapeutic work.

Whilst appreciating these important views, I am aware that diagnoses can be helpful, as they provide a definition of the concern, clarifying the circumstances under which it occurs and the ways in which it manifests itself (Gergen, Hoffman, & Anderson 1996).

I have learned from clients that diagnosis, in addition to its pathologising potential, can also have the opposite, normalising, effect. Not only can it can provide clarity about what is happening, it can also take pressure off the individual by putting the issue into a wider context. For example, on hearing my diagnostic summary of her presenting problems as "vaginismus", one client was relieved and empowered, having previously thought something peculiar to her was happening due to her abnormal response. The diagnosis assured her that this was a phenomenon well known to professionals that has established treatment procedures. Similarly, many clients felt empowered on hearing the phrase "spectatoring" used in sexology to describe the experience of watching oneself during sexual activity in the context of sexual performance anxiety. This is usually accompanied by a worry that something will go wrong which in itself becomes a barrier to sexual functioning. Clients can feel relieved and normalised by the naming of these processes.

Both a diagnosis and systemic exploratory questioning are important in developing a comprehensive picture of clients' experiences, such as:

"Who is most concerned?"

"How is it a problem?"

"What does it mean to you to have this problem?"

"What does it mean to your partner for you to have this problem?"

"How has it impacted on your life?"

It can be empowering to highlight the double edge of diagnosis using systemic questioning to emphasise clients' choice: "Many research studies on large international populations of men have shown high prevalence of erectile dysfunction worldwide. Does this finding more worry you (given how prevalent the problem is) or more reassure you (given it is so common)?" Sharing such diagnostic findings (Hackett et al 2007) can support clients' feeling of belonging to a large community of similar functioning people rather than being in an isolated minority, outside the healthy population of "perfect performers" (Zilbergeld 1999).

SYSTEMIC APPROACH

Qualitative research
Emotional, cognitive, behavioural, relational, cultural dimensions
Neutrality, curiosity and irreverence
Circular and reflexive positioning
Socially constructed realities
Exploratory interventions
The client is the expert
Deconstruction

SYSTEMIC PSYCHOSEXUAL THERAPY

Qualitative and quantitative research
Emotional, cognitive, behavioural, relational, cultural and physical dimensions
Neutrality and normative judgements
Linear, circular and reflexive positions
Socially constructed truth and facts
Exploratory and instructive interventions
Both the client and the therapist are the experts
Diagnosis and deconstruction

SEXOLOGY

Quantitative research
Physical and medical dimensions
Normative judgements
Linear causality
Truth, facts, scientific evidence
Instructive interventions, direct, educational input
The professional is the expert
The relevance of diagnostic categories

Concluding reflection

Different perspectives and concepts from sexology and the systemic approach were reviewed and reflected on in terms of their usefulness when applied synergistically. "Both/and" was a guiding principle in this integration demonstrating how these different disciplines, typically operating separately, could be applied when combined, each enriching the other, as illustrated by the diagram above.

Each of these approaches is complex and it is not necessary for psychotherapists to have extensive expertise in sexology in order to usefully incorporate sexual issues within their clinical practice. This chapter has hopefully illustrated the possibilities of integrating the systemic approach with knowledge from sexology. In my opinion such integration could also be relevant to other therapeutic approaches. Psychotherapists of various different orientations typically do not feel "experts" with sexual issues and thus do not address sexual topics leaving it to specialist services. I sympathise with this practice and in the past have resorted to such separation of sex from the rest of the human experience myself.

Yet, in qualifying as a psychosexual therapist, I have come to believe even more strongly in the potential of the systemic approach to contribute in this area. Psychotherapy training programmes could provide specific knowledge on sexual functioning, dysfunctions, and the range of effective treatments available, enhancing therapists' expertise not in becoming psychosexual therapists treating sexual dysfunctions but in working more comprehensively with sexual issues. However individual practitioners can also make a sea change in expanding their practice into this area by proactively taking small steps, such as: applying their existing knowledge and skills to sex and sexual relationships, and expanding their insights through reading and attending professional events. In so doing, it is possible to broaden psychotherapy practice through opening up a discourse on sex thereby gaining the necessary knowledge to address various sexual issues but also to be sufficiently informed as to when to make an appropriate referral to specialist services. My hope is that implementation of these ideas would constitute a significant move in the direction of shifting beliefs and practices with respect to inclusion of sexual issues within the field of psychotherapy to the benefit of our clients.

References

Anderson, Harlene (2000). Becoming a Postmodern Collaborative Therapist: A clinical and theoretical journey. *Journal of the Texas Association for Marriage and Family Therapy*, 5(1) 5–12.

Attwood, Joan, D, & Weinstein, Estelle (1989). The Integration of Sex Therapy Techniques with Marital and Family Therapy. *Australian and New Zealand Journal for Family Therapy*. 10(3), 161–168.

Bancroft, John (2009). *Human Sexuality and its Problems*, 3rd ed. London : Churchill Livingstone.

Basson, Rosemary (2000). The Female Sexual Response: A Different Model. *Journal of Sex & Marital Therapy*, 26(1), 51–65.

Burr, Vivien (2003). *Social Constructionism*. 2nd ed. Hove. New York: Routledge.

Cecchin, Gianfranco (1987). Hypothesising, Circularity and Neutrality Revisited: An invitation to curiosity. *Family Process*, 26(4), 405–14.

Cecchin, Gianfranco; Lane, Gerry & Ray, Wendel (Eds.) (1992). *Irreverence: A Strategy for Therapists' Survival*. London: Karnac Books.

Chalker, Rebecca (2000). *The Clitoral Truth: The World at Your Fingertips*. New York: Seven Stories Press.

Cornwell, Max (1989). 'Falling in Love with Ideas', an interview with Luigi Boscolo. *Australian and New Zealand Journal of Family Therapy*, 10(2), 97–103.

Foucault, Michel (1976). *The History of Sexuality: The Will to Knowledge*. Volume 1: An Introduction. London: Allen Lane.

Gergen, Kenneth J.; Hoffman, Lynn & Anderson, Harlene (1996). Is Diagnosis a Disaster? A Constructionist Trialogue. In Florence W. Kaslow (Ed.), *Handbook of Relational Diagnosis and Dysfunctional Family Patterns* (102–118). Oxford: John Wiley.

Hackett, Geoff; Dean, John; Kell, Phil; Price, David; Ralph, David; Speakman, Mark & Wylie, Kevan (2007). *Guidelines on the Management of Erectile Dysfunction*. British Society for Sexual Medicine.

Hare-Mustin, Rachel T. (1994). Discourses in the Mirrored Room: A postmodern analysis of therapy. *Family Process,* 33, 19–35.

Iasenza, Suzanne (2004). Multicontextual Sex Therapy with Lesbian Couples. In Shelley Green, Douglas Flemons (Eds.) *Quickies. The Handbook of Brief Sex Therapy*. New York: W.W.Norton.

Iasenza, Suzanne (2010). What is Queer About Sex? Expanding Sexual Frames in Theory and Practice. *Family Process*, 49: 291–308.

Markovic, Desa (2007). Working with Sexual Issues in Systemic Therapy. *Australian and New Zealand Journal of Family Therapy*, 28(4), 200–209.

Markovic, Desa (2010). A Case of Enhancing Sexual Confidence; Both the Client and the Therapist are the Experts. *Australian and New Zealand Journal of Family Therapy*, 31(1) 13–24.

Markovic, Desa (2011). *A Model of Integration Between Systemic and Psychosexual Therapy*. North American Society for Psychotherapy Research, Canada, paper presentation.

Markovic, Desa (2013). Multidimensional Sex Therapy: A Model of Integration between Sexology and Systemic Therapy. *Sexual and Relationship Therapy*, 28(4), 311–323.

Masters, William H. & Johnson, Virginia E. (1966). *Human Sexual Response*. Boston: Little, Brown.

Maturana, Humberto R. (1988). The Search for Objectivity of the Quest for Compelling Argument. *The Irish Journal of Psychology*, 9(1), 25–82.

Pearce, W. Barnett (2007). *Making Social Worlds: A Communicational Perspective*. London: Blackwell Publishing.

Radovanovic (now Markovic), Desa (1994). Prisoners of Identity: Interview with Dr Gianfranco Cecchin. *Human Systems, The Journal of Systemic Consultation & Management*, 4, 3–18.

Selvini-Palazzoli, Mara; Boscolo, Luigi; Cecchin, Gianfranco & Prata, Giuliana (1980). Hypothesising–Circularity–Neutrality: Three Guidelines for the Conductor of the Session. *Family Process*, 19(1), 3–12.

Schnarch, David (2000). Desire Problems: A systemic perspective. Chapter 2. In: Sandra Leiblum, & Raymond C. Rosen (Eds.), *Principles and Practice of Sex Therapy*, 3rd ed. (17–56). New York: The Guilford Press.

Tiefer, Leonore (2004). *Sex is Not a Natural Act and Other Essays*. 2nd ed. Boulder, Colorado: Westview Press.

Tomm, Karl (1987). Interventive Interviewing: Part II. Questioning as a Means to Enable Self-Healing. *Family Process*, 26(2), 167–183.

Tomm, Karl (1992). *Ethical Postures in Therapy*. KCC London workshop.

Weeks, Gerald & Gambescia, Nancy (2000). *Erectile Dysfunction: Integrating Couple Therapy, Sex Therapy, and Medical Treatment*. W.W.Norton. New York. London.

Weeks, Gerald & Gambescia, Nancy (2002). *Hypoactive Sexual Desire. Integrating Sex and Couple Therapy*. W.W.Norton. New York. London.

Weiner, Linda, & Avery-Clark, Constance (2014). Sensate Focus: Clarifying the Masters and Johnson's model. *Sexual and Relationship Therapy*, 29(3), 307–319.

White, Michael (2007). *Maps of Narrative Practice*. W. W. Norton & Company: New York.

World Association of Sexual Health (WAS) (2014). *Declaration of Sexual Rights*.

Wylie, Kevan R., DeColomby, Pierre, & Giami, Alain (2004). Sexology as a Profession in United Kingdom. *International Journal of Clinical Practice*, 58(8), 764–768.

Zilbergeld, Bernie (1999). *The New Male Sexuality*. Revised edition. New York, Toronto, London, Sydney, Auckland: Bantam Books.

26
When You Say, "It's not Sickness, it's Love" there will be a Powerful Change of Context

Mia Andersson

With this chapter I invite the reader to follow me in an essay on the Milan affiliate Gianfranco Cecchin's contribution to systemic praxis during a time of shifting stages in the development of systemic thinking. Gianfranco Cecchin and Luigi Boscolo, his partner at Il Centro Milanese di Terapia della Famiglia, identify this development as being, *"from the first cybernetics through second cybernetics to the profession's present concern with the nature of the observer and self-reflexivity"* (Campbell & Draper 1991, p.ix). This identification of various cybernetic stages matters for the therapist's perspective and arrangement of the therapeutic context; in first order cybernetics, the focus is on the client system, whereas in the later orders, the involvement of the observer in the situation and the nature of the observer are included in the observation. From now on Cecchin makes a vital distinction between "seeing *the system*" and "to *see* systemically".

Cecchin devoted himself to refine the arrangement of the therapeutic context with attention to the concepts of "contingency of interaction" (Maturana 1985) and "coincidental correspondence" (Gadamer 2003, p.50); what emerges is due to the interaction, not to any party's ambition or ends. Although the new is brought forth by the communication, the perspectives of both parties matter, as they come into play in the process. Eventually Cecchin would claim, "Therapy occurs in the interplay of the prejudices of therapist and client – a cybernetics of prejudices" (Cecchin et al 1994, p.8).

Due to this understanding of the therapeutic process, Cecchin did not really think interventions would worsen the situation – since people don´t do what we tell them anyway. However the tendency of clients to marry their diagnoses was a concern that made him commit himself to the development of a non-pathologising perspective and language. That way he could keep an active stance as a therapist through the turbulence of shifting stages. The title of this essay is inspired by an interview with Cecchin, a passage of which is quoted below (Campbell & Draper 1985). There he tells some imaginary therapists that if they say to a client "It's not sickness, it's *love* ..." then there will be a powerful *change of context*. The passage conveys Cecchin's awareness both of the tyranny of language (Abrahamsson 2000, p.24) and of the need for a change of *context* – not people.

After an introduction in this chapter on the therapist's perspective, three further sections follow. The first is based on Cecchin's publications from 1985, where his voice is for the first time distinguishable from the voice of the Milan team through to the last book he wrote with Garry Lane and Wendel Ray in 1994. The second section is based on three interviews from the end of the twentieth century. Both sections are illustrated with examples from my own praxis. The last section, in search for what's next, discusses some late comments that reflect Cecchin's non-pathologising perspective and language.

The perspective matters

Sometimes we cannot change the context because it is too powerful. It is at a higher level: cultural, political, institutional, and you as a therapist have no influence. The context is fixed by a lower level with implicative force which reinforces the first level, but there is the possibility that the implicative force can become so powerful that it changes the higher context. There is this duality. You as a therapist can do something about this movement. When you say, "It's not sickness, it is love, probably you shouldn't come here because we are therapists, but as long as you continue to believe it's a sickness you should continue to come", that introduces a powerful change of context.

(Campbell & Draper 1985, p.283)

I have called this essay, "*When you say it's not sickness it's love, there will be a powerful change of context*" in order to highlight the importance of the therapist's perspective and language. Cecchin's use of context in this interview I understand as synonymous to systemic premises or belief systems. The same year as the book with that interview was published, systems theorist Humberto Maturana presented his epistemology at a seminar week in Oxford (Maturana 1985). He said, "*Whenever people suffer, something has got in the way of love*" and "*We will perturb people differently if we operate from the domain of love*". These statements are utterly important in my work with severe eating disorders (Andersson 1995, p.9). From this point in time I have steered away from the construction of anorexia as sickness and invite clients to explore how their self-starvation is connected to the dimension of love.

Cecchin also refers to Maturana. He states that we perturb a system differently from a systemic-relational perspective – with its focus on anthropologist Gregory Bateson's patterns that connect – than we do if we approach it from lineal-causal explanations which, according to Bateson, "*have the effect of terminating dialogue and conversation*" (Cecchin 1987, p.406). In his struggle for an ethical and aesthetical orientation within therapy, where the therapist is active yet not imposing his own bias on the client, Cecchin suggested that we look for how what people do is right and in which context it makes sense.

Already during my training in Milan in the early 1980s I was struck by Boscolo and Cecchin's awareness of the power of mental constructs. Especially three aspects of their teaching are crucial for this essay. Firstly, they warned to *never marry your hypotheses*. Later, Cecchin would stress that we, as therapists, are responsible for what we believe because it has consequences. This awareness lies behind concepts such as aesthetic curiosity, systemic irreverence and cybernetics of prejudices. The second aspect I learned from my training in Milan in 1981 was *clients marry their diagnoses*. In the end, Cecchin completely lost confidence in diagnoses and began to see them as nothing more than classifications in the head of the therapist just to orientate themselves (Soderlund 1998, p.1). As we shall see, Cecchin continued to elaborate on a non-pathologising alternative – to talk with people about eccentricity as a choice that is understandable (Abrahamsson 2000, p.24). The third aspect of importance of the Milan School for this essay was the saying, *it is easier to let go of a friend than of an enemy*. This is close to the concept of positive connotation, probably the most powerful invention by the original Milan team (Selvini Palazzoli et al. 1978, p.55-66). It has the power to open up, because it only adds an aspect to whatever has been denoted "bad, mad or sick" without demanding a complete reformulation or quest for change, and so its positive message can deconstruct underlying premises that block evolution.

Cecchin's publications from 1985–1994

Although Cecchin's work has its roots in the Milan research team and their therapy based on Bateson's cybernetics, I have chosen to take my starting point in the introductory quotation by Cecchin published in 1985. He set out to elaborate on Bateson's cybernetics of self; on how systemic premises emerge from ongoing interactions within a system (Bateson 1972, pp.280-308). Premises can be most powerful in people's constructions of self and self-in-relation. Cecchin, who strongly believed that the wish to be right – especially right-in-relation – is a guiding force in what people do, realised that those who come to therapy have constructed themselves as wrong, wrong-in-relation. Furthermore, according to Bateson, some systemic premises have the power to block evolution. This is consistent with another of Cecchin's observations; people come to therapy for they are stuck because of some systemic premises.

The shift to second order cybernetics within the field took off with the work of Humberta Maturana and Francisco Varela. When Maturana presented his epistemology in Oxford in 1985, he upset his audience with his sayings, "*Instructive intervention is impossible*" and "*It is the client system that decides what it accepts as an enticement for change*". In the event that people do what therapists tell them to do, it is because people will pick interventions that already fit the system (the "fit theory") and not because we tell them to do so. Ideas that prove to be useful for the clients emerge from the contingency of interaction, not from any particular intervention or ambition of the therapist.

Cecchin's comment on the shift to second order cybernetics can be read in *Milan Systemic Family Therapy*, "*The paradise of the first order cybernetics is gone*" (Boscolo et al 1987, p.18). The therapist now has to examine the effect of what Maturana formulated, "*How you are involved in a conversation that changes relations.*" The Oxford week is echoing in Cecchin's reflections on the need for increased awareness of the presence and activity of the therapist/observer; what we do may lead to improvement or deterioration, especially to improved or deteriorated relations.

Some years earlier the original Milan team had published their famous paper on three guidelines for the conductor of the session, "Hypothesizing, Circularity, Neutrality" (Selvini Palazzoli et al 1980). However, as a consequence of the epistemological shift, the concept of neutrality was attacked. In a revisited version with the subtitle, "An Invitation to Curiosity", Cecchin replies, "*In order to avoid the trap of oversimplifying the idea of neutrality, I propose that we describe neutrality as the creation of a state of curiosity in the mind of a therapist*" (Cecchin 1987, p.405). He claims that there is a need for an aesthetic frame within which curiosity may be enhanced (Cecchin 1987, p.408). With reference to the Oxford week he continues, "*Specifically, drawing on the work of*

Maturana, the kind of curiosity produced from a lineal-causal frame incorporates the notion of 'instructive interaction'; curiosity within an aesthetic frame does not", and, "An aesthetic science ..., with a focus on curiosity, 'gives up' the attempt to direct people" (Cecchin 1987, p.409). Aesthetic curiosity in therapy is best understood from the following description, "*When we are curious about the patterns or relationships of ideas, people, events, and behaviours, we perturb the system with which we are interacting in ways that are different from perturbations based on our attempts to discover a correct description/explanation (that is, causal connections)*" (Cecchin 1987, p.409).

In *Irreverence*, Cecchin, Lane and Ray set out to explore their ideas in the postmodern era, where there was no longer just one explanation to things, and all sorts of models appeared within the field of therapy. The book connects to Cecchin's work on aesthetic curiosity, but most interesting I find the authors' description of how they suffered from doubts about which route to choose in the epistemological turbulence – a non-intervention or an active one (Cecchin et al. 1992, p.52). Eventually they had enough of doubts and decided to become irreverent to all models. This choice is in line with philosopher Hans Georg Gadamer's work on coincidental correspondence; the therapeutic conversation is like any normal conversation where people engage without ends, and where new ideas emerge in the very process.

Their next book, *The Cybernetics of Prejudice*, takes its starting point in second order cybernetics; the behaviour of all parties involved in a process is being shaped by that very process, and "*the meaning of any behaviour is found within the context of the subsequent behaviour it evokes*" (Cecchin et al 1994, p.8). Again they work in line with Gadamer, this time with his dialogic hermeneutics; how people receive something new is determined by established structures or, with Gadamer's term, prejudices. Cecchin, Lane and Ray work with the concept of prejudice more or less synonymously with Bateson's premises, especially when they look into the therapists' reluctance to take in what does not correspond with their belief system. Now the authors return to their doubts with a completely different attitude; as therapists they can "afford the *luxury* of doubt more easily than the family" (Cecchin et. al 1994, p.24). I can still hear Cecchin saying "*we are the ones who can afford not to be in the right*". This freedom to give up their hypotheses is supported by Gadamer's definition of prejudices as "*simply conditions whereby we experience something – whereby what we encounter says something to us.*" (Cecchin et al 1994, pp.7-8).

The concept cybernetics of prejudices has to do with networks of ideas involved in the situation. Therapy happens when the prejudices of the therapist and those of the family interact. In fact it is *"the relationship between the prejudices of the client and the therapist that is the heart of therapy"* (Cecchin et al 1994, p.17). However *"when prejudices become interlocked in a mutually reinforcing way, nothing can change"* (Cecchin et al 1994, p.39). Usually we do not realise how our prejudices blind us. Maturana expressed this, *"We are not aware that we are not aware"* and Cecchin claimed that when we think that the clients are stuck *we* are the ones who are stuck. Finally the authors arrived at a *"post-ideological orientation in therapy ... **based on the luxury of doubt"*** (Cecchin et al 1994, p.27, emphasis mine). They also offer a definition of this orientation, *"When one is able to deconstruct one's own mythologies of change, therapy and influence, then one is free to engage in a lively, ironic and irreverent improvisational interaction. **This is the essence of a post-ideological orientation in therapy**.*" (Cecchin et al 1994, p.33; my emphasis).

An example
The story of Maria, diagnosed with anorexia, is a good example of someone who had married her diagnosis. After several years in and out of the hospital Maria had lost confidence in the methods of the clinic. Nevertheless the medical explanations had an authority for her; Maria had learned that anorexia is a sickness and that in order to get well she would have to fight the agony connected to eating. Since she could not eat sufficiently, she believed she would have to live with this sickness for the rest of her life.

Maria's parents spoke of her as loving and highly sensitive to other people's needs, devoted to make everyone happy. Yet, in the recursive interaction with the world, this empathic young woman had judged herself as insufficient in various relationships, and thus constructed herself as wrong-in-relation. My hypothesis was that Maria's self-starvation protected her from an inner chaos due to the contradiction between her negative self-image and the positive image other people presented. Perhaps Maria had perceived previous treatments as a threat to the illusionary safety anorexia provides. If so, this could be a reason for her not cooperating in previous programmes.

In the beginning of her therapy with me Maria would cling to the idea that her condition was a sickness and that she was a hopeless case because, with Cecchin's words, the context at a higher level was impossible for her to contradict. Therefore I decided to try what he suggests – do something that would introduce some change of context. I set out to explore Maria's belief system, especially her experienced insufficiency in relations. Through my curiosity of her relational reality, there was a shift from "sickness" to "love". Eventually the connection between Maria's self-starvation and her need to always be right-in-relation began to emerge.

The idea that Maria might be able to get out of her prison first hit her mother. In line with Bateson's notion that paradoxes dissolve with time, Cecchin held that we can never know when, how or where change will happen – only *that* it will happen. A change can start in any part of the system and spread from there. In Maria's case, change started with the mother who, without at first being aware of it, had got the message: if anorexia is an existential choice, then it must be possible also to let go of it. Again I recalled the voice from my Milan training, "*It´s easier to let go of a friend than of an enemy*". Often when this kind of insight happens, it is followed by a sudden exhaustion. This is what happened in the case of Maria's mother. She told her daughter about her exhaustion and that Maria must hold on to their agreement or take responsibility for her own life and leave home.

In the following session when the mother recounted this episode, I asked her if, in that moment, she saw Maria's anorexia as an illness. "No" the mother answered, "*I had taken on the new perspective – and must have felt that **she** had actually come to the point where it would be possible for her to hold on to our agreement*", and she smiled, "*otherwise I would **never** say so*". "I bet not," I replied, "*Mothers don't fail a sick child!*" Maria later told me that, in the moment it happened, she had noticed a completely new state of mind in her mother. That made her feel really safe and the anorexic voice in her head miraculously shut up. She was free to eat and commented, "*At the time I couldn't imagine that this would ever happen!*" The security Maria had found in her anorexia was now replaced by the security in her relation to her mother.

During our evaluation, Maria's mother said that it was difficult to tell other people what had been helpful. For her the sessions had just been like *normal conversations* – exactly the expression Gadamer uses about therapy. The father told me that he had expected to get both tools and homework, but that it had not been necessary. Now they could see Maria's self-starvation as possibly her only way to some self-acceptance when her negative self-image had got in the way of love, of her understanding of herself as the loving person she really is.

Cecchin and some interviews published 1998–2000

> *People lock themselves in. They build their own prisons through premises. It is very difficult to get into them. New information is taken up and transformed to fit in to the known pattern. It makes the premises stronger. The prison is strengthened. If you try to get in you are cast out. If you don´t try to get in then nothing happens. What you can do is to be engaged. In this way people can be as they are. Intense realities emerge from intense relationships. They become engaged in their own reality and can find their own ways out of the situation. Nothing new needs to be added.*
> (Cecchin 1999, Video: *A Bopper in Training and Therapy*)

This quotation is a transcript from a video where Cecchin gave his systemic view on therapy. It is a wonderful example of his way to handle a therapeutic paradox, when people come to therapy because they are stuck, but every attempt to get them unstuck seems futile due to hermeneutic loops; anything new is perceived as a threat to established premises and as a consequence the premises become even stronger. If something new is taken in anyway, it is immediately transformed to fit established patterns. I believe this is why Cecchin talked so passionately about therapy as the arrangement of a context that only subtly conveys that change is possible.

When prejudices become interlocked in a mutually reinforcing way, it is not only pointless, it is even counterproductive, to come up with proposals for change. On the other hand, as Cecchin puts it, *if you don't try to get in, then nothing happens*. Here, like in the first quotation, Cecchin is keen to convey that we *can do something*. We can engage in the reality of the other. This message is furthermore reinforced by the addition, *intense realities emerge from intense relationships*. One aspect of intense relationships that Cecchin stresses, is that the therapist can be of strong opinions. In a late interview for *New Therapist*, "Prejudiced about Prejudices", he even focuses on the inevitability of opinions, *"You always have some opinions about what is going on and your opinions are going to have an influence."* (Soderlund 1998, p.1). This awareness made Cecchin recommend therapists to make constructive use of their prejudices – put them on the table and try them out but discard them as soon as they prove not to be useful in the clinical situation.

As we have seen, Cecchin concluded that we are the ones who are stuck when we think that the clients are stuck. It is in such cases we need the luxury of doubt, so that we can discard our hypotheses, preferences and other prejudices. Cecchin, Lane and Ray worked with our accountability or readiness to take responsibility for what we believe and how we arrange the therapeutic context, "*If you are not first willing to become aware of your own prejudices and how they come into play in relation to your clients, you will inadvertently set into motion an escalating process in which the very thing you hope to reform grows worse the more you try to change it*" (Cecchin et al 1994, p.42). However, if we engage ourselves with aesthetic curiosity, the clients may get engaged and curious too. Or, as Maturana says, "*to help the other reflect is, in the long run, the only thing you can do*" (Maturana quoted in Andersson 1990, p.29).

In another late interview, Cecchin told the Swedish psychiatrist Erik Abrahamsson that he was working on a new concept – eccentricity, "*I want to define the deviant as eccentric, people who choose a deviant way of life. To talk with people about deviances is what we do all the time – can we have **a different type of conversation, not to use the language of pathology and isolation**, but the language of eccentricity, to talk about eccentric behaviour: you are an unusual person, you have your own style*" (Abrahamsson 2000 p.24; my translation and emphasis).

An example
In an evaluation of her therapy a young woman, Eva, confirms Cecchin's later ideas such as the engagement in the client's reality as an option in stuck situations, the potential value of the therapists own prejudices if we evaluate them in the actual situation, and the possibility to avoid the language of pathology and isolation when we talk with people about their behaviour as, although somewhat eccentric, an act that makes perfect sense in its logical-relational context.

Eva was so thin at the age of fifteen that her doctor in the clinic feared she might die. As Eva resisted all forms of treatment the situation was most critical. In that situation the social worker involved referred her to me and she accepted family therapy in combination with medical care from her GP. Soon Eva also developed intense bulimic binges and severe self-harm. Her negative self-image was constantly reinforced due to her hermeneutic hell; recursive loops of perceived failure dominated her interaction with the world. In the therapy most of the messages from me were transformed in the same manner, as Eva could hear only what fitted her negative structures.

My only chance was to engage in Eva's reality in the hope that she would also get engaged in exploring it. I was curious to know how she connected her symptoms to other aspects of her life. This was crucial for she got really curious too. Eventually I could juxtapose her negativity with my impression of her as a colourful girl, who behaved in somewhat eccentric ways, but who had got herself all wrong. Eva first rejected my perspective but was eventually challenged by the contradictory images. That freed her to explore and accept herself as, what I call, "positively different, or deviant".

Eva's evaluation can be summarised in a few distinct points:

- *You tuned down the sickness and focused on me.* Nothing was more important for Eva's process than the tuning down of the "sickness". Slowly she could see how her symptoms were connected to other crucial aspects of her life and, therefore, understandable.
- *You said that I had completely misunderstood something vital about myself – and that made all the difference.* To Eva, my engagement to get to her centre, led to a growing sense of her personal value. Bit by bit, she engaged in a conversation on how she had mistaken her negative self-image for who she really was.
- *You said tough things – and I needed that.* Here Eva refers to the many occasions when I challenged her negative premises about herself and her potential and especially about her eating disorder as a condition she would never get out of.
- *You were so damn sure – and that meant a lot.* I am especially happy for this point in Eva's evaluation. It highlights how we are responsible for what we believe. Most likely my faith in Eva's potential to find her ways out of her prison of premises made the difference between further deterioration and improvement in her case.
- *All of Eva was allowed to come out.* Eva especially appreciated my invitation to see herself as a sensitive and relational human being who tried her best to feel safe, or secure. The existential-systemic perspective helped her liberate herself from her eating disorder. Now she could explore her potentials and become who she really was.

Interestingly Eva did not mention my work with the family system. I think that my systemic perspective – that I was *seeing* systemically –

was more important for her understanding than my focus on the family. Also I believe it was important that I never pushed for change, just arranged a context that subtly conveyed that change is possible.

What's next? – increased use of a non-pathologising perspective and language

Cecchin, who was always alert to the risk that therapists inadvertently might contribute to a situation where clients marry the diagnoses, continued to counteract our tendency to marry our hypotheses. As we have seen the non-pathologising perspective was a concern for him already in 1985. His awareness of how hypotheses, preferences, prejudices – and especially our preoccupation with diagnoses and sickness – becomes part of the therapeutic context is well expressed in a late interview, "*Even the way we* **look** *at something, influences it*" (Soderlund 1998, p.2; my emphasis).

Not only the non-pathologising perspective but also a non-pathologising language is an issue of increasing importance in Cecchin's later thinking. In his interview with Abrahamsson, he suggests that we talk with our clients about their choice of lifestyle instead of using the language of pathology, "*The systemic thinking offers a solution; the positive connotation of the acceptance of the responsibility to become crazy gives a certain dignity to the deviancy: they [the clients] behave strange but not sick or incompetent. It is a choice.* **To become anorectic is a choice**. *When you talk with clients and say that they have made a choice that is understandable, they agree with you*" (Abrahamsson 2000, p.24; my translation and emphasis).

These late interviews, as well as the video interview from 1999, show how central the idea of arranging a powerful change of context, or premises, was in Cecchin's thinking. The postmodern era offered him a possibility to play with various levels of abstractions instead of accepting fix descriptions of the various states where people get stuck. Up to this point in time Cecchin had stressed that such states are temporary and will eventually be gone. Now he found a new freedom to challenge all sorts of mythologies about influence and change. He and his co-authors arrived at the post-ideological orientation in therapy, where people engage in an improvisational interaction where nothing new needs to be added. Instead it is in the very interaction, through conversation, that new ideas are brought forth, ideas that neither therapists nor family members would come up with on their own.

Despite these insights and despite the deterioration and even pathology that our involvement might inadvertently entail, Cecchin stressed an active stance as a therapist. The key words however are engagement and aesthetic curiosity, not intervention and change. Here I need to repeat a favourite quotation, "*An aesthetic science ... with a focus on curiosity 'gives up' the attempt to direct people*" (Cecchin 1987, p.408). Even in a situation when prejudices of the family and prejudices of the therapist interlock it is possible to get out of the deadlock – if only we are willing to deconstruct our mythologies of influence and change and realise that we are the ones who can afford not to be in the right.

In this chapter, I have explored a few themes of special importance in my work with severe eating disorders: the non-pathologising perspective, a post-ideological orientation in therapy (Cecchin et al 1994, pp.27–33) and the therapist's aesthetic and active engagement in the client´s reality. With my examples I have shown how these themes can make a difference in seemingly hopeless situations. When Maria's mother took on the non-pathologising perspective, the anorexia in Maria's head was miraculously gone. When the parents talked about therapy as a normal conversation "without tools and homework", it is in line with Maturana's and Gadamer's work; the new is brought forth in the conversation. Also in Eva's process, the tuning down of the sickness was crucial. Her eating disorder was no longer mystifying; it was no longer a condition that had struck her for no reason, a condition from which she would recover only if she accepted the nutrition programme in the clinic. Apparently, it was the challenging of the sickness as well as my engagement in Eva's reality, my frankness and my faith in a positive outcome that made a difference to her.

Both the transformation of Maria's mind set and Eva's insightful evaluation of her therapy can be seen as confirmations that the therapist's perspective and engagement is what really matters. I do think that their examples support my strong belief that, with the introduction of an alternative to a fix description or sickness, the actual state can be experienced more as a quest or tendency in the domain of love than a definitive state. My hope for the future is that more case examples will give further evidence that a non-pathologising perspective and language and a post-ideological orientation in combination with an active stance can bring about a change of context powerful enough for people to find their own ways out.

References

Abrahamsson, Erik (2000). *Till tals med Gianfranco Cecchin.* Svensk Familjeterapi, 2, 20–24.

Andersson, Mia (1990). *Hur ser du på terapeutens arbete Humberto? Interview with H. Maturana.* Svensk Familjeterapi, 1, 28–34.

Andersson, Mia (1995). Mother–Daughter Connection: The healing force in the treatment of eating disorders. *Journal of Feminist Family Therapy,* 6(4) 3–19.

Bateson, Gregory (1972). *Steps to an Ecology of Mind: Collected Essays in Anthropology, Psychiatry, Evolution, and Epistemology.* New York: Dutton.

Boscolo, Luigi; Cecchin, Gianfranco; Hoffman, Lynn & Penn, Peggy (1987). *Milan Systemic Family Therapy.* New York: Basic Books.

Campbell, David & Draper, Ros (Eds.) (1985). *Applications of Systemic Therapy: The Milan Method.* New York: Grune & Stratton.

Campbell, David & Draper, Ros (Eds.) (1991). *New Systemic Ideas from the Italian Mental Health Movement.* London: Karnac Books.

Cecchin, Gianfranco (1987). Hypothesizing, Circularity, and Neutrality Revisited: An invitation to curiosity. *Family Process,* 26, 405–413.

Cecchin, Gianfranco; Lane Gerry & Ray, Wendel (1992). *Irreverence: A Strategy for Therapists' Survival.* London: Karnac Books.

Cecchin, Gianfranco; Lane, Gerry & Ray, Wendel (1994). *The Cybernetics of Prejudices in the Practice of Psychotherapy.* London: Karnac Books.

Cecchin, Gianfranco (1999). Gianfranco Cecchin. "A Bopper in Training and Therapy." Presented at *Gianfranco Cecchin's Eyes – 10 Years After.* Il Centro Milanese di Terapia della Famiglia 04-1-2014.

Gadamer, Hans Georg (2003). *Den Gåtfulla Hälsan: Essäer och Föredrag.* Ludvika: Dualis Original presentation: Über die Verborgenheit des Gesundheit. Milan International Summer School, Montisola 1981.

Maturana, Humberto (1985). *Epistemology: How Do We Know and What Is to Know.* Oxford Conversations. Kensington Consultation Centre, London.

Selvini Palazzoli, Mara; Boscolo, Luigi; Cecchin, Gianfranco & Prata, Giuliana (1978). *Paradox and Counterparadox.* New York: Jason Aronson.

Selvini Palazzoli, Mara; Boscolo, Luigi; Cecchin, Gianfranco & Prata, Giuliana (1980). Hypothesizing, circularity, and neutrality: three guidelines for the conductor of the session. *Family Process,* 19, 73–85.

Soderlund, John (1998). Prejudiced About Prejudice: An interview with Gianfranco Cecchin. *New Therapist* 30.

Notes on Contributors

Georgios Abakoumkin

I am an Assistant Professor of Social Psychology at the Department of Early Childhood Education, University of Thessaly, Greece. I have graduated in psychology from the University of Tübingen, Germany, and was awarded a Ph.D. degree in Social Psychology from the Panteion University, Greece. My research interests include social cognition issues (e.g., preference and choice), intragroup processes (e.g., group performance) and interpersonal relations (e.g., social relations and health).

Taiwo Afuape

Being an African working class woman is central to my work as a Lead Clinical Psychologist and Systemic Psychotherapist for the Tavistock and Portman NHS Foundation Trust in South Camden Community Child and Adolescent Mental Health Service (CAMHS) and for Central and North West London NHS Foundation trust in a Psychology/ Psychotherapy Adult Mental Health Department. Previously I have set up community psychology services for transitional populations – women escaping domestic violence, homeless people, people misusing substances, travelling communities of Roma and Irish heritage and refugee people – and worked for 7 years in a Human Rights charity for survivors of torture. I have also managed an adult mental health Systemic Service. In addition, I have written a book entitled *Power, Resistance and Liberation in Therapy with Survivors of Trauma*, as well as co-edited 2 books, one about Liberation Practices and the other about a responsive approach to working in an Urban CAMHS.

Notes on Contributors

Mia Andersson

I work as a psychologist and psychotherapist and I trained at Il Centro Milanese di Terapia della Famiglia in the early 1980s and was from early on part of the Milan network. For the last three decades I have been running my own systemic centre for eating disorders in Stockholm, and have finished a work on my experience of "Anorexia therapy" at the University College of Sodertorn, a centre for practical knowledge, where I am now in the process of writing my masters thesis. I have presented at various international family therapy congresses over the decades and published on my work with mother-daughter relationships as the healing force in the treatment of eating disorders (*Journal of Feminist Family Therapy*, 1995). My earlier qualitative research in Sweden covered family therapy from the families perspective with cases of eating disorders with the Danderyd Hospital and Knowledge Centre for Eating Disorders. My focus on third order cybernetics and my main thesis, with reference to Gianfranco Cecchin, is that a non-medical perspective on eating disorders introduces a powerful change of context.

Francesca Balestra

I am an Italian postdoctoral researcher in clinical and social psychology. I also work in private practice as a family and couple therapist, and I collaborate in research and training activities at the Bologna Family Therapy Centre. My research is focused on communicative and interactive processes. I developed these interests almost eight years ago, when I started to collaborate with Laura Fruggeri at the University of Parma, Italy. Since then my research has addressed the interpersonal and communicative processes of co-construction that take place between therapist and clients in psychotherapeutic encounters. In conducting these investigations I embrace constructionist and dialogical approaches, and I adopt integrative and transdisciplinary research methods, especially qualitative and observational methods. I believe that process research can enhance therapists' relational competences, fill the gap between manuals and everyday practice, and help clinicians in promoting generative and transformative conversations with their clients.

Nora Bateson

I love complex systems and since most of life is comprised of them, I seem to work in a wide range of places. I am a filmmaker, writer and educator, as well as President of the International Bateson Institute based in Sweden. In every thing I do I try to bring the question "How we can improve our perception of the complexity we live within, so we may improve our interaction with the world?" I do this through my work as an international lecturer, researcher and writer, as well as filmmaking. The fire that drives my work is the aspiration that my work will do some little good toward bringing the fields of biology, cognition, art, anthropology, psychology, and information technology together into a study of the patterns in ecology of living systems. Maybe – if we could see more complexity, (we being humanity), we might be less destructive toward each other and nature. I directed and produced the documentary film, *An Ecology of Mind*, a portrait of my father, Gregory Bateson. As the daughter of an anthropologist and with a degree in Southeast Asian Studies I am no stranger to the delicate and difficult task of cultivating trans-cultural learning. Cross-generational, and cross- cultural communication can be easily misunderstood or stereotyped. I try to widen comprehension of dignity, and bring complexity to notions of identity, respect, and how to broach the existing patterns of polarity between "cultures". Meanwhile, the IBI, integrates the sciences, arts and professional knowledge to create a qualitative inquiry of the integration of life. I have been fortunate to have gathered a impressive team of international thinkers, scientists and artists to generate this innovative form of inquiry, which I call: "Transcontextual Research". Memberships and awards: Board Member: Tallberg Foundation, Fellow of Lindsifarne Foundation, Bateson Idea

Group (BIG), Club of Rome, Great Transition Foundation, Human Potential Foundation, Awards: Sustainable Thompkins Ecology Award, Winner Spokane Film Festival, Winner Santa Cruz Film Festival, Media Ecology Award.

Electra Bethymouti

I work as a psychologist, systemic & solution focused trainer and supervisor, crisis mediator. I was trained in Systemic Solution Focused Therapy in Spain with one of the founders of the field, M. Beyerbach. I later spent some years training and working in the team of J. L. Linares as a therapist and researcher in the field of systemic family therapy in psychosis. I have also applied systemic thought in my work with homeless people, prisoners and victims of violence, as well as in the field of crisis intervention in mass disasters. At present I work as a private practitioner and as a trainer for various systemic institutes in Greece and abroad. I am involved in socio-political initiatives for the rights in the field of (mental) health and I am a member of the Social Solidarity Clinic of Thessaloniki.

Andrea Davolo

I am a systemic/social constructionist therapist, supervisor and consultant. I completed my PhD within a European project in Social Representation and Communication and completed my psychotherapeutic training at the Centro Bolognese di Terapia della Famiglia. Since 2007, I have been working as Psychologist at the Immigrants Health Centre of Parma (Italy), where I work with immigrants families and refugees that have been victims of war, collective and political violence. The theoretical framework I refer to is a combination of systemic, dialogical, ethno-psychological and clinical-political ideas. I also train and supervise professionals of educational, health and social agencies with respect to the intercultural issues, cultural mediation and health promotion in multicultural contexts. I collaborate with the Centro Bolognese di Terapia della Famiglia.

Lucia De Haene

I am Assistant Professor at the research group of Education, Culture and Society, Faculty of Psychology & Educational Sciences, KU Leuven, Belgium. In 2009, I obtained my PhD at the University of Leuven with a dissertation on parent-child relationships in the context of forced migration, including an analysis of the role of narrative methodologies in research with participants with a history of organized violence. My current research focuses on family and community psychosocial sequelae of organized violence, forced migration, and exile  and process analyses of psychotherapeutic and community-based interventions in host societies. Closely connected to my academic work, I am engaged in family therapeutic work with refugee families in the Faculty's clinical centre, where I coordinate a specific clinical service for refugee clients with three collaborators under my supervision.

Jane Dutton

 I am a Consultant Family and Multi family Therapist at the Anna Freud Centre , London, where I am also the Lead in Systemic Development. Previously I was the Service Lead of the former Marlborough Family Service, London, where I worked for 12 years. I was born in London, and although lived outside the UK for some time, have lived and worked in East and North London for most of my adult life, and think of myself as a Londoner. My route into systemic work (qualifying as a family therapist at the end of the 1980s) was through social work, to which I remain strongly committed.

Notes on Contributors

Laura Fruggeri

I am a systemic/social constructionist therapist, supervisor, consultant and researcher. I teach Family Psychology at the University of Parma and I am on the Faculty of the Centro Bolognese di Terapia della Famiglia. I am External Examiner of the PhD and Master programs at the Tavistock Clinic. I am member of the Editorial Advisory Board of several national and international Journals in the family studies field and I have presented at several national and international conferences, seminars and training courses. I have conducted and published several studies on: symbolic and communicative processes in the construction of interpersonal relationships in different contexts: families, health and social services, educational agencies; relationships and processes in non traditional families; Interactions and transitions in everyday family life; research methodologies and procedures for the study of family transitional processes; process analysis of therapeutic conversations; dialectical/dialogical supervision.

Don Boardman

I am a Senior Family Therapist/Supervisor and completed my systemic training in Clanwilliam Institute in 2002. I have worked in Hesed House Psychotherapy Service for seven years. At the start of 2011, I began to collaborate with Padraic Gibson, Director of Hesed House, in researching the efficacy of an Advanced Brief Strategic Therapy model. (Padraic is responsible for introducing this model to Ireland). I am particularly inspired by the early pioneers in the systemic field and feel a particular affinity to the work of Paul Watzlawick. Through my research and practice I endeavour to channel the same spirit of creativity and adventure which early systemic practice was immersed in. I try to ground my systemic work within a scientific method, namely looking for what works in helping clients to resolve their difficulties as quickly as possible. I wish to acknowledge the guidance, support and wisdom of two other systemic mentors who along with Padraic Gibson have helped challenge and shape my therapeutic efficaciousness and they are Dr Ed McHale and Dr Imelda McCarthy. The ongoing care and support which I receive from my family, only proves how far short words fall in conveying his gratitude.

Padraic Gibson

As a psychotherapist l work and live in Dublin with my partner Annmarie and my two boys, Miles and Aaron. I also have the pleasure of working regularly in Italy and the UK, where I have also had the pleasure of training at The Tavistock Clinic with some amazing teachers such as Bernadette Wren, Charlotte Burck and Reenee Singh. My current research interests are in pragmatic interventions for psychological suffering and in building a more rigorous understanding of the effects logic (formal and informal) have on constructing problematic human interactions. Currently director of The Bateson Clinic, Clinical Director of Hesed House, a community based therapy service and co-founder on The OCD Clinic ® International. In September, 2016 my last book "winning without fighting' will be transformed into a masters programme on SEBD, in Dublin City University, where I am currently lecturer. Part of my year is spent in Tuscany, Italy, where I am a senior clinical associate, researcher and lecturer at the clinical school of specialisation in Psychotherapy with Professor Giorgio Nardone.

Gill Goodwillie

I am a consultant family and systemic psychotherapist and supervisor in private practice. I specialised in working in Child and Adolescent Mental Health having worked in the National Health Service (NHS) as professional lead in Family Therapy for fifteen years. I have a range of roles as a clinician, senior lecturer, doctoral research supervisor and pre-

viously manager within the National Health Service (NHS), Higher Education, Local Authority and Voluntary Sectors, in a career spanning forty years. I was a past Head of Counselling for an organisation affiliated to the Westminster Pastoral Foundation (WPF). I am a member of the Editorial Board for *The Journal of Psychological Therapies in Primary*

Care, reviewer for *Human Systems: Journal of Systemic Practice* and I am also an EMDR practitioner.

Therese Hegarty

I began my career as a primary school teacher and worked in Dublin for 24 years, taking a particular interest in supporting children showing social and emotional difficulties. In 2000, feeling constrained by the work I was allowed to undertake within the role of teacher, I left education and undertook a Masters in Family Therapy. On completion of this course I established a community based Family Therapy service in the community where I had worked as a teacher. I was never really able to leave education however and I now lecture in the Froebel Department of Primary and Early Childhood Education, Maynooth University, where I am working hard to develop a new B Ed programme, lecturing in Social Personal Health Education and drawing on active and experiential methodologies. I also introduce students to reflective practice and narrative practice. I was widowed in 2006 and I have three adult children and one grandson.

The garden is my therapy and I am happiest when I walk or swim or talk with good friends. The picture shows me in the woods in County Wicklow, Ireland.

Marie Keenan

I am a Forensic and Systemic Psychotherapist, Restorative Justice Practitioner, Researcher and Lecturer at the School of Social Policy, Social Work and Social Justice, University College Dublin and a member of the Advisory Board of UCD's Criminology Institute. My recent publications include Child Sexual Abuse in the Catholic Church: Gender, Power and Organizational Culture, (2012) Oxford University Press, Broken Faith: Why Hope Matters (2013) Oxford: Lang, with Pat Claffey and Joe Egan (Eds) and Sexual Trauma and Abuse: Restorative and Transformative Possibilities? (2014), Dublin: UCD.

I have served as Chairperson of the Irish Family Therapy Association of Ireland, on the Board of the Irish Penal Reform Trust, on the Advisory Group for the implementation of the Guidelines on Child Sexual Abuse for the Irish Episcopal Conference, and on the Expert Group [Ferns 5] set up by the Department of Health and Children to advise the Minister for Health and Children on the feasibility of establishing country-wide services for the treatment of adolescent and adult males who had perpetrated sexual offences. I have also served on several advisory panels for Religious Orders in Ireland. I have taught and led specialist workshops in a range of universities and training institutes in Dublin and have presented my research and clinical work in the United Kingdom, Finland, Turkey, the United States of America, Australia and South Africa. Specialising in the area of crime, sexual trauma and sexual offending I conducted research on Roman Catholic clergy who had sexually abused minors and on the Church's response to the problem of child sexual abuse. I was the Principal Investigator of a Facing Forward/UCD collaborative research project on sexual violence and restorative justice and was a Senior Researcher and Co- principal Investigator with KU Leuven on a Daphne III funded project on an international research project on Developing Integrated Responses to Sexual Violence: An Interdisciplinary Research Project on the Potential of Restorative Justice. I am a regular contributor to discussions on radio, television and in the print media on these and other social problem

Christopher Iwestel Kinman

I was born in Ibadan, Nigeria and have lived in numerous places throughout my life, including England, Michigan, Chicago, and – in Canada – Saskatchewan, Alberta and British Columbia. Currently, I reside near the city of Vancouver. Family therapist, writer, photographer, poet... there are many descriptions which could be applied to me. Throughout my whole life I have felt a strong connection with what Gregory Bateson calls the Creatura – the world of all that is living, a world of relations. In my work, and through life, I search for connections that sustain and give life. I love my work as a family therapist. For over 23 years now, I have also been working directly with the Sts'ailes First Nation, which resides at the confluence of the Chehalis and Harrison Rivers in Southwestern British Columbia. Recently I was honoured with the gift of a new name from the elders at Sts'ailes. This name is Iwestel, which means one who

Notes on Contributors

guides. I am also a professor with City University of Seattle Canada, in Vancouver, where I teach family therapy, work with addictions, among other subjects. In 2012, I created and premiered a film about family therapy pioneer, Lynn Hoffman. The film is titled, "All Manner of Poetic Disobedience: Lynn Hoffman and the Rhizome Century". I have two graduate degrees, a Master of Science in Marriage and Family Therapy, and a Master of Divinity and am currently enrolled in a PhD. Program with Simon Fraser University, in Burnaby, BC. Through my working life I have been a consultant to a variety of human service organisations, a speaker and workshop presenter, and have facilitated numerous training events for a variety of groups -- both professionals and community members. Besides my home country of Canada, I have presented and consulted in Portugal, Mexico, the United Kingdom, the Czech Republic, and the USA.

Vicky Kokkini

I have been working as a teacher of theatrical education at a primary school since 2004. I have a degree in Theatrical Studies by the National Kapodistrian University of Athens and I am currently a postgraduate student in the field of Educational Sciences at the Department of Early Childhood Education, University of Thessaly. I have also studied music, I hold a diploma in flute by the National Conservatoire and I have been a member of Peristerion Philharmonic Orchestra since 2008.

Andrew Larcombe

I am a 61 year old male originally from the United Kingdom who has lived in Vancouver Canada for the last 35 years. My ancestry is English and Scottish. I work as the clinical supervisor of a counselling team in the Downtown Eastside neighbourhood of Vancouver. I have worked for twenty years in this inner-city area in a variety of locations and roles. I have a background in psychiatric nursing and social science. I have training in narrative therapy and self-regulation therapy. For a number of years I have developed an interest in community education. I have presented workshops on mental health and addictions to community organisations and I have worked as an instructor in a counselling certificate program. In the last two years I have designed and presented in-service workshops on Trauma Informed Practice (TIP) in the healthcare organisation that I work for.

Desa Markovic

After ten years practicing as a Clinical Psychologist in Belgrade, Yugoslavia, I moved to London in 1991 to pursue studies in Systemic Family Therapy at Kensington Consultation Centre (KCC), qualifying both as psychotherapist and supervisor. Since then, I have held senior academic posts on postgraduate psychotherapy programmes at various training organisations in London, such as KCC, Relate, Central School of Counselling and Therapy, and the Institute of Family Therapy, as well as the Porterbrook Clinic in Sheffield. I have worked as a systemic and psychosexual therapist in different contexts including psychiatric hospitals, psychosexual clinics and private practice. My interest in psychosexual therapy developed from a growing awareness, as teacher and practitioner, that sexual issues continue to be marginalised both in psychotherapy training and clinical practice. This realisation led me to specialising in psychosexual therapy at Sheffield Hallam University followed by doctoral studies at Birkbeck College. In recent years I have promoted the possibilities for integration between systemic therapy and sexology, two fields that have traditionally been separated and fragmented at the levels of theory, practice, research, and training. To this end, I have developed a Multidimensional Model that integrates these two areas. It embraces multiple perspectives, highlighting the complexity of human sexuality and sexual relationships and provides material for expanding the theory and practice of the systemic approach. This research activity has led to my further publications in the field, international conference presentations and the development of modules on psychotherapy and psychosexual therapy courses. I have given lectures and presentations on this work at numerous national and international conferences such as The North American Society for Psychotherapy Research, The European Society for Psychotherapy Research, The European Federation of Sexology and several World Association of Sexual Health bi-annual conferences. In 2014 I was awarded fellowship from SSSSR (Sheffield Society for the Study of Sexuality and Relationships) for my contribution to sexology. Currently I am Programme Director for Psychotherapy and Counselling at Regent's University London where I have developed a Module on Systemic and Sexual Therapy.

Notes on Contributors

Imelda McCarthy

I work as a systemic/collaborative therapist and supervisor at the Fifth Province Centre in Dublin. This 'centre', which is in my family home, also includes a weekly meditation group and individual/group conversations on consciousness (social/spiritual) development. I have worked under the guidance of Spiritual Teacher Sri Vasudeva for 17 years, and am Spiritual Director of their meditation community in Ireland. In the academic and therapy fields, I am on the faculties of the TAOS Institute PhD Programme, the Houston Galveston Institute, the G & I Institute (Czech Republic), Context (Berlin), the Institute for Systemic Studies (Hamburg) together with Clanwilliam Institute and Hesed House (Dublin). My writings on the Fifth Province have been published and presented in over twenty countries and translated into nine languages and I still moderate the Fifth Province Facebook page. I am one of the co-founders of the Family Therapy Association of Ireland and of the first family therapy training programmes in Ireland. I am on the editorial boards of the Journal of Family Therapy (UK), Human Systems (UK), the Journal of Community Work and Narrative Therapy (Australia) and the International Journal of Collaborative Therapies (USA). I co-edited a book with Carmel Flaskas and Jim Sheehan, *Hope and Despair in Narrative and Family Therapy* which was published by Routledge in May 2007. It is great to be seeing *Systemic Therapy as Transformative Practice* come to fruition!

Monica McGoldrick

I am Director of the Multicultural Family Insititue and on the clinical faculty of the Department of Psychiatry at the Rutgers Robert Wood Johnson Medical School in New Jersey. I have been teaching, training and presenting internationally for over forty years and my books include, *Ethnicity and Family Therapy* (3rd Ed.), *The Expanded Family Life Cycle* (5th Ed.), *Genograms* (3rd Ed.), *Living Beyond Loss* (2nd Ed.), *Re-Visioning Family Therapy: Race, Culture and Gender*

in Clinical Practice (2nd Ed.), *Women in Families*, and *The Genogram Journey: Reconnecting With Your Family* (2nd Ed. of *You Can Go Home Again*, 2011). My newest book, *The Genogram Casebook* (2016) is published by W.W. Norton.

Efrosyni (Frosso) Moureli

I work as a psychiatrist, group analyst, systemic therapist and trainer, member of the editing committee of the Greek Systemic journal Metalogos for 12 years until recently. I have used systemic thinking and practice in many fields as Mental Health Centres, psychiatric clinic, families with psychotic member, schools as well as social contexts. At the present I work privately, I teach in an systemic Institute, I am a member of the Social Medical Centre of Thessaloniki and of the movement against the gold mining in N. Greece.

Katerina Nanouri

I have a degree in Philosophy, Education and Psychology by the National Kapodistrian University of Athens. Since 2012, I have been a postgraduate student in the field of Educational Sciences at the Department of Early Childhood Education, University of Thessaly. I have worked as a secondary education professor in Literature at a private setting for several years.

Ann-Margreth E. Olsson

I hold a Professional Doctorate in Systemic Practice from the University of Bedfordshire and am a trained social worker (BSc and Master), supervisor and manager (MSc) as well as pedagogue (Master). Currently I am employed as a Senior Lecturer in Social Work at Kristianstad University. I am a Swedish representative in the NATO Technical

Notes on Contributors

Team on "The impact of Military Life on Children from Military Families" and pioneer in Sweden as researcher in the field of military families. Social services, coaching pedagogics and counselling, military families; soldiers, veterans and their extended families; children's participation, 'Barnahus' (Children Advocacy Centers), social worker's investigational work and parenting support programs constitute my major fields of research and publication. My academic affiliations include Research Platform for Collaboration for Health, CYPHiSCO – Children's and Young People's Health in Social Context, Nordic network for Barnahus (Children's House) Research, ERGOMAS – European Research Group on Military and Society and ISPCAN – International Society for the Prevention of Child Abuse and Neglect. My professional trajectory includes top managing positions in social services and health care in Sweden and being CEO of AMOVE AB, a private consulting firm focusing on coaching, supervision and organisational development.

Marcelo Pakman

I am an Argentinian community psychiatrist, psychotherapist and family therapist living in the USA since 1989. While maintaining a community based systemic clinical practice, I have given lectures, courses, seminars and workshops in more than 100 cities of North and South America, Europe and Asia. Since 2000 I have coordinated a summer intensive Spanish course attended by practitioners of many countries. In my teaching and writing I have worked on situations of poverty, violence and ethnic dissonance, on the politics of community mental health and human rights, on testimony and memory. In the last years I have elaborated a critical-poetic conception of psychotherapy articulating my long time interest on the clinical, social critique and philosophy, and focused on the micropolitics of everyday life and of psychotherapy, on transformative poetic events during therapeutic processes, and on the emergence of discontinuous poetic events that deviate from dominant micropolitics.

Hugh Palmer

I am a UKCP Registered Systemic Psychotherapist, based in Pocklington, a market town nestled in the Yorkshire Wolds between York and Hull. I was a lecturer at the University of Leeds from 1994-2000, and after a couple of years working in New Zealand, lectured at the University of Hull from 2003-2012. I recently taught on the Masters in Relationship Therapy for the Relate Institute, and still have a close relationship with Relate, having developed their on-line CPD courses for mental health and bereavement. I currently work part-time as a Senior Systemic Psychotherapist (Family Therapist) in the NHS, working with children, young people and their families. I have a long-standing interest in the work of Gregory Bateson, which led to my work around the aesthetics of therapy incorporating being human as well as the scientific and theoretical.

Dimitra Pouliopoulou

I work as a psychologist, systemic therapist, trainer in non-formal educational settings for adults, youngsters and persons with disabilities, member of the Solidarity Social Medical Centre of Thessaloniki – Greece. After ten years living in Italy, where I studied psychology at the University of Florence, I moved back to Greece in 2007 where I got specialised in systemic therapy at The Institute of Systemic Thinking and Psychotherapy, in Thessaloniki. Throughout my years of study and practice, and till today, I have collaborated with, and worked within, a variety community-based services and organisations; psychiatric units, mental health and social care services in the public sector, also for people who would experience psychosis and extreme distress; in non-formal education contexts for people with disabilities – particularly visual impairment – youngsters and adults. My interest is oriented mainly to the Open Dialogue approach, as well as towards other dialogic and reflecting processes and collaborative approaches to therapy.

Notes on Contributors
Vikki Reynolds

I'm an activist/therapist working to bridge the worlds of social justice activism with community work & therapy, and shoulder up teams of folks working in the margins alongside minoritised and marginalised people. I have supervised and worked as a therapist with refugees and survivors of torture, anti-violence counsellors, mental health and substance misuse counsellors, housing and shelter workers, activists and alongside gender and sexually diverse communities. I am an Instructor with VCC, UBC, Adler University and with City University of Seattle, Vancouver in the Masters' Program where I received the Dean's award for Distinguished Instruction. I have written and presented internationally on the subjects of resistance to 'trauma', ally work, justice-doing, a supervision of solidarity, ethics, and innovative group work. My book, entitled *Doing Justice as a Path to Sustainability in Community Work*, is available for free download along with interviews, keynotes, and articles on my website (www.vikkireynolds.ca).

Cathy Richardson/Kinewesquao

I am a Métis woman with Cree and Dene ancestry. I live in Montreal, Canada and work as an Associate Professor at the Université de Montréal in the School of Social Work. I participate in teaching, writing, research and Indigenous activism. I am a co-founder of the Centre for Response-Based Practice, advancing praxis that helps people in their recovery from violence in a spirit of dignity and social justice. I have served as a delegate to the United Nations Permanent Forum on Indigenous Issues and am currently engaged in research projects to address structural violence against youth in Canada.

Peter Rober

I am a clinical psychologist, family therapist and family therapy trainer at Context -Center for marital and family therapy (UPC KU Leuven, Belgium). I am full professor in family therapy at the Institute for Family and Sexuality Studies (medical school of K.U. Leuven, Belgium). My research interest areas focus on family therapy with children and on the therapy process. I did a lot of work around the use of self of the therapist and the therapist's inner conversation. Furthermore, I'm interested in better understanding silences and secrecy in families. I published several articles in international family therapy journals. Since 1992, I have presented international workshops on family therapy with children and adolescents, as well as on the therapist's inner conversation.

Ernst Salamon

I have been a clinical psychologist, systemic therapist, supervisor and consultant in Sweden for over 40 years. During that time I co-developed the nationally and internationally known Commission Model with two colleagues, Mia Andersson and the late Klas Grevelius. These days I enjoy painting and drawing and spending time with my five grandchildren. This is a self-portrait.

Gail Simon

My early career was in therapeutic work with children and families in statutory and third sector settings. I came to systemic practice through social work in the early 1980s when I trained in family therapy using structural, strategic and early Milan approaches. I undertook further training at the Kensington Consultation Centre (KCC) in London in the early 1990s. In 1990, Gwyn Whitfield and I co-founded The Pink Practice as a response to oppressive psychothera-

peutic practices against the lesbian, gay and queer communities. Systemic thinking was a real help in the fight against pathologising theory and social constructionism helped further in critically situating theory in ideological contexts. I have been teaching and supervising therapy for many years and then embraced practitioner research which I find absolutely inspiring! Lots of people think research is dull until they find out how many forms of inquiry there are which echo the values and activities of their own practice. My doctoral research was on "Writing (as) Systemic Practice" in which I experimented with dialogical writing styles to reflect my conversational and ethical practice in therapy, supervision and education. Now I lead the Professional Doctorate in Systemic Practice at the University of Bedfordshire and enjoy researching the extraordinariness that is involved in human systems and writing and editing for professional journals and for the new systemic practice publishing tent, Everything is Connected Press. I co-edited *Systemic Inquiry. Innovations in Reflexive Practice Research* (2014) with Alex Chard. I am part of the Måfå Research Group which writes about and creates collaborative dialogical installations.

Ged Smith

I am a Family Therapist working for two NHS Trusts in the Liverpool area of England, working in both Children and Adult services. In addition to this I offer many forms of systemic supervision to individuals, teams and agencies across a wide area including Universities and Mental Health Teams around the UK. My Professional Doctorate explored ways of challenging hegemonic masculinity in family therapy, and this, alongside issues of power and gender are of great interest to me. I hope to bring this into therapy sessions, forever exploring ways of engaging people in open discourse, challenging and being challenged.

Umberta Telfener

I am a clinical psychologist with a degree in Philosophy and one in Psychology. I am an adjunct professor for the PhD Course in Health Psychology of the University La Sapienza of Roma and have worked in a Public Health Centre for ten years and in private practice since 1979. As a teacher of the Milan Family Therapy School (Boscolo & Cecchin), I act as a supervisor and a teacher of systemic practices in Italy and abroad. I have written and edited many books and articles among which a systemic dictionary built as a dialogical hyper-text supervised by Heinz von Foerster, my mentor (Sistemica, voci e percorsi nella complessità, Bollati Boringhieri, Torino 2003). I love reading, travelling, jazz, walking in nature and have visited shamans in many places of the world. You can visit my website www.systemics.eu, and my blog online for the Italian newspaper, *Corriere della Sera*: http://blog.iodonna.it/umberta-telfener/

Eleftheria Tseliou

Since 2011 I have been an Assistant Professor in Research Methodology in Education at the Department of Early Childhood Education, University of Thessaly, Greece. I am also a systemic family therapist with experience in training and supervision in systemic family therapy. I hold a first degree in Philosophy, Education and Psychology and an MSc in Clinical Psychology by the Aristotle University of Thessaloniki, Greece and also an MSc in Family Therapy and a Ph.D. in Psychology by the Institute of Psychiatry, King's College, University of London. My interests lie in the development of reflexive and collaborative practices in research, psychotherapy and education. My research interests include the study of counselling / psychotherapeutic process and the study of academic discourse in higher education by means of discourse analysis methodology.

Fany (Fotini) Triantafillou

I work as a psychiatrist, systemic and psychoanalytic therapist, trainer and supervisor. I was born in Mytilini Lesvos, the land of poets and philosophers, nowadays a hosting place for people who try to escape from war. I studied Medicine and was specialised in Psychiatry in Thessaloniki, Greece. Next, I found myself in the Psychoanalytic Psychotherapy training with The British Association of Psychotherapists in London. Just before coming back to Greece, I fell in love with systemic thinking and especially Cecchin's construction of it. I consider Gianfranco Cecchin my mentor and a great inspirer. After returning to Greece, we co-created with some good friends and colleagues a public Mental Heath Centre (of Western Thessaloniki), a place in which we approached difficult problems within a problem-ridden community by learning and developing systemic thinking and practice. Gianfranco and other great friends helped us generously. I retired from the MHC Director's post in 2008. As it turns out, that Mental Health Centre facilitated Thessaloniki to become a place for union and exchange of people interested in systems. Next, we created the Systemic Association of Northern Greece, and some years later, we invented and created the first systemic journal in Greece, *Metalogos*, of which I have been a co-editor for some 12 years now. Since 2012, *Metalogos* has been bilingual (Greek and English) and on-line only. For the last ten years, I have been collaborating with The Institute of Systemic Thinking and Psychotherapy, in Thessaloniki. One of my latest love and occupation is video construction...

Valeria Ugazio

I am director of the European Institute of Systemic-relational Therapies (EIST) (www.eist.it) in Milano, and Professor of Clinical Psychology at the University of Bergamo, Italy. Introduced to the family therapy field by Mara Selvini Palazzoli, my first mentor, I participated with immediate enthusiasm in what was to become the "Milan Approach" and taught in the "Centro Milanese di Terapia Familiare" directed by Luigi Boscolo and Gianfranco Cecchin until I founded EIST in 1999. The inspiring idea which has guided me until now has been to develop a systemic interpretation of intersubjectivity. The semantic polarities theory, set out in Semantic Polarities in The Families. Permitted and Forbidden Stories (2013, New York: Routledge) realises the first step towards this objective. I am currently interested in developing systemic therapeutic approaches and interventions coherent with the semantic polarities perspective and specific for families and individuals, facing phobic, obsessive-compulsive, eating disorders and depression.

Fani Valai

I am a primary school teacher. I hold a degree in Education from the University of Ioannina, Greece and I am currently attending a postgraduate program at the Department of Early Childhood Education, University of Thessaly in the area of innovative design and implementation of educational material. I have a strong interest in pedagogical issues concerning students with cultural and linguistic diversity and for the last few years I have been working in preschool and primary school settings at the area of school inclusion for Roma children.

Justine Van Lawick

I am a clinical psychologist, family therapist and director of training at Lorentzhuis, the centre for systemic therapy, training and consultation in Haarlem, the Netherlands. I am a senior trainer in the Netherlands and abroad. My areas of interest focus on addressing violent behaviour and demonisation in couples, couple groups and families – with compassion for all the involved family members and without blame. My latest project addresses multi-family work with fighting divorced parents and their children. Another area of interest of mine is working with marginalised families. Finding power and vitality in the middle of tragedy is in the centre of my work. Some of my published texts include: Van Lawick & Bom (2008) Building Bridges: Home visits to multi-stressed families where professional help reached a deadlock, *Journal of Family Therapy*; Intimate Warfare (2010), with Martine Groen, Karnac Books (English); *No Kids in the Middle: Dialogical and Creative Work with Parents and Children in the Context of High Conflict Divorces* (2015) with Margreet Visser, Australian and New Zealand Journal of Family Therapy; and Van Lawick (2013); and *Couple and Family Dynamics and Escalations in Violence in Contemporary Issues in Family Studies: Global Perspectives on Partnerships, Parenting and Support in a Changing World* edited with Abela, A. & J. Walker, Wiley-Blackwell.

www.ingramcontent.com/pod-product-compliance
Lightning Source LLC
Chambersburg PA
CBHW051534230426
43669CB00015B/2587